About the volume:

Science, both as a practice and as a way of knowing the natural world, is of recent creation. For six centuries before the creation of science, nature was explored and discussed in Christian Europe within the discipline known as 'natural philosophy', a God-oriented discipline. The present book investigates the origin of two versions of 'natural philosophy', those created by two of the Orders of friars, the Dominicans and the Franciscans, in the early thirteenth century. It also argues that these natural philosophies were both created to help meet specific religio-political needs of the thirteenth-century Catholic Church.

The famous medieval conflict between 'science' and 'religion' is in fact a construct of the nineteenth century. The medieval discipline of natural philosophy, by contrast, was one in which nature was explored in the cause of defending Roman Catholicism – fighting heresy and promoting lay spirituality.

About the authors:

Roger French and Andrew Cunningham both teach in the Wellcome Unit for the History of Medicine, which is part of the Department of the History and Philosophy of Science in Cambridge University.

Before Science

For Luis García Ballester

Before Science

The Invention of the Friars' Natural Philosophy

ROGER FRENCH and
ANDREW CUNNINGHAM

Published by
SCOLAR PRESS
Gower House
Croft Road
Aldershot
Hants GU11 3HR
England

Ashgate Publishing Company
Old Post Road
Brookfield
Vermont 05036–9704
USA

British Library Cataloguing in Publication Data

French, Roger
Before science: the invention of the Friars' natural philosophy
1. Religion and science — History 2. Philosophy and religion — History
I. Title II. Cunningham, Andrew
261.5'5'0902
ISBN 1–85928–287–3

Library of Congress Cataloging-in-Publication Data
French, R. K. (Roger Kenneth)
Before science: the invention of the friars' natural philosophy
by Roger French and Andrew Cunningham.
p. cm.
ISBN 1–85928–287–3 (alk. paper)
1. Philosophy of nature—History. 2. Friars. 3. Philosophy, Medieval. 4. Science, Medieval. 5. Nature—Religious aspects—Catholic Church—History of doctrines—Middle Ages, 600–1500. 6. Catholic Church—Doctrines—History. I. Cunningham, Andrew, Dr. II. Title.
B738.N3F74 1996
189—dc20
ISBN 1 85928 287 3 95–47878
CIP

Typeset in Sabon by Bournemouth Colour Press and printed in Great Britain by Biddles Ltd., Guildford.

Contents

Illustrations

Preface

The theme of this book, one of mutual scholarly interest, derives from discussions together in the summer of 1985. After further preliminary investigation we divided the research and writing between us. However, we take joint responsibility for all the failings of the work.

In a work such as this, it is necessary to bring into discussion events from well over a thousand years of history. No one can be an expert over the whole area, or be *au fait* with all the current concerns of specialist historians. So we are sure that specialists in other areas of medieval history may still find our necessarily broad statements, especially in the earlier chapters, sometimes lack the nuancing and the reservations they themselves would give them.[1] This is unavoidable. We would simply ask them to be patient with us, and to keep in mind the larger argument which we are putting forward.

The personal positions of historians with respect to religion should be irrelevant to the neutral stance they seek to take in their professional work, and this is the situation to which we have aspired. But the history of science, as a historical discipline, has been built on the dividing-off by historians of the seemingly 'religious' from the seemingly 'scientific'. Our book does not do this. Thus at least one earlier reader of our text, a historian of 'medieval science', has assumed that it must be a work of Christian apologetics, seeking to rehabilitate the reputation of the medieval Roman Catholic Church with respect to the history of science, and that we are therefore opposed to the liberal traditions of thought in the academic world which have developed over the last two centuries. Those who know us will recognize that nothing could be further from the truth, and we trust that a dispassionate reading of the book will confirm this.

Note

1. Dr Magnus Ryan of All Souls College, Oxford, has read the whole text and advised us on a number of points of expression to do with the socio-political structures of the period where the medievalist might reach for his trebuchet, and we are grateful for his attentions; we have followed his advice where we could, without prejudicing our argument.

Nihil magis difficile est, quam semel insitam et ab omnibus susceptam opinionem evellere, novamque introducere.

Julius Caesar Arantius

Introduction

The thirteenth century was the century of the friars, men living by a religious Rule, like monks, but out in the world instead of being confined in a monastery. There were many varieties, including Crutched Friars, Austin (Augustine) Friars and Friars of the Sack. They came in several colours, including black (the Dominicans), white (the Carmelites) and grey (the Franciscans). So popular did the founding and joining of Orders of friars become, that eventually the Pope had to call a halt to the creation of new brotherhoods and to suppress some of those already formed. The friars saw themselves as acting directly in the service of the Pope: defending Catholic orthodoxy and papal sovereignty throughout Christendom, and acting as missionaries going out beyond Christendom, to North Africa and India and as far away as Tibet and China, to convert the heathen to the true religion, Roman Catholicism.

Among the Orders of friars, the most important at the time and subsequently were those founded by St Dominic and St Francis. Dominic and Francis were given the unique privilege amongst latter-day saints of being 'adopted' into the Holy Family, and the papacy promoted their cults. In the iconography of the medieval Church many paintings show Dominic or Francis, or both, present in scenes depicting episodes in the history of the Holy Family, while many others show members of the Holy Family present in scenes depicting episodes in the lives of Dominic and Francis. Their relationships were with the two most important members of the Holy Family. Dominic was taken to have a special relationship with the Mother of Christ. In legend Dominic had received from Mary's own hands his scapular – the strip of cloth worn over the habit, hanging from the shoulders, and symbolizing the acceptance of the yoke of Christ. Dominic is also said to have received the tradition of the rosary from Mary's own hands. Francis, in turn, was held to be in a special relationship with Christ, and his life was held to mirror that of Christ himself, even to the extent of receiving the stigmata in his hands, feet and side like Christ had done. Francis is also held to have invented the custom of displaying a miniature crib in churches at Christmas, with the new-born Christ placed within it. The extraordinary reputation these two saints acquired indicates how important were the services that Dominic and Francis gave to the Catholic Church by the founding of their respective Orders at a most critical period in the history of the

Roman Catholic Church, and how grateful the Popes and the hierarchy of the Church were to them. It was celebrated in the traditions of both Orders that Pope Innocent III had had a dream before meeting each saint, in which the respective saint was, quite literally, stopping the collapsing Church from falling.

The Orders of friars originated at the same period and in the same areas as the first universities. Scholars have long been aware that individual members of the Orders founded by Dominic and Francis – the Dominicans and the Franciscans – played an important role in the study of nature in thirteenth-century Europe. For instance, the central role of the Dominicans St Thomas Aquinas and Albert the Great (Albertus Magnus) in assimilating the works of Aristotle, including the nature books, and rendering them amenable to Roman Catholicism, has long been appreciated. Similarly, scholars have long celebrated the Franciscan Roger Bacon for making major contributions in promoting the importance of the study of mathematics and, together with other Franciscans, in developing a science of 'optics' in the thirteenth century.

But while the friars have been, in a general way, included in the stories told by historians of 'medieval science', no one to our knowledge has hitherto looked at the *basis* of the friars' interest in nature: why they were interested in nature at all, and what particular areas and aspects of nature each Order was interested in. This is what we investigate here. The picture which will emerge will indicate that the Dominicans and the Franciscans each had very particular and compelling reasons for being interested in the study and promotion of knowledge of nature, and that these reasons determined very precisely what they studied and how they studied it. The Dominicans and the Franciscans were interested in different aspects of natural study, and for different, though closely related, reasons. Moreover, it will become clear that the basis of the respective interest in nature of both Orders lay in the very particular political and social concerns of twelfth- and thirteenth-century Europe. In particular, as we shall show, the specific ways in which the members of each of these Orders approached and developed the study of nature in the thirteenth century was of a piece with the larger political and social goals for the defence and development of Catholic Europe that each Order had adopted for itself, and followed from them.

Our approach has the effect of moving the focus somewhat from the more customary concerns of historians of 'medieval science', who have tended to tell a story in which texts and ideas are central, concentrating on adventures of texts (the 'transmission' and 'assimilation' of Greek and Arabic texts into Latin), on conflicts between -isms (such as Aristotelianism and Platonism), on the internal developments of ideas in various natural sciences, and on the growth and structure of institutions such as the universities. Historians of 'medieval science' have not been so interested in social and economic structures and organizations, or in individual and group motivation, emotion and ambition – that is, in the reasons why people did the things that they did, such as investigate nature, seek out texts, write new texts. These questions are of central concern to the focus we have adopted here.

Thus, while our story is about ideas and texts, it is also about sex and violence. It is about sex perverted and sex renounced, about violence undertaken to uphold Christianity and to exterminate those holding beliefs threatening that faith. For ours is a story about power: physical and legal power over peoples' bodies, and intellectual power over their minds. It is a story about struggles over how people should live and what they should think in a particular society at a very precise moment in its history.

Our present study will, we believe, be a positive contribution to the discipline of the history of science. We hope that it will also be seen as an interesting story in its own right. But for historians concerned with the subject-area of 'medieval science' we hope it will be useful in another way too, since it suggests a route out of the difficult issue of the historical relations of 'science' and religion. For what we present is a study of men of religion, with precise and explicit politico-religious goals and interests in the real world, engaging in the study of nature – and doing so *because of* those politico-religious concerns.

The traditional story told of the development of science has been one of a centuries-long hostility and incompatibility between religion and the study of nature. The progress of science over the centuries has therefore usually been presented by historians as the result of a progressive *separation* of the study of nature from religion: only as and when religion retreated to its proper sphere could science develop properly and freely. So the historian of science was not surprised to find the two apparently intermingled in medieval texts, as in those of our thirteenth-century friars, for in his view the separation of religion and science had not yet fully taken place by the medieval period. Hence the category of the 'friar-scientist', in the persons of Aquinas, Albertus, Roger Bacon and others, did not seem to present any contradiction. In recent decades, however, although the historian of science still sees it as his or her duty to find and identify true instances of 'science' in medieval writings yet, wishing to be more alert and sympathetic to the context in which knowledge was produced in the past, he or she has come to appreciate (rather than dismiss) the religious and theological context in which he or she finds that 'science'. So the general consensus amongst historians of science today could be expressed as: 'the science of medieval people was highly religious', or 'religion was the matrix in which science was shaped in medieval times'. This new attitude (which amounts in effect to a reversal of the previous attitude about the historical relation of religion and science) has meant that historians today are no longer so certain that the advance of science went hand in hand with the decline of religion, nor are they any longer in consensus about the historical relationship of science and religion.[1]

However, even in this new, more sympathetic approach there is a basic assumption still being made and which our study suggests needs to be questioned. The assumption is that these medieval people were practising science (in the sense in which we customarily use that term today), and that their expression 'natural philosophy', *philosophia naturalis*, essentially meant the same thing to them as our expression 'science' means to us.[2]

In this context we hope our present study will highlight the highly *religious* nature of thirteenth-century natural philosophy, and the religio-political motivation of those who created and studied it, and thus help us to understand and appreciate the identity of natural philosophy for its first practitioners.[3] One thing at least should become clear: that for its practitioners, such as our friars, natural philosophy was concerned with studying nature *as created by God*, and was both evidence of some of the attributes of God and also a route to a closer knowledge of and spiritual communion with God. Natural philosophy was a study in which the central concerns were the detection, admiration and appreciation of God's existence, goodness, providence, munificence, forethought and provision for His creation. Thus natural philosophy was not simply some religious (or religiously motivated) early version of modern science, but had its own identity, which we can perhaps retrieve if we pay sufficient attention to the context, motives and practice of those who created it and then pursued it as an enterprise in its own right and with its own unique identity.[4]

Notes

1. For a recent attempt to find a consensus on the issue, see David C. Lindberg and Ronald L. Numbers, *God and Nature: Historical Essays on the Encounter Between Christianity and Science*, University of California Press, 1986.
2. The issue is complicated by the fact that medieval people used the term '*scientia*' for certain theoretical disciplines and to characterize and distinguish between different kinds of knowledge. *Scientia* is also the historical source of our modern term 'science'. But the medieval and the modern terms do not mean the same thing(s): there is some overlap in their

meanings, but the differences in their meanings must be recognized as being as important as the areas of similarity.

3. Although there are many modern scholarly historical works which use the term 'natural philosophy' in their titles, scholars do not seem to have seen it as necessary to define medieval natural philosophy as such, or discuss the way or ways in which natural philosophy differed from modern science.
4. For the current state of the historiographical discussion on relations between 'medieval science' and religion, see the review article by David C. Lindberg, 'Medieval Science and its Religious Context', *Osiris*, 1995, **10**, pp. 61–79.

CHAPTER ONE

Philosophy and true philosophy

Introduction

Natural philosophy, both as a practice and as a subject-area, was created in early thirteenth-century Christian Europe. The natural philosophy that we are concerned with in this book was created by thirteenth-century Christians in order to serve as a weapon to defend Christianity against the threats that they perceived it was then facing, and to promote particular Christian religious practices. It was produced by amalgamating in certain ways Greek philosophy (especially that of Aristotle) with Christianity. Thus to understand the nature of the natural philosophy of the friars and others in the thirteenth century, it is necessary for us to look first at Greek philosophy and at Christianity, and at the role of the study of nature and the natures of things within them. This will also help make clear the identity of philosophy (of which natural philosophy was in the medieval centuries a part) and thus distinguish it from 'science' as we know and practise it today.

Philosophy

'Philosophy' means the pursuit or study of wisdom (*philo-sophia*), and as the Greek writer Diogenes Laertius wrote of it around AD 250 in his *Lives of the Philosophers*, 'Thus it was from the Greeks that philosophy took its rise; its very name refuses to be translated into foreign speech'.[1] Today we do not practise philosophy in the way that the Greeks did. To its first Greek practitioners and their successors, philosophy was a unitary and integral study. But today when historians and other academics look at Greek philosophy, we naturally enough tend to see it through the spectacles of our own interests and our own, modern, academic disciplines. Hence we unwittingly divide it up into present-day subject-areas. Thus we turn what was a unitary and integral practice into so many separate practices, such as 'ethics', 'politics', 'science', 'biology', and so on, which reflect the modern divisions of the academic world and academic knowledge. And although we certainly have an academic discipline today which is called 'philosophy', it deals with only a fraction of the range of topics and issues which constituted its Greek predecessor.

It also has different aims. So we must beware of projecting back the boundaries and concerns of modern philosophy on to Greek philosophy, for that would lead us to misunderstand it. We must equally beware of treating Greek philosophy simply as an amalgam of early versions of many modern-day disciplines, for Greek philosophy predated the creation of all such disciplines.

Philosophy was a quintessentially Greek enterprise. It was first practised in the Greek city states around the Ionian Sea. The earliest Greek philosophers we know about were Thales, Anixamander and Anaximenes of the seventh and sixth centuries BC. We refer to these early philosophers today as the 'pre-Socratics'. Although their beliefs and doctrines have to be pieced together from 'fragments' (that is, references to them in later writers), it has been the customary consensus of historians that they 'were searching for the one source, the *physis* or nature, whence come the scattered particulars of everyday experience'.[2] The high point of Greek philosophy is associated with the lives and work of three men in particular: Socrates (*c*.469–399 BC), his pupil Plato (*c*.427–*c*.347 BC), and Plato's pupil Aristotle (*c*.384–322 BC), all active in Athens. The practice of Greek philosophy continued for centuries after the death of Aristotle, though not in such an original and investigative manner. For philosophy was practised, by a certain cultivated class of men, throughout the regions which were conquered by Alexander the Great (Aristotle's pupil), since these areas became 'Hellenized' and Greek-speaking. Many of the areas of the Near East which later constituted the Roman Empire were thus Greek-speaking, and hence philosophy could be practised in them. While most Romans prided themselves on their practical and down-to-earth attitude, and distrusted Greek philosophy, nevertheless a number of eminent Romans also adopted Greek philosophy and, like Cicero (106–43 BC), tried to spread the practice amongst their fellow Romans. The philosophical sects which most flourished after the death of Aristotle were those of the Platonists (or as we now call them, 'neo-Platonists') and those of the Stoics. Aristotle himself had a few immediate followers, and his school, the Lyceum, continued in existence for some years. But his writings are thought to have been lost shortly after his death, and were not recovered until about 70 BC.

We may gain some sense of the range and content of Greek philosophy in the period from Socrates to Aristotle simply by looking at the conventional titles of Aristotle's own works. There are books on logic, on ethics, on politics, on rhetoric, on poetics, and on metaphysics. Thus far it might appear to resemble the range and content of modern-day philosophy. But Aristotle also produced books on physics, on the heavens, on animals, on generation and corruption, on meteorology, and on the soul. These subjects definitely do not fall under the modern-day discipline of philosophy. And all these topics (and others) were, in the tradition of Greek philosophy, part of a unitary and integral enterprise for Aristotle.

What was that integral enterprise – Greek philosophy – about? It certainly was concerned with the nature of things and their causes and, in the hands of someone like Aristotle, it was about actually making efforts to acquire sure and certain knowledge about the natures of things (their *physis*). But this was simply a means to an end. For Greek philosophy was centrally about something else, something higher. It was about *how to live properly*.[3] It has been said of Socrates that 'he professed a new *sophia* [wisdom], the wisdom of thinking well, a wisdom of the inner man who lived what he thought: the true philosopher'.[4] The inner man – the soul – of the philosopher, according to Socrates,

> will not ask philosophy to release her [from pleasure and pain] in order that in the very process of release she may deliver herself up again to the thraldom of pleasures and pains, doing a work only to be undone again, weaving and in turn unweaving her Penelope's web. But she will calm passion, and follow reason, and dwell always with her, contemplating the true and the divine and that which is beyond appearance and opinion, and thence deriving nourishment. Thus she seeks to live while she lives, and after death she hopes to go to her own kindred and to that which is like her, and to be freed from human ills.[5]

For Plato too, the true philosopher is the person who is freed from slavery to his senses, who pursues true virtue and wisdom. Aristotle, whose version of philosophy had much more of consideration of the physical world in it, also thought of philosophy as being the way to reach the well-being of the soul. So we may say about Greek philosophy that its practice consisted of a continual, unending, series of studies and enquiries and practices which shape a man to live properly.[6] It is a *paideia*, a shaping.[7] But more than this. As a modern writer has elegantly put it, discussing Plato:

> in the eyes of Plato, philosophy was an essentially practical spiritual process. It was not theory or practice, science or life, nor even theory applied to practice, science applied to life, but both in one – the striving of the soul to purify and ennoble itself, to make itself all beautiful within. There is no right understanding of the philosophy of Plato possible if we forget that he regarded it as primarily a process, the true life of the spirit, the soul making of itself a divine poem, the highest music ... Philosophy was, according to Plato, not only essentially practical, but also essentially one, and one because all ideas led up to the idea of The Good.[8]

What is true of Plato's concept of philosophy here is equally true of that of Socrates and that of Aristotle and that of other Greek philosophers. Greek philosophy was about The Good, The Beautiful, The Divine: *this* is what the philosopher seeks, what he wishes to know, what he tries to follow, what he seeks to contemplate and be at one with. Philosophy was primarily an inner experience, akin to a religious experience, and was therefore centrally concerned with the soul and its well-being. The philosopher achieves a certain state of mind; he does not seek to change the world outside himself.

What of the role and importance of 'nature' or the 'natures of things' in this Greek philosophy?[9] While every philosopher agreed about the general goal of philosophy, they did not all accord the same role to investigating the natures of things in helping one achieve that goal. Something of the range of positions can be illustrated from the views of Socrates, Plato and Aristotle respectively. Our source for the opinions of Socrates are the dialogues of Plato, in which Socrates is cast as the main speaker. In one of these dialogues, *Phaedo*, Plato has Socrates say that in his early life he had turned philosophy from the study of the external world typical of the Ionian philosophers, to the study of man and the purposes of human action in society. He had done this because the sort of explanations offered for natural phenomena seemed only to account for the how and not the why of things. What he wanted was an explanation in terms of some guiding Intelligence, which brought things about with some aim in view and for some purpose. But the philosophers such as Anaxagoras, in Socrates's view, did not look for 'the power which in arranging them as they are arranges them for the best ... That it is really the Good and the Right which holds and binds things together, they never reflect'.[10]

Plato, the disciple of Socrates, had a greater role for the study of the natures of things in his philosophy, though not in the form in which things are visible and experienced here below, but in their purest and highest form, in the form – or 'Forms' – in which they truly exist, and of which this world we see and experience is but an imperfect shadow. In this sense, for Plato, nature (*physis*) is precisely the expression of The Divine, The Beautiful, The Good. The natures of things exhibit the workings of soul (*psyche*). Thus the study of the natures of things is a way of reaching the goal of philosophy (The Good) because the nature of things is itself an expression of The Good. Plato's views on the importance of the natures of things and on how the natures of things came to be and for what purpose, was particularly influential in later centuries, for his *Timaeus* was the only one of his dialogues continuously available in the 'medieval' centuries. The *Timaeus* is an account of how the universe came into being: it is a creation story. The universe was brought into existence by the Demiurge to fulfil certain goals, and in bringing it about the Demiurge made all things for the best. The *Timaeus* is not central to our present-day way of looking at Plato and his philosophy, but it was for many centuries taken as his central work. For its readers it represented a fulfilment of the truly philosophical approach to understanding the natures of things that Socrates had supposedly been seeking when a young man, but been unable to find: one which speaks of Mind, and of goals and of purposes. It was a 'teleological' account, that is, one which speaks in terms of goals (*teloi*) or purposes.

But by contrast with his pupil Aristotle, Plato had very little role for the actual investigation or consideration of the natures of things in his philosophy. The 'Forms' were, for Plato, simply for contemplation, freed of any taint of the material versions of them which could be found in the universe accessible to our senses. In the philosophy of Aristotle, by contrast, the investigation of the natures of things plays a major role. Aristotle agreed with Plato that the essence of natural things lay in their forms. But for Aristotle the forms were not celestial, but resided in the physical things themselves. When Aristotle used the term *physis*, 'nature', it was almost always the nature *of a thing*, the animal, plant or mineral he was considering. What made the physical world Good and reaching to the Divine, was the expression of the nature of a thing as – in the case of animals and plants – it grew, developed and expressed itself in the form of the complete thing itself.[11]

So, in developing and (in part) opposing the views of his teacher Plato, Aristotle agreed that the unchangingness of the heavens was indeed worthy of the philosopher's attention, and he wrote on the perfect circular motion of the heavens in *On the Heavens*. But he also argued that the same sort of eternal divine verity was discernible here on earth, in that very area where Plato thought there was nothing but change and impermanence:

> Of the beings such as are composed by nature – the ones we call ungenerated and imperishable for all eternity, and the others we say partake of coming-to-be and passing-away – it so happens that while the first ones [i.e. the heavenly bodies] are worthy and divine, there are very few views (*theoria*) of them available to us because, if we try to investigate these beings – even those we long to know about – that which is clear to perception is very scanty. It is easier for us to acquire knowledge about the perishable plants and animals because we live among them, since one can acquire much knowledge about each kind that exists if one cares to take enough trouble. And each of them has its charm. For even if we grasp only a little bit about the heavenly bodies, yet by the excellence of the knowledge it is more pleasurable than all the things around us (just as seeing a fleeting glimpse of our loved ones is more pleasurable than seeing many other things large and clearly), nevertheless with respect to the

> others [i.e. the earthly beings] since we know more and better about them they have superiority in knowledge [over what we know of heavenly things]. And furthermore, by being nearer to us and more similar in nature, they make some compensation for the philosophy about heavenly things.
>
> As we have already treated the heavenly bodies, giving our opinion about them, it remains to speak about animal nature leaving out nothing as far as possible, neither nobler nor less noble. For even with animals which are not pleasant to look at, nevertheless the nature at work in them holds extraordinary pleasures for those who are capable of recognising the causes and are philosophers by their natures ... in all of them there is something of nature and of the Beautiful. For the non-random, the for-something's-sake is in the works of nature most of all; and the thing because-of-which it is composed, or has come-into-being – its purposes (*teloi*) – are part of the Beautiful.[12]

Thus with Aristotle we find the sublunar physical world and the study of sublunar natures of things given a central role in philosophy: the true philosopher investigates and understands the things of the physical world as the expression and embodiment of the Beautiful, 'the non-random, the for-something's-sake', that is, the full and regular expression of the natures of things.

But even with Aristotle the interest in the natures of things is an interest exclusively theoretical, even though the information is to be gained empirically. Aristotle does not want to modify the natures of things, much less harness the natures of things to man's material interests; he simply aspires to *wisdom* about them as an approach to the Divine. This was the case with all later Greek philosophers too, whether they were neo-Platonists, Stoics or Cynics: they all saw nature or the natures of things as, in some sense and to some degree, an expression of the Good and the Beautiful, and they none of them wanted to master or exploit the natures of things as scientists do today.

The 'religious' nature of Greek philosophy needs to be stressed. For our modern, a-religious, understanding of what constitutes philosophy can lead us to fail to notice the central spiritual and ethical function and point of Greek philosophy for its practitioners. Not only did Greek philosophy resemble a religion in its aims (though not in any ritual practices), but it was also used as a form of religion by its practitioners, for its practical concern was with living the good life, and with the welfare of the soul and its relation to the Divine.[13] And this was the root of the Greek philosopher's interest in the natures of things, for the physical world could be seen as an expression of the Divine, and its study as leading to the Divine, and the soul's welfare as lying in the perception of this. Some Greek philosophers believed that Greek philosophy actually originated as a version of a religion, one highly influenced by

Zoroastrianism.[14] Thus Greek philosophy definitely did not arise as a rejection of religion, as our conventional story about it claims that it did (and as our modern version of philosophy actually did originate, many centuries later), but as a continuation of religion by other means, as it were.[15]

As an example of the practice of philosophy as a way of life of a quasi-religious kind, we may take the philosophical sect of the Stoics. The Stoics believed there is an active principle of the world, which is the *logos* – the Word, or Reason (it is *logos* as in 'logic'). We need (they claim) to live in accordance with natures of things. The virtuous man therefore conforms his will to the divine *logos* and lives in passionless calm detachment from self and from worldly interests. This is to follow Stoic philosophy. And this tranquillity of soul is achieved by an active process of philosophizing. Seneca, a Roman who lived in the first century AD and who is perhaps the best known of the ancient Stoics, wrote to this effect, saying that philosophy consists not in words but in actions, it is not a mental diversion but a way of life, a way of life which seeks tranquillity of soul:

> Philosophy ... forms and shapes the mind, it orders the life, it determines actions, it shows what is to be done and what is to be left undone, it sits at the helm and guides the ship of life through all dangers. Without philosophy no man can live free of fear and without cares ... One must philosophize! Whether the rule of fate fetters us with inexorable law, whether God as governor of the universe has determined everything, whether human life is set in motion by accident, without a plan, and is determined by a throw of the dice – philosophy must be our protection. God willing, it will exhort us daringly to obey fate. It will teach us to accept chance.[16]

Seneca saw the divine law as expressed in the natural world. There is no implied distinction here between 'natural' and 'unnatural', for Seneca uses the Latin term *natura* as equivalent to the Greek *physis* and still very much as the 'nature of things'. Seneca wanted to free his co-practitioners of Stoicism from fear of divine retribution or divine wilfulness, and emphasized the orderliness of the physical world. By this he meant what we mean today by 'naturalness': it is the regular fulfilling of their natures that makes things 'natural'. Thus Seneca's *Natural Questions* explain in natural terms the things that the ancients most associated with the vengeance of arbitrary gods and goddesses – lightning, earthquakes, floods, and so on. The naturalness of these things meant they were understandable to the human mind and therefore not to be feared; and their naturalness in no way conflicted with the abstract divinity of the *logos* that they expressed.

The Stoics sought *ataraxia*, peace of mind, through their acceptance of what was natural as a result of the logos. The same is true also of the philosophers who held that the world was made up of atoms. Their views were rejected by Aristotle on the grounds that the atoms moved randomly and hence without purpose: for him this was unphilosophical. But the atomists were not pursuing a 'scientific' view of the world, for their purpose was to persuade man that the action of the atoms was, above all, not guided by the gods. The gods existed, but had no power, arbitrary or just, over man. The aim of the atomistic philosopher Epicurus was to relieve man of the fear of the gods and enable him to achieve ataraxia, as a basis for living the good life, the life of the true philosopher.

The association of Greek philosophy with 'religious' goals was so intimate that it is hardly surprising to find that it was apparently none other than the philosopher Plato who coined the term 'theology', when discussing the ways in which the poets refer to the gods.[17] Aristotle too uses the term 'theology', when discussing the types of philosophy: 'There must be three theoretical philosophies – mathematics, physics, and what we may call theology – since it is obvious that if the divine is present anywhere, it is present in beings of this sort.'[18] 'Beings of this sort' are those which can exist separately by themselves (unlike the beings that mathematics deals with), and which are not subject to movement or change (physics deals with the beings subject to movement and change). Thus 'theology' deals with those beings possessed of a real individual existence, yet which are eternal and immutable, and these are of course the divine First Movers; these First Movers produce the eternal, regular, perfect motion of the heavenly bodies, and are thus 'the causes of so much of the Divine as appears to us'.[19]

The view of 'nature' and the natures of things which the natural philosophy of the thirteenth century after Christ was to present was significantly different from the view and deployment of natures of things that we have just been looking at in ancient Greek philosophy – even though natural philosophy was in large part to be built on Greek philosophy. Thus it was not simply a matter of the practitioners of this new enterprise, natural philosophy, taking up the discussion of the natures of things at the point where the Greek philosophers had left it off. For natural philosophy (as we shall see in later chapters) had different aims, boundaries and context than Greek philosophy had had.

But there were certainly some very important and basic features of the Greek philosophers' attitude to the physical world which were to be reflected later in natural philosophy (in addition to any simple information about the physical world that would be available to the natural philosophers from the work of the Greek philosophers). These fundamental features, common both to most of Greek philosophy and to thirteenth-century natural philosophy, all stem from the essentially 'religious' origin and nature of Greek philosophy, and appealed to the essentially Christian nature of natural philosophy in the thirteenth century.

First, the basic attitude to the nature of things is *teleological*, concerned with the goal-directedness both of the natures of things and of a more abstract or collective *logos*, and seeking in the latter's goal-directedness the presence of Mind and Intelligence. Everything in both these senses of 'nature' is for the good, and has a good goal to which it aspires. Second, there is a total obsession with *soul*. Some philosophers believed that the activities of soul can be discerned in the motions of the heavenly bodies and in the bodies of animals; all believed that the human soul is the true man. Third, there is the constant desire on the part of the Greek philosopher when looking at the physical world, to find *eternal regularities* present in it, whether the perfect, eternal, unchanging, circular motion of the heavens, or the persistence of the species in animals, which is the recurrence of their natures. Finally there is the habit of most Greek philosophers of seeing the cosmos as worth exploring and discussing because it is *beautiful*, as an aspect of The Good, The Beautiful, The Divine, as evidence of a divine Mind. All these we shall see adopted also in natural philosophy. Indeed they were exactly the sort of thing which made Greek philosophy a suitable and attractive basis for the men of the thirteenth century, as Christians, to use as a foundation on which to build this new enterprise of theirs: natural philosophy. All of these features come from the 'religious' nature of Greek philosophy, and it is in this (and not in any supposedly 'scientific' character) that they were to be attractive to men of the thirteenth century.

True philosophy

So much, for the moment, for Greek philosophy. We turn now to Christianity, which some of its early adherents referred to as 'the true philosophy', since they thought that it really achieved the goals that Greek philosophy only aimed at.

Christianity was begun by the Jewish followers of Jesus, claiming that he was the Messiah or Christ as foretold in the Jewish scriptures. They claimed also that he had been crucified, and that he had risen again from the dead. They claimed that he was the Son of God made flesh (incarnate). Thus Christianity was, from the start, a revealed religion, with a set of doctrines which had been given authoritatively and which one had to believe in order to be a Christian. These doctrines are not open to empirical proof or disproof, or to the test of reason or logic: they are, by contrast, mysteries, and gain their authority from being so.

Initially, Christianity arose out of Judaism. The early Christians therefore treated the Jewish scriptures as basic to their own 'true' Judaism – Christianity – for in these scriptures the coming of a Messiah was foretold; and hence Christians inherited the sacred texts of the Old Testament as part of their own sacred texts. And with these they inherited a creation story, as told in Genesis, about the origin of the universe in a moment (or, more properly perhaps, in a week) of creative activity by the one true God. In this story the world was portrayed as the immediate creation of God, and was filled with His living creations (His 'creatures'), which were good:

> And God said, Let the waters bring forth abundantly the moving creature that hath life, and fowl that may fly above the earth in the open firmament of heaven. And God created great whales, and every living creature that moveth, which the waters brought forth abundantly, after their kind, and every winged fowl after his kind: and God saw that it was good.[20]

But the early Christians did not succeed in convincing their fellow Jews that their Jesus was the Messiah foretold. Thus Christianity became a 'heresy' of Judaism, and was obliged to develop separately from it. So Christianity did not become even a branch of Judaism. Instead Christianity – taking with it the Jewish scriptures, including the creation story of Genesis – became 'Greek'. It first spread amongst Greek-speaking ('Hellenized') Jews. The stories of the life of Christ, the Gospels, were all first written in Greek (though Christ himself had spoken Aramaic). All the other texts which came to constitute the New Testament were also all first written in Greek. And then St Paul, who was himself a Greek-speaking Jew, led the campaign to spread the Christian message to non-Jews – that is, to 'Greeks'.

The consequence of these early events in the history of Christianity was that, from its origin, Christianity was in large part formed by Greek – that is, by philosophical – culture. The philosophical basis of Christianity (and all philosophy in the western tradition was basically Greek, of course) is evident throughout the New Testament. For instance, the opening words of St John's Gospel speak in terms of the Stoic conception of God as the *logos*: 'In the beginning was the Word (*logos*), and the Word was with God, and the Word was God. The same was in the beginning with God.' Then there is the whole business of the soul. The human soul, as we have seen, was central to the enterprise of Greek philosophy, especially Platonism, which concerned itself with the heavenly origin of the soul, with its career, its fulfilment and its well-being, and also with its afterlife. Yet the concept of the soul plays virtually no role at all in Judaism.[21] Thus it came about that Christians came to be credited with souls because Greeks credited themselves with souls, and indeed with eternal souls in order to make sense of Christ's words on the life everlasting and the kingdom of heaven. Hence the soul became central to Christianity because it had been central to Greek philosophy.

The work of depicting Christianity as the fulfilment of Greek philosophy appears to have been begun by St Paul, as in his famous sermon at Athens. Paul was waiting for some companions when he felt moved to speak out and declare Christianity to be the fulfilment of Greek philosophy:

> Now while Paul waited for them at Athens, his spirit was stirred in him, when he saw the city wholly given to idolatry. Therefore disputed he in the synagogue with the Jews, and with the devout persons, and in the market daily with them that met with him. Then certain philosophers of the Epicureans, and of the Stoicks, encountered him. And some said, 'What will this babbler say?' other some, 'He seemeth to be a setter forth of strange gods': because he preached unto them Jesus, and the resurrection. And they took him, and brought him unto Areopagus,[22] saying, 'May we know what this new doctrine, whereof thou speakest, is? For thou bringest certain strange things to our ears: we would know therefore what these things mean'. (For all the Athenians and strangers which were there spent their time in nothing else, but either to tell, or to hear some new thing.)
>
> Then Paul stood in the midst of Mars' hill, and said, 'Ye men of Athens, I perceive that in all things ye are too superstitious. For as I passed by, and beheld your devotions, I found an altar with this inscription, TO THE UNKNOWN GOD. Whom therefore ye ignorantly worship, him I declare unto you. God that made the world and all things therein, seeing that he is Lord of heaven and earth, dwelleth not in temples made with hands ... For in him we live, and move, and have our being; as certain also of your own poets have said, "For we are also his offspring". Forasmuch then as we are the offspring of God, we ought not to think that the Godhead is like unto gold, or silver, or stone, graven by art and man's device ...'. And when they heard of the resurrection of the dead, some mocked: and others said, 'We will hear thee again of this matter'. So Paul departed from among them. Howbeit certain men clave unto him, and believed: among the which was Dionysius the Areopagite, and a woman named Damaris, and others with them.[23]

Christianity teaches the truths of the God 'unknown' by you followers of Greek philosophical sects, Paul says, you Epicureans and Stoics; Christianity teaches the God in whom we live and move and have our being, and of whom even your – Greek – poets have spoken.[24] This was Paul's message to the Greeks. Some Greeks believed him. Thus eventually Christianity became a non-Jewish (that is, a 'Greek') religion. It is of great interest that when Paul preached that day on Mars' Hill, 'Dionysius the Areopagite' was amongst those who believed Paul's message about Christianity being the fulfilment of Greek philosophy, for we shall be meeting Dionysius again many centuries later, this time playing an important role in the creation and content of the natural philosophy of one Order of friars.

But what was to be the proper relationship between this 'true philosophy' (Christianity) and the Greek philosophy to which it owed so much? Did 'true philosophy' need philosophy, or was philosophy an irrelevance to 'true philosophy'? Was Greek culture and philosophical education to be necessary for the true Christian? Was the truth of revelation, as offered by Christianity, to be dependent on or require support from reason, as offered by Greek philosophy? These were highly important questions in the early centuries of Christianity, for on their resolution depended the direction that Christianity would take, and there was much conflict about them. Moreover, many of the controversial doctrinal questions for early Christianity arose from the Greek (philosophical) origin of many of its concepts, and they were not easy to resolve without recourse to Greek philosophical ways of thinking. But some parties insisted that the revealed truths of Christianity should not depend for their interpretation on the reasoned truths of Greek philosophy.

The inner conflict over the proper role of Greek philosophy in Christianity was important when Christianity came under attack from the second century. In this situation, some Christians thought that resort to the argument that Christianity was simply the fulfilment of Greek philosophy, would disarm the attackers. For Greek philosophy was still very influential in Roman culture. Christianity could, they hoped, be explained via Greek philosophy, and with its legitimacy thus shown, surely the persecutions would cease. In this manner reasoned the so-called 'apologist' Fathers of the Church, such as Justin Martyr and Aristides of Athens.[25]

Most prominent amongst those claiming the indispensability of Greek philosophy for the comprehension and practice of Christianity were two of the 'Greek Fathers' of the Church, Clement of Alexandria and Origen, both of whom were active in Alexandria in the years around 200. Clement argued the case in his *Miscellanies* (*Stromata*). In a chapter entitled 'Plato's opinion, that the chief good consists in assimilation to God, and its agreement with Scripture', Clement quotes Plato as saying that because there is evil on this earth we should 'fly away from earth to heaven as quickly as we can; and to fly away is to become like God, as far as this is possible; and to become like him, is to become holy, just and wise'.[26] For Clement there is complete consistency between (Platonic)

Greek philosophy and Christianity: the *logos* who became incarnate in Christ spoke through Plato as well as through Moses:

> the barbarian and Hellenic philosophy has torn off a fragment of eternal truth not from the mythology of Dionysius, but from the theology of the ever-living Word. And He who brings again together the separate fragments, and makes them one, will without peril, be assured, contemplate the perfect Word, the truth.[27]

So, for Clement, philosophy 'was given to the Greeks, as a covenant peculiar to them – being, as it is, a stepping-stone to the philosophy which is according to Christ'.[28] Clement applied his neo-Platonic philosophical skills to seeking the mystical sense concealed, he believed, beneath the letter of the Scriptures. As a modern commentator has written, for Clement 'finding the deeper meaning is thus the process by which God gradually, by means of parable and metaphor, leads those to whom God would reveal himself from the sensible to the intelligible world'.[29]

Origen too promoted the use of Greek philosophical works for the proper understanding and practice of Christianity. He wrote to Gregory, a student of his, urging him

> to direct the whole force of your intelligence to Christianity as your goal ... And I would wish that you would take with you on the one hand those parts of the philosophy of the Greeks which are fit, as it were, to serve as general or preparatory studies for Christianity, and on the other hand so much of Geometry and Astronomy as may be helpful for the interpretation of the Holy Scriptures. The children of the philosophers speak of geometry and music and rhetoric and astronomy as being ancillary to philosophy; and in the same way we might speak of philosophy itself as being ancillary to Christianity.
>
> It is something of this sort perhaps that is enigmatically indicated in the directions God is represented in the Book of Exodus as giving to the children of Israel ... [30]

Thus Christians who used Greek philosophy in this way were, according to Origen, like the Israelites in captivity in Egypt, to whom God had said, through the mouth of Moses:

> And I will give this people favour in the sight of the Egyptians: and it shall come to pass, that, when ye go, ye shall not go empty: but every woman shall borrow of her neighbour, and of her that sojourneth in her house, jewels of silver, and jewels of gold, and raiment: and ye shall put them upon your sons, and upon your daughters; and ye shall spoil the Egyptians.
>
> ... And the children of Israel did according to the word of Moses; and they borrowed of the Egyptians jewels of silver, and jewels of gold, and raiment: and the Lord gave the people favour in the sight of the Egyptians, so that they lent unto them such things as they required. And they spoiled the Egyptians.[31]

To use Greek philosophy – 'Egyptian gold' – was thus merely to obey God's own instructions. It was to 'spoil' (that is, despoil) the valuables of non-Christians for the benefit of Christians. We shall be hearing more about this 'Egyptian gold' later.

Origen also pursued the approach evident in Clement of Alexandria, to finding the true – that is, the mystical – meaning of the literal text of scriptures, which it was thought must underlie them. He developed the allegorical exegesis of scripture, whereby every passage of scripture can be analysed into a literal and one or more spiritual meanings for Christians. According to Trigg, Origen claimed that the Bible

> contains three levels of meaning, corresponding to the three-fold Pauline (and Platonic) division of a person into body, soul, and spirit. The bodily level of Scripture, the bare letter, is normally helpful as it stands to meet the needs of the more simple. The psychic level, corresponding to the soul, is for those making progress in perfection ... It was, of course, with the third level of meaning, the spiritual, that Origen was chiefly concerned. Spiritual interpretation deals with 'unspeakable mysteries' so as to make humanity a 'partaker of all the doctrines of the Spirit's counsel ... '.[32]

So for Origen and other Greek 'Fathers' of the Church, proper Christianity, at least for full initiates, was not possible without Greek philosophy – 'Egyptian gold'.

However, other Christians began to see the Greek philosophical heritage of Christianity not as the potential cure for present ills, but rather as the cause of them, especially of schisms between Christians. Tertullian (*c*.160–*c*.220, active at Carthage and Rome, and writing around 197), a contemporary of Clement of Alexandria and Origen, wrote in opposition to their teachings, that 'philosophy is the core of worldly wisdom, the rash interpreter of God's nature and plan. In fact, the heresies themselves are secretly nourished by philosophy'.[33] In a most famous challenge, Tertullian asked: 'What has Athens to do with Jerusalem? what has the Academy [of Plato] to do with the Church?' Tertullian called Aristotle, the great philosopher, 'that wretched inventor of dialectics'.[34]

By about AD 300 the split ran largely along linguistic lines between those who claimed that Greek philosophy was irrelevant and even threatening to Christianity, and those who claimed that Greek *paideia* is fundamental for the education of a Christian if he is to understand the point and purpose of Christianity. Those who were Greek by language and lived in Athens, Alexandria or the east of the Roman Empire, tended to favour the view that cultivation of Greek philosophy was essential for the good Christian; such was the case with Clement of Alexandria and Origen. Those who were Latin by language and lived in Rome or the west or south of the Roman Empire tended to regard it as irrelevant to the good Christian, and possibly dangerous; Tertullian, for instance, although he had a 'Greek' education, wrote mostly in Latin. This split in attitude became institutionalized in a split in the Church, and it corresponded to and in part arose from a political split in the Roman Empire.

The greatest of the Latin Fathers of the Church, St Augustine (353–430), epitomizes in his own life and writings the issue of the relation of Greek philosophy to Christianity. Augustine was a teacher of Latin rhetoric. Like other Romans he distrusted Greek philosophy. He spent nine years among the Manicheans, a sect professedly Christian, but who maintained that there is not one God (as conventional Christians believed) but two 'principles', a good principle and an evil principle. This world and all that is in it was made, they claimed, by the evil principle. Augustine came particularly under the influence of the Manichean teacher Faustus. Questions about the nature of God and the origin of evil – issues made central to him by the Manicheans – continued to preoccupy Augustine in later life. Augustine came to Christianity in an unexpected way, and one which was to have considerable historical consequences, given the continual great importance of his writings in Latin Christendom. This is his own account of the sequence of his conversion:

> And Thou, willing first to shew me, how Thou *resistest the proud, but givest grace unto the humble*, and by how great an act of Thy mercy Thou hadst traced out to men the way of humility, in that Thy WORD was made flesh, and dwelt among men: – Thou procuredest for me, by means of one puffed up with most unnatural pride, certain books of the Platonists, translated from Greek into Latin. And therein I read, not indeed in the very words, but to the very same purpose, enforced by many and divers reasons, that *In the beginning was the Word, and the Word was with God, and the Word was God: the Same was in the beginning with God: all things were made by Him, and without Him was nothing made* ...
>
> And I had come to Thee from among the Gentiles; and I set my mind upon the gold which Thou willedst Thy people to take from Egypt, seeing Thine it was, wheresoever it were. And to the Athenians Thou saidst by Thy Apostle, *that in Thee we live, move, and have our being, as one of their own poets had said*. And verily these books [i.e. of Plato] came from thence ...
>
> And being thence admonished to return to myself, I entered even into my inward self, Thou being my Guide: and able I was, for Thou wert become my Helper. And I entered and beheld with the eye of my soul, (such as it was,) above the same eye of my soul, above my mind, the Light Unchangeable ... He that knows the Truth, knows what that Light is; and he who knows It, knows eternity ...[35]

Thus Augustine's conversion, according to this account of his, was via reading 'some books of the Platonists', which to his mind spoke of the very same revelation as the one he then found in the Bible, especially in the Gospel of John. He came to the realization, therefore, that evil is not created by God, but is only apparent, and that *this* world bears proof of the existence and goodness of the one true God: 'And I heard, as the heart heareth, nor had I room to doubt, and I should sooner doubt that I live, than that Truth is not, *which is clearly seen being understood by those things which are made*.'[36]

These Platonic books were, as he said, like 'Egyptian gold', the gold which the Lord urged the Hebrews to take with them from their captivity among the Egyptians. This is the function that the Greek philosophical works had for Augustine, and which could thus legitimate their use by later Christians: the conversion testimony of Augustine himself showed that the Greek philosophical works were valuable for Christianity. As Augustine wrote, the very name 'philosopher' means 'lover of wisdom'; God is wisdom; therefore the true philosopher is a lover of God.[37] Thus, where Augustine had initially thought that Greek philosophy was *superbia* (vanity), and so not suitable for a Christian, after his conversion via the works of the Platonists, he came to the conclusion that *superbia* founded on faith became *sapientia*, true wisdom.

The double legacy of the Roman Empire

The fate of Greek philosophy within Christianity – the relevance of 'Egyptian gold' to the proper practice of Christianity – depended crucially on the fate of the Roman Empire. And it was the political changes in the West in the centuries following the collapse of the Roman Empire, which called into being the Orders of friars and made natural philosophy necessary.

When the old Roman Empire – the political, economic and social empire based on Rome, that is – melted away, it left two shadows behind: a version of the Empire, and two Churches whose form, nature and organization owed an enormous amount to the model of the Empire. They are both important for our story. Their histories are intertwined, but let us deal first with the Church.

Perhaps the most basic problem facing early Christianity had been whether it was to be a personal or a communal religion. Many people thought the Second Coming was imminent, and that personal salvation and personal religious experience were all-important. Amongst these the most important group were the Gnostics, whose beliefs and activities are still coming to light as the Nag Hammadi scrolls are interpreted.[38] The

Gnostics were highly mystical in their beliefs and practices and heavily indebted to Greek (especially Platonic) philosophy.[39] They believed in the Divine Mother, and had their own Gospels and other texts. But in some tragic events now lost to us, the Gnostics were defeated by rival Christians, and their texts were destroyed and their beliefs outlawed. Other people thought that Christianity was properly a communal and catholic religion depending on a priestly hierarchy, and these are the ones who won the early internecine battles. Hence by the AD 200s Christians had already arranged an informal organization of bishops, priests and deacons.

Christianity had come under intermittent persecution from the Roman rulers since the beginning of the second century. Though there were long periods when it was safe to practise Christianity openly, Christians were basically seen as traitors to the Roman state. They showed this outwardly by their refusal to perform rites of worship toward the Emperor, for they maintained of course that there was only one true God. As their enemy Celsus put it, writing about AD 180:

> If everyone were to do the same as you, there would be nothing to prevent him [the Emperor] from being abandoned, alone and deserted, while earthly things would come into the power of the most lawless and savage barbarians, and nothing more would be heard among men either of your worship or of the true wisdom.[40]

The persecutions were heaviest in the reign of Diocletian, in the two years before his abdication in 305.

Yet, despite these persecutions Christianity became, to all intents and purposes, the 'official' religion of the Roman Empire in 313. For the Emperor, Constantine, had supposedly just seen a vision – a cross of light against the sun, with the message, 'In this conquer'. As is the way with emperors and dictators, the faith of the leader became the faith of the followers. Thus suddenly Christianity now rose to the challenge of being the faith of an empire. In its turn it was to harry unbelievers and promote and protect the faith throughout the whole Empire. Christianity was now to extend (or be extended) to all the citizens and subject-peoples of Rome, without exception: to be 'Roman' was to be Christian.

To this end the Church developed its organization, which was directly based on that of the Empire proper. The local church leaders (bishops) had at first been directly chosen by their local clergy and laymen; the bishops within each of the 'provinces' of the Empire had then begun to meet together. Hence the imperial administrative regions, the provinces, were taken as natural units for Church organization. When the provinces then came to be grouped together by the Emperor for administrative purposes into larger units, so the meetings of bishops followed these new large groupings, and each came to be dominated by a particular bishop: each came to be treated as a major 'diocese'. The most important such dioceses were Rome, Alexandria, Constantinople, Antioch, Jerusalem and Carthage: between them they comprehended the territory of the Roman Empire. Beyond the area of the Empire, however, the Church had to send groups of missionaries (as to Ireland and England), who created large churches ('minsters') to use as missionary centres, and the most important of these came to be the seats of bishops, and the location of other sees was decided on by the administrative needs of local lay rulers.

Now it so happened that shortly after he had made Christianity the state religion, Constantine had set up a new capital in the east for the Roman Empire. Settling his government at Byzantium in 330, he renamed this ancient Greek town 'New Rome', but it came to be known as 'Constantinople'. Less than a century later the old capital, Rome, was overrun by barbarians and thenceforth Rome and most of the rest of the western territories were marginal to the concerns of the Empire now based in Constantinople. It had only one firm foothold of influence remaining to it on the Italian mainland: its local centre of imperial government, its 'exarchate', at Ravenna, which it had reconquered.

The Roman Empire at Constantinople was a 'theocracy': the rule of God. As Steven Runciman writes:

> It saw itself as a universal Empire. Ideally it should embrace all the peoples of the earth, who, ideally, should all be members of the one true Christian Church, its own Orthodox Church. Just as man was made in God's image, so man's kingdom on earth was made in the image of the Kingdom of Heaven. Just as God ruled in Heaven, so an Emperor, made in His image, should rule on earth and carry out His commandments. Evil had made its way into God's creation, and man was stained with sin. But if the copy – the Greek word was *mimesis*, 'imitation' – could be achieved, with the Emperor and his ministers and counsellors imitating God with His archangels and angels and saints, then life on earth could become a proper preparation for the truer reality of life in Heaven ... the Emperor [was] in Byzantine eyes the Viceroy of God, the sacred head of the peoples of the earth.[41]

There is no question here of the separation of Church and State, or even of a thorough-going distinction between them. Following the example of Constantine himself, subsequent Emperors continued to convene and participate in the meetings of bishops, and to have a special relationship with the Patriarch of the Church. This practice continued right through to the final collapse of the Byzantine Empire in the fifteenth century. Although there were to be quarrels around this issue, the Emperor in Constantinople was always seen as the image of God, and in that sense as the head of the Church.

Constantine had acted in this spirit from his first days as a Christian for, in his role as Emperor, he convened universal Church councils to resolve certain disputes amongst Christians and got the bishops to establish once and for all what the proper doctrines and discipline (that is, the practice and daily life) of Christians should be. One highly controversial issue of doctrine was the view of Arius, who was maintaining that since God is an unknowable monad, the Son cannot be in the same sense God. The Platonic Greek philosophical basis of this view is obvious. But Constantine had no time for such disagreements. He said to Arius and Arius's bishop and rival, Bishop Alexander of Alexandria:

> You ought not to have raised such questions at all, and if they were raised, not to have answered. For such investigations, which no legal necessity imposes, but the frivolity of an idle hour provokes, we should – even if they are made for the sake of a philosophical exercise – lock up within our hearts and not bring forward into public gatherings.[42]

Constantine presided over the Church councils of Nicea of 325 and 327, which produced creeds (statements of orthodox Christian belief) and canons of discipline. The system of ecumenical councils did not however, despite Constantine's intentions, succeed in quelling dispute and promoting harmony within the Church.

Thus the Roman Empire survived: it survived for another thousand years, but based in Constantinople not Rome. And because it was thus now based in a Greek-speaking region, so the everyday language of the Empire became Greek. Latin survived in use for legal and administrative purposes for some time: the great codification of Roman law, drawn up at the command of the Emperor Theodosius II (438) and revised by command of the Emperor Justinian (promulgated in 534), was in Latin – though the Justinianic additions to it were in Greek. But Greek was now the language of the Empire. And hence Greek became the natural language of the Church in the eastern dioceses (Constantinople, Antioch, Jerusalem, Alexandria). As those dioceses came to be whittled down by the expansion of Islam in the seventh and later centuries to just that of Constantinople, so the 'Byzantine empire' (the diocese of Constantinople) came to be the sole area where the 'Greek' church held sway. Having Greek as their native tongue, and maintaining a tradition of secular education on the ancient Greek model, the Byzantines were able not only to preserve the ancient Greek writings, but they kept them in continual use as well. To put the matter at its most direct: both Aristotle and Plato continued to be read and discussed. They were read and discussed as philosophers. They were also read and discussed as pertinent to the understanding and interpretation of Christianity. The religious and spiritual traditions and the doctrines of the Greek Church were profoundly shaped by this fact. The greatest church in Constantinople, for long the greatest church in Christendom, was called 'St Sophia'. It was not, however, dedicated to a human saint, though there were several candidates of that name. It was dedicated to 'the Holy Wisdom' (*he hagia sophia*), that is to Christ as the incarnate Word of God. It is a peculiarly Greek concept, it is 'sophia' as in 'philosophy' (philo-sophia) 'the love of wisdom'. It would be another thousand years before such a dedication of a church would be thinkable in the West.

Meanwhile in the West the old Roman Empire simply collapsed. If we need a precise date as marking the final demise of the Roman Empire in the West, we may take 476, when a barbarian general deposed the Emperor. The decay of the western Empire was a by-product of a catastrophic economic slump. For the next 500 years Europe as a whole continued to suffer. The population decreased all over the area of the former Empire. The 'villa', the unit of Roman agricultural production, was abandoned. The area of land under cultivation decreased: forest spread again over many areas once cultivated. Virtually every Roman town, including the Eternal City great Rome itself, ceased to be occupied. The unitary territory of the former Roman Empire fragmented politically under the impact of invasions. From having been an empire based on towns, Europe again became almost exclusively rural. Literacy became confined to a tiny proportion of the population: primarily to the clergy of the Roman Catholic Church (and only to some of them at that). And, as one might expect, such conditions of economic contraction and retreat produced a state of learning equally destitute of liveliness and innovation.

Constantinople was the New Rome and head (so its Emperor believed) also of the Christian Church. In the West, however, although the political empire of Old Rome simply fell apart in the fifth century, yet the imperial religious organization, Christianity, survived. As early as the fifth century (Leo I, Bishop of Rome 440–61), the Bishop of Rome – the traditional capital of the Empire and the place where St Peter himself was buried – came to claim that Old Rome was the sole and proper head of the Christian Church, and that he, the Bishop of Rome, was the heir to St Peter. Though Rome was as yet a long way from being free from eastern imperial control, there were thus now two Churches, one east and one west, both claiming to have absolute jurisdiction over the territories of the (former) Roman Empire – and hence over each other. As Christianity was initially practised in the local language, the eastern Church spoke Greek (as we have seen); but the western Church spoke Latin. From about AD 400 there was a standard version of the Scriptures available in Latin, for that is when St Jerome was finishing his version, which much later came to be known as the 'Vulgate', the version 'in the common tongue'. But over the next few centuries literacy became less and less common in the West, and Latin fell out of use in favour of local languages. The western Church, however, continued to use Latin as the language of worship. Eventually the skill of reading and writing came to be possessed almost exclusively by higher Church officials. This is why Latin – dead as a common language on the demise of the Empire in the West – nevertheless continued as the language of literacy and of learning in the West. Thus the Roman Church came to speak a language different from the (vernacular) languages of its own members, and one different again from that of the Church in Constantinople. In time the 'Latin' Church, indeed, ceased to be able to understand Greek at all, with Greek being spoken only in Ravenna (the Byzantine enclave) and in Sicily and the 'boot' of Italy. Henceforth there were to be two sets of church 'Fathers', Latin (such as Augustine and Jerome) who were accessible to the Latin Church, and Greek (such as Origen and Clement of Alexandria) who were not. The Greek philosophers, Plato and Aristotle, were no longer read in the Latin west, copies of their works were no longer even possessed: inevitably therefore they could not be called on to assist in the understanding and interpretation of Latin Christianity. Hence Latin Christianity came to have no time or room for the assistance of Greek philosophy. Even neo-Platonism was a subject of interest only to a very few. And of course almost all the ancient writings on the natures of things were Greek. They too were thus no longer available to the Latins of the West, and had no role in their culture.

The successive Bishops of Rome – 'pope' ('papa', 'father') as they came to style themselves – were never happy with their subjection to Constantinople, and especially to an Emperor who claimed to be able to adjudicate on spiritual and religious matters. Certain of the Popes actively sought to break the link which tied Rome to Constantinople. Foremost amongst them were Gregory II (715–31) and Leo III (795–816) who between them, it has been argued, ran a papal campaign to 'emancipate' the (Roman) Church from the (eastern) Empire.[43] In the course of this campaign of 'emancipation', one of the eighth-century Popes caused to be written a famous (and later notorious) document, the so-called 'Donation of Constantine', which was long regarded as authentic. In it is described how, centuries before, the Emperor Constantine had given to the Bishop of Rome supremacy over all other dioceses, had given him the Lateran Palace in Rome as the papal headquarters, and the city of Rome and territories of Italy as his patrimony. Now, in the 700s, these Popes flattered and cajoled the new rulers of the Franks, Pepin the Short and his sons, to win 'back' and then become 'defenders' of these supposedly papal territories. Among these territories was Ravenna, the seat of (eastern) imperial government in Italy. But while the Franks did win 'back' these territories for the papacy from the Lombards, the Pope then expected them to be 'defended' against the claims of the Emperor in Constantinople. In return for this help, and on the pretext of there being a vacancy on the imperial throne in Constantinople, the Pope then rewarded Pepin's most famous son, Charles the Great (Charlemagne) with the title of 'Emperor of the Romans' on Christmas Day 800.

Thus in addition to there being two Churches of the old Roman Empire, a 'Greek' one and a 'Latin' one, there were now two Roman Emperors, a 'Greek' one in Constantinople, and a 'Latin' one – the Holy Roman Emperor – in the West, each taking their legitimacy from, and confirming the legitimacy of, their respective Churches. In the West the Pope had not only begun to formally annoint this new Emperor, but he had to all intents and purposes created the post itself. What the Pope had in mind was an Emperor who would be subject to the papacy in spiritual matters; what Charlemagne had in mind in accepting the title, however, seems to have been something more akin to the role of the Emperor in the theocracy in Constantinople. In later centuries this difference in their understanding of the point of the position of Holy Roman Emperor was to lead to extensive disputes between Emperor and Pope, centred on the question of which of them had the ultimate right to appoint the other.

With the existence, from AD 800, of two Churches, two Emperors and two Empires, we can leave the eastern Church and Empire and now concentrate on the western, where our story continues. But it is important for us to remember that hostilities continued for centuries between the Churches of east and west, the Pope continually calling for the submission of the eastern Church to his own supremacy. It is also important for us to remember that although the eastern Empire and Church now entered a state of long decline, yet still all the best books, the Greek ones, were part of the everyday culture of Constantinople, but were known not at all in Rome or the West. Even in the court of Charlemagne at Aix-la-Chapelle (790–814), where learning was respected and scholars promoted, the ancient texts which were so laboriously copied out in the new 'carolingian' form of writing, were Latin (that is, Roman) works, not Greek.[44]

Thus Christianity, as we have seen, was partially Greek in its origin, and the predominant Greek influence on it in its beginning and in subsequent centuries was from the Platonic and Stoic traditions. Through the collapse of the Old Roman Empire, the western branch of the Church – the Latin Church – abandoned this philosophical tradition as a live input into understanding the Bible and Christian doctrine. As we shall see in later chapters, when Greek learning was reintroduced to the West, and came to be reincorporated into Latin Christianity, the predominant form of Greek philosophy used would be not Platonic, but Aristotelian. It was inevitable therefore that there would not be total compatibility between Christianity and this form of Greek philosophy.

Natural philosophy, a new subject, was to be constructed in the thirteenth century by reapplying Greek philosophy to Christianity. As we have seen, all the concern with the natures of things was Greek and philosophical. For the promotion of a study built on Greek philosophical concern with the natures of things, it was necessary that people either had their own twelfth- and thirteenth-century reasons for wanting to revive Greek philosophy, or they felt they needed to apply arguments from and about the natures of things to their own twelfth- and thirteenth-century concerns. Greek philosophy was not revived because it was marvellous, nor just 'because it was there', nor 'for its own sake', nor for some simple 'love of learning', nor even because the people of medieval Europe felt backward compared to their more civilized neighbours. It was revived in order to serve the interests and concerns of twelfth- and thirteenth-century men; it was therefore revived in a way peculiar to the Latins of the twelfth and thirteenth centuries.

Notes

1. For the early part of our account of Greek philosophy we use the excellent article by I.C. Brady, 'History of Philosophy (Ancient Philosophy)' in the *New Catholic Encyclopedia*, McGraw-Hill Book Company, New York, 17 vols, 1967–79, vol. 11, pp. 303–10. The quotation from Diogenes Laertius (1.4) is on p. 303.
2. Ibid., p. 304.
3. Some faint trace of this meaning, in its Stoic sense, is still preserved in modern English usage when we speak of someone having a particular 'philosophy of life', or of someone accepting misfortune 'philosophically', or even in the concept of a 'philosophy of' marketing or whatever; this kind of usage in modern English is quite distinct however from discussion of philosophy as an academic discipline.
4. I.C. Brady, op. cit. According to Plato, 'Socrates awakened Athenians to the care of their souls through the practice of *elenchos*, which made them aware of their own ignorance', William Jordan, *Ancient Concepts of Philosophy*, London, Routledge, 1990, p. 70.
5. Socrates in *Phaedo* by Plato, 84 a–b, in the translation of Benjamin Jowett.
6. As a modern philosopher has written, pointing up the difference between Greek and modern philosophy, 'the [Greek] philosopher leads a particular, distinctive and valuable lifestyle. Socrates devoted his life to the practice of *elenchos*. The Platonic philosopher cultivates death, contemplates the Form of Beauty, and practises politics (applied philosophy) in the ideal state. The Aristotelian philosopher aims either to lead the life of practical wisdom in a *polis* with his friends, or, perhaps, to spend his life in

theoretical contemplation. All the Hellenistic schools of philosophy promise the philosopher personal happiness, and believe that happiness arises from the correct orientation towards the world; the Stoics believe the process of orientation is largely natural; the sceptics think we must learn the impotence of reason and argument; only for Epicurus does the correct orientation have to do with learning certain truths – those truths, however, point us away from reason and towards the authority of the child and the senses. For ancient philosophers, then, the value of philosophy lies as much in a particular lifestyle and in the practice of philosophy as in the particular conclusions we reach through our skills in argument. And here indeed ancient philosophy does differ from its modern counterpart'. Jordan, *Ancient Concepts of Philosophy*, p. 176.

7. Werner Jaeger, *Early Christianity and Greek Paideia*, Cambridge, Mass., The Belknap Press of Harvard University Press, 1961.
8. Robert Flint, *Philosophy as Scientia Scientiarum: and a History of Classifications of the Sciences*, Edinburgh and London, Blackwood, 1904, pp. 68–9 (capitalization of 'The Good' added).
9. 'Greek philosophy had been a means of recognizing "the Divine" from its very beginnings, a fact of which our modern history of Greek philosophy has lost sight almost entirely, during the era of positivism and naturalism in which these grandiose systems of nature were interpreted as the first attempts of the human mind to create modern science', Werner Jaeger, 'Greeks and Jews', in his *Scripta Minora*, 2 vols, Rome, Edizioni di Storia e Letteratura, 1960, vol. 2, pp. 169–83, see p. 171.
10. We follow here the paraphrase of F.M. Cornford, *Before and After Socrates*, Cambridge University Press, 1932, repr. 1979, pp. 1–3. The passage he is referring to in the *Phaedo* is 96–99; our quotation is from 99c, as translated by Benjamin Jowett, with capitalization of the Good and the Right added.
11. This issue is dealt with in more detail in Chapter 4.
12. Aristotle, *Parts of Animals*, Book 1, c. 5 (644 b 25–645 a 26), as translated for us by Christine Salazar.
13. Edgar Wind, in *Pagan Mysteries in the Renaissance*, Oxford University Press, 1980 (first published 1958), p. 3, writes of Plato's seventh *Letter*, that 'instead of disclaiming for his philosophy any kinship with [common mystical initiation] rites, Plato declared on the contrary that philosophy itself was a mystical initiation of another kind, which achieved for a chosen few by conscious inquiry what the mysteries supplied to the vulgar by stirring up their emotions. The cleansing of the soul, the welcoming of death, the power to enter into communion with the Beyond, the ability to "rage correctly", these benefits which Plato recognised were commonly provided by mystical initiations were to be obtained through his philosophy by rational exercise, by a training in the art of dialectic, whose aim it was to purge the soul of error'. Such Platonic religio-philosophic attitudes and practices were put back into direct practice in the Renaissance.
14. See F.M. Cornford, *From Religion to Philosophy. A Study in the Origins of Western Speculation*, Sussex, Harvester Press, 1980 (first publ. 1912); Jaeger, 'Greeks and Jews'.
15. The view that the Greeks were the first rationalists who separated religion from science/philosophy, underlies most modern work in history of science

and in history of philosophy; for instance it is basic to W.K.C. Guthrie, *A History of Greek Philosophy*, Cambridge University Press, 6 vols, 1962–81. Compare Jaeger, quoted in note 9 above.

16. Epistle XVI, as cited by Eduard Lohse, *The New Testament Environment*, London, SCM Press, 1976, p. 249. 'Non est philosophia populare artificium nec ostentationi paratum. Non in verbis, sed in rebus est. Nec in hoc adhibetur, ut cum aliqua oblectatione consumatur dies, ut dematur otio nausia. Animum format et fabricat, vitam disponit, actiones regit, agenda et omittenda demonstrat, sedet ad gubernaculum et per anticipitia fluctuantium derigit cursum. Sine hac nemo intrepide potest vivere, nemo secure ... philosophandum est: sive nos inexorabili lege fata constringunt, sive arbiter deus universi cuncta disposuit, sive casus res humanas sine ordine inpellit et iactat, philosophia nos tueri debet. Haec adhortabitur, ut deo libenter pareamus, ut fortunae contumaciter; haec docuebit, ut deum sequaris, feras casum'; Latin text as given in the Loeb edition, vol. 1, pp. 104–6.

17. *Republic*, 379 a 5: '... it is most important that the tales which the young first hear should be models of virtuous thoughts ... The founders of a State ought to know the general forms in which poets should cast their tales, and the limits which must be observed by them'

'Very true ... but what are these forms of theology that you mean?'

'Something of the kind, I replied: – God is always to be represented as he truly is, whatever be the sort of poetry, epic, lyric or tragic, in which the representation is given ...'; as translated by Benjamin Jowett. See also L.P. Gerson, *God and Greek Philosophy*, London, Routledge, 1990.

18. Aristotle, *Metaphysics*, 1026 a 18 seqq., as given in Clement J. Webb, *Studies in the History of Natural Theology*, Oxford, Clarendon, 1915, p. 15.

19. Webb, p. 15. This division of philosophy was known to the people of the Middle Ages through a mention of it in Chapter 2 of Boethius's *De Trinitate*; see Ralph McInerny, 'Beyond the liberal arts', in David L. Wagner, ed., *The Seven Liberal Arts in the Middle Ages*, Bloomington, Indiana University Press, 1983, 248–72, see p. 250.

20. Genesis 1.20–1.

21. See, for instance, the article 'Soul', in *New Catholic Encyclopedia* (note 1 above), vol. 13, 447–64, esp. 'Soul (in the Bible)' by W.E. Lynch, pp. 449–50: 'there is no dichotomy of body and soul in the Old Testament. The Israelite saw things concretely, in their totality, and thus he considered men as persons and not as composites. The term *nepeš*, though translated by our word soul, never means soul as distinct from the body or the individual person. Other words in the Old Testament such as spirit, flesh, and heart also signify the human person and differ only as various aspects of the same being ... The term ψυχή is the New Testament word corresponding with *nepeš*. It can mean the principle of life, life itself, or the living being. Through Hellenistic influence, unlike *nepeš*, it was opposed to body and considered immortal.' See also Erwin Rohde, *Psyche. The Cult of Souls and Belief in Immortality among the Greeks*, London, Kegan Paul, 1925.

22. 'Areopagus' means 'Hill of Ares', Ares being the Greek god of war, equivalent to the Latin god of war, Mars. Hence it is also referred to as 'Mars Hill', as later in this passage. A legal council met here, and appears

to have had the power to appoint lecturers – as perhaps with St Paul here. The 'Dionysius the Areopagite' referred to at the end of this passage may have been a member of this council. See the entry 'Areopagus' in James Hastings and John A. Selbie, eds, *Dictionary of the Bible*, Edinburgh, Clark, 1909.

23. Acts 17.16–34, Authorised Version.
24. Eduard Lohse identifies one such 'Greek poet' as Cleanthes, with his early Stoic poem to Zeus; *New Testament Environment*, p. 245.
25. See for instance Henry Chadwick, *Early Christian Thought and the Classical Tradition*, Oxford, Clarendon Press, 1966; Robert M. Grant, *Augustus to Constantine: The Thrust of the Christian Movement into the Roman World*, London, Collins, 1971, ch. 7.
26. Clement, Book II, ch. xxii, citing Plato *Theatetus* 176b; the Plato as translated by Benjamin Jowett. For the text of Clement see *Ante-Nicene Christian Library: Translations of the Writings of the Fathers down to 325 A.D*, edited by Revd Alexander Roberts and James Donaldson, vols 4 and 12, vol. 12, p. 75. On Origen we follow Joseph Wilson Trigg, *Origen: The Bible and Philosophy in the Third-Century Church*, London, SCM Press, 1985, 54–66.
27. *Miscellanies*, Book I, ch. xiii.
28. *Miscellanies*, Book VI, ch. viii.
29. Trigg, *Origen*, p. 61.
30. Origen's Letter to Gregory, as translated by Menzies in Allan Menzies, ed., *Ante-Nicene Christian Library: Additional Volume*, Edinburgh, Clark, 1897, pp. 295–6, see p. 295. The Gregory to whom the letter is addressed is possibly Gregory Thaumaturgus.
31. Exodus 3.xxi–ii; 12.xxxv–vi.
32. Trigg, *Origen*, pp. 125–6; see also Beryl Smalley, *The Study of the Bible in the Middle Ages*, Oxford, Blackwell, third edn, 1984 (first published 1941), pp. 1–14.
33. Cited from Tertullian's *De Praescriptione Haereticorum*, by Norman Kretzmann, 'Reason in Mystery', in *The Philosophy in Christianity*, ed. Godfrey Vesey, Cambridge University Press, 1989, pp. 15–39, see p. 20.
34. Quoted by W. Le Saint in the article 'Tertullian', *New Catholic Encyclopedia*, vol. 13, pp. 1019–22, see p. 1019. On Tertullian see also Timothy D. Barnes, *Tertullian: A Historical and Literary Study*, Oxford, Clarendon, 1985.
35. *The Confessions of S. Augustine*, translated by E.B. Pusey, Oxford, Parker, 1838, pp. 117–21; passages in italics are quotations from the Bible. For the Latin original see *S. Aurelii Augustini Confessiones*, ed. M. Dubois, Oxford, Parker, 1888.
36. Ibid., p. 121.
37. Augustine wrote that, 'In considering "natural" theology, it is necessary to enter discussions with philosophers, whose very title if we translate it into Latin means "lover of wisdom". Now if God, through whom all things were made (as divine authority and truth witness) is wisdom, then the true philosopher is a lover of God'; 'cum philosophis est habenda collatio: quorum ipsum nomen si latine interpretemur, amorem sapientiae profitetur. Porro si sapientia Deus est, per quem facta sunt omnia, sicut divina auctoritas veritasque monstravit, verus philosophus est amator Dei', *City of God*, Book 8, ch. 1, (Migne, *Patrologia Latina*, vol. 41, pp. 225–6) our translation.

38. On the Gnostics, see the excellent work of Elaine Pagels, *The Gnostic Gospels*, London, Wiedenfeld and Nicolson, 1980. She discusses in particular the relation of Gnostic thought, and its defeat, to political circumstances.
39. Yet, even though the Gnostics were so 'Greek' in their concerns, it seems that they were not at all interested in the 'rational' dimension of Greek philosophy, nor in 'the natures of things' in the manner of Greek philosophers such as Aristotle.
40. Celsus, quoted from Robert M. Grant, *Augustus to Constantine: The Thrust of the Christian Movement into the Roman World*, London, Collins, 1971, p. 115.
41. Steven Runciman, *The Byzantine Theocracy*, Cambridge University Press, 1977, pp. 1–2.
42. As cited in A.H.M. Jones, *Constantine and the Conversion of Europe*, London, English Universities Press, 1948, repr. 1964, p. 145.
43. Walter Ullmann, *The Growth of Papal Government in the Middle Ages: A Study in the Ideological Relation of Clerical to Lay Power*, London, Methuen, 1955.
44. However, a few works were translated from Greek somewhere in the Carolingian Empire, for instance Pseudo-Dionysius was sent to Louis the Pious by the Eastern Emperor in 827, and translated by John Scotus Eriguena. The importance of this work is discussed in Chapter 9.

CHAPTER TWO

The air of towns

The commercial revolution

The Orders of friars were created as a response to the problems created by the vibrant, rich, urban society of Europe at the beginning of the thirteenth century. The approaches to natural philosophy that the Orders of friars created were also responses to the problems of wealth, power and belief in that society, and cannot be properly understood outside that context that gave rise to them. Money makes towns, and then towns make heresy.

The changes in the economy of Europe were slow in making their appearance and gradual in producing their effects. The court of Charlemagne had been an untypical bright spot in a bleak world. For in general, for centuries after the collapse of the old (western) Roman Empire, Europe was lawless, distressingly poor and benighted. By comparison with contemporaneous life in the Byzantine Empire or in the rising Islamic Empire on the south and eastern shores of the Mediterranean, life in central and northern Europe was hard and deprived. By present-day standards the condition of life for most people even in 1200 was one of dire poverty, but compared to any time in the previous five centuries, the society of 1200 was a wealthy one indeed. The improvement had started in the mid-900s. Over the period of two centuries the changes were of such a magnitude that they deserve both the epithets they have recently been given: 'The commercial revolution' and 'The industrial revolution'.[1] No one knows why this economic revival happened: ultimately it may have been due to a change in climactic conditions. This upturn in the fortunes of Europe was to continue for four centuries, until the Black Death of 1348. In the traditional historical terminology for this period, what thus distinguishes the 'Dark Ages' (culturally deprived) from the 'High Middle Ages' (culturally flourishing) is precisely this economic improvement, this commercial and industrial revolution.

Everywhere the population began to increase: England's population, for instance, may have increased threefold between the Norman invasion in 1066 and the Black Death in 1348. The feudal 'manor' or 'demesne' became the primary unit of agricultural production. Waste lands were resettled, and virgin and marginal lands were increasingly brought under cultivation. Agriculture became more productive: the area under cultivation was increasing, the yield of crops was improving, and the rotation of crops seems to have been practised more effectively. This in turn led to some improvement and innovation in machines, changes which were also possibly a response to a shortage of labour. Water-mills and windmills became common, as did tidal mills. In England the Domesday Book reveals the existence of over five and a half thousand mills in 1086. The horse was given, for the first time, a padded collar, and it has been estimated that this made it twelve times more efficient than its Roman predecessor; thus for the first time horses could be employed in agriculture, and in the north they were put to pulling the new heavy (wheeled) plough, with which heavy northern soils could be brought under cultivation. The new three-field rotation system allowed for the growing of oats to supply the horses, who were given (again for the first time) metal shoes to enable them to work harder longer, which a race of smiths and their forges arose to supply.

Europe was wealthy again. This massive change in the material conditions of life transformed the face of Europe. It made new initiatives and ways of life possible. It facilitated a cultural efflorescence. It led to changes in what people believed – in, that is, what was taken to be true about both this world and the next. It led to violent disputes to control the wealth of this world, and its people. And, as this world got richer and more comfortable to live in, so more and more people chose, for one reason or another, to flee or reject it. This age of wealth became for many an age of self-imposed poverty. Some people deliberately adopted poverty as a way of life as a protest against the values and beliefs of this society. As we shall see, our heretics were amongst these. Others adopted poverty as a strategy to meet such dissidents on their own ground, and to thus be able most effectively to defend the beliefs and organization of Roman Catholicism against its opponents. This is what the Dominicans were to do. Others again, while they adopted poverty as a protest against materialist values, used it as a means to free their bodies and minds from the encumbrances which usually prevented people from living the true spiritual life of a Roman Catholic Christian. This was to be the attitude of the Franciscans, who set out to be poor as Christ had been poor, and spiritual as Christ had been spiritual, and hence enable themselves to defend and promote true Christianity against its detractors, and to be a model for true Christian living.

There is no convenient term in common usage among historians to refer to this period of economic and cultural flourishing in Europe, especially in the south-west band around the Mediterranean, and its intellectual and religious dimensions. 'Medieval' covers too long a period, of up to a thousand years. Moreover, 'Middle Ages' and 'medieval' are descriptions given long after the time and by people who wanted to denigrate the period and the events which happened in it; the terms were intended to indicate a 'middle' period of cultural decline between the high points of Antiquity and the Renaissance.

The term we have chosen (and we are aware of our temerity in doing so) is, instead, 'Troubadourean'. One of the reasons for doing so is that it is built on a contemporary category, and reflects the place where the central events of our story started: Occitania or the Languedoc, where the troubadours sang. We should stress that we shall be using the term 'Troubadourean' in a temporal and cultural sense, as described above. The term does, however, have some relation directly to one of the leaders of the friars, St Francis, who was familiar with troubadour poetry and is, and was, often known as 'God's troubadour'.

Feudal control and papal authority

Control in Europe over men's lives and minds in post-Charlemagne Europe, was both political and ideological, and the heresies, when they came, were challenges to both the political structure of feudalism and the claims of the papacy to ideological primacy.

The most important legacy of Charlemagne's rule was a side-effect of the collapse of the Carolingian Empire: the social-political-economic system we now refer to as 'feudalism'. This came to be dominant by 1100 in most of the western parts of the old Roman Empire, and was practised by lay and religious landowners alike. Feudalism – at the risk of oversimplifying a very complex set of issues, still under fervent debate by historians – is a structure of land-holding: land, and its produce, is in effect let for life in return for fealty (loyalty) and certain services. Initially those services were primarily military: the 'fee', a given area of land, had to supply on demand one fully equipped warrior (a knight) for the lord's service. All land (except common land) had this burden on it. Whoever held the land (or a fraction of it) was liable to provide the military service (or the appropriate fraction of it) either in his own person, or in the person of someone else, or in cash or kind. The forms of social and political relations followed from this structure of land-holding. Land was granted as a favour (not sold or rented) by one person to another; the granter was thereby the superior and the grantee the inferior, and this relationship persisted throughout the tenure of the land. Hence the holder of the land regarded its owner as his lord, paid him the deference due to a lord, fought on behalf of his lord when required, submitted himself to his lord's administration of justice. A warrior class of 'knights' came into existence, which developed its own codes of combat and honour – 'chivalry', the code of the warrior who rides a horse (*cheval*). The knights had their ceremonies of admission to knighthood, their oaths, their ceremonial tests and exercises (the tournament), and the deeds both true and mythical of their heroes were celebrated in song by 'troubadours', especially the song (*chanson*) about Roland, Charlemagne's companion, and the songs about King Arthur and his knights.[2]

Land was always granted complete with its occupants, its peasants. Ultimately of course the whole system of seigneurial control was sustained on the backs of the peasantry, confined on the manors of their lords, providing labour services on the lord's demesne, scraping a living for themselves from their small strips of land, providing a proportion of the produce of their little holdings to the lord, and subject in everything to the whim or justice of their lord. They were serfs – virtual slaves.

On the peasants fell another, greatly hated, burden: tithes. In these centuries it became the norm and the law for every piece of land to give a tenth of its produce (or equivalent) every year to the Church. It was this which provided the basic income of the whole Church organization.[3] The tithe was due to the local – the parish – church and was paid locally in kind (often being stored in great tithe barns); the incumbent of the local church took what was due to him, and passed the rest on to his ecclesiastical superiors. This is how the thousands of church buildings and thousands of parish priests were supported.

Most churches were originally established and built by landowners. But in the tenth and eleventh centuries, ownership of them increasingly passed into religious hands, either to a bishop or, more frequently, to a religious house. The parish and its church were pieces of realizable and income-yielding property, for virtually every piece of land in Europe was bound to pay tithes to one church or another. The outgoings of a church included the upkeep of the fabric, the maintenance of a priest, and the relief of the local poor and sick. (Increasingly it was taken for granted that monks – God's poor –

were the natural recipients of this money.) Because the parish was a piece of property producing an income, so people came to have an interest in ensuring that the bounds of each parish were established beyond doubt, and they were walked regularly just to make sure. As property, parish revenues and churches could be given away. If a landowner donated a parish church to a monastery (as many did) to ensure the saying of prayers for his soul, then he intended that church to produce an income for the monastery. The income of each parish church had to exceed its outgoings. Hence the greater part of the income of many parish churches came to be appropriated by the religious houses for their own support; they often appointed priests as vicars ('stand-ins') on small pay to run the place.

As it was a piece of real estate, it was important that the parish church should not be owned by its incumbent, its priest, for he would inevitably want to make it heritable, so that he could pass it on to his son. It would then cease to be of profit to its original owner. This has been seen as one (though only one) reason why, from the eleventh century on, the celibacy of the priesthood came to be preached and promoted as an important point of discipline in the western Church, which it had not been hitherto. A priest must have no sons.[4]

A mighty expansion in monastic institutions took place from the tenth century – the very period of the economic expansion.[5] Monks and nuns are the 'regular' clergy; unlike ordinary priests, they live according to a 'Rule'. Most monks were not in priest's orders, and hence could not officiate at Mass or take services. The religious life secluded from the world, either as individuals (hermits, anchorites), or in communities, was a traditional manifestation of Christianity, and common since the fourth century. In the West the 'Rule' of St Benedict (written *c.*530) was for centuries the model for monastic life. The Rule specified the daily round of services, worship, meditation, spiritual reading and manual work to be carried out by the monks or nuns of the community; it called for total obedience, for personal poverty, for chastity. We shall be hearing more later (Chapter 3) of the nature of the learning necessary for and typical of this religious life. The primary task of the monk was *opus Dei*, God's work: that is, communal worship. 'Never departing from His guidance, continuing in the monastery in His teaching unto death, through patience we are made partakers in Christ's passion, in order that we may merit to be companions in His kingdom', as St Benedict wrote in his Rule.[6]

The first movement of monastic expansion flowed out from the monastery of Cluny in Burgundy. These Cluniacs followed the Rule of St Benedict, with even greater stress on and splendour in the conduct of the services, the liturgy. By 1200, except in Germany, there were hundreds of 'daughter' houses owing allegiance to Cluny – more than 500 of them in England alone. The spread of Cluniac houses was matched in the early 1100s by other monastic movements. The hermit life was revived, most notably by the Carthusians, who took their name from their mountain house at La Grande Chartreuse. Then again there was competition from a new movement of people claiming to follow the Rule of St Augustine: Austin or Augustinian canons, and Premonstratensians. Finally there was founded in this period the great order of the Cistercians, led by St Bernard of Clairvaux in the early decades of the twelfth century, and following the Rule of St Benedict – but literally interpreted. This meant two things in particular: a more ascetic way of life than the Cluniacs (St Bernard was reportedly particularly hostile to the jewels and coloured glass of Cluny);[7] and a greater concentration on manual work. Cistercian monasteries were supposed to be self-sufficient on their estates; they were only too successful, rapidly becoming very rich farmers of sheep and cultivators of vineyards.

> In their sincere desire to flee the worldly and commercial life of the cities the Cistercians went to live in areas 'remote from the habitation of man'. But by attempting to become independent of the outside world, they created an economic empire based on a highly centralised administration and on up-to-date technological expertise.[8]

Of all the monastic orders the Cistercians were the least drain on the resources of the secular society; indeed, they became so rich that their wealth tempted secular rulers to reverse the usual direction of giving, and to call on them for various loans and gifts.

This expansion in the number of monasteries and regular clergy coincided both with the great increase in population and with the economic expansion, and also with a change in the pattern of inheritance amongst families who owned land. It had been usual, for kings as well as lesser landowners, to divide their land amongst their children. Now, however, it came to be normal over most of Europe to adopt 'primogeniture': everything goes to the eldest son, little if anything to any other children. This served to keep estates and kingdoms intact, but of course it left the younger children unprovided for. One place they could go was into a monastery or nunnery. As Professor Brooke writes, 'This is perhaps to us the most surprising feature of many monasteries of the early eleventh century, that a large number of their monks were not there of their own volition, at least in the first instance'.[9] There they would be provided for for life; they would have no claim on the family estate; and they would not breed (and thus produce further claimants). To enter a religious house was not to step down from one class to a lower. For life within a monastery or nunnery was a microcosm of the hierarchical structure of the outside world. Then as now, birth was important if one was to become an abbot, prior or Mother Superior. And in all monasteries there were other people to do at least some of the hard work: the Carthusians of La Grande Chartreuse, where the brothers lived secluded from the world in a distant mountain retreat, and secluded from each other in their individual cells, had servants, while the Cistercians on their great farms and granges had a whole class of lay brothers, with different roles and aspirations from the monks who could read, and these lay brothers undertook the greatest share of the manual work.

The monastic building programme was on an almost unbelievable scale in this century. Apart from their role as religious centres, therefore, we must see the monasteries and nunneries of Troubadourean Europe as serving to mop up some of the surplus wealth of Europe, especially in the 1100s. But we must also see them as absorbing up some of the surplus population – the population which, if allowed to breed normally in the world, would have affected the stability of that world. This absorption was done in the name of a greater asceticism and religiosity, of a retreat from the world and its riches and temptations. But that asceticism with respect to the values of the outside world could only go so far. When the Pope granted Waldo, a merchant of Lyons, permission in the 1170s to form a community of poor preachers, he insisted that Waldo swear that he did not believe all the rich were in hell.[10] The values of the world could be denied, but not condemned.

Although the Pope was acknowledged to be the head of the Roman Church now, he hardly ran a centralized clerical empire. It is in this period that the Popes set out to extend their control down to the parish priests, and to standardize and enforce doctrine, discipline and ritual. The most important Pope in all this, and the one who proved the strongest and most successful at getting his own way, was the one whose appointers gave him the delightfully inappropriate name of Innocent III (Pope 1198–1216). He is the one who first clearly saw his post as that of Vicar of Christ. As he announced in his inaugural sermon:

> Who am I and of what lineage that I should take my place above Kings? For to me it is said in the Prophets, 'I have this day set thee over nations and over the kingdoms, to root out and pull down, and to destroy, and to throw down, to build and to plant'. To me it is said in the Apostles, 'I will give unto thee the keys of

> the kingdom of heaven; and whatsoever thou shalt bind on earth shall be bound in heaven; and whatsoever thou shalt loose on earth shall be loosed in heaven'. The successor of Peter is the Vicar of Christ: he has been established as a mediator between God and man, below God but beyond man; less than God but more than man; who shall judge all and be judged by no one.[11]

Despite these grandiose ambitions, it was in practice a real problem for the Popes to win the right to appoint bishops, or even the lesser right of approving their appointment. For bishops were usually appointed by their chapters at the suggestion, or under the pressure of, the local ruler. The rulers wanted men who were of use to them as administrators. But bishops regarded themselves also as responsible for the conduct of services, good order, right belief, the protection of church property against lay encroachment, the protection of the special jurisdictional status of the clergy (the 'benefit of clergy'), and the running of the church courts of their diocese. Hence they had a double loyalty – which was sometimes tested – to their local secular ruler and also to the ruler of the Church, the Pope. In this period bishops usually took it on themselves to build, rebuild or enlarge a building for their chair (*cathedra*) of office, that is, a cathedral (or *duomo*), and we shall see later something of its pertinence to natural philosophy (Chapter 10). In the same way as the Popes were trying to gain control over the bishops, so each bishop in this period was engaged in trying to gain control over the appointment of the parish priests of his diocese; as parish churches were private property, and the right to appoint parish priests also lay in private hands, this was a difficult matter, and the bishops had to content themselves with approving (or not) lay appointments, and with the right to remove incapable or unorthodox incumbents.

The Popes were also concerned with the establishment of doctrinal orthodoxy and disciplinary uniformity throughout their earthly empire, and this is a matter to which we shall be returning. It was only in the 1150s (by Peter Lombard in his *Sentences*) that the 'sacraments' were set and established at seven: baptism, confirmation, the eucharist (mass), penance, extreme unction, (holy) orders, and matrimony. It was only in 1215 that a council of the Church approved the work in which they were set out. Marriage and sex were particular concerns of the papacy at this period. That marriage should be for life, and that it was only legitimate if sanctioned by the Church, were novelties being brought in now, as was the celibacy of the priesthood (as we have already seen).[12] The cult of the Virgin was also taken to new heights. The Pope now, in the 1180s, also asserted a papal monopoly in the creation of saints, which was formalized in 1234: only the Pope and his officials could detect sainthood. The rise and rise of the Pope, the man who now claimed to be the direct descendant of St Peter and who called himself the Vicar of Christ, can be illustrated by the Councils of the Church held under the Pope's leadership. The first such Council of the entire western Church was held at the Lateran (the Pope's home in Rome) in 1123: the very fact it took place here marked the fact that the Roman Church was now free from eastern control. Within less than a century, in 1215, the fourth Lateran Council was held, and at this Innocent III had many of the central doctrines and points of discipline confirmed for the Roman Catholic Church, including the obligation on every Catholic to take the sacraments of penance and mass once a year at least, and a ruling on what it is that is happening in the mass. Thus the holding of the Fourth Lateran Council indicated that by 1215 the Roman Catholic Church was run by the Pope in Rome.

It is evident that many people had an interest in maintaining the stability of this system. Everyone at the top of this system – even abbots, priors and bishops – were from the same class, and had the same interests. All of it, including all forms of church and religious life, was built on the profits from agricultural land and on the values of the country. And although, as we have seen, most of the population of Europe at this period lived under feudalism, locked on to the land, feudalism itself was no bar to the 'commercial' or 'industrial' revolution: indeed the intensification of manorial agriculture under feudalism provided the surplus that made forms of life possible beyond the needs of sheer survival. But the vitality of the 'commercial revolution' did not derive from the feudal countryside, although it depended on the surplus the countryside produced. Instead it was to be found in the towns – entities which did not fit the feudal structure and hierarchy.

Town air

The towns of Troubadourean western Europe constitute one of the most visible and long-lasting effects of the great economic revival of the period. They are important for our story because certain of the towns were the very places where the major problem arose to which the creation of the orders of friars was intended to be an answer, for towns bred heresy.

The towns spelled 'freedom': they acted as oases of (relative) freedom from all the restrictions and most of the obligations that fell on all the lower orders in the feudal system. Thus they were places – the only places – where 'free' thought was possible. The significance of Troubadourean towns in their own time is summed up in the traditional saying, 'Town air makes free', for any serf who succeeded in living in a town undetected by his master for a year and a day was (at least in theory) thereby rendered free for life. A town-dweller had no master, not in the feudal sense.

All over western Europe towns again became centres of settlement. In some places people again moved back to the sites of old Roman towns. In others, little villages 'just growed' until they became towns. These we might consider towns of 'organic' growth, and are in themselves spectacular evidence of the new wealth and energy of the society. But in addition to such appearances and reappearances of towns, many feudal landowners, from kings down to abbots, deliberately set out on policies of building quite new towns.[13] This phenomenon is visible in connection with the reclamation of the Low Countries, with the colonization east of the Elbe, in England, Wales and Gascony, and elsewhere.

These artificially created 'new' towns exhibit the basic features and attractions of all town life all over Europe, and may be used by us here to understand the role of towns in Troubadourean Europe in general. In the creation of a 'new' town, a feudal lord would have his men choose and mark out a site for settlement, and announce (sometimes with a written charter) the freedoms or 'liberties' of the town. The plots available for prospective burghers to come and build on would be let at an annual rate. What was in it for the lord? A town on his property was a potential source of much wealth, for the outlay of very little money. He 'farmed' it in several ways: he charged rents for the house-plots, he charged market dues, he charged for the administration of justice, he used it (or hoped to use it) to sell his surplus produce to. What, on the other hand, was in it for the burghers? Potential residents were interested in two kinds of freedom, which could only be found in towns. First there was freedom *from*, from feudal duties and restrictions: for to hold property by burgage tenure was to hold virtually as a freeman. Then there were all the freedoms *to*: the freedom to hold property at all, and also to be able to pass it on to one's heirs; the freedom to marry off one's daughter without paying a feudal tax; the freedom to set up in business without interference, and so on.

Most important of all was the freedom to trade. For at the centre of all towns, both 'new' and 'organic', there was a market-place; the market-place was the centre of Troubadourean urban life. This distinguishes the Troubadourean town totally from an old Roman town. The Troubadourean town was primarily a commercial centre, with a market at its core; the Roman town had been primarily an administrative centre, with a forum at its core. Indeed the market was more important to such Troubadourean towns even than the church: all 'new' towns had a market, and were built around that market, but not all of them had a church. For such towns were often founded at a distance from existing centres of settlement, and on land less productive for agriculture. A town founded on an old Roman road, or on a river bank, for instance, would thus be on a feature already being used as the boundary between parishes. An extreme example of this phenomenon is Royston in Hertfordshire (England): founded in the 1180s, it was set at a crossroads used to mark the boundaries of no less than five parishes. It was three hundred and fifty years before the townspeople of Royston had a parish church of their own.

The most important product that the merchants traded 'internally' between the different regions of Latin Europe was wool, in both its raw and woven states; but those who wove the wool and traded the finished cloth flourished most. The leading towns in this industrial and commercial activity, the towns which recovered quickest and which became dominant, were those of two areas: Flanders in the north; and, in the south, an area which flourished even more, and which included northern Italy, Provence, and the south of France: Languedoc. The towns of the latter area were also those most in touch with the flourishing Byzantine and Islamic empires across the Mediterranean lake, with which they traded on behalf of Latin Europe.

Technically, even in northern Italy, these towns lay in the domains of feudal overlords. The Holy Roman Emperor believed he was the supreme overlord of them all. But by the twelfth century these towns had turned the tables on their rulers, and had set themselves up as the masters of their respective hinterlands. Within the southern towns (that is, the Italian and those of Languedoc and Provence) government was by the 'commune'; governments, as Lopez has put it, of the merchants, by the merchants and for the merchants: 'Each town harrassed the feudal rulers of its district, debauched their serfs by offering employment and protection, eroded the land around their castles, and finally forced them to become members of the commune as the only alternative to total ruin.'[14] In the communal organization of towns, the first group to seek autonomy and outside recognition was always the merchant guild: thus the town authorities were often coextensive with the merchant guild. The most successful of these southern towns now functioned as independent states – city-states – going to war against claimants to overlordship in order to defend their political liberty, going to war against each other in order to defend their commercial freedoms. The 'liberty' they were defending was not simply the liberty to organize their own political affairs: it was also the liberty to trade freely. The towns had a tumultuous and eventful time defending their interests against the outside world. As an astonished northerner recorded of the Lombard cities in 1154:

> almost all the land is divided between the cities, and they all compel their bishops to dwell among them, and it is almost impossible to find any noble or magnate, even in so wide an area, who does not obey the orders of his city ... they far surpass all other cities in the world in wealth and power. They are helped to this position not only, as we have said, by their industrious habits, but also by the absence of their Princes [i.e. the Emperors], who usually stay on the other side of the Alps ... they scarcely ever receive their Prince with the respect which as subjects they ought willingly to show him; nor do they obediently accept what he has ordained ... unless he brings up a large force of soldiers and they are compelled to feel his authority ... Among the cities of this people, Milan now holds first place ... not only because of its size and plentiful supply of valiant men, but also because it has subjected to its authority two neighbouring cities which lie on the same arc of land, Como and Lodi ... [15]

In northern Italian cities two parties developed. The Ghibbelines were constituted mainly of the old nobility from the countryside, and were the 'imperial' party, for they hoped the Emperor would one day restore their privileges; the Guelphs were the party for the urban interest, and for a defence against the Emperor they looked to the only available alternative power, the papacy.

There were struggles for political power within these and other towns too – that is to say, new claims for political autonomy of one class from another, or claims to a share in running town affairs. The communes of the Italian towns were rarely stable for long. Ruling families and would-be-ruling families were often at outright war with each other. To defend themselves each family put up one or more huge towers in the city, the highest rising to as much as 97 metres; the period around 1200 has been described as 'the age par excellence for the construction of towers'.[16] A couple still survive, leaning precipitously, in the heart of Bologna, while San Gimignano is still a forest of them, though more than 50 have been destroyed. Increasingly also the merchant class came under pressure from the craft guilds, and in the 1200s such guilds were grudgingly therefore

2.1 Medieval towers in Bologna

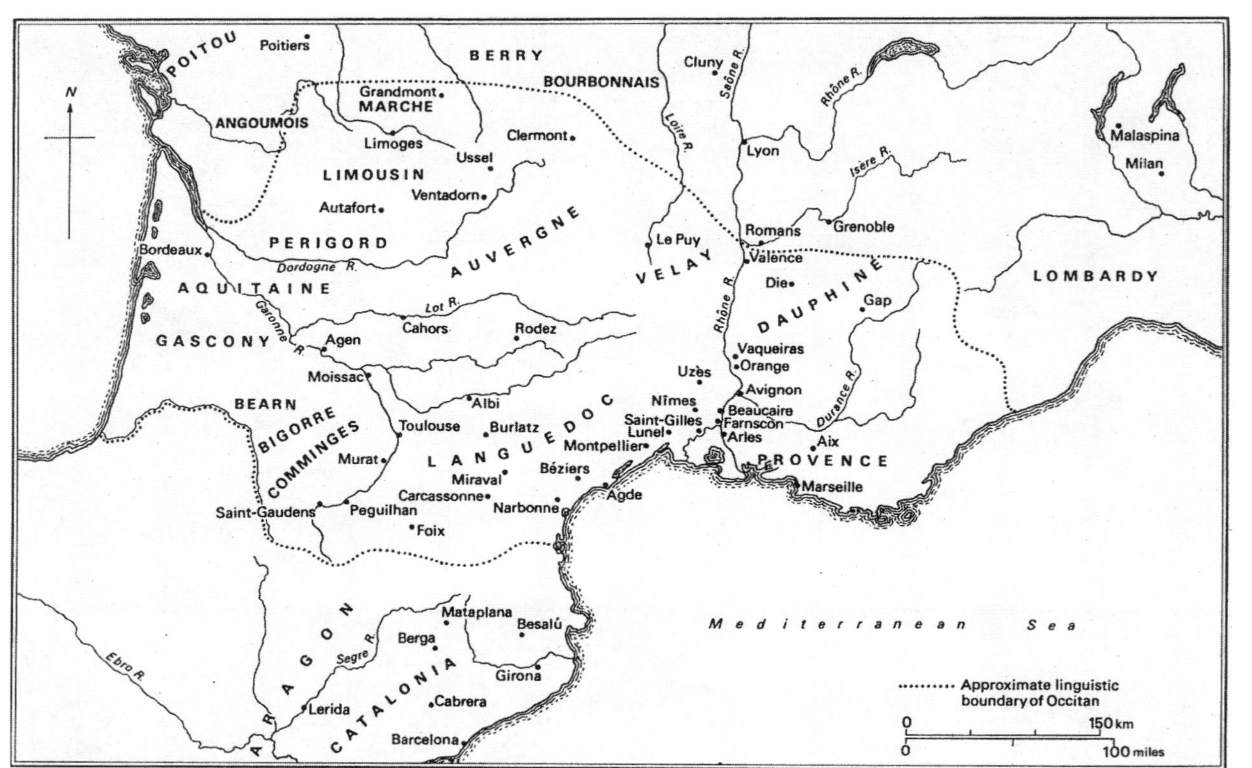

2.2 Map of Occitania

admitted to share power. Although these autonomous towns often waged and suffered from disastrous wars, this warfare was not all just energy dissipated in pointless destruction; for warfare was, for these towns, both a product and symptom of their commercial ambitions and success.

The Languedoc town of Toulouse can be taken as an example of such development.[17] We do not choose it at random, for it will play a most important part in our story. From around 1100 it was developing along the lines of a north Italian city; that is to say, it was progressively usurping the prerogatives of its feudal lord, the Count of Toulouse. From about 1170 to 1190 the Count fought back, but without success, and what had hitherto been a town subject to his feudal authority now began to act like a fully-fledged city state, claiming autonomy for its own affairs. Around the year 1200 pressure from within led to a more 'populist' structure of government. And then, led by the new popular consulate, the town in 1202–05 engaged in wars against other towns and villages in its region, to try and create an area of the local country over which it was dominant. Thus, within a century, Toulouse had gone from being a town subject to a feudal lord, to being an autonomous city making forceful claims to the allegiance, produce and markets of the surrounding countryside and its residents. In the case of Toulouse this was to be the peak of its emulation of the Italian cities: its development was to be rudely and suddenly stopped in its tracks, for reasons we shall return to later.

Conclusion

We have seen that the rise of twelfth-century western Europe to economically buoyant status went hand in hand with the rise of struggles to rule that society. The primary struggle – and the one which has left many documentary traces – was between the Popes and lay rulers. It might appear from this that the interests of the papacy and lay rulers were fundamentally opposed: as if there was in this period a political struggle between Church and State, and indeed this is how the political history of this period is customarily written.[18] But there is a strong sense in which both the Pope and the local rulers were actually on the same side. For they had a common interest in maintaining a hierarchical society. At the bottom of the hierarchy were the peasants, the serfs. Both lay rulers and the church had serfs – virtual slaves – as the lowest and commonest grade of tenant and if anything it was the church landlords (such as abbots) who were the harder masters of their serfs. So both kinds of ruler lived off the same tenurial system, and shared a general interest in its continuance. And both parties claimed to be governing in God's name, and to be doing His work. Of course the Pope and lay rulers had their differences: but they were differences between them as rival rulers; they had few essential differences in world-view. They differed on who should rule the world, not on what kind of world it should be, or whether it should be ruled by people like themselves.

In practice it was one of the functions (though not an intention) of the Church to provide the ideology – the belief-system, attitudes, world-view – which supported and promoted this state of affairs. The language of social expression too was that of the Church. To put it in modern-day terms, the primary language of social expression was 'religious'; but such a formulation is somewhat misleading, because it implies that there was a modern-style divide between the 'political' and the 'religious'. The Christianity preached and practised by the twelfth-century Church was, naturally enough, a Christianity which supported the social and political structures of feudal society. It did not challenge them, nor was it neutral with respect to them. The Church was the source of the moral values of that society: it is not therefore surprising to find that its leaders spoke about people's duties, not of their rights; of their obligations, not of their freedoms; of obedience, not of autonomy; of suffering, not of self-fulfilment, as being the human lot in this world. And the rewards in the hereafter were limited too, for salvation was for the few, not the many: monks could earn it, the rich could buy it (by giving endowments to the Church), but it was not available to the poor.[19] Yet the poor were, by their lowly position, the ones most firmly bound to subscribe to the values and doctrines of this society. Such moral values are obviously political in import. At different times the Bible has been deemed to demand different ways of life of men in Christian society. In Troubadourean times, those who had the power and authority of interpreting the Bible believed it called for a feudally ordered society. Their view long prevailed, because they and their agents also had a virtual monopoly on being able to read the Bible at all.

Thus the Pope and lay rulers were equally opposed to any form of internal dissent. If any new form of organization was to be created they wanted it to be ideologically correct, they wanted it to function within the orbit of their power. This is what made towns such a problem: they were highly valuable for the improvement of a ruler's income, yet they were difficult to control, and they kept trying to escape from their overlord and to claim 'freedom' for themselves. No wonder 'commune' was such an unwelcome term to the ears of

Troubadourean rulers. Similarly, when independent centres of teaching came into existence, as we shall see in the next chapter, the 'powers that were', both the Pope and lay rulers, were deeply concerned with the orthodoxy of their members. Again, if anyone was to put forward an alternate interpretation of the Bible, and to claim on that basis that men in Christian society should therefore be pursuing different ways of life, then both the Pope and lay rulers would be hostile to such people. They might even be prepared to share the work – be the two 'arms' – of rooting such evils out of society: of, in other words, physically eliminating the people who professed them. A protest against the ruling ideology was (and was correctly interpreted as being) a threat to those who profited from that ideology. And given that that ruling ideology was expressed in 'religious' terms, it was natural that protests against that ideology should be expressed in the same language – that, in other words, such protests should appear as *heresies*. A heresy is, of course, the opposite of an orthodoxy. The people in whose interest such a revolt would be, and who were most able to promote such a revolt, were those most 'free' from the feudal control of lay ruler or Pope, and those with greatest access to alternative ways of thinking and living. These people were the town dwellers, and especially those professional travellers, the merchants. It is in towns, the richest, most 'free' and most successful towns, the towns of Languedoc, Provence, and northern Italy, that we will find the greatest and most dangerous 'heresy' of these years.

Notes

1. Robert S. Lopez, *The Commercial Revolution of the Middle Ages, 950–1350*, Cambridge University Press, 1976, and Jean Gimpel, *The Medieval Machine: The Industrial Revolution of the Middle Ages*, London, Gollancz, 1977, much of the account of economic revival below comes from these two works; Lynn White, Jr., *Medieval Technology and Social Change*, Oxford University Press, 1962. See also Robert Latouche, *The Birth of Western Economy: Economic Aspects of the Dark Ages*, London, Methuen, University Paperbacks, 1967 (original French edition 1956), for a perspective from Roman to Dark Age to 'High Middle Age' conditions.
2. See Richard Barber, *The Knight and Chivalry*, New York, Harper and Row, 1982 (originally published 1970).
3. In general see Colin Platt, *The Parish Churches of Medieval England*, London, Secker and Warburg, 1981.
4. Georges Duby, *The Knight, the Lady and the Priest: The Making of Modern Marriage in Medieval France*, London, Allen Lane, 1984 (original French edition 1981). Henry Charles Lea, *An Historical*

Sketch of Sacerdotal Celibacy in the Christian Church, first edition, Philadelphia, Lippincott, 1867.

5. 'From 900 to 1050 ... is the period in which monastic influence rose to its peak in the political and social life of western Europe. Yet the number of monasteries and monks was comparatively modest; in population and variety the century following 1050 is the age of growth.' Christopher Brooke, *The Monastic World, 1000–1300*, London, Paul Elek, 1974, p. 85.
6. As given in Ernest F. Henderson, editor and translator, *Select Historical Documents of the Middle Ages*, London, Bell, 1925, p. 274.
7. Dom M. David Knowles, *Cistercians and Cluniacs: The Controversy between St Bernard and Peter the Venerable*, Oxford University Press, 1955; G.R. Evans, *The Mind of St Bernard of Clairvaux*, Oxford, Clarendon Press, 1983.
8. Gimpel, *Medieval Machine*, p. 47.
9. Brooke, *Monastic World*, p 87.
10. Brooke, *Monastic World*, p. 184.
11. As quoted in Sidney R. Packard, *Europe and the Church under Innocent III*, New York, Russell and Russell, 1927, repr. 1968, p. 15.
12. Marina Warner, *Alone of All Her Sex: The Myth and the Cult of the Virgin Mary*, London, Picador, 1985 (first published 1976), pp. 144–6; Duby, *The Knight, the Lady and the Priest*.
13. Here we are indebted especially to Maurice Beresford, *New Towns of the Middle Ages: Town Plantation in England, Wales and Gascony*, London, Lutterworth, 1967; much of the information in the following paragraphs comes from here. See also Colin Platt, *The English Medieval Town*, London, Secker and Warburg, 1976.
14. Lopez, *Commercial Revolution*, pp. 69–70. On the ascent of the communes see also Lauro Martines, *Power and Imagination: City-States in Renaissance Italy*, London, Allen Lane, 1980, esp. chs 1–4.
15. Otto of Freising, *Gesta Friderici Imperatoris*, Book II, ch. 13, as translated in Brian Pullan, *Sources for the History of Medieval Europe from the Mid-Eighth to the Mid-Thirteenth Century*, Oxford, Basil Blackwell, 1966, pp. 177–8.
16. Martines, *Power and Imagination*, pp. 37–8.
17. We follow John Hine Mundy, 'Urban Society and Culture: Toulouse and Its Region', in Robert L. Benson and Giles Constable, eds, *Renaissance and Renewal in the Twelfth Century*, Oxford, Clarendon, 1982, 229–47, esp. 229–30.
18. The conflict of powers showed itself most in the so-called 'investiture controversy', over who had the right to invest bishops with their symbols of office – the Pope or lay rulers (especially the Emperor). This began in the pontificate of Gregory VII (Hildebrand) in 1073 and lasted into the thirteenth century. It was a contest eventually won by the papacy. The view of the political history of this period as revolving around, and as essentially consisting of, a great conflict between Church and State, was very important in the nineteenth century, and has similar roots and purposes as does the tradition of seeing the history of 'science' as a great conflict between Church and free intellectual enquiry (represented by Science), a historical tradition which also blossomed in the nineteenth century. Although we are heirs

to both these historiographic traditions, we need not be misled by either.

19. See Brooke, *Monastic World*, p. 85; see also Christopher Brooke, *Medieval Church and Society, Collected Essays*, London, Sedgwick and Jackson, 1971, p. 153.

CHAPTER THREE

Sapientia and *scientia*: the cloister and the school

Learning before the *studium*

The development of book learning in the twelfth and thirteenth centuries has usually been treated by historians somewhat monolithically, and the story that they have been most interested in telling is one of the simple 'transmission' and 'assimilation' of ancient Greek texts. Learning, and the promotion of learning, were of great importance to both of the two major Orders of friar, the Dominicans and the Franciscans. The natural philosophy of the friars was built on writings from Greek antiquity, as well as on the Bible and the Fathers. The friars created *studia* within their own Orders in which they taught their members natural philosophy and other subjects, and they also entered the *studia* created by the secular masters, which they saw as a rival form of learning which needed to be controlled. In order to understand and appreciate the precise nature of the friars' interest in learning, and to understand something of its later impact on the universities, it is necessary to distinguish the different approaches to learning evident in twelfth- and thirteenth-century Europe.

The earliest form of education in post-Roman Europe was that provided in the *monastic schools*, from around the sixth century until long after Troubadourean times. Education provided in a monastery was not usually a bishop's concern, for the monasteries in his diocese owed him no allegiance, and he had no rights over them. The teaching of their own novices was something all monasteries provided for, and the teaching was usually in the hands of the 'novice master'. The point of this education was to train future monks for their job as monks, that is for the life of prayer, services, meditation and contemplation of God. This was 'God's work', *opus Dei*. The monk's task was liturgical and spiritual, and therefore his monastic education was for liturgical and spiritual purposes. It consisted primarily of learning to read and to write, and the primary and central text which the monk learnt to read was the Bible, the 'Sacred Page', together with the (Latin) Church Fathers. Such learning was intended to provide the monk with 'wisdom', *sapientia*.

It was generally accepted that the Bible contained all knowledge, sacred and profane, that was necessary for man. But there was a problem. The harmony between God, man and the natural world had been broken by man's Fall, and so man's understanding of God was now defective.[1] It followed that in causing the Bible to be written, God used a level of expression that could be understood by man, but which did not express the higher truths which man in his reduced state was incapable of receiving. So it was generally believed that there was more to the Bible than the literal meaning of its words. It was held that the Bible, in addition to its literal meaning, had a spiritual meaning, for some aspects of the Greek tradition of Origen and Clement for finding the mystical meaning of scripture (as discussed in Chapter 1) were available to Latin monks through the works of the Latin Fathers, St Jerome and St Augustine.[2] Often an analogy was drawn between the Bible and the human body, composed of matter (the literal meaning) and soul (the spiritual). Sometimes the spiritual meaning was taken to include the allegorical, in which the literal events of the Bible were taken to symbolize a greater spiritual truth, or to be parables with a higher moral meaning, or to foreshadow the later events of the New Testament.[3] We may illustrate some of these points by an example given by Hugh of St Victor, who is commenting on the Biblical passage 'Be careful, for your enemy the Devil, like a lion, prowls around'. By taking *leo* to allegorically denote *diabolus*, Hugh tells the reader, we at once understand the meaning of the text rather than merely the literal meaning of the words 'lion' and 'devil'. What gives us our greater understanding is partly our 'natural' knowledge of lions: the nature-of-lions.[4]

In rising from the literal meaning of the Scriptures to a higher, and often very personal contemplation of God, the monk had a number of tools to help him. These included things that we now think of as 'scholastic' such as commentaries, expositions, glosses and scholia. For the monk, however, these were modes of patristic exposition, and only later came to be adopted by the schools and hence became 'scholastic'.[5] It was in handling these tools that the basic disciplines of a secular education became useful. In particular we should take note of the technique of *distinctio*. This was a method of arriving at a knowledge of a term by dividing off or 'distinguishing' the various meanings that it could have. In reading the Bible the several meanings of a word such as *seculum*, 'world', would be discovered by extensive reading to discover the sense in which it was used in different passages, and thus what senses were potentially available for it in any one passage, perhaps one whose allegorical meaning was being sought.

In addition to the basic reading and writing, it was possible, though in no way obligatory, for monks to be taught the so-called 'seven liberal arts'. There are the three arts of language, grammar, rhetoric and dialectic/logic, and the four arts of number, arithmetic, geometry, astronomy and music. The 'seven liberal arts', as a group, date from late Roman times, though much of their content was of course ultimately derived from Greek sources.[6] They were 'liberal' arts because they had been thought to be the ones best suited to train the 'free' (*liberalis*) Roman man for public life. In the monastic world these liberal arts were known about in a very indirect way: through late Roman writings such as Martianus Capella's stylistically difficult *The Marriage of Philology and Mercury* of the fifth century.[7] Languages, grammar and history were useful to understand the literal sense and arithmetic for the number symbolism that often appeared in allegorical interpretations. 'Natural' knowledge of plants and animals was useful to understand the symbolic way these creatures were used in the Scriptures. Dialectic could be used in helping to establish true doctrine and rhetoric for preaching. The dialectic was composed of fragments of the 'old logic' of Aristotle, found in Boethius and the 'natural knowledge' in paraphrases and excerpts from such authors as Pliny. The purpose of bringing in this secular learning was to unlock the knowledge contained at one or other level of the Bible. But these liberal arts were, as might be expected, seen as only marginally relevant to the life of prayer, services, meditation and contemplation of the monastery. The point needs to be stressed that monastic use of Latin, monastic divine reading and divine contemplation were all concerned with man's moral relationship with God. There was no consideration of nature as evidence of God in the Creation.[8]

The seven liberal arts were of much greater relevance to another kind of education: that available in the *cathedral school*. From the early 800s church councils (Châlons 813, Aix-la-Chapelle 817) insisted that every cathedral should have a school to educate its young clerks. Of these Tours and Chartres became much the most famous. Charlemagne issued several decrees that all cathedrals and monasteries in the Empire should have a school. These cathedral schools were usually the only ones anywhere.

But in practice not all cathedrals maintained schools, nor was the history of any one school necessarily continuous. We know of the existence of such schools from around the year 1000, with Bishop Gerbert (945–1003, Pope Sylvester II 999–1003) founding one at Reims and Bishop Fulbert (bishop 1006–28) founding one at Chartres cathedral. The high point of the influence of the cathedral school was in the period *c.*1100 to *c.*1180, when there were important schools at a whole range of cathedrals in and around Paris, and stretching to the north: Notre-Dame, Chartres, Orléans, Reims, Laôn, Tours, Cologne, St Gall, Liège, and elsewhere. The most famous masters who taught in cathedral schools included Fulbert and Gerbert, and in the twelfth century William of Conches, Thierry of Chartres and, most important of all, Peter Abelard.

Cathedral schools existed primarily for the education of the clergy of the diocese, and for future administrators of the diocese and kingdom, since many royal administrators were bishops and other clerics. Such administrators were required for the growing amount of diocesan administration that the extension of episcopal power was entailing. Moreover, the bishops had taken on themselves the right to promote all teaching in their dioceses, and to control who could teach by 'licensing' teachers. The bishop's Chancellor usually looked after this task of licensing teachers. The point of this was to promote, and control, the teaching of the doctrines of the Catholic Church throughout the diocese, right down to parish level.

There was another reason why the schools should produce a scholar with a training different from that of the enclosed monasteries. In promoting Innocent III's attempt to strengthen the influence of the papacy within the Church, teachers like his friend Stephen Langton at Paris (later Archbishop of Canterbury, 1207–28) were convinced that a reorganized Church would regenerate society and free the Church from secular powers. Langton taught his students that the clergy should not abandon themselves to contemplation, that the civil power should not appoint civil servants to high ecclesiastical office, and that the Pope was the arbiter between equal secular powers (for example the King of France and the Emperor).[9] In such a world there would be abundant employment for able and practical students of men like Langton.

The seven liberal arts would provide a prospective administrator with skills of argument and numeracy. But it was believed that an education in the seven liberal arts also taught virtue. For instance Robert, son of Hugh Capet, and future King of France, was sent by his father *c.*1000 to Gerbert to learn 'enough knowledge of the liberal arts to make him pleasing in the eyes of the Lord by the way he practised all of the holy virtues'.[10] Similarly, Bishop Fulbert claimed that teaching in the liberal arts enables young people 'to learn virtue' and for young clerics to 'prepare to vanquish the army of vices'.[11]

The kind of knowledge which was taught in cathedral schools, using the seven liberal arts, was known as *scientia*, that is human knowledge, knowledge about the world (at the theoretical level), and knowledge which can be shown to derive from firm principles. This is in contrast to the *sapientia* taught in the monasteries. The difference between *sapientia* and *scientia* is here expressed by Honorius of Autun, writing in the mid-twelfth century in a work called 'On the Exile of the Soul and on Its Homeland; or, On the Arts':

> Just as for the people of God there was an exile in Babylon, while Jerusalem was their homeland, so ignorance is the exile of the inner man though wisdom (*sapientia*) is his homeland ... The route from this exile to the homeland is *scientia*, for *scientia* deals with earthly matters, while *sapientia* deals with divine matters. One should pass along this route not by steps of the body, but by desires of the heart. Indeed this route leads to the homeland through the ten directing arts and through the books cleaving to the way and serving it like so many towns and villages along a road.[12]

Scientia and the liberal arts in general became popular in the twelfth century among wandering scholars, who would attend the masters at the cathedral schools for certain elements of their education. John of Salisbury for instance, who later became personal secretary to the Archbishop of Canterbury, spent a number of exciting years listening to the masters in and around Paris:

> When, still but a youth, I first journeyed to Gaul for the sake of study, in the year following the death of the illustrious King of the English, Henry [I], 'the Lion of Justice', [i.e. in 1136], I betook myself to the Peripatetic of Pallet [i.e. Peter Abelard] who was then teaching at Mont Ste. Geneviève. The latter was a famed and learned master, admired by all. At his feet I learned the elementary principles of this art [i.e. logic], drinking in, with consuming avidity, and to the full extent of my limited talents, every word that fell from his lips. After his departure, which seemed to me all too soon, I became the disciple of Master Alberic, who had a very high reputation as the best of the other dialecticians. Alberich was in fact a most bitter opponent of the Nominalist sect. After thus passing almost two full years at the Mont, I had, as instructors in this art, Alberich and also Master Robert of Melun ... After working with the aforesaid masters for two full years, I became so accustomed to pointing out the topics, rules and other elementary principles, with which teachers stock youthful minds ... that with youthful lack of reflection, I unduly exaggerated my own knowledge. I took myself to be a young sage, inasmuch as I knew the answers to what I had been taught. However, I recovered my senses, and took stock of my powers. I then transferred, after deliberation and consultation, and with the approval of my instructors, to the grammarian of Conches [i.e. William of Conches, teaching at Chartres]. I studied under the latter for three years, during which I learnt much.[13]

John of Salisbury's account of his youthful travels is very revealing and informative about intellectual life in the cathedral schools at the time. He studied in Paris and in Chartres, and the central study he pursued was that of logic (or dialectic), one of the seven liberal arts. The study of logic was suddenly very important in the twelfth century, being made so primarily by Peter Abelard (1079–1142), the 'Peripatetic' (that is, follower of Aristotle) from Pallet. Peter and others were using the so-called 'Old Logic' of Aristotle, the *Categories* and the *On Interpretation*.

They used the *Isagoge* of Porphyry of the third century AD as translated by Boethius in the sixth century as a guide to Aristotle's logic, together with certain other late Latin writings by Boethius on Aristotle's logic and on the syllogism. The immediate result of this making logic pre-eminent was a celebrated public quarrel between 'nominalists' and 'realists', between those who claimed that 'universals', that is terms such as 'man', 'house' etc. are mere names, mere intellectual conveniences, and those who claimed that they are realities having an existence independent of the individual instances. In the passage cited from John of Salisbury above, Abelard appears arguing the case for nominalism, whereas Alberic is a realist.

Argument was central to logic, and arguments could be taken either from authorities or from reason itself. This was a radical innovation. Every issue could be subjected to logical (or 'dialectical') discussion, and every side of the case could be put and defended. Contradiction or apparent contradiction between authorities or between reason and authority was deliberately sought out: that was the whole point of this discipline of logic.[14] Thus what made logic so very exciting and indeed potentially dangerous in the twelfth century was not the inner content of logic itself, but the fact that it could be used to raise, and perhaps resolve, questions about Catholic doctrine: does God exist? is the soul immortal? what are the relations of the three parts of the Trinity? in what way is God present in the Eucharist? ... and so on *ad infinitum*. That is to say, a certain aspect of Greek philosophy – logic, as originated by Aristotle – was now being used to discuss, raise questions (*questiones*) about, point to the ambiguities of (and perhaps even resolve) features of Christianity and Christian doctrine which themselves arose largely from the (Platonic and Stoic) Greek philosophical roots of Christianity. Logic, the *scientia* of strict reasoning, was seen by Peter Abelard and others as the essential key to such philosophizing, so much so that logic/dialectic was in their eyes synonymous with philosophy itself. And their claim was that philosophy in this sense is essential to a proper understanding of divine matters, and for reconciling the apparent contradictions in the Bible and in what the Church Fathers had said.

This application of philosophy – understood primarily as logic/dialectic – to divine matters led to the creation of a new discipline by Peter Abelard and others: *theology*. The term 'theologia' is Greek and, as we saw in Chapter 1, was first used by Plato, and then by Aristotle.[15] Peter Abelard did not have these works of Plato and Aristotle available to him, and had probably come across the term in the works of Boethius or Dionysius. But although it was an old word, Peter Abelard's application of it was new. For theology to him, and then to generations of others, was a matter of *dialectical argumentation*, not of insight gained by meditation, nor the decisions of episcopal or other authoritative sources. This 'theology' was therefore quite different from the *sapientia* of the monasteries. For in this 'theology' mystery and revealed truth were to be investigated by the test of reason. This 'theology' was a new, God-centred subject, for which the seven liberal arts – and especially logic – were to be essential bases. Theology was the application of *scientia* to the understanding of the nature of God and of the Christian religion. Pagan learning had thus been brought back as essential for understanding the divine.

All this was wildly exciting, because the invention of theology meant that every doctrinal position could be argued about, and every conclusion drawn about doctrine was potentially heretical. This scholastic theology has therefore rightly been seen as a time of relative 'free-thinking', given Abelard's view that 'by doubting we come to inquiry, and by inquiry we perceive truth'. As Charles Homer Haskins has remarked, in Abelard's approach 'the emphasis upon contradiction rather than upon agreement and the failure to furnish any solutions, real or superficial, tended powerfully to expose the weaknesses in the orthodox position and to undermine authority generally'.[16] So many issues were thrown into doubt, as by Peter Lombard's *Sentences* which opposes seeming contradictory statements on Christian doctrine of the Fathers to each other, or Peter Abelard's own *Sic et Non* (Yes and No), that the Pope felt obliged to determine a list of orthodox positions and issue them in 1215.

Increasingly, as teaching in the schools moved further from the contemplation typical of the cloister, pagan philosophy was brought in. It was frequently referred to as 'Egyptian gold', like the gold and valuable items that the Jews in captivity had borrowed from the Egyptians before quietly stealing away: it was not theirs; it was not holy; it was a lesser truth than revelation; but it was uncommonly useful. The analogy, earlier used by Origen and Augustine as we saw in Chapter 1, was now again used from the middle of the twelfth century up to the attempt by Gregory IX in 1231 to emasculate the philosophy of Aristotle to make it suitable for use in the university of Paris.

But these new disciplines, *philosophy* (that is, understood now primarily as meaning *logic*) and *theology*, were not introduced without opposition. A number of people were opposed to making these innovations fundamental to the knowledge of the divine, and the opposition was expressed both in terms of the redundancy of these new subjects for the authentic religious life, and on the grounds that the discussion, questioning and argumentation that were basic to logic and theology were leading people away from Christian truth and into heresy. In this way the twelfth-century dispute over the relevance of these subjects replayed the disputes of earlier Christian centuries over the role of pagan learning for Christians.

The most famous twelfth-century opponent of the use of 'Egyptian gold' (pagan philosophy) was St Bernard, abbot of Clairvaux (1091–1153). He succeeded in getting Peter Abelard tried by a Church council at Sens in 1141, where his teaching on the Trinity and other matters was condemned as heretical. He also brought Gilbert, Bishop of Poitiers, to trial on similar charges in 1147, claiming that Gilbert asserted the heresy that the Divine Nature did not become incarnate. St Bernard was not a killjoy opposed to innovation of any kind. His complaint was quite correct: the study of the liberal arts and theology really were diversionary from the religious life of the monastery. St Bernard was concurrently involved in promoting a radical reform of monastic life among the Cistercians, bringing the monastic life back to the ideal originally taught by St Benedict. The true teacher of the religious, St Bernard claimed, was the Sacred Page:

> What did the holy Apostles teach us? These are our masters, who ... teach us even today ... They do not teach the art of fishing ... of the reading of Plato, or to entangle in arguments with Aristotle, nor to be always learning and never come to the knowledge of the truth. They have taught me to live.[17]

It is not the teaching of the schools but the teaching of the Apostles to which one must be attentive, says Bernard: the Apostles teach truth, not doubt and uncertainty.

Under the threat that *sapientia* would be replaced by the new *scientia*, others argued similarly that all the philosophy one needed could be derived from the Bible itself, and thus one could avoid the pagan philosophy of the ancient writers. Jacques de Vitry, preaching to students in about 1200 and reacting against the new use of Greek and Arabic works on nature, claimed that the traditional divisions of philosophy according to Origen – moral, natural and 'inspective' – could all be found in the Bible, in the books of that most wise man, Solomon. The book of Proverbs teaches moral philosophy, natural philosophy is to be found in Ecclesiastes, which teaches (said Jacques) the vanity of the physical world of the Creation, and the need instead to know and love the Creator, while the Song of Songs teaches us that only eternal things should be valued and contemplated, which is the central lesson of inspective philosophy.[18] Thus the three books of Solomon provided all the necessary wisdom, the philosophy or *sapientia*, of the Church.

Students who had been introduced to the logic of Aristotle and his commentators, and to the new study of theology, went on to other walks of life, primarily in the Church or the administration of Church and

State. Primed by their education they were, naturally enough, aware that there were works by the Greeks which were not available to them, and that there might be works by the Greek philosophers of which they had not even heard, but which might be relevant to the pursuit of the seven liberal arts or to theology.

It is in this context that we find Latin Christians first actively looking for texts of the Greeks, and seeking to make them available in Latin.[19] They found these texts, as we might expect, at the expanding edges of the Latin world. For, driven by the economic and demographic forces which made Troubadourean Europe an expanding and growing economy, Latin Christendom, the least sophisticated culture, was extending into and beginning to colonize and trade with the fringes of the two much more sophisticated cultures: Islam and the Byzantine Empire.

It was trade that took the Venetians to Byzantium, and there James of Venice and others came across Greek texts and undertook some translations from the Greek in the early 1100s, such as the *Posterior Analytics*. Indeed, the expansionist demands of trade were so strong as to lead Venice to take over Byzantium entirely in the course of the Fourth Crusade.

In Spain the Christians were waging a war of so-called 'Reconquest' (*Reconquista*), progressively displacing the Muslims and planting Christians in their place; by 1085 Alphonso VI of Castile had captured the city of Toledo in the centre of the country; Christians were brought in to settle this frontier state, and a new bishopric was made there. When Peter of Cluny (the Venerable), on a visit to Spain in the 1140s, paid Robert of Chester and Hermann of Carinthia to translate Koranic materials from Arabic to Latin, it was because he believed that the first step in converting the infidel was to learn his doctrines; later the Archbishop of Toledo was to have the text retranslated by one of his Toledo canons.[20] So we find that Toledo was, especially in the middle and second half of the twelfth century, something of a centre for the translation of Greek works from Arabic to Latin, and as the Reconquest progressed in the thirteenth century so translation came to be undertaken also in Cordoba and Seville. Scholars trained in the cathedral schools, such as Hermann of Carinthia and Gerard of Cremona, came to Spain hunting for particular manuscripts. Gerard of Cremona, for instance, was drawn to Toledo by his desire to see Ptolemy's *Almagest*, an astronomical work, which he could not find among the Latins; he learnt Arabic and translated many works up to his death in 1187.[21] Daniel of Morley was in Toledo at the same period, 'hearing' Gerard of Cremona translate the *Almagest*. In contrast to the excitement of translation in Toledo, Daniel found on returning to Paris and England that the contemporary study of Roman law, and the ignorance of Aristotle and Plato, was stultifyingly boring. When he met the Bishop of Norwich, he answered his questions on astrology by writing a treatise on the upper and lower worlds, in about 1175. It begins with the story of the 'Egyptian gold'[22] (We look at Daniel's account of nature in the next chapter.)

Often enough translations from the Arabic were made with the help of Jewish scholars. For example Michael Scot (who, like Mark of Toledo, had the Archbishop of Toledo as a patron) was helped by Abuteus Levita. Alfred of Shareshill was taught by Salomon Avenraza. The Jewish communities of Languedoc, Provence and northern Italy were large and could find good use for Arabic medicine and astrology in translation.[23] So where there was a Jewish text intermediate between the Arabic and Latin, it was because the Jewish version had a value, some practical use, to its translator.

When the Crusaders took the Holy Land and established the 'Latin Kingdom of Jerusalem' there in 1099 in another act of expansion, the settlers here too came across some Greek works in Arabic, and some translations were undertaken. Adelard of Bath is thought to have brought back a copy of Euclid's *Elements* from Syria in the early 1100s, together with astrological and computational works.

The fourth main area of expansion of Latin Europe in the twelfth century was in south Italy and Sicily where the Normans created a Latin kingdom from the 1050s. The original population here spoke Greek and in Sicily many also spoke Arabic since there was a large Arab population and the island had been under Arab rule until its capture by the Normans. Hence the court of King Roger II (*c.*1093–1154) became a centre of translation and study. Here mathematical and astronomical works were translated from Greek to Latin. Some of the Greek Fathers of the Church were translated now, as by Burgundio of Pisa in the early 1100s, including the writings of St Basil, Chrysostom and John of Damascus, to assist in developing that new study, theology. Manfred, King of Sicily from 1258 to 1266, supported translation in the interests of good government. *Scientia*, he said, is a necessary spice, giving justice and moderation to the legal and military duties of a king. It was for this reason, he said, that he commissioned translations of Aristotle and others from the Greek and Arabic.[24]

The texts people were looking for were those which related to the studies of the seven liberal arts, and philosophy, and here they were keen to translate works of Muslim scholars as well as those of ancient Greeks. Amongst the first works sought out and translated were further logical works by Aristotle – the so-called 'new logic'. Hence they somehow found Boethius' hitherto unknown sixth-century Latin translations of the *Prior Analytics* of Aristotle, together with his translations of

Aristotle's *Topics* and *On Sophistical Refutations*.

Mathematical and astronomical works, such as Ptolemy and Euclid were also sought out and translated.[25] For 'astronomy' we must very often understand 'astrology', since mathematics and observation, the characteristics of the study of the heavenly bodies, are the essential tools of predictive astrology. Mathematical studies had particular uses in an expanding economy such as that of Latin Europe. The astrolabe could be used profitably in navigation and surveying; and arithmetic, practised with the new Arabic numerals, was similarly of use in trade. Moreover, the medical man used 'astronomy' in calculating critical days and 'astrology' in prognosis.

Thus the translations from the Greeks, whether direct from Greek to Latin, or indirectly from Arabic to Latin, did not happen by chance, nor simply through some vague 'thirst for knowledge', nor because the texts simply 'became available' to the Latins. The time and the place and the nature of the desire were very specific, and an integral part of the economic and political expansion and growth of Troubadourean Europe.

The work of translation was in no way centrally co-ordinated, so it depended on the initiative and idiosyncratic decisions of individual scholars and their patrons. It occupied only a few generations. The most important ancient Greek whose works were translated now was Aristotle. Virtually all his works extant in Greek or Arabic were translated into Latin at this period, and hence became available to scholars. But there was very little Plato translated. Plato's *Timaeus* was already available, and continued to be so, but there was little else. One reason for this is that the Arabs had had little use for Plato in their own studies, so there was little available for the Latins in Arabic. But this was not the case with the Byzantine Greeks. So this suggests that the twelfth-century Latins themselves did not see Plato as being as desirable as Aristotle. In a way this was to be a bit of a pity because, as we saw in Chapter 1, the philosophy of the New Testament is primarily Platonic. Now, therefore, the Plato-based New Testament was about to be expounded via the philosophy of Aristotle! It is hardly surprising therefore that the logical works of Aristotle (the set of works known as the *Organon*, literally the 'instrument' of thinking) which in theology and philosophy was now to be applied to God's Book, did not fit the purpose perfectly.

The *studium*

By the years around 1200 the cathedral schools and other teaching licensed by the bishop were giving way to a new form of institution, the *studium* or, as it later came to be called, the university. There was a *studium* at Paris by the 1190s (though it was 'officially' recognized by the King only in 1200), in Oxford a little later and at Cambridge in or around 1209. Such *studia* were not founded by individuals, but by the simple coming together of masters who arranged to teach students for fees, and who arranged their affairs in their common interest. It was like a guild, devoted to teaching and run by the masters of the craft; and when the student had been trained to teach he was given his final tests and then admitted to the mastership, whereupon he was himself able to practise this craft. From their early years the masters of the *studia* found it politic to get the backing of the Pope, the Emperor and other local rulers. Hence, although neither the papacy nor the bishops had founded any of the original *studia*, yet they came to take it upon themselves to authenticate the teaching offered in the *studia*. Hence the right to teach anywhere, the *ius ubique docendi*, awarded by the chancellor, was authenticated and made realizable by papal and episcopal validation. In a way this was a simple extension of the bishops' claim to license all teaching in their diocese. If we take Oxford as our example, it appears that the Bishop of Lincoln, in whose diocese Oxford fell, first appointed his own chancellor to oversee both the *studium* and the town in 1209, and then shortly afterwards the masters chose their own chancellor – who thus became their representative to the bishop. Similar developments happened at other *studia*. But although the ecclesiastical hierarchy took a close interest in the *studia*, it is important to remember that the Church did not found the *studia*. That is, the *studia* were creations of the market-place, responding to felt needs for teaching and learning by twelfth- and thirteenth-century people, and not imposed from above by the Church. Hence the content and order of studies within the *studia* was arranged by the masters, and taught to meet the needs of prospective students.[26] And although many of these students would later seek careers in the Church, the subjects offered at the *studia* were not simply ones which would be of most direct use to future ecclesiastical administrators, priests and bishops. Nor was the teaching available limited to subjects that the Church was concerned with. As Professor Powicke has written: 'The medieval universities provided a vocational training for clerks in the broad sense of the term – for notaries, secretaries and the clerical handyman, for civil and canon lawyers, for medical men and for the intellectual elite, the theologians and philosophers.'[27] Thus the teaching of the *studia* certainly contained subjects which were thought necessary for future clerics, but it also contained other subjects. The Church sought to control and approve the curriculum, but it had had no hand in initially creating it.

By the mid-thirteenth century, the first *studia* had begun to develop a number of faculties. The fundamental faculty was that of arts. This had developed out of the seven liberal arts as taught in the cathedral schools. The mastery of the subject-matter of this faculty made one a 'Master of Arts', a title still used today. But the liberal arts content of this faculty soon came to be largely replaced or outweighed by what were known as 'the three philosophies'. One of these was to be natural philosophy. Hence the arts faculty very early came to be also known as the Philosophy faculty. Within a few decades it came to be accepted that completion of the course of studies in the arts faculty was essential before one could move on to any of the other faculties, which thereby came to be seen as the 'higher' faculties. In some but not all *studia*, medicine was one of the higher faculties; in a place like Padua it was not a 'higher' faculty but was to all intents and purposes merged with the arts/philosophy faculty. In some *studia*, law was one of the higher faculties, either civil law or canon law or both; and, again, at some *studia*, such as Bologna, it was the only higher faculty, whereas as at Paris its study was impossible (since the Pope banned it in 1219). And then in some *studia* theology was one of the higher faculties. In the thirteenth century there was a faculty of theology only in Paris, Oxford and Cambridge. But whether or not there was a theology faculty at a given *studium*, everyone regarded theology as the highest faculty. Indeed they regarded theology as the Queen of the Sciences, and theology continued to be seen like this for the next 600 years. It was Queen because it dealt with the highest study available to man, and it was a Science (*scientia*) because of course, like the other *scientiae*, it dealt in theory and it was built on sure and certain principles.

We have seen the origin of the seven liberal arts (and particularly of logic) and of theology, itself built on logic, as deriving primarily from the cathedral schools. Law and medicine, now adopted into the schema of the *studium*, had different origins as learned studies. Civil law had been taught by free masters at Bologna from about 1100, and took as its basic text the Code of Justinian which was the encoded law of the Roman Empire. Canon law was also early taught at Bologna. This studied the law of the Catholic Church, and took as its central text the *Concordance of Discordant Canons* (= the *Decretum*) drawn up by Gratian (1139–42), part of the purpose of which was to harmonize and regularize the papal decrees.[28] Medicine, as a subject taught other than by example and one to one, took its origin in Salerno, where it was taught from *c.*985 to *c.*1225.[29]

The mode of teaching of all subjects at the *studium* was 'scholastic', that typical of the schools. This was built on the model of the kind of logic taught by Abelard, and also on the teaching of law at Bologna.[30] In both cases this involved a deep acquaintance with a number of basic texts, and the development and exercise of commentary, *questiones*, and disputing – the skills of arguing positions in order to determine the truth which underlay the apparent contradictions of those basic texts. This approach was used in logic and in law where, to a modern eye, it seems appropriate. It was, as we have seen, also applied in theology. But it was also used in medicine and, in the course of time, in the 'three philosophies' – including natural philosophy – where, to the modern eye, it seems inappropriate. For to a modern it seems that the best way of resolving the truth about medicine or nature is to look at nature and to investigate nature at first hand. This did not seem to be so obvious to the men who taught and learnt at the *studium* of the thirteenth century, among whom were the friars. It is because of such differences that we should hesitate in identifying the natural philosophy of the *studium* with the natural science of today.

Lest we be tempted to look for spurious continuities and create for ourselves a continuous 'history of learning' in the West, it is desirable to stress once more the novelty of everything that was being taught in the thirteenth-century schools and then in the *studia*. The seven liberal arts (the trivium and the quadrivium), as a group, were new in late Antiquity, and had not been pursued in this way in ancient Greece, though they were built on the learning of ancient Greece. Theology was a new subject, built up on logic in the twelfth century, though the name of the new discipline was taken from Plato. Canon law was new, having recently resulted from papal efforts to regularize Church law. Civil law too, as a subject for study, dates from the late Roman Empire, and as a medieval subject certainly owes its origin to the discovery of a manuscript of the *Digest* of Justinian in Montecassino in the 1080s. Medicine, both as a communally taught subject, as a subject built on a particular set of texts, and as a subject built on logic, was new in the centuries around 1150, even though the basic texts of *studium* medicine were ancient Greek and Roman Greek in origin. Finally, the 'three philosophies', natural, moral and metaphysical, were also new in the thirteenth century, both as a set of 'philosophies' and as a way of dividing up the one coherent domain of philosophy, even though they used the ancient Greek writings of Aristotle as their basic texts. It is clear from the way in which these subjects were taught in the thirteenth-century *studium*, and from the fact that they were taught in the thirteenth-century *studium*, that these subjects were meeting thirteenth-century needs, in a Christian society. Hence in general, and also in the specific case of natural philosophy, it was inevitable that the friars and the masters of the thirteenth-century *studium* would not read Aristotle strictly 'Aristotelically', that is as the Greeks had read him or as he had intended to be understood by the Greeks.

As we shall be seeing in later chapters, the friars played a significant role in shaping the curriculum of the secular *studia*, even though they had played no part in creating them. Their particular goal was the faculty of theology, and members of the two main Orders of friars, Dominicans and Franciscans, quickly got themselves inserted into the limited number of teaching posts in theology. For this they were much resented by the secular masters and open warfare, as we shall see, went on between the friars and the masters for many years. Theology, the pinnacle of studies in the *studium*, to a certain extent set up what the curriculum in the lower faculty, that of arts, should consist of. So, by entering the theology faculties, the friars had an influence on *studia* curricula out of all proportion to their numbers.

Not only did the friars seek influence over the *studia* of the secular masters, but they adopted the model of the *studia* for their own internal educational organizations. Dominicans and Franciscans were trained within their Orders in *studia* which shadowed those of the secular masters, and were often located in the same towns. We shall hear more about these later.

But most important for our purposes, the friars had a great influence on the shaping of the new discipline of natural philosophy as it was taught in the *studia* of the masters. For, as we shall be seeing, the friars created natural philosophies for their own purposes, and which expressed their own interests as friars, and these were influential on the secular masters in their own decisions about what constituted proper natural philosophy. For instance, some of their members of the Order of Dominicans, and in particular St Thomas Aquinas and Albertus Magnus, produced great commentaries of the works adopted as the basis of *studium* natural philosophy – the works of Aristotle – commentaries whose interpretations became, in time, basic to the interpretation of Aristotle promoted in the schools.

Notes

1. B. Smalley, *The Study of the Bible in the Middle Ages*, third edn, Oxford, Clarendon Press, 1984, p. 26; G.R. Evans, *The Language and Logic of the Bible: the Earlier Middle Ages*, Cambridge, 1984, p. 1.
2. Smalley, *The Study of the Bible*, pp. 12–13.
3. Ibid., p. 10; Evans, *Language and Logic*, p. 5.
4. C.H. Buttimer, ed., *Hugonis de Sancto Victore Didascalicon. De Studio Legendi*, Washington, 1939, p. 97.
5. Smalley, *The Study of the Bible*, p. 26.
6. On their late Antique origin see *Martianus Capella and the Seven Liberal*

Arts, edited and translated by William Harris Stahl, Richard Johnson and E.L. Burge, 2 vols, New York, Columbia University Press, 1971, 1977, vol. 1, esp. p. 95: 'between Varro, in the first century B.C., and Martianus [in the fifth century AD], there is no evidence that any handbook of the seven liberal arts was written; yet, contemporary with Martianus, Augustine started one; in the next century Cassiodorus compiled one, while Boethius wrote on many of the subjects, discussed the basis of the liberal arts, and appears to have coined the term "quadrivium" ... '; compare the same work, p. 90, which asserts (but does not document) an ancient Greek origin for the seven liberal arts.

7. Ibid. See also William H. Stahl, *Roman Science: Origins, Development and Influence to the Later Middle Ages*, Madison, University of Wisconsin Press, 1962.
8. E. Gilson, *History of Christian Philosophy in the Middle Ages*, London, 1980, p. 176.
9. Smalley, *The Study of the Bible*, pp. 249–51.
10. Quoted in Georges Duby, *The Age of the Cathedrals: Art and Society, 980–1420*, translated by Eleanor Levieux and Barbara Thompson, University of Chicago Press, 1981, p. 18 (original French edition 1966–76).
11. Loren C. Mackinney, *Bishop Fulbert and Education at the School of Chartres*, Indiana, The Medieval Institute, University of Notre Dame, 1957, pp. 34–5, n. 111, quoting Fulbert's letters.
12. Migne, *Patrologia Latina*, vol. 172, p. 1243, our translation. We are grateful to Dr S. Kusukawa for bringing this passage to our attention.
13. John of Salisbury, *The Metalogicon of John of Salisbury: A Twelfth-century Defense of the Verbal and Logical Arts of the Trivium*, translated with an Introduction and Notes by Daniel D. McGarry, Berkeley, University of California Press, 1955, pp. 95–7. 'Metalogicon' is a term coined by John of Salisbury.
14. On the techniques and content of logic and disputation see John Marenbon, *Later Medieval Philosophy (1150–1350): An Introduction*, London, Routledge and Kegan Paul, 1987; *The Cambridge History of Later Medieval Philosophy from the Rediscovery of Aristotle to the Disintegration of Scholasticism 1100–1600*, eds Norman Kretzmann, Anthony Kenny, Jan Pinborg, Cambridge University Press, 1982.
15. The term was used in this 'Platonic' sense by a number of the Greek Church Fathers. On later knowledge of it, see Ralph McInerny, 'Beyond the Liberal Arts' in David L. Wagner, *The Seven Liberal Arts in the Middle Ages*, Bloomington, Indiana University Press, 1983, pp. 248–72; Marenbon, *Later Medieval Philosophy*, pp. 56–60. On Abelard inventing theology, see Jean Leclercq, 'The Renewal of Theology', in Robert L. Benson and Giles Constable, *Renaissance and Renewal in the Twelfth Century*, Oxford, Clarendon Press, 1982, pp. 68–87: 'Abelard would give a new meaning to the word *theology*, by expressly associating it with intellectual research pursued according to a method calling more freely upon one of the liberal arts: dialectic'; the high point in the creation of theology was 'the twenty-five-year period from approximately 1125 to 1150', ibid., pp. 68, 70. See also Hastings Rashdall, *The Universities of Europe in the Middle Ages*, eds F.M. Powicke and A.B. Emden, Oxford University Press, 3 vols, 1936, repr. 1958 (original edition 1895), ch. 2,

esp. p. 43: 'Abelard was the true founder of the scholastic theology'. With respect to the claim there that Peter Abelard invented theology, it should be noted that although in earlier centuries there was discussion of God and the nature of God, and other topics which from the twelfth century came under the new discipline of 'theology', yet before that time they were not and had not been 'theology' in the sense in which Abelard meant the term and in which the term has been used since the time of Abelard.

16. Abelard as quoted in Haskins *The Renaissance of the Twelfth Century*, Cambridge, Mass., Harvard University Press, 1927, p. 354, Haskins himself on p. 355.
17. From a sermon for the feast of St Peter and St Paul, as translated by G.R. Evans, *The Mind of St Bernard of Clairvaux*, Oxford, Clarendon Press, 1983, p. 13.
18. See S.C. Ferruolo, *The Origins of the University*, Stanford University Press, 1985, p. 250.
19. The main sources on which we rely for who translated what where are Haskins, *The Renaissance of the Twelfth Century*, ch. 9; and more recently our knowledge has been brought up to date by Marie-Thérèse d'Alverny, 'Translations and Translators', in Benson and Constable, R*enaissance and Renewal*, pp. 421–62.
20. The papacy continued to support Arabic studies for this purpose in the thirteenth century. For example Gregory IX provided for ten scholars of Arabic and other oriental languages in Paris in the interests of converting the infidel, *Chartularium Universitatis Parisiensis*, ed. H. Denifle, OP, Paris, 1889, vol. 1, p. 212. Likewise the Dominicans maintained special schools (like the *studium Arabicum* in Tunis) for those who travelled in the East for the purposes of conversion. See D. Lindberg ed., *Science in the Middle Ages,* University of Chicago Press, 1978, p. 73, 77; *Chartularium*, vol. 1, pp. 317–20. For Peter of Cluny see R. Lemay, *Abu Ma'shar and Latin Aristotelianism in the Twelfth Century*, Beirut, 1962, p. 16 and Smalley, *The Study of the Bible*, p. 81. There were also Christian writings in Near Eastern languages pursued by Peter of Cluny, who requested translations from Peter of Toledo and Peter of Poitiers (his secretary). David Lindberg, 'The Transmission of Greek and Arabic Learning to the West', in Lindberg, *Science in the Middle Ages*, p. 87.
21. R. Lemay, *Abu Ma'shar*, p. 16.
22. Karl Sudhoff, 'Daniels von Morley Liber de naturis inferiorum et superiorum', *Archiv für die Geschichte der Naturwissenschaften und der Technik*, 1917, 8, pp. 1–40 (with text). See further on this in Chapter 4.
23. Lindberg, 'Greek and Arabic Learning', p. 68.
24. He sent these to the masters of Paris, so that they could add *scientia* to the quadrivium (he refers to the masters as driving a team of four horses, the *quadrigae*). See *Chartularium*, vol. 1, p. 435.
25. See for example Lindberg, 'Greek and Arabic Learning', pp. 60, 66, 69.
26. See Ferruolo, *Origins of the University*, p. 262, for the competition between masters for students, and the frequent 'poaching'. For selection of masters by students, see also R.W. Southern, 'The Schools of Paris and the School of Chartres', in Benson and Constable, *Renaissance and Renewal.* Certainly for masters of arts teaching was a commercial proposition (the case was sometimes made that theologians should not charge fees) and a new translation containing material attractive to students might also be

seen as commercially valuable. The material benefits of a functioning *studium* were clearly seen in the thirteenth century by civil powers (see Pearl Kibre, *Scholarly Privileges in the Middle Ages*, Medieval Academy of America, 1961), and these lie behind the attempts by Charles I of Sicily and Henry III of England to entice masters and scholars of Paris to their respective countries. (*Chartularium*, vol. 1, pp. 119, 501).

27. F.M. Powicke, *Ways of Medieval Life and Thought: Essays and Addresses*, London, Odhams, 1949, p. 198.
28. See Josiah C. Russell, *Twelfth Century Studies*, New York, AMS Press, 1982; ch. 8 'Gratian, Irnerius, and the Early Schools of Bologna'.
29. See P.O. Kristeller, 'The School of Salerno', *Bulletin of the History of Medicine*, 1945, **17**, pp. 138–94.
30. See, for an example of law reasoning as taught at Bologna, the judgement of Pope Innocent III on the relative claims of the rival claimants to the throne of the Holy Roman Empire in 1200, in Pullan, *Sources for the History of Medieval Europe* pp. 194–200.

CHAPTER FOUR

Nature before the friars

The autonomy of nature

The *scientia* of the schools, which we met in the last chapter, included interpretations of some parts of Greek philosophy. The men of the schools saw that the Greeks had discussed something that emerged in Latin translation as *natura*, 'nature' in one sense or another. There were dangers here for a Christian society, for 'nature' in Greek philosophy often had characteristics attributed to God in the twelfth-century West and was often used to designate some sort of autonomous principle. Let us see how the problem started.

What the Greek philosophers wrote about was determined in part by the actions attributed to the gods of the traditional pantheon. Not that the Greek philosophers were pious men in the traditional sense. Quite the contrary, for they all, of whatever school, agreed that the gods had *no* influence on the lives of men. Lightning was not the vengeance of Zeus upon man. The earth was not shaken by Poseidon. The winds blew and the rains came not from the will of the gods, but from nature. There were more theories about the cause of lightning than philosophers who wrote about them, and all the explanations agreed only in being natural. That was the point: when Greek philosophers talked about nature they were not engaging in an exercise in reaching the final physical truth of a matter, but in teaching that the gods had no part in it. This was essentially an act of faith, and many philosophies were god-free religions, even concerned with 'the divine' in an abstract way.

The philosophers also disagreed about what 'nature' was, except that it replaced the gods. The spectrum of belief ranged from the purposeless particles and void of the atomists to the goal-directed teleology of Aristotle's *physis*, but in view of its role 'nature' had a unique importance in philosophy. It was an autonomous principle of generation or change. Freeing the people from fear of the gods and offering 'nature' in their place was not popular with the political masters of the people or with the official religion that was part of their rule. Nature in this sense was still less attractive to Christians, whose God was omnipotent and the Creator of all things. It was no accident that Aristotle's philosophy of nature was forgotten about in the Christian West and the atomist verses of Lucretius survived only in a handful of manuscripts. Christianity had no room for nature as an autonomous principle.

But this began to change in the twelfth century. Apart from Plato, whose demiurge could be seen as an anticipation of the notion of Creation, and whose discussions about the natural world had accordingly survived, there were fragments of other philosophies that touched on the natural world to be found, and the search for more became more intense as the century grew older. It soon became clear to a Christian society that explanations involving 'nature' acting in some autonomous way could be at odds with the prevailing ideology, and twelfth-century philosophers got into trouble with the authorities, just as ancient ones had done. There were many pressures at work in society for the regulation and modification of what was recovered from ancient sources, and especially the doctrine of the autonomy of nature. Part of the story of this chapter is about that regulation and modification: that is, about the ways of solving the problem of the autonomy of nature. The problem reached crisis proportions by the end of the century, and a new way of solving it had to be found. That is the subject of the next chapter.

Scientia and *natura*

Our story is about natural knowledge and we must see here how part of *scientia* became *naturalis*. We shall see in subsequent chapters that the natural philosophies of the two major Orders of friars differed greatly from each other and we shall in the present chapter see how they also differed from what had gone before. It is tempting then to think that they both had their own way (a 'philosophy' in the modern sense) of looking at the same thing ('nature'). With such a view it would seem proper to look first at other views about nature in the period before the friars in order to emphasize the novelty of their approaches.

But the matter is not as simple as that. We must first think about what *we* mean by 'nature' before we too readily read back some modern usage to the twelfth and thirteenth centuries. We are all aware that the word 'nature' in English can be applied to individual things or kinds of things, for example when we say that it is in the nature of a cat to catch mice. Secondly for us it more readily means 'the natural world' or 'mother nature' in some form or other. But such a meaning was far less common or powerful in the ancient world and Middle Ages than might be supposed. Indeed, there is a sense in which 'nature' as we understand it did not exist as a category for most twelfth-century learned men. It was not, that is to say, that their ways of approaching and understanding a given something differed, but that most of them did not see anything for which there was a need to approach and understand. They saw, of course, the physical world they lived in. It was their temporary habitation while in this life, hoping for the next. It was God's creation as revealed in Genesis and expounded in the hexameron literature of the Fathers. But it was not always 'nature' as an organizing or fecund secondary principle between God and His creation. In contrast, as we shall later see, the friars *did* see 'nature' as something that had a place in a scheme of God and Creation.

There were two main sources for twelfth-century doctrines about 'nature'. The first was the physical works of Aristotle, and especially those on animals. In the *Generation of Animals* in particular Aristotle was concerned to refute what he saw as the materialism of those philosophers whom he chose as his intellectual predecessors. He accordingly rejected their accounts of how animal bodies developed, accounts which relied largely on the properties of the matter composing the bodies. His own explanation rested on the Form of the adult male of the species which used appropriate matter and drew out the characteristics of the adult animal from it. The Form of the adult living animal was its soul and its *physis*, 'nature', and the causality of generation was not material but final, that is, purposeful. For Aristotle, 'nature' was always the nature-of-the-thing and he never used *physis* as a general principle external to the animal. His animal books are studies of the natures of each animal.[1]

Latin writers like Seneca and Pliny used the Latin term *natura* to translate the Greek *physis* and although both writers to a certain extent treat of 'nature' as a general principle yet their term is, much more often than their modern translators allow, the nature-of-things, *rerum natura*. Where Seneca and Pliny used 'nature' in the general sense it seems probable that the term derived not from an Aristotelian philosophy but from a Platonic tradition, in which a demiurge had not only put the world together but continued to manage it. This is clear too in the second-century medical and philosophical writer Galen. He wrote in Greek, and what his Latin translators always rendered as *natura* was both *physis* and *demiourgos* as equivalent. But this is Galen's deliberate conflating of the Platonic creative principle with the *physis* of the physical philosophies, particularly that of Aristotle. Other writers kept the two separate. The demiurge was not *physis* and Pliny for example does not make it clear whether *natura*, even in the general sense, was or was not a deity. As we have seen, the Christians adopted a Platonic form of philosophy partly because a creative demiurge could be identified with the omnipotent God of the Jews, and there was little use for 'nature' as a general creative principle. The early Christian centuries were more concerned, for example, with the two 'natures' of Christ – the human and the divine – than with the natural world.[2]

But the doctrine of nature-of-the-thing was not clearly known to the West until the thirteenth century. It was not popular even in antiquity and many preferred the more anthropomorphic image of a creator, such as Plato's demiurge, to explain how the world and its contents came to be. Aristotle's world had been eternal and the processes he described by which the corruptible bodies of living things were renewed was part of that eternity. Plato's demiurge in contrast, like a workman, *made* things, out of something simpler and for the first time, at least originally. Plato's doctrines and the *Timaeus* in which they were expressed were better known than Aristotle in the Middle Ages, and it is very probable that the notion of 'nature' as an autonomous and generative principle was derived ultimately from Platonic roots. This is the second source for twelfth-century doctrines about 'nature'.

The medievals could construct their view of the physical world also from neo-Platonic sources. During the earlier medieval period the Roman Catholic Church's perception of the world rested largely on that of St Augustine. He had been for nine years a 'hearer' of the Manichees and their doctrine of dualism of God and Devil (see Chapter 1). When he turned away from it, it was not to Platonism itself, for the Platonic distinction between body and soul was too close to the Manichean distinction between the evilness of matter, *hyle*, and the goodness of soul. Instead he turned to a version of Plotinus' neo-Platonism, which emphasized God's creating the world by emanation, so that God and world were almost one. In this view too there was little room for 'nature' as a separate principle and little reason to give special attention to the natural world.

But this changed in the twelfth century. As more Greek and Arabic texts – including much deriving from Aristotle – were sought out the term 'nature' came to be used in a number of different ways. The most important were the two mentioned above, the enduring and powerful meaning of 'nature-of-a-thing' and nature as a principle, perhaps in some way personified. As we examine the writings in which people expressed these two meanings of 'nature' they seem to be of three kinds. Those who wrote on the natures of things most often were writing philosophically. They read the literal meaning of the physical world and expressed it in plain, if dialectical language. The *physicus*, the medical man and the translators fall into this group and were drawn to the Aristotelian *libri naturales*. In contrast the monastic writers tried to reach a knowledge of the nature of things, especially those near God, by contemplation rather than by dialectic. They used an elaborate language full of metaphors and allegories and thought a literal reading, whether of the natural world or of the Sacred Page, was merely preliminary. Thirdly, the poets too used an elaborate language of allegory and much more than the other groups were inclined to discuss nature as a general principle, even as a personalized allegorical figure, with semi-divine characteristics including rationality and providentiality.

But this came close to giving some sort of autonomy to Nature. Care had to be taken by those who wrote about Nature as an allegorical figure not to give her too many of the attributes of God as Creator. This was done by portraying nature as the submissive agent of God with a special task of maintaining the species of living things that God had originally created. This meant that God was not directly concerned with the generation of ignoble animals, which was instead overseen by Nature. It is in this way that Nature as an allegorical female figure in the words of the poets had powerful resonances in the minds of those who were concerned more prosaically with the natures-of-things: Nature saw to the generation of things. When all went well – when it was natural – Nature was faithfully perpetuating God's species. If anything went wrong then Nature had either made a mistake or was playing games (*ludi naturae*), neither of which could have been attributed without impiety to God. Nature was not only an allegorical generative and normative figure but a symbol of birth itself: *natura* is literally 'birth', a revealing and development of the individual (it is derived from *nascor*, 'to be born'). This is just what Aristotle's nature-of-a-thing was: the unfolding of the attributes that made a thing what is was; the teleological goal-finding of natural change; the coming to be of plants and animals and their quiddity. Thus these two meanings of 'nature', approached by different intellectual routes and expressed in different language, link at a point – the essential natures of things – that was to be central to the two natural philosophies of the two main Orders of Friars.

Nature as allegory

One way of avoiding the dangers of positing nature as an autonomous principle was the use of allegory. By the twelfth century this was an old device among Christians, having been used by Boethius for his figure 'Philosophy'. The even older *Physiologus* supplied a series of natural wonders that were essentially allegories about the truths of the Christian story, played out among animals. The details of the animals derive in part from philosophy, and the Aristotelian nature-of-the-animal often plays its part in illustrating a Christian truth. But now that the purpose is religious rather than philosophical, an animal is not restricted to a single essence or quiddity and can have a 'second nature' (or even third) if it can be used to illustrate another truth.[3] It would have been plain to all readers that Christ himself spoke in parables, a form of allegory, either to hide its meaning from the wrong people or to indicate a higher 'moral' reading.[4] Particularly in the later twelfth century 'nature' was also often dealt with as personified, particularly by the poets of the school of Chartres.[5] This was not a technique of the philosopher or the medical man or with those who for one or other reason favoured Aristotle's view of 'nature' as the nature-of-things, or who preferred a literal reading of the physical world. Instead, the monastic device of allegory was often used to portray nature as a sort of Platonic demiurge squeezed into a Christian context. Personifications of this sort were used not only by Boethius but by Martianus Capella for his Mercury and 'Philology' (a source for Western astrology), and their interest to us is that both 'nature' and 'philosophy' later have uses characteristic of the twelfth century.

It is in such language that Bernard Sylvester (in mid-century), Alain of Lille and others treat nature as bountiful, beautiful, allegorical, Platonic and yet a true servant of the Creator, often abused by man, but capable of showing him the true morality of life. Bernard Sylvester's prosimetron *Cosmographia*, written in the 1140s, was a model for later writers. Much of Bernard's information about the natural world, but not his use of allegory, comes from the *physici* and *medici*. His subject-matter is that of the hexameron literature, which since patristic times had discussed the six days of creation.[6] When Creation came to be seen as Nature, Biblical commentary on Genesis took a new form. Here, in the work of Bernard, Nature complains in tears to Noys (*nous*, God's providence) about the confusion of matter in the original chaos. Noys separates the elements and arranges a (very Platonic) ensouled world. As Noys sets about producing man, Nature departs to find Urania, working astrologically among the stars, and Physis, in the sublunar world. Physis has two daughters, Theorica and Practica: the reference is to medicine,[7] and we are reminded that medicine and astrology formed a complete account of the physical world. Nature's job is the lesser creation: to make material copies of the eternal (Platonic) ideals of things. She is *mater generationis*,[8] almost our 'mother nature'. As we shall see in the case of Alain of Lille, nature is thus the viceroy of God, whose hands are not to be contaminated with the baseness and evil of matter.

Another allegorical view of nature is given in John of Hauteville's *Architrenius* (about 1184).[9] This is the story of a man who seeks consolation for his lost youth by seeking true knowledge from Lady Nature. He travels over a countryside allegorically representing deficient education (partly in Paris) to Thule, where ancient philosophers direct him to Nature and natural knowledge: natural knowledge existed at the very edges of the world.

Reading the Sacred Page and Nature literally

Directly opposed to the allegorical and poetical treatment of 'nature' was the literal reading given to the physical world and the Sacred Page and sometimes both by translators and philosophers. 'Philosophy' in the twelfth century was knowledge of things human and divine and a literal reading of this kind could generate the danger of treating nature as autonomous. For William of Conches, the grammarian of Chartres, philosophy was the true knowledge of all things that exist, whether incorporeal or visible, that is, of God and His creation. This philosophy was primarily about God: this is William's purpose in practising philosophy. In twelfth-century Christendom philosophical knowledge that did not relate to God was not simply useless or impious knowledge, it was not knowledge at all. It was not only that God granted some knowledge to man, but also that the meaning of all things could only be grasped in the light of their relationship to their Creator: William saw divine design in the world.

But William the grammarian was also inclined to look at the literal side of things.[10] Perhaps this was because he *was* a grammarian, and he certainly too had a particular interest in medical matters: it was the doctors' stock in trade to know about the physical world and its microcosm, the body. William held that the various stages of philosophy – being a human enterprise – are imperfect, or what is the same thing, man cannot know God directly. Man is fallen, and his powers are weak. In fact William and the philosophers were in a similar position to the monks: just as the latter used the devices of allegorical and spiritual reading of the Sacred Page to enable imperfect man to approach God's true meaning within the page, so our grammarian and the philosophers were using *philosophy* to approach a knowledge of God from the physical world of nature and from profane writings. It is this all-encompassing nature that made 'knowledge' or 'philosophy' a single enterprise in twelfth-century schemes of knowledge.

William saw God as the creator-craftsman, the *artifex* without whose will the naturally disparate elements within nature would fly apart. This is not allegory, and William believed on the literal level that the elements were opposites that naturally repel each other. Some held, he said, that 'elements' meant the opposing and irreducible qualities of hot, wet, cold and dry; but he draws his notion of element from Constantine the African, whose medical *Pantegni* he used in about 1130. William, although a teacher of grammar, was in fact well read in medical matters. He calls himself a *physicus*, a term he uses also for Constantine: it meant for him a man whose duty was to look at the ultimate natures-of-things. The term is derived from *physis*, and clearly implies that William the grammarian was concerned with a literal reading of the natural world. He also knew that central text of medieval medical education, the *Isagoge* of Joannitius,[11] where also the nature of the elements is discussed. But the nature books of Aristotle were not yet in use in Salerno, and William was distant from contemporary centres of translation where Aristotle's physical doctrines might become known. William's conclusion (it was not Aristotle's) is that the irreducibility of the elements means that they are atomic.[12] (The same notion could be read into the *Timaeus*, which William had glossed.[13]) For William the stars too are elementary (in contrast to Aristotle's doctrine that they were quintessential) and are animated, part of a chain of intelligences reaching down to man through aerial and watery demons. Through such (distinctly unAristotelian) linkages the bond between the upper and lower worlds, the subjects of William's unified philosophy, were established.

So William's medical and philosophical interests encouraged him to think literally about the world. He makes an important distinction that we have not met before: while the *physicus* (he says) looked at the ultimate natures of things, the duty of the *philosophus* was to consider these in the light of creation – for example how God had arranged matter after chaos. So for William, the philosopher has a higher role, and a more Christian one than that of the pagan philosophers of antiquity: philosophy is becoming domesticated in a Christian world. In expressing his physical, medical and philosophical interests William was not of course ignorant of the techniques of allegory and so on in the reading of the Sacred Page, but he saw the essential unreality of the allegorical figures like Mercury and Philology, used by others.[14] (He similarly removed the *involucrum* of higher meaning from the words of the Bible.[15])

But William the grammarian did not convince everyone. Another William, Abbot of St Thierry, was not alone in believing that there was a special grace (that of Latin study of the Sacred Page) in the cloister that gave true understanding in contemplation as the last stage in knowing God. In such an understanding arguments taken from nature were 'physical', merely the first stage, corresponding to a literal reading of the Sacred Page, in a process that might pass through allegory and symbolism to divine knowledge. William of St Thierry, the abbot, was accordingly horrified to find that William, the grammarian, did not rise above the literal level of reading the Sacred Page, for example in interpreting 'in a physical sense' the story of the creation of Eve from Adam's rib. The Abbot wrote to St Bernard of Clairvaux complaining that, following Abelard, William of Conches 'brings forward a new philosophy, confirming and multiplying what he [Abelard] had said'.

Continuing, the Abbot pours scorn on William of Conches as a *physicus* and a *philosophus* who 'philosophises physically about God' (particularly on the persons of the Trinity and the birth of Christ):

> Then in a philosophical, or rather physical way describing the creation of the first man, he first says his body was not made by God but by nature and that his soul was given to him by God, and afterwards that the body was in fact made by spirits, which he calls demons, and by the stars. In another place he seems to follow the opinions of some other fatuous philosophers who say that nothing exists beyond bodies and the corporeal; that there is no God in the world besides a concourse of elements and a natural temperament, and that this is the soul in the body; in another he is a manifest Manichee, saying that the soul is created by the good God, but the body by the Principle of Shadows.[16]

So William of Conches, our grammarian, represented everything that was detested by the defenders of monastic wisdom and the *lectio divina*. He did not rise above the literal, he argued dialectically and physically about the divine, he raised nature as a generative and autonomous principle[17] that contended with God in creation and, worst of all, he seemed to be a dualist, a Manichee like those who had tempted St Augustine and whose descendants were even now threatening orthodoxy from Constantinople to northern Italy, Languedoc and Provence. Bernard, a man of considerable influence,[18] was convinced, and William had to recant.[19]

This encounter provides important evidence of the hostility of the orthodox to the use of 'nature' as a separate principle. While the nature-of-a-thing could be readily subsumed within God's means of creating or arranging the world, 'nature' as a separate generative principle looked dangerously heretical. Whether William of Conches was or was not a 'manifest Manichee' he was seen by William the Abbot as in some way equating 'Nature' as an autonomous principle with demons and even with the Evil Principle of the Manichees.

That the autonomy of nature led to the neglect of God in the schools was clear to the monks even when nature was Plato's.

> Non est scola vanitatis
> Sed doctrina verititatis;
> Ibi nomen non Socratis
> Sed eterne trinitatis.
> Non est Plato vel Thimeus
> Hic auditur unus deus

sang Hugh of St Orleans[20] during the years – the 1130s – when William of Conches was putting his philosophy of the world together: the cloister, unlike the schools, [particularly those of Paris] is not a school of vain learning, but has the doctrine of truth; here is not the name of Socrates, but of the eternal Trinity; it is not Plato or Timaeus who is heard here, but the One God. In other words Hugh thought that philosophy, especially that which looked towards the physical world, ought to be replaced by contemplation of a God who is a Trinity, but nevertheless single, unlike the God of the Manichees. Verse of this kind was a new weapon in the Troubadour centuries, but not much of it was on the side of the monks. For example, Abelard the scholar was defended against the monastic Bernard by a Goliard poet who was in favour of scholastic teaching, even within the monasteries. This poet's Apocalypsis Goliae tells how Golias was led by Pythagoras to the land of the classical philosophers and poets, carefully avoiding the corruption of the monks.[21] It was the poets and the schoolmen, not the monks, who explored that part of philosophy that was concerned with the physical world, or 'nature' in certain senses of the word.

Natura naturans and *natura naturata*

Another way in which the difficulties of the old doctrine of nature as an autonomous principle could be met was by radically transforming it into a Christian doctrine. It could be done historically, by showing that Greek philosophy had been a sort of preparation for the final revelation of Christian truth. This depended on insisting that *philosophia* embodied knowledge as a whole, of things both divine and human. This meant that old philosophy could be seen as the same kind of enterprise, a seeking of knowledge of God, but in itself a lower and earlier form of knowledge. For example Hugh of St Victor[22] made his account of knowledge as a whole a historical one. His *Didascalion*[23] (written before 1141) is partly a history and reading guide in the arts as a preliminary to theology and partly an idealized account of the studies at the school at St Victor.[24] The views of Pythagoras and Plato on the soul are therefore for Hugh parts of philosophy (as is the theory behind even so practical an art as agriculture) even though incomplete parts of truth. He represented the origins of philosophy as a search among the Greeks for the Immutable. This prepared the human mind (he says) for the reception of Christian truth: the ultimate Immutable is God, followed, in Hugh's account, in descending order by the upper and lower parts of His creation, as cause and effect. These two together are in fact 'nature'.

This is an important and distinctive use of the term. One way out of the difficulty of the autonomy of nature was to identify nature as an aspect of God's activity, so that God in His actions in making and controlling the world could be called *natura naturans*. In this case, God's creation became *natura naturata*, the passive and material side of 'nature'. This latter device, to equate *natura* at least in part with creation, came to be used by the friars, and something very similar is employed here by Hugh of St Victor. His 'nature' was double, for God – says Hugh – created the sempiternal heavenly bodies and the immutable underlying material substance of things. The actual physical sublunary world of the senses, which is the outward mutable form of the primordal substance, is 'the work of nature', in Hugh's words. His meaning is that corruptible objects have their causes not directly from God, but indirectly, through the heavens.

It was partly because the physical objects of the sublunary world are not the direct creation of God that *physica*, 'study of nature', is not high on Hugh's hierarchy of the kinds of knowledge (which includes the seven arts). It is partly too, because the ultimate aim of philosophy for Hugh, the religious remedying of man's imperfections, was not to be achieved by studying the causes of physical things. We have concentrated on the 'natural' part of Hugh's framework of knowledge but, as in the case of most of his contemporaries, it was not central to his concerns. *Physica* was a small part of theoretical philosophy, and Hugh's historical treatment provided a variety of ways in which theoretical philosophy had been divided. For Hugh, what ultimately succeeded these, all of which rise no higher than literal understanding of words, is the allegorical and tropological interpretation of the Sacred Page, a much higher level of understanding and truth. Philosophy as a whole was therefore practical in two areas: to prepare the soul for its future life by remedying its defects with *scientia*; and to reform the cathedral clergy, for the Victorines were intended to be scholars while the monks 'pray and mourn'.[25]

Hugh gave great importance to the literal reading of the Scriptures as the basis of the spiritual reading. A literal and dialectical reading could be argued about, and disputation as used by the Victorines was part of the means whereby they decided, in the schools of the twelfth and thirteenth century, what 'nature' was. It is important to note that the *Aristotelian* version of 'nature' as the natures-of-things had not yet come into currency. Aristotle was still the logician; and one of the things that attracted the students to the schools was disputation. Disputations were practical and entertaining exercises in dialectic and were accordingly absent from the quiet of the cloister (as observed by, for example, Peter of Celles writing in the 1160s):[26] for the monks dialectic for argument was superficial learning. But in the schools the dialectic that made Abelard a popular teacher, and which was informing the new theology, could be turned also to the physical world. At least as early as the 1170s the formal roles within the disputation of the *respondens* and *opponens* had become established, and Godfrey of St Victor, a successor to Hugh, provides a neat image of Aristotle the dialectician as the fencing master who gives out the weapons and armour together with instructions for their use.[27] In this image the dispute between the swordsmen is in philosophy, the content of which Godfrey identifies with the seven liberal arts. Of these, the quadrivial arts relate to the physical world, but it is still Plato who is the philosopher of what is natural, of the upper world, the macrocosm, and of the body of man, the microcosm. By the later twelfth century the distinction used by the Victorines between 'nature' (God and the celestial world) and 'the works of nature' (the sublunary world) was common to many writers.

New philosophy and Christianity

The western understanding of *natura* began to change radically during the second half of the twelfth century. A number of scholars interested in physical and mathematical *scientiae* were attracted to places where translation from the Arabic was going on. These *scientiae* included medicine, astronomy and astrology. Little difference was seen between the last two of these and astronomy was often seen as the mathematical doctrines needed to practise astrology. However intellectually interesting these *scientiae* were, they had the considerable added attraction that they were useful. The doctor generated part of his professional image on this ability to prognosticate and judicial astrology was soon to become a thriving trade. Westerners were predominantly interested in making translations in these two fields, both 'physical' in the sense of being about the natural world. But new and different dangers arising from the autonomy of nature accompanied these interests. Churchmen too were interested in the new philosophy and other Arabic beliefs, largely because of the need to monitor them.

The main problem was the autonomy of nature. The medical man and the astrologer had little need to rise above their interest in nature and to treat it as a stage in knowing God, as the theologians did. The Archbishop of Toledo sponsored translations from the Arabic at the Christian frontier in Spain; had he wished to defend and propagate the faith it was as well to know the literature of the enemy.[28] In the Christian world it was accepted that God as Creator occupied the ultimate place in a hierarchy of existence, controlling a range of beings down to man and beyond. The Arab Muslims however held that this hierarchy was one of intelligences, to the first of which God gave the power of creating the inferior and all that came below.[29] This distanced God from man and went a long way to allowing the separate existence of an autonomous principle of nature. It was a doctrine too that opposed the earlier western teaching that nature *was* God, as *naturans*.

Everyone could agree of course that God had chosen to work through secondary principles in the physical world, and that one of these might be 'nature' in some sense. It was a common feature of many interpretations of 'nature' that the celestial bodies were part of the apparatus by which the lower world (perhaps 'the works of nature') was governed. This made the search for Arabic astrology, under way in the first half of the twelfth century,[30] even more interesting. But a full-blown astrological theory was an apparatus in which 'nature' could look not only an autonomous but a necessary principle, acting according to rules that made prediction possible.

In adopting predictive and mathematical astrology, the westerners therefore had to be careful. In the first place they had to change the Arabic texts in important ways. It was necessary to alter the calendar from Islamic to Christian. Second, the Arabic doctrine of the Great Conjunctions gave importance to long cyclic periods of history, for example 960 years: these had to be fitted into extant Biblical chronologies, beginning with creation. It was more necessary than ever for the Christians to insist that Nature was the celestial world, God's creation, and the Works of Nature the perceptible arrangement of the substance of the physical world. The celestial bodies were taken in the West to be agents of God's will for the lower world: the motions of the upper world were the direct cause of the changes in the lower. The incorruptible celestial bodies caused generation and corruption amongst the mutable elements of the lower world. Generation of animals happened in the lower world but was caused in the upper. Hermann of Carinthia called knowledge of the upper and lower worlds *scientia naturalis*[31] and his interest, and that of and many others in this *scientia* was of course that, because the relationship of the upper and lower worlds was causal, events on earth could be predicted. The centre of attention was Ptolemy's *Almagest*, which contained both astrological techniques and the mathematical astronomy on which they rested. It was the ambition of Christians like Hermann and the Englishman Robert of Chester to discover and translate the work. Gerard of Cremona found it in Toledo and began (with help) to translate it, at the same time making it known to an audience.[32]

This 'class' around Gerard included Daniel of Morley, another Englishman with astrological interests. During a brief journey home he came to discuss the matter with the Bishop of Norwich. The bishop was interested in, and probably anxious about, astrology. Not only was it partly pagan – a *doctrina Arabum* – but it appeared to be deterministic. Daniel, writing up his reply to the bishop in a book (between 1175 and

1185) was at pains to answer both criticisms.[33]

> No one should be disturbed that in dealing with the creation of the world on the basis of what has been said, I call for evidence the gentile philosophers and not the fathers of the church, because although the former are not included among the faithful, yet since some of their works are full of faith they should be drawn to our doctrine. Whence we also, who are mystically liberated from Egypt, are ordered by the Lord to borrow from the Egyptians vessels of silver and gold.[34]

As for the bishop's second worry, that of determinism, Daniel recalls that he had himself been much concerned about this aspect of Arabic astrology, but had succumbed to the arguments of Gerard of Cremona that the causal effects of the planets was often thwarted by the material nature of the lower things.

The 'nature' that Gerard had been searching for in Arabic sources covered the upper and lower worlds as cause to effect. It was predictive, and thus useful and interesting, but not so determinist as to run into Christian theological opposition. It was subordinate to the worship of God. Under such terms could the utility and interest (and both Gerard and Daniel were excited by it) of this philosophy of the upper and lower worlds be accepted into Christendom. Daniel's *philosophia* had also to meet these conditions. Although physical, and a literal reading of the natural world, yet its purpose, like that of other twelfth-century philosophies, was to perfect man's nature, overcoming, says Daniel, the weaknesses man has in being partly corporeal. The world for Daniel was the image of God's will and the central concern of Daniel's philosophy was how the created world worked, causally and predictively. It was a Christian and a philosophical world, created *ex nihilo*, not by a rearranging of extant matter or by a Platonic demiurge or by delegated intelligences. Both upper and lower parts were created at the same time in order to perfect the cause-effect relationship between them. But Plato figures large as The Philosopher in Daniel's philosophy. To him are attributed the four causes, efficient, formal, material and final, that we think of as Aristotelian. But they are also very Christian causes, for God, says Daniel, is the efficient cause, His wisdom the formal, His goodness the final and the four elements the material (to which scheme we may compare Gundisalvi's additional spiritual causes). Indeed, Daniel represents Aristotle as presenting two ultimate causes only. These are 'principles' or original causes, and the context of Daniel's discussion is Creation: the two principles are unity and diversity; or God and nature; or (in the Greek terms of which Daniel does not approve) *nous* and *hyle*. Daniel does not know of, or chooses not to follow, Aristotle's nature books. In his account, the *physici* who look at the natural world are concerned with (unAristotelian) questions about the relationship of the elements. Daniel certainly knew some of Aristotle's physical works, but may not have known in all cases who wrote them. He used *On the Heavens and Earth* in Gerard's translation, but does not mention Aristotle. *On Sense and the Sensed* is, however, attributed to Aristotle, while *On Generation and Corruption* is the work of 'the philosopher'. Apart from two small spurious works, no other of Aristotle's physical treatises are mentioned, and it has been argued that Daniel was familiar with these works only through the paraphrase made by Avicenna.[35] Daniel's 'nature', then, consists of God's immutable laws by which the upper world causes and 'complexions' the lower. The mechanism of this causality and of complexioning is the subject of the second part of Daniel's tract. This is *astronomia*, consisting of eight related *scientiae*: astrological judgements, medicine, physical nigromancy, agriculture, sleight of hand (*prestigia*), alchemy, 'images' and the *scientia* of mirrors and glasses.

In short, Daniel's philosophy of nature has the same purpose, the remedying of man's defects, as those we have been looking at, while its subject-matter is quite different. Like others too it is directed towards God-and-his-works and is (like them) a religious exercise. This perhaps came to be emphasized as the Muslim material was adapted for a Christian culture; and like many Christians his technique of adaptation was to show how the new details were an extension to the extant Christian view of nature.

Another way of neutralizing the threat of the autonomy of nature appeared as Aristotle's doctrines were found, at first anonymous, in Arabic physical writings. This was to treat these doctrines as literal readings of nature and subject them to a process that paralleled the discovery of spiritual meaning in the literal reading of the Scriptures.

This was the technique adopted by Archdeacon Dominic Gundisalvi, an important figure among the translators. He worked with the patronage of the Archbishop of Toledo in the middle of the century. In Toledo they were at the boundary between Christian and Muslim Spain and thus more likely than most in Christendom to become familiar with Arabic texts. Historians have treated Gundisalvi largely as a translator and consequently as an agent in a process of transmission. Our interest is in what motivated Gundisalvi – and his patron – to select certain texts from what was available among the Arabs, and then to translate them.

What Gundisalvi made of his chosen Arabic texts depended on what was in his mind already. Part of this was knowledge of the rather scant history of western writings, including the tradition of the seven liberal arts. More important were the beliefs and disciplines of his Church, which was not only, as Christian, opposed to Islam, but was the Church of a people who were locally actively antagonistic to the Muslims and would have been doubly sensitive to differences in belief.

This aggressive use of philosophy was one of the reasons for learning it, a religious reason we shall meet again with the friars. Here, in the twelfth century, we must note that philosophy had a widely recognized purpose, also religious. Let us examine what Gundisalvi thought it was. When – shortly after 1150 – he wrote his *De Divisione Philosophiae*[36] which borrows extensively from the Arabs Alfarabi, Algazel and Avicenna, the result is not a translation but a careful mixture of these writers and the more homely Boethius and Isidore, the whole adjusted with some sophistication to twelfth-century Christianity. Like other writers on the topic of the kinds of knowledge Gundisalvi makes extensive use of the technique of *distinctio*,[37] dividing and subdividing the topic 'knowledge' until the categories are clear, but very numerous. The result looks like a mass of fine distinctions, but in fact Gundisalvi's argument is plain throughout. It is that the basically Aristotelian philosophy he has met in the Arabic commentators provides further illustration and explanation of the beliefs of Christianity.[38] Now, we could tease apart his 'distinctions' to show precisely what he meant by *philosophia* and *scientia naturalis*, but in fact this on its own would not help very much in looking for his reasons for writing or the resources that were used by the friars in their natural philosophy. We should be looking at what knowledge was for, as well as what it was about, in Gundisalvi's text and in the thirteenth century. He wrote, he said, to supply true wisdom, *sapientia*. The use of which was, simply, the perfection of man.

According to Gundisalvi it was in fulfilling this purpose of philosophy – to perfect man – that we recognize its divisions, the *scientiae*. Some of these *scientiae* were cultivated to look after man's material needs. Of these, some had been invented by man, like the seven liberal arts (he added that the subjects of the trivium were necessary for communication). Other *scientiae* (and here the quadrivial subjects would fit) help man's soul reach the truth. Another, divine *scientia*, had been given directly to him – said Gundisalvi – in the Sacred Page. The theoretical side of philosophy was to know the truth and the Good, and the practical side was to live the good life. All of these things were the work of God, and so Gundisalvi can adopt a definition of all philosophy as an assimilation (*assimilacio*, 'making similar') of man to the works of God. In Gundisalvi's eyes philosophy achieved this by allowing man to perceive the truth of things.

This truth – said Gundisalvi – in relation to physical things, the natural world, was perceived by recognizing the four natural causes described by Aristotle, at the centre of Aristotle's account of *physis* and the nature-of-a-thing. It was by means of these four causes that Aristotle explained how things came to be as they are, that is, how their 'natures' became manifest. These causes were fundamental to the later natural philosophy of at least one Order of the friars and to the *studia*, and we must see how the pagan 'Egyptian gold' of philosophy was refined by Gundisalvi for use in a Christian society.

Aristotle had said that everything had a material cause, the matter of which it was composed; a formal cause that gave it shape; an efficient cause, the immediate agent producing it, and a final cause, the purpose it was to serve – that is, how it acted in accordance with its 'nature'. But to fit Aristotle squarely into a Christian framework, Gundislavi extended all these physical and 'literal' explanations of natural change into a single mode of explanation, the spiritual. He added a spiritual cause to each of Aristotle's. Thus the 'corporeal' formal cause was Aristotle's Form, while the spiritual formal cause was the power lodged by God in the celestial regions to control generation and corruption, growth and age, health and disease and other changes in the material sublunar world. Similarly the final cause was double, the 'corporeal' being Aristotle's and the spiritual being the union of body and soul so that man may see the truth of perceptible things, and live accordingly in justice and sanctity in the knowledge of the Creator – the 'good life' that was the practical purpose of philosophy. In a similar way Gundisalvi doubled the Aristotelian categories of Substance and Accident, producing corporeal and spiritual forms. This led the true philosopher, he said, to recognize himself and the first Substance created directly by God. Subsequent Accidents to the Substance resulted in categories, species and individuals. Truth was known to Gundisalvi, in effect, through Aristotelian categories, which described the real world, in Christian terms.

To produce a 'spiritual Aristotle' in these two ways was to render Aristotle's philosophy acceptable to Christendom. That was a condition Gundisalvi had to satisfy, but his purpose was something else: he wanted to show that the old philosophy in modern dress (that is, in the Arabic commentators; Gundisalvi was not reading Aristotle directly) was an illustration and extension of Christian truth. In such an enterprise the fact that Aristotle had said that the world was eternal came to be a problem for some Christian apologists. Gundisalvi however, solved the problem by exploring further ways in which Christianity could embrace philosophy. He used a number of *distinctiones* of 'eternity' which in a Christian world included meanings not available within Greek philosophy but with deep significance in relation to a Creation that included the beginning and ending of time. In other words Gundisalvi is again spiritualizing Aristotle. Here for Gundisalvi there is a single philosophy, with a single subject: God-and-His-works: this subject was divided into things without beginning or end (God as Creator and Trinity), things created before time (the angels and [first] matter, *hyle*), things created with time (the celestial bodies and the elements), which are 'sempiternal' in being without end, and, lastly, everything else, which was created during time. Some of the latter, like souls, are without end, but other natural and artificial things are transient. So, by choosing the right distinction for 'eternity' and for 'world' (the celestial bodies and the elements) Gundisalvi has explained away the problem of Aristotle's eternal world by combining it with Christian principles and obtaining a richer overall picture.

This scheme of creation was the framework of Gundisalvi's classification of the *scientiae* that belonged to philosophy. Neither the content nor the purpose of the 'natural' *scientiae* could be divorced from the purpose of philosophy as a whole, which was to perfect man, both in soul and in mode of life, in the light of the knowledge that philosophy supplied. It was around this framework too that Gundisalvi arranged the whole of the Aristotelian *libri naturales*. This scheme was the arrangement of topics from the abstract to the concrete, from the unmoved to the moved, from that without to that with matter. Or in other words from metaphysics or theology to mathematics and to *scientia physica sive naturalis*. Here Gundisalvi came closest to Aristotle by locating each of the (named) *libri naturales* on a scale from abstraction from, to involvement with, matter and motion. Gundisalvi took most of this from Alfarabi, and although we have reference to *On the Heavens and Earth*, *On Generation and Corruption*, *On the Soul* and the two animal books (together with works of other authorship on plants and minerals) yet Aristotle is not clearly identified as their author. Nor did Gundisalvi identify his Arabic sources.[39] The result of both was that his Christian readers would not have known where to look for any amplification of what he said in his text and so would not have recognized an 'Aristotelianism' as distinct from a 'Gundisalvism'. The same absence of an -ism can be noted in the Latin translations of Albumasar's astronomy, sometimes said to have been a major vehicle for the introduction of Aristotelianism into the West (before 1180).[40]

The work of Gundisalvi was known by others who wrote on the divisions of the sciences, like Daniel of Morley, or who were also concerned with teaching, like Robert Kilwardby. It seems then that in the second half of the twelfth century a number of people were interested in a philosophy that could be found among the Arabs, and which included a new way of discussing the physical world. It does not seem to have been much earlier than the beginning of the thirteenth century that it was widely known that the source of this was Aristotle. Only then was it the case that to identify Aristotle with parts of the new philosophy made his *libri naturales* worth searching for.

To summarize the place of Gundisalvi in the discussion of nature in the period before natural philosophy we can see that he represents one way of thinking about the natural world as part of a whole philosophy. He extended Christian doctrine and the use of the seven liberal arts within it by the use of the 'Egyptian gold' of pagan philosophy. His purpose was the Christian one of demonstrating how to perfect the person. His material was a second-hand and unacknowledged Aristotle and first-hand but equally unacknowledged Arabic commentators. The result was a manner of thinking about the physical world that was much more elaborate than that of the quadrivial arts. *Scientia naturalis* for Gundisalvi was the knowledge of concrete (not abstract) things, in the heavens and on earth, together with their motion. It was 'knowledge of the natures of things', not 'knowledge of nature', and although it had Aristotle's causality and so on as its principles, they were not principles of a generalized Nature, and not principles that could be given much status in a Christian world-view. Gundisalvi's concern was with the nature of philosophy rather than with its practice, and without direct citation of Aristotle and without urgent need of Aristotle's physical works, no widespread adoption of Egyptian gold followed Gundisalvi's writing.

Nature and medicine

The medical man has a special place in the topics dealt with in this chapter. He had a particular technical meaning for the term *natura*. He read the physical world literally. He had practical reasons for employing a philosophy of nature derived from Aristotle. Although intimately bound up in the theory of medicine, medical 'nature' could still be seen by outsiders as autonomous and the doctor as devoid of a proper respect for God. Like the astrologer the medical man had a professional reason to look at the physical world and less reason to look above it. His special concern was with the microcosm, the body of man, made from the same elements as the bigger world. In the earlier part of the twelfth century, before the *studia*, it was the physician who could claim to be best informed on the single *scientia* or philosophy of the upper and lower world. He was professionally obliged to consider the physical world, its airs, waters and places, in which his patients were found. And he had very practical uses for astrological prediction – prognosis from the moment of decumbiture (when the patient took to his bed) and the calculation of critical days. There is little doubt that the medieval physician gained in reputation from the elaborate display of astrological theory with which he could impress his patients.

So it was the professional concern of the medical men with the physical world (already established in astrology)[41] that explains why they first came to study the Aristotelian texts on the natural world. Thus while Hugh of St Victor, about 1140, made no connection between *physica*, knowledge of the physical world, and *medicina*, yet subsequently the medical man so completely adopted natural knowledge that his subject became physic and he became the physician. Thus when Daniel of Morley said 'He who condemns astronomy destroys medicine' the word he used was *physica*, not *medicina*.[42] (His argument was primarily that the prediction of critical days is based on an understanding of the astrological role of the moon.)

In these ways medical teaching was a natural route by which a knowledge of the natural world reached those whose philosophical interests required it. By the time of Bartholomaeus of Salerno in the later part of the twelfth century, Aristotle was available again and in a less anonymous fashion than had been the case with Gundisalvi. Bartholomaeus disparaged the mode of exposition of current western medical works and proposed to remedy it by the use of the introductory *Isagoge* of Joannitius 'of Alexandria', and by reference to Aristotle's *Physics* and *Metaphysics*. The *Isagoge* is for Bartholomaeus *medicina*, that is, part of *physica*, the subject-matter of Aristotle's nature books. *Physica* in turn is part of *naturalis scientia*, itself a part of philosophy. The other parts of philosophy, said Bartholomaeus, are moral and rational; and by giving each a theoretical and practical side, he produced a comprehensive scheme of human knowledge that gives medicine a secure relationship to the new, Arabic-Greek rational philosophy. And if a rational medicine that gave explanation was more attractive to patients and students than the older and more empirical *medicina* of simples and purges, then we have one reason for the reputation of late twelfth-century Salerno as a medical centre, and a reason why its medical commentators, anxious to become better – more attractive – teachers, made use in plain language of the 'Egyptian gold' of Aristotle's nature books.[43]

Another important Salernitan teacher was Urso, who also chose to follow Aristotle's nature books. In his commentary on the *Aphorisms* of Hippocrates there are many echoes of Aristotle's *Meteorology* and *On Generation and Corruption*.[44] In his *De Commixtione Elementorum* Aristotle is mentioned explicitly in connection with the *Physics*, *On Generation and Corruption* and *On the Soul*. The sources for Urso and his colleague Maurus appear to have been Greek-to-Latin translations rather than the Arabic-to-Latin used by Daniel of Morley.

In Bartholomaeus's Salerno of the 1160s and 1170s there was an established curriculum of medical books to be read, known as the *Articella*,[45] the medieval textbook of medicine, and the teaching proceeded by way of the master's commentaries on these texts. The curriculum invariably began with the *Isagoge*, and it is possible, as Kristeller suggests[46] that the other texts were added in explanation of it. Certainly the *Isagoge* was often thought of as an introduction to the *Tegni* of Galen, invariably another component of the curriculum and in effect an introduction to all of Greek medicine that came to be used in the Middle Ages. Thus a teacher like Maurus at Salerno had to explain the underlying doctrines on which these texts rested. Commentaries in use before 1160 show that the Aristotelian *libri naturales* – the nature books – were in use in Salerno. That these books were not yet in use in other kinds of teaching elsewhere did not mean that they were not available elsewhere, simply that they were of most use in medicine. To explain what lay behind the terse sentence of the *Isagoge* when it described the naturals, the Salernitan commentators found Aristotle's physical works extremely useful. From them they could explain why there were four elements and four qualities, how from these the complexions of the homogeneous parts of the body came about, how the simple parts built up into organs, and how the organs exercised their faculties. After a brief opening definition of medicine, the *Isagoge* lists the seven 'naturals'. They are the elements, mixtures, composed parts, organs, faculties, functions and the spirit.[47] That is to say, they were the components of the body, its structure, driving powers and actions: in short, its nature. Thus the medical man's particular and technical use of the term *natura* is at root the nature-of-the-thing meaning given to *physis* by Aristotle.

In addition to the naturals, the *Isagoge* listed a number of 'non-naturals'. These were so called because they were not part of the body's nature. To us, with our notion of Nature as the natural world and its principles, they seem natural enough – changes in the air and winds, exercise, diet, sleep, baths and so on – but for the Greek medicine in which they originated they were not part of the body's *physis*, not part of the nature-of-the-body. The scheme was complete with a listing of the three 'contra-naturals'. Their designation indicates that they were the things that damaged the *physis* of the body, not that they acted against any Nature in any wider sense. These were disease itself, the cause of disease and the accidents that followed disease. Since disease was often thought of as damaged function, these things were contra the nature-of-the-body as it tried to express itself in the functioning of the body.

So 'nature' in medicine at the end of the twelfth century meant something different, but clearly related to Greek philosophy. It was an elaborate conception but it was open to objections related to those about the autonomy of nature. That is, those who gave a great deal of attention to nature were often said by others not to give enough to God.[48] The monks and others who criticized the new dialectical education of the schools[49] were even more affronted by the formal teaching of medicine.[50] Moreover, medicine was seen as a lucrative *scientia*, practised as a trade and without the mind passing from the Creation to the Creator: it was, in the terms we have been using in this chapter, merely at the literal level of reading the physical world.[51]

The nature of things: Alexander Neckam

We have seen that the principle that nature was autonomous, derived in two ways from Greek philosophy, was inconsistent with Christian doctrine and that those who wished to use it had to modify it in one way or another. The problem reached a crisis with the view of the natural world taken by the Albigensian heretics, as we shall see, and solving it became an urgent necessity for the friars. They solved it by two devices similar to those we have met in this chapter, making nature part of God, and returning to Aristotle's view of nature. Finally, in this section we look at an author who was close in time to this crisis, who knew of the heretics, and of Aristotle's view of nature and who himself wrote 'on the natures of things'.

This was the English scholar Alexander Neckam. He avoided the dangerous autonomy of nature by ignoring it. His book (probably written between 1197 and 1204), *De Naturis Rerum* is not, as has been claimed, a natural history,[52] that is, a description of 'nature', but is a treatment of the individual natures of things. But they are not Aristotelian natures. It was not that the physical works of Aristotle were not available to Alexander. Indeed, it has been claimed that he was a significant figure in having early knowledge of the physical works.[53] His own words make it clear that some of his contemporaries did read the physical works, but with some discretion. 'Acute investigators of subtle things can be called "observers through windows" when they enquire into the natures of things through subtle and fine reasoning. Therefore the rectors of the schools close the doors in the streets while they read clandestine lectures to a few listeners ... with a lowered voice.'[54] Not only was this reading private, continues Alexander, but in some cases also secret, the readers storing up such knowledge until a suitable moment for its use.

Alexander's knowledge of such things came from his experience of the schools of Paris and Oxford in the last three decades of the twelfth century. He is able to ignore the autonomy of nature by writing at a higher level than the philosophers. His purposes in writing become clearer when we see that his book is an introduction to a commentary on Ecclesiastes. Following Origen, Alexander divided the books of Solomon – the sapientals (*Proverbs*, *Ecclesiastes*, *The Song of Solomon*, *Wisdom* and *Ecclesiasticus*) – into three 'philosophies', of which *Ecclesiastes* is the equivalent of *physica*.[55] This is why the 'natures of things' is pertinent to a commentary on *Ecclesiastes*; but even so it is not Alexander's purpose to linger on the details of the creatures he describes. He is not, he says, writing *philosophice aut physice* but morally, and his purpose is to lead the mind of the reader from the natures of things to their origin, God as opifex, God as *summa natura*: the ultimate 'nature of a thing'. It is for others, he says, to follow the 'golden chain of Homer' and argue philosophically from the particulars of things to universals. So Alexander's evident love of the physical world leads him directly to the love of God, without the intervention of philosophy, and without the essential early step of such a philosophy, the literal reading of the physical world. The philosopher's world, of the four elements, is transitory, he argues, for after the Day of Judgement air and fire will cease to exist. The seven liberal arts, although useful, lead to vanity if indulged to excess, and trespass upon theology. He writes, indeed, in an elaborate prose style suitable for a biblical allegorist, quite unlike the plain style of a philosopher or translator. His first chapter sets up the task of reconciling the two biblical accounts of Creation. In the beginning God created heaven and earth; but also in the beginning was the Word. A spiritual interpretation of the Sacred Page allows Alexander to equate the light that God allowed to exist at the beginning of Creation with Christ himself, the great light that illuminates the shadows – the allegory for those without faith, who do not understand (Alexander here writes in the present tense) is that they are condemned to eternal night if addicted to the works of the shadows. 'The works of the shadows' means a literal and philosophical concern with the physical world and Alexander seems to be making an allusion to the Dark and Evil Principle of the Manichees that Abbot William saw reflected in the philosophy of William of Conches. In short, Alexander is writing a monastic commentary, not a scholastic one; it is allegorical, discontinuous and invites contemplation on the mysteries of faith.[56] As for whether it was Light or the Word that was first in the world, we shall see that the topic was fundamental for the different views about the natures of things taken by the two Orders of friars.

We have seen that twelfth-century views of 'nature' – whatever the *distinctiones* of that term – were centrally to do with God, with man's relation to Him and man's attempt to lead the good life as a Christian philosopher. The dangers of seeing nature as an autonomous principle, inherent in literal readings of the physical world and in the trades of medicine and astrology, were seen and avoided. Whether in reading the Sacred Page, in describing the parts of knowledge – philosophy – or in describing God's relationship with Creation, all of our authors were looking at nature as an aspect of divinity, not as the separate subject of a separate intellectual enterprise. This theocentricity was to be continued into natural philosophy: natural philosophy was to be about God, and for the friars it was to be about God in very special ways.

Notes

1. See Roger French, *Ancient Natural History: Histories of Nature*, London, Routledge, 1994.
2. See for example J.A. Weisheipl, 'Aristotle's Concept of Nature: Avicenna and Aquinas', in L.D. Roberts, ed., *Approaches to Nature in the Middle Ages*, New York, 1992, p. 138.
3. Thus the ant has three natures: to proceed in a line with its fellows, to bite the grain of corn it carries in half, so that it will not germinate when stored, and to distinguish between edible and inedible grains. These supply respectively a moral about the foolish virgins, the wisdom of separating the spiritual from the carnal and of rejecting a foreign creed. For the *Physiologus* see the edition by F. Sbordone, Milan, 1936, which gives the Greek text. A Latin version is supplied by F.J. Carmody, 'Physiologus Latinus versio Y', *University of California Publications in Classical Philology, 12*, (7), 1941, pp. 95–134.
4. It was not clear to the medievals whether Christ spoke indirectly, in parables, to confine his message to the initiated or to enable the vulgar to grasp its essence. See Stephen L. Wailes, 'Why Did Jesus Use Parables? The Medieval Discussion', *Medievalia et Humanistica*, ns, **13**, 1985, pp. 43–64.
5. The school of Chartres was deliberately set up to combine *scientia* with *eloquentia*. 'Eloquence' was classical usage, and it may be that the late antique notion of nature informed the Chartres attitude to the natural world. Bernard of Chartres established that secular studies – our Egyptian gold – had a place alongside Christian learning. Stock argues that the Chartres idea of nature as the ability of creatures to reproduce their kind was embodied in glosses in Gratian's *Decretum* to explain natural law. See B. Stock, 'Science, Technology and Economic Progress in the Early Middle Ages', in Lindberg, *Science in the Middle Ages*, pp. 1–51.
6. The hexameron of Thierry of Chartres represents a genre of literature that varied from commentaries on Genesis to literal readings of nature; Abelard and Hugh of St Victor also wrote hexamerons. See R.S. Avi-Yonah, *The Aristotelian Revolution: A Study of the Transformation of Medieval Cosmology, 1150–1250*, Harvard University, unpublished Ph.D. dissertation, 1986 (University Microfilms International). Thierry's *Heptateuch* is the result of an ambitious scheme to bring together into a single book the best of the liberal arts, and so represents an ideal scheme of knowledge in the pre-*studia* schools. Grammar, for instance, is treated

allegorically, but the collection does not give a twelfth-century synthetic view of nature. See G.R. Evans, 'The Uncompleted Heptateuch of Thierry of Chartres', *History of Universities*, 1983, **III**, pp. 1–13.

7. C.S. Lewis, *The Allegory of Love. A Study in Medieval Tradition* (first published 1936), Oxford, 1977, p. 94.
8. Quoted by B. Stock, *Myth and Science in the Twelfth Century. A Study of Bernard Silvester*, Princeton University Press, 1972, p. 6.
9. S.C. Ferruolo, *The Origin of the University*, Stanford University Press, 1985, p. 119.
10. William of Conches, *Philosophia Mundi*, ed. and trans. (into German) by G. Maurach, Pretoria, 1980. See also H.R. Lemay, 'Guillaume de Conches' Division of Philosophy in the Accessus ad Macrobium', *Mediaevalia*, **1** (2), 1975, pp. 115–29, which supplies the text. William's literal reading of the physical world has prompted some historians to discuss his 'science', a term asserted to be interchangeable with 'natural philosophy': see for example Joan Cadden, 'Science and Rhetoric in the Middle Ages: The Natural Philosophy of William of Conches', *Journal of the History of Ideas*, **56**, 1995, pp. 1–24.
11. William of Conches, *Philosophia Mundi*, p. 21. He also knew three other works of the *Articella*, the Hippocratic *Aphorisms* and the works on urines by Isaac and Theophilus. See E. Jeanneau, *Note sur l'Ecole de Chartres*, Chartres, 1965 (also available in *Bulletin de la Société Archéologique d'Eure-et-Loire* (4è trimestre 1964: Mémoires, t. xxiii).
12. William of Conches, *Philosophia Mundi*, pp. 18, 20.
13. M-T., d'Alverny, 'Translations and Translators', in Benson and Constable, *Renaissance and Renewal*, p. 425.
14. Jeanneau, *Note*, p. 30. William may have been antagonistic to knowledge of parts of Aristotle's physical account of the heavens, rather than ignorant of it, as R. Lemay, *Abu Ma'shar and Latin Aristotelianism in the Twelfth Century*, Beirut, 1962, p. 187, implies.
15. Cf Stock, *Myth and Science*, p. 30, whose argument is slightly different. On allegory in general, see Lewis, *The Allegory of Love*.
16. Deinde creationem primi hominis philosophice, se magis physice describens, primo dicit corpus ejus non a Deo factum, sed a natura, et animam ei datam a Deo, postmodum verum ipsum corpus factum a spiritibus, quos demones appellat, et a stellis. Ubi in altero quidem stultorum quorumdam philosophorum videtur sententiam sequi, dicentium nihil prorsus esse praeter corpora et corporea; non aliud esse Deum in mundo quam concursum elementorum, et temperaturam naturae; et hoc ipsum esse animam in corpore: in altero manifestus Manichaeus est, dicens animam hominis a bono Deo creatam, corpus vero a principe tenebrarum. Migne, *Patrologia Latina*, vol. 180, cols 333–40; 340: our translation. See also Etienne Gilson, *History of Christian Philosophy in the Middle Ages*, (first published 1955) London, 1980. This must have accentuated the problems that Bernard found with William of Conches' account of nature.
17. See Stock, *Myth and Science*, p. 243. On Chartrian notions of nature and creation, see J.M. Parent, *La Doctrine de la Création dans l'Ecole de Chartres*, Paris/Ottowa, 1938.
18. G.B. Lardner, 'Terms and Ideas of Renewal', in Benson and Constable, *Renaissance and Renewal*, pp. 1–33. See also J. Leclerc, 'The Renewal of

Theology' in the same volume, pp. 68–87.

19. William's *Dragmaticon* is the revised version of his *Philosophia Mundi*, omitting much of the literal and physical reading, for example of the account of the creation of Eve.
20. Quoted by Ferruolo, *Origins of the University*, p. 106.
21. Ferruolo, *Origins of the University*, p. 107.
22. Hugh, the refounder of the abbey, and his uncle had arrived in Paris in the second decade of the twelfth century, Hugh bearing the bones of St Victor and his uncle money for new buildings. J. Taylor, *The Origin and Early Life of Hugh of St Victor: An Evaluation of the Tradition*, Indiana, Notre Dame, 1957, p. 67.
23. C.H. Buttimer, ed., *Hugonis de Sancto Victore Didascalicon. De Studio Legendi*, Washington, 1939; Hugh's preface.
24. The Parisian Abbey of St Victor was in character and learning somewhere between the monasteries and the schools. Victorines were not monks but canons, living under a rule based on that of St Augustine for secular clergy.
25. Beryl Smalley, *The Study of the Bible in the Middle Ages*, Oxford, Blackwell, third edn, 1984 (first published 1941), p. 83.
26. Ferruolo, *Origins of the University*, p. 87.
27. Godfrey of St Victor, E.A. Synan, trans., *The Fountain of Philosophy: A Translation of the Twelfth-Century Fons Philosophiae of Godfrey of St Victor*, Toronto, The Pontifical Institute, 1972, p. 23.
28. Translations were necessary to counter the claims and attacks of different sects and religions. Mention of Arabic learning for this purpose was made in note 20 of the previous chapter. But the Greek learning of the Byzantines could also be a problem. Hugh of Honau, visiting Constantinople, urged Hugo Etherianus to translate Greek works on the nature of Christ to remove 'dangerous doubts' that the Latins had adopted from Greek sources. Moses of Bergamo, at a theological disputation in Constantinople in 1136 with the translators James of Venice and Burgundio of Pisa, stressed the *utility* of translations from the Greek. See d'Alverny, 'Translators and Translations', p. 432.
29. See Henry Corbin, *History of Islamic Philosophy*, trans. L. and P. Sherrard, London and New York, 1993, esp. chs 4 and 5, part 1.
30. The mathematical aspects of astronomy were dealt with in the quadrivium, and although a distinction was often made between calculation and prediction (which came close to a denial of free will) the distinction between astronomy and astrology is partly an invention of later historians of things 'scientific'.
31. Hermann was the twelfth-century translator of Abu Ma'shar (Albumasar). Lemay, *Abu Ma'shar*, p. 49. Despite Lemay's insistence on Abu Ma'shar's Aristotelianism, this is certainly not an Aristotelian version of 'natural science'. And despite Abu Ma'shar's (implicit) Aristotelianism, his account of matter, form and substance is somewhat Platonic.
32. Lemay, *Abu Ma'shar*, p. 16.
33. A. Birkenmajer 'La role jouée ... ' in *Études d'Histoire des Sciences et de la Philosophie du Moyen Age* (Studia Copernicana, 1), Warsaw, 1970. The term *doctrina Arabum* is Daniel's; K. Sudhoff, 'Daniels von Morley Liber de naturis inferiorum et superiorum', *Archiv für die Geschichte der Naturwissenschaften und der Technik*, 1917, 8, pp. 1–40 (with text).
34. Neminem etiam moveat, quod de creatione mundi tractans super his, que

dicuntur, non patres catholicos sed gentiles philosophos in testimonium voco, quia licet tales inter fideles non connumerentur, quedam tamen eorum verba, cum sint fidei plena, ad nostrum doctrinam trahenda sunt. Unde et nos, qui mistice liberati sumus ab Egypto, a domino iubemur, mutuari ab Egyptiis vasa aurea et argentea.; Sudhoff, 1917, p. 7 (our translation).

35. Birkenmajer, 'La role jouée ...'.
36. Gundissalinus, *De Divisione Philosophiae*, in C. Baeumker and G.F. von Hertling, eds, *Beitrage zur Geschichte der Philosophie des Mittelalters*, Münster, 1906, vol. 4. Gundisalvi is also known as a translator of Arabic physical books, working with the slightly mysterious figure of the Jew 'Avendauth'. Between 1151 and 1166 he translated Avicenna's commentary on the *De Anima*, which may have provided a resource for the heresy of David of Dinant. Indeed, Gundisalvi translated parts of Avicenna's *Shifa* based on the Aristotelian physical works, in which some scholars recognized the doctrines as Aristotle's. See David Lindberg, 'The Transmission of Greek and Arabic Learning to the West' in D. Lindberg, ed., *Science in the Middle Ages*, University of Chicago Press, 1987; G. Théry, OP, 'Autour de decret de 1210: 1 – David de Dinant. Étude sur son pantheisme materialiste', *Bibliothèque Thomiste*, VI, Kain, 1925, and d'Alverny, 'Translators and Translations'.
37. Distinctions based on citation of text and on dialectical analysis of terms were used in a number of subjects. For example the *allegationes* of twelfth-century civilist glosses on Justinian are similar to the Sacred Page distinctions of the monastic commentators. See for example S. Kuttner, 'The Revival of Jurisprudence', in Benson and Constable, *Renaissance and Renewal*. Twelfth-century problems that are of concern to us in this book, like the existence of evil and the status of the devil, were also tackled by the *distinctio* technique. Thus Simon of Tournai faced the questions of whether the devil was to be hated, even though he was part of God's creation. Since the devil was the source of evil, and God the source of all good, did God punish the devil? See J. Warichez, ed., *Les Disputationes de Simon de Tournai*, Louvain, 1932, p. 62, disp. 18. Simon was probably a pupil of Odo of Soissons, whose own 'questions' on texts were more in the older, monastic style. Simon's dialectic was, as we would expect from the date at which he worked, Aristotelian; but in addition he was amongst the first to use Aristotle's works on the soul and on metaphysics (in their Toledan translations). This is amongst the first appearances of the Egyptian gold of pagan philosophy. There is, however, very little knowledge of Aristotle's physical works in Simon's writings. For our purposes it is useful to note that for him transubstantiation is miraculous and outside the course of nature, taking place by virtue of the ceremony as a whole. See also F. van Steenberghen, *Aristotle in the West. The Origins of Latin Aristotelianism*, Louvain, 1970, p. 115.
38. Compare the use of philosophy in Christianity by Clement of Alexandria and Origen in Chapter One.
39. To examine Alfarabi's text would take us beyond the scope and purposes of this book. We should note however that like his western successors Alfarabi said that all areas of knowledge lead to the divine. For the place of astronomy in Gundisalvi see C.A. McMenomy, *The Discipline of Astronomy in the Middle Ages*, University of California, Los Angeles,

unpublished Ph.D. thesis (University Microfilms International, 1984).

40. Lemay, *Abu Ma'shar*, makes a great deal of Abu Ma'shar's Aristotelianism. However, Aristotle is cited by name so rarely in the text that no western reader would have any idea of the source of the new doctrines.
41. The close connection between astrology – the study of 'nature' in our present sense – and medicine means that it is almost certainly no accident that the first translation of Ptolemy's *Almagest* was made, about 1160, by a Salernitan medical student: Lindberg, *Science in the Middle Ages*, p. 72. On the use of Aristotle in Salerno, see also D. Jacquart, 'Aristotelian Thought in Salerno', in P. Dronke, ed., *A History of Twelfth-century Western Philosophy*, Cambridge University Press, 1988, pp. 407–28. The connection was also expressed for example by Bernard Sylvester (he believed the two subjects to be the chief of the *scientiae*) and was no doubt encouraged by increasing knowledge of Albumasar's astrological *Introductorium*. This 'introduction' was translated twice, in part by John of Seville in 1133 and wholly by Hermann of Carinthia in 1141. At the beginning of the work Albumasar links medicine and astrology as universal subjects. His description of the object of medicine (to explain the natures and motions of elementary and mixed bodies on the basis of necessity and accidents) makes the medical man not only a *physicus* (as with William of Conches) who explores the natures-of-things but one who works with Aristotelian principles. But the important point for our story is that Aristotle is not mentioned by Albumasar and his doctrines are unattributed. No Christian reader of the *Introductorium* would know where to look for an amplification of Albumasar's view of the physical world.
42. Sudhoff, 'Daniels von Morley', p. 32. See also Stock, *Myth and Science*, p. 27. John of Salisbury uses the single term *physici* for the medical men and those concerned with the natural world; L. Thorndike, *A History of Magic and Experimental Science*, New York, Macmillan, 1923–58, 8 vols. II, p. 168.
43. P.O. Kristeller, 'Bartholomaeus, Musandinus and Maurus of Salerno and Other Early Commentators of the "Articella" with a Tentative List of Texts and Manuscripts', *Italia Medioevale e Umanistica*, 1976, **19**, pp. 57–87. See also P.O. Kristeller, 'Philosophy and Medicine in Medieval and Renaissance Italy' in S.F. Spicker, *Organism, Medicine and Metaphysics*, Dordrecht, 1978.
44. The term is Birkenmajer's: 'La role jouée ... ' p. 41.
45. The name *Articella* seems to appear only late in the history of the collection. It was printed several times up to the 1530s. The edition of Lyons, 1519 is used here.
46. Kristeller, 'Early commentators', pp. 57–87.
47. Res vero naturales sunt septem scilicet elementa: commixtiones: compositiones: membra: virtutes: operationes: et spiritus; f.iir.
48. See for example John of Salisbury, *Polycraticus*, in Migne, *Patrologiae Cursus Completus*, vol. 199, Paris, 1855, pp. 415–75 (book II); 475. Another critic of the doctors for their mercenary trade and belief in the autonomy of nature was Alfred of Shareshill, who translated and commented on some of the *libri naturales* at the end of the twelfth century. See his *De Motu Cordis*: C.S. Barach, ed., *Excerpta a Libro Alfredi Anglici De Motu Cordis item Costa-ben-Lucae De Differentia Animae et Spiritus*,

Innsbruck, 1878, p. 94.

49. For example Cistercians and others were actively seeking to increase their numbers, and saw the attraction of the schools to students as an obstacle to recruitment; see Ferruolo, *The Origins of the University*, pp. 68–78.

50. The superiority of cure of souls over cure of body was clear for example to Peter the Chanter and Stephen Langton, who attacked medical students. See J.W. Baldwin, *Masters Princes and Merchants*, 2 vols, Princeton University Press, 1970, vol. 1, p. 85.

51. Various church councils during the twelfth century accordingly prohibited regular clergy from learning medicine. See J.D. Mansi, *Sacrorum Conciliorum Nova et Amplissima Collectio*, vol. 21, Venice, 1776, cols 459 and 528. See also Ferruolo, p. 303.

52. Alexander Neckam, *De Naturis Rerum*, ed. T. Wright, London, 1863. It is misleading to think of Neckam as a 'naturalist', as does for example C. Raven, *English Naturalists from Neckam to Ray*, Cambridge University Press, 1947. On the date of Alexander's book see also B. Lawn, *The Salernitan Questions*, Oxford, Clarendon Press, 1963, p. 31.

53. A. Birkenmajer, *Études d'Histoire des Sciences et de la Philosophie du Moyen Age* (*Studia Copernicana*, 1), Warsaw, 1970, which includes the same author's 'La rôle jouée par les médecins et les naturalistes dans la réception d'Aristote aux XIIè et XIIIè siècles', p. 5: Alexander 'in effect' quotes Aristotle's work on generation and corruption. Alexander was in the circle of Alfred of Shareshill, who clearly did use the physical works, and who dedicated his book on the motion of the heart to Alexander. Alexander was also familiar with the medical commentaries of Urso of Salerno where also the physical works were being used. See also R.W. Hunt, *The Schools and the Cloister. The Life and Writings of Alexander Nequam*, Oxford, 1984, pp. 68–71; Lawn, *Salernitan Questions*, p. 32; see also John Blund, *Tractatus de Anima*, ed. D.A. Callus and R.W. Hunt, London, 1970, p. iii.

54. Hunt, *Schools and Cloister*, p. 68.

55. See Hunt, *Schools and Cloister*, p. 81. On Origen see Chapter 3.

56. Indeed, Alexander seems to have wanted to become an Augustinian monk. He is said to have abandoned an attempt to become a Benedictine when it was met only by a pun on his name: 'Si bonus es, venias; si nequam, nequaquam' (Neckam, Wright's edn of 1863, preface). Alexander's book, although not prescribed reading in Paris, was popular, and its price was regulated: *Chartularium Universitatis Parisiensis*, ed. H. Denifle, OP, Paris, 1889, vol. 1. p. 644. He taught in Oxford during the last decade of the twelfth century. See R.W. Hunt, 'English Learning in the Late Twelfth Century' in *Essays in Medieval History*, ed. R. Southern, London, 1968. p. 107.

CHAPTER FIVE

Heresy and Dominic

In the last chapter we saw how and why knowledge about nature could exist in twelfth-century Europe. We saw that different groups – canons, monks, masters, poets – all had a certain interest in discussing 'nature' in some sense, but each took a different view of what constituted proper knowledge. This chapter looks at these issues in an extreme form, where the knowledge of one group was heresy to another, and where two new groups – the two major Orders of friars – were put together to fight for one form of belief. It was a question of control of knowledge. What mattered was which group had the power, whether political, economic or indeed military, to insist upon their own knowledge and suppress that of other groups. The knowledge we are dealing with here is that about the 'Egyptian gold' of philosophy, about deep theological principles and about nature. The groups are Cathar and Catholic Christians, masters in the *studia* and above all the new Orders of clergy, the friars.

The autonomy of nature, so likely to be read into Aristotle's physical works, offered a constant temptation to argue physically about the divine. We saw that William of Conches attracted a good deal of *odium theologicum* for doing so within a Platonic framework, and an Aristotelian apparatus offered even more temptation. The well-known bans at Paris on the reading of Aristotle of 1210[1] and 1215 were the result of small groups of people succumbing to that temptation. One group was that of the followers of David of Dinant, not far from Paris, where David's views, and his followers, were declared heretical by the Archbishop of Sens and the Bishop of Paris. The condemnation included a prohibition upon reading 'the books on Aristotle about natural philosophy',[2] and those of his commentators, upon which David's doctrine was built: *libri Aristotelis de naturali philosophia*.[3]

David's book was called *De Tomis* (Albertus Magnus called it *De Atomis*) or *De Divisionibus*. It was concerned with the logical process of division[4] and its application to God, the soul and the natural world. Now, for David, the natural world is Aristotelian. David has read the *Metaphysics*, the *Physics* and *On the Soul* or at least parts of them in a florilegium or similar collection of excerpts[5] and he talks of form and matter in an Aristotelian, not a Platonic way. By arguments derived from Aristotle's *Metaphysics* and *Topics*, he proves matter, soul and God to be the same. Matter and soul, he says, must be either the same or different.

But if they are different, they must have some common substrate in which alone can differences be apparent. Another argument used by David was that soul can understand both matter and God, but since the intellect can only understand the intelligible by substantial, not accidental, conjunction, therefore the substance of mind, matter and God must be the same. David also argues that as the opposite of Being can only be non-Being, all Being must have an underlying identity, *materia prima*.

David wrote as a logician rather than a theologian. It was the first of many cases where an artist, in developing the knowledge of his group, brought it into conflict with the knowledge of other groups, here the doctrine of the Catholic Church as interpreted in this part of France.[6] The ban was repeated in the Courçon statutes for the university of Paris of 1215.[7]

Also included in the ban of 1210 was the work of Amalric of Bene. Here, around Amalric, was another group in the early years of the thirteenth century, with their own knowledge of God and the world that clashed with the knowledge of a larger and more powerful group. It was localized, being centred at Corbeil, just to the south of Paris. Amalric was a logician and a teaching master and among those condemned to life imprisonment were Dudo, his priest and a student of theology for ten years, some other students who had completed their arts education and who were theology students of long standing, and a number of priests holding livings to the south of Paris. Amalric himself was by now dead, but the bishops ordered his body to be exhumed, excommunicated and reburied in unconsecrated ground. The heresy of Amalric and his followers was primarily to assert that the persons of the Trinity were separable and that God had existed alone and incarnate in Abraham, was joined by His son in the incarnation of Christ and finally by the Holy Spirit, represented by the followers themselves of Amalric. This, they thought, was the final state of affairs until the end of the world; that is, that there would be no final resurrection, and they poured scorn on the teachings of the Paris masters on the question of resurrection. It followed that in this final state of the world, God was to be identified with the physical world, being as much in and of the stones of the natural world as in the bread on the altar. So Amalric, by another route, had reached the same conclusion – the materiality of God – as David of Dinant, and so shared in his condemnation.[8]

Heresy in Occitania

Being small and localized, the groups of David of Dinant and Amalric of

Bene were easily suppressed. It was a very different matter with the dualist heresy of the Cathars, spread from Constantinople to Occitania – that is, to the region of Provence and Languedoc.[9] This was a new kind of heresy which 'was itself massive and provoked a massive reaction of the Church', a crisis comparable to the reformation.[10] The scale of the heresy was great and its threat is central to our account. Certainly the Church was badly frightened and acted accordingly.[11] It took a fully blown crusade to stop the heresy, and Gilson has said that it 'broke the religious unity of the Western world'.[12] That is the point: crusades against Saracens (Muslims) were a matter of religion, politics and warfare, they were aggressive and the battles were distant. The heresy in contrast was at home and the battle against it had to be turned from defence to aggression (and matters of religion and politics had to be settled by warfare). Innocent III thought that the danger posed by the Cathar threat was greater than that from the Saracens, and most agreed.[13] The urgency and closeness of the threat demands that we look at the location and nature of the response.

Provence was not then part of France. It had been, as its name suggests, the great 'province' of the Roman Empire. Its language, Provençale, was not French, nor the related Spanish, but a separate development from the original Latin. It was indeed a separate civilization, prosperous, town based and courtly. Medieval poetry, as distinct from medieval imitations of classical verse, flourished and developed at the hands of its troubadours. On the other side of the Rhône from the Troubadours' *Proensa* lay Languedoc, where the town of Toulouse was free of its feudal overlord, the count, and attempted in the manner of Italian cities to create a city-state by taking over neighbouring towns and villages.[14] The two areas were in great, and ultimately fatal, contrast to the Europe further north. There in the north the social system was more feudal, and so based on the holding of land, on the agriculture of that land and on the military obligations of its holders. With little trade and small money economy, the northern towns were less important and in the literal sense, there was less civilization. Paris was a notable exception, and plays a major part in our story.

So the people of the south, and particularly those of Toulouse, were different. There were those among them too who differed in religion. They regarded themselves as 'Good Christians' and their opponents as the *Catholici*. Part of the attraction of their kind of Christianity was the extreme asceticism adopted by their leaders, the Perfects, *perfecti*. Living on frugal diets and with few material possessions, the Perfects were in obvious contrast to the indulgent prelates attacked even by the orthodox Alan of Lille.[15] The Perfects were also learned. The Good Christians saw no reason to change their mode of life in order to match that of outsiders. They saw it as different, and they sought to defend it when pressure was applied.

To outsiders their social life seemed morally lax to the point of sexual perversion, and their religious beliefs eccentric and dangerous. And they were irritatingly well off. The Catholics regarded these Provençals as heretics, having adopted the Albigensian version of the Cathar heresy. The heresy had come from Constantinople[16] and had arrived in the West by way of Bulgaria, and the French for 'Bulgar', meaning the believer and practitioner of Catharism, complete (as we shall see) with his unnatural sexual practices, came into English as 'bugger'. To think of the loading that word has always carried in English is to catch some of the antagonism aroused by Catharism. Part of our story is this tale of sex and violence in the thirteenth century, in which the violence was excessive and the sex unnatural.

There were a number of symptoms of Catharism that the Church found alarming, largely because they removed the Cathars from Catholic control. The Cathars had a Bible in the vernacular, so that it could be widely read by people who thus did not need a priest to interpret it to them from the Latin. They could, in other words, be independent of the orthodox Church. Indeed, the Cathars were opposed to a hierarchical priesthood; and some of these Bibles differed from the Vulgate by including heterodox matters of eastern origin. Moreover, most Cathars rejected the Old Testament, at least in part. The Cathars, holding that all matter was evil, did not build churches and hence gave little evidence to an outsider of their activities. They were defended in Languedoc by the local aristocracy, particularly the Count of Toulouse, and even by the local bishops. It was a heresy of the urban élite. It is said that Catharism was spread[17] by cloth merchants and doctors, both of whom had professional reasons to travel from house to house (where the religion was practised) and to talk with the women of the household, who were very significant in the religion. In a word, it was very difficult for the Catholic Church to take effective action against it. For many years the Cathar Church existed openly, with, for example, convents for women *perfectae* which acted as centres of activity. The Cathar Church even, like the Catholic Church, held a Council, at Saint-Felix de Caraman[18] where Niquinta (or Nicetas) of Constantinople acted as 'pope'. The Council had been arranged by the Cathar Church of Toulouse, to whom Niquinta addressed a sermon. Niquinta claimed to be the head of the Cathar Church in Constantinople, and he now proceeded to consecrate new bishops, making sure all were extreme dualists, which seems not to have been the case before. This was between 1167 and 1177, after a series of councils of the Catholic Church had failed to suppress the heresy. The papacy of the Catholic Church, which was itself still in the process of securing its own power – even of appointing the bishops – viewed this new 'Pope' and newly strict heresy with considerable alarm.

Heretical belief

The Catholics identified the Cathars with the Manichees of the early Christian centuries. This gave the Catholic Church a ready-made set of arguments that had first been rehearsed by St Augustine, particularly those of his work against Faustus.[19] This derivation of Catharism from Manicheeism is almost certainly correct, and on its long journey, chronologically and geographically, the heresy had developed variations. What was common to them all was their view of evil. All agreed that evil was so apparent in the world that it could not be the work of a truly good God. It must, they argued, be the work at least of demons or fallen angels, whom God had created but could no longer control. At their most extreme, and increasingly as they came under attack at the beginning of our period, the Cathars adopted a radical dualism: they believed in two Gods, one good, the other evil. Both were eternal, or at least would continue for ever. It followed that the good God was *not* omnipotent, since the evil god had created, and retained power over, all physical things. The good God's creation was limited to the kingdom of heaven, the angels and the human soul. The problem of evil was central. Since all matter was evil, the Cathars did not use the ceremonies of the Catholics. They thought that baptism with material water was useless, and practised a baptism of the spirit upon becoming one of the *perfecti*. They held that the laying on of hands was of no significance, since hands were material. Some allowed the ceremony of breaking bread before a meal, holding that bread, although material, could carry a blessing. Others did not allow it,[20] and none at all allowed that bread or wine could substantially change into the flesh and blood of Christ. Indeed, the doctrine of transubstantiation was more formally defined at the fourth Lateran council of 1215[21] and this suggests that it was so defined and written down as a hardening of the Church's doctrine in the face of heresy. The sacraments of the Cathars, as a very obvious part of their procedures, highlighted the difference between the practices of the two churches. Later, the Dominican Rayner Sacconi angrily said that the Cathar sacraments were a mockery of those of the Catholic Church, as apes imitate men.[22]

Since, for the Cathars, matter was evil, it followed that man too was partly evil, for his body was the creation of the evil principle or god. The religious objective through life was to cleanse the soul from its material taints until one was ready for the final baptism of spirit, the *consolamentum*, which most people took late in life. This made the believer one of the *perfecti*, who almost entirely neglected the needs of the body to finally release the soul. If in illness the body of a Perfect was too weak to enable him to utter the Lord's Prayer, he refused to take nourishment, and so committed a sort of liturgical suicide. In contrast, the bulk of believers, holding that matter was evil, were little concerned at the moral level about its actions. Their bodies were evil, and what mattered above all was their souls, particularly after taking the *consolamentum*. Before taking it, it was scarcely possible to avoid the lusts of the flesh, even though evil. Marriage was regarded as institutionalized fornication and less desirable than casual sexual encounters simply because of the sexual opportunities it offered. Sexual generation was thought to be very evil because it depended on lusts of the flesh, and so the religious would eat nothing sexually generated like meat or eggs. It followed too that young children were very evil, being born of sexual generation and being composed very much of matter from which the soul had had little time to free itself. At least in the opinions of outsiders, it was for this reason that the Cathars indulged in every kind of sexual activity that did not produce offspring. Perhaps otherwise there would have been more of them. The Cathars themselves used to calculate that there were no more than 4000 of their number in the world.

Alain of Lille: nature and dialectic against heresy

The heresy of the Cathars and the evil that they saw in the natural world provoked a response from many amongst the groupings of people we have met. Alain of Lille was a scholar and poet whose well-known 'The Complaint of Nature', *De Planctu Naturae* (before 1182)[23] is directed against the heretics. Alain (born about 1128) was a pupil of Thierry of Chartres, became a master of theology and lived into the thirteenth century as a bitter opponent of the Cathars. He became involved in the campaign against the heresy, probably while teaching in Montpellier. He died in 1202 in Citeaux, the home of the Order, the Cistercians, that had first preached against the Cathars. In his youth theologians had argued about the nature of universals and the use of dialectic in theology: an intellectual and spiritual world that was radically changed by the upsurge of heresy by the time he was teaching theology in Paris in the 1190s.[24]

Alain's prosimetron form – a mixture of verse and prose – was imitated substantially in later medieval poetry.[25] Troubadour and Goliard poetry indeed, like that of Chartres, was often concerned with Nature in a personalized way as a generative vital force.[26] Much of it too was concerned with knightly honour and chaste love: chaste because illicit, and because chaste, unproductive. Illicit and unproductive in love, it shared a third characteristic with the heresy that lies behind the friars' natural philosophy, for both flourished in what was soon to become the south of what is now France.

Alain of Lille's Nature is the personalized, semi-divine manager of the natural world.[27] Personalized and perhaps with something of a Platonic demiurge, Nature comes between the Christian God and His creation. This is managed in Alain's text quite neatly by Nature as 'vice-regent of God' arranging the primordial matter of God's original creation so as to produce the physical world: the Creator is not denied His creation, and is content to leave the details to a deputy. In Alain's allegorical verses Nature speaks to him in words that are the Platonic ideals of actual words. She appears to him from heaven dressed in clothes that carry the moving images of the parts of the natural world, from the animals of the zodiac to the fish in the sea. Alain uses the classical names for the winds and the heavenly bodies, Favonius, Phoebus, Juno, Jove, and the characters attributed to the animals – the slyness of the fox, the servility of oxen – are very much like those of the late Greek poets like Aelian.

So Nature for Alain is Greek, and fits into the Christian view of the God-Creation universe rather uneasily. It is one of the purposes of allegory to make such a thing possible at all. Nature herself has to tell Alain she is not detracting from God's omnipotence as a creator: she is His lowly disciple, and in being herself created and multiple, and in working with pre-existing materials to produce transient works in someone else's name, she is in all things distinct and inferior to God. God's creation of man is not only the original creation of the primordial matter and the creation of the Idea, but also the making of the physical man into a higher order of being. Nature takes on characteristics unattributable to God. Nature, not God, is for Alain responsible for such an evil as death, for example. And Nature is not only Greek for Alain, but Platonic. We have seen she speaks to Alain Platonically: truth is a matter of Platonic forms; it is God whose Ideas provide the (Platonic) models for the animals, but Nature who arranges for the perpetuation of those Ideas by physically forming the mortal individuals, 'cloaking matter with form';[28] the individual's powers and vices are located in the body as Plato had described: in all, Plato is The Philosopher. Alain, like Godfrey of St Victor, notes Aristotle only for his subtlety of argument.[29] And personified Nature is not only for Alain Greek and Platonic but also Christian in a rather particular way: Nature is the Mother of All Things but nevertheless, Alain stresses, she is a virgin. Part of Nature's virtues are those of Mary.

Why does Nature appear to Alain in tears? What is her complaint, *planctus?*[30] It is that men are forgetting her. We must remember that for people like Alain, Nature was not only generative, taking as her special role the generation of men and animals to preserve God's original Ideas, but she was normative: Nature laid down what was normal, ordered, organized and thus natural. Alain addresses Nature as the author of Natural Law, the bringer of true government, beauty and form. So what has gone wrong? In a word, the answer is that man – heretical Cathar man – has become unNatural. It is not merely that his lust has broken through Nature's *normative* bounds of moderation, but that he fails to perform Nature's other great concern, that of reproducing individuals to maintain the perpetuity of God's Idea for the species. Nature explains to Alain with more tears that men made themselves effeminate by shaving close, plucking their eyebrows and taking great care of their hair. The language in which Alain puts Nature's complaint about this has an elaborate and clever analogy with which he covers but does not hide the sexual perversions of the heretics, an analogy of grammar, where nouns in the Latin sentence have genders (three), and where by the rules and misrules of grammar the nouns are joined by a copula, properly or improperly. By linking two masculines together, or two feminines, to say nothing of neuters and of joining one noun to itself, Nature, in Alain's words, can express all kinds of sexual activity that deviate not only from Nature's rule of normality, but from her intention that the species should be propagated.

To summarize, Alain's reaction to the heresy was to invoke a Platonic view of the world, and Catholic faith. In this work he was not aware, or chose not to use, the views of Aristotle and the commentators on nature: Aristotle is still for Alain the logician only.[31] The first book of Alain's *On the Catholic faith, against the Heretics of His Own Time, Especially the Albigensians*[32] is written against the Cathars (Gilson says this is the first tract of a newly defensive church)[33] and it proceeds almost entirely by quotation of the Sacred Page. In the single citation from philosophy, Plato is the philosopher.[34] Like most other opponents of the Cathars, Alain uses his sources to show in opposition to the Cathars that the natural world is good. It is Plato and 'the philosophers' who understand, Alain assures his readers, that 'the magnitude of things' means the power of God; the beauty of things is correspondingly His wisdom, and the order of things His goodness. This work was written later than the *Planctu*, after about 1182, and probably after Alain had been involved in a campaign of preaching against the heretics. We shall see below that preaching was a new weapon of the Catholics against the Cathars, and it was no doubt for preaching that Alain made collections of *distinctiones* which, he said, made clear all the levels of interpretation of the Sacred Page.[35]

In writing allegorically, of course, Alain is relating his work to the higher levels of interpretation of the Sacred Page. It is this that often links the elaborate prose of the monastic commentators and of the 'philosophical poets'. Alain's *Anticlaudianus*[36] is another allegory of Nature complaining about depraved man, and Alain proclaims that he is writing on all three levels,[37] literal, allegorical and moral. His purposes could not have been achieved by limiting himself to the lowest of these, the literal, the level of language to which the philosophers confined themselves.

So we have seen that a literary man of the late twelfth century found two weapons with which to fight the Cathar heresy in allegorical verse and in arguments from the Sacred Page. We do not know whether Alain's *De Planctu* had any effect among the Troubadours of the south, many of whom seem to have been in sympathy with the Cathars and whose own songs were hardly Platonic in Alain's or any other sense. Nor can we suppose that arguments from the Sacred Page were particularly effective, for the heretics had a different Sacred Page in disregarding the Old Testament and making what the Catholics saw as perverse *distinctiones* on the terms of the New.

It was useless, in other words, to use as a weapon a citation from a text that one's opponent regarded as either without proper meaning or diabolically inspired. Some common ground had to be found on which the opinions of the Cathars could be faced. This third weapon was found in arguments based on reason. Alain and others used this weapon. His *Rules of Sacred Theology* (*Regulae de Sacra Theologia*) excludes all arguments from doctrine and the Sacred Page. The text reflects in an extreme form the new systematic and dialectical theology of the schools. It proceeds from self-evident truths by a series of rules:[38] every *scientia* says Alain, has its own rules, like those of grammar, dialectic, rhetoric, ethics, *physica*, arithmetic, music, geometry and astronomy. In each case the rules are different (those of *physica*, for instance, are aphorisms). Theology, the new school subject, is a *supercelestis scientia* and its rules are subtle, hidden and noble. Alain sets them out, aided by self-evident truths, those 'common conceptions of the soul, with which every rational man will agree, having once met them', *communi animi conceptiones*. There is a Monad, states Alain's first rule. Supercelestially there is unity, subcelestially, plurality. The Monad as Unity produces another, Equality; the union of Unity and Equality constitutes the Third Person of the Trinity. God is alpha and omega, but they are not parts of Him; God as uncompound is single; He is an intelligible circle whose centre is everywhere and whose boundary is nowhere. All these points are marshalled against the dualism of the Cathars. Alain likewise continues, arguing against the view of evil held by the Cathars, that all created things are good, all *scientiae*, even including magic, because these too are created. It is abuse of these that is evil, and the misuse of magic is paralleled by the worse misuse of doctrine by the Cathars.[39]

Alain's *planctu* was matched by the slightly later verse that Alexander Neckam added to his work on the natures of things. As part of a geographical eulogy he describes Toulouse, 'Well defended, powerful and rich', but now known for an evil, a notoriety that came from a depraved doctrine.

> Our times do not have happy outcomes and this
> Principal error perverts doctrine, law, faith.
> A race once shining with light,
> Why do you ruin yourselves in the shadows?
> Why do you follow the errors of Faust and the Manichees?
> That dark Lucifer of yours creates nothing.[40]

When Alexander cries sadly, E*rgo Tolosa vale ... ergo dolosa peri* it is the cry of a monastic commentator who sees nature wronged. The remedy for him however is not in a new view of nature – as we have seen, it was not his business to speak philosophically or physically.

But Alexander's was not only a monastic and poetical mind. He had learned and taught in Oxford and Paris and was knowledgeable about the arts, laws, medicine and theology. Before he became abbot of the Augustinians at Cirencester in 1213 he wrote out a concerted defence of orthodoxy, his *Speculum Speculationum*.[41] It was prompted, he said, principally by his desire to confute the Cathars. He intended to do so by bringing logic to the aid of theology, his second purpose in writing. He was of the generation in which the use of the New Logic had matured and was seen as very widely applicable. The Old Logic in the hand of someone like Adelard had been popular and exciting because of the power of argument in conferred, and the New Logic seemed even more powerful. Like Alain, Alexander saw advantages of attacking the heretics with a logic that seemed to reflect the very mechanism of the soul's reasoning powers, rather than the Sacred Page that had little authority with the heretics.

But in practice Alexander's logic is not very distant from the Sacred Page. He does not quote the Bible as *authority*, with chapter and verse locations, but uses many of its unlabelled commonplaces as self-evident axioms. These are similar to the 'common conceptions of the soul' but based on a text that was sacred and very familiar, never losing its self-evident authority. His chief target is naturally the Evil Principle. He argues dialectically that two Principles, as beginnings, would be impossible, since one would be superfluous and the other diminished; there cannot be two unbounded Immensities; only one Beginning is possible and that is the *summum bonum.* His argument is partly a reduction to absurdity based on biblical axioms. For example, he argues that since God is a Trinity, two Gods would be six persons. Of which Father would be the incarnate Son? Which Spirit moved over the face of the waters? Which God created the heavens and earth?[42]

In a similar manner he draws absurd conclusions about the heretical belief that the Evil Principle made corporeal things, including the human body, and that the Good God made spirits, including the human soul. If this were so, how could man be a natural and proper combination of body and soul? How would the two Principles administer punishments and rewards to their creations? At death, does God withdraw the soul from the body or the Evil Principle remove the body from the soul? How can a final resurrection take place? More philosophically, does the soul vivify the body or does the body draw life from the soul? What about actions of the body that depend on the soul, like speech – do the two Principles *co-operate* in producing them? *O impotentia, O defectus, si rerum principium in hac re egeat ope alterius!*[43]

In short, like many other critics of the Cathars, Alexander saw the evilness of the physical world and of its creator as the most offensive part of their doctrine. As a man who was learned in most of the studies of the schools he chose to make his attack with logic on its own or as applied to theology; he did not choose to use philosophy. Evil, he says logically, is a corruption of good, and so can only exist in a good thing (free will is good but may lead to some evil). A *summe malum*, supreme evil, could not exist on its own because its nature would be destroyed in its corruption; since what is eternal is good, evil is not eternal; what is not eternal has been created. Occasionally Alexander uses the natural objects of philosophy to illustrate his arguments, for he was after all the author of a *De Rerum Natura.* He takes from Aristotle the doctrine that animals are composed of body and soul, but it is from the logical works, not the physical. His purpose is to enquire sarcastically of the heretics whether we must suppose that toads are rational in possessing a soul created by the good God and whether making the soul of a worm is better than creating the physical world. Alexander undoubtedly knew of the physical works of Aristotle, how they were read in Oxford and Salerno, and here he uses *De Anima* and the *Metaphysics.* We may suppose that he read the *De Motu Cordis* dedicated to him by Alfred of Shareshill and was familar with the philosophical and medical doctrines explored there. But for him, a man reflecting on a life of study and now in a cloister, the most potent weapon against the Cathars was not a philosophy of nature but a dialectical theology.

Pure goodness

A book that was important in the battle against the Cathar heresy, and one which brings us closer to the Dominicans' argument, was the *Liber de Causis*. It is a translation of an Arabic work that is based on neo-Platonic sources, primarily Proclus. But in the West it was attributed to Aristotle. It appeared to explain fully Aristotle's understanding of the relationship between God and the world, an understanding which was often thought to be somewhat defective in Aristotle's *Metaphysics*.[44] It became available some time between 1167 and 1187, just when the Cathar heresy was seen as a major threat by the Catholics. It was known first as *Exposition of Pure Goodness* (*De Expositione Bonitatis Purae*) and so seemed tailor-made to use in the battle against the Cathar conception of evil. This was probably the reason that it was later used in the universities. (It was the subject of detailed commentaries by Roger Bacon, Albertus Magnus, Thomas Aquinas, Siger of Brabant and Giles of Rome.)[45] Its utility for the Catholic cause was even noted in the major surviving Cathar text.[46] These circumstances – the battle against heresy – ensured that the book was much more celebrated in the West than in the East of its immediate origin.

As a weapon against the Cathars the *Exposition of Pure Goodness* was used alongside Alain of Lille's *Rules of Sacred Theology* and Nicholas of Amien's *Art of the Catholic Faith*. Like them it uses no arguments from the Sacred Page. It is, like them, based on the dialectical reasoning of the schools. Like them it is a collection of propositions whose conclusions are cumulative and which seem to owe something to the geometrical method of the schools.

Its argument is that pure goodness descends from a single good God. This is demonstrated by the chain-of-causality argument, that nothing is self-causing and every local cause can be ultimately traced back to uncaused ultimate cause. The causality is not at all Aristotelian. In other words the book was used extensively not because it (wrongly) carried the name of Aristotle, and certainly not because it was part of some process of 'transmission' of his works. Rather, it was because the book could be used for the same purpose that Aristotle's nature books happened to be useful for: correction and maintenance of Catholic belief.

Indeed, in an Aristotelian context, the 'causes' discussed by the *Exposition of Pure Good* sound odd. What do we mean by man? asks the book. We consider him to be a being and to be live. 'Being' and 'live' are then treated as causes of 'man'. The more distant the cause from man, the more important the cause is: 'being' has precedence over 'live', which cannot be without it. In such a scale of causality 'man' is least, for he can be removed and 'living being' remains. Remove 'being' and nothing remains. It follows that of all causes, those most distant are the most important, and the ultimate single cause the most important of all.

In this work goodness flows down from the First Cause in a way that looks to us, but not at first in the thirteenth century, as unAristotelian. The ultimate cause existed before eternity, which it created; created with eternity was Being, and then Intelligence; and created after eternity was Soul. The first Intelligence gave rise to second Intelligences, and the essence of all Intelligences is the pure goodness of the first cause. Intelligence contains soul, soul contains nature and nature contains generation. In a very unAristotelian way, forms are held by Intelligence, and it is through them and through generation that pure goodness descends to material objects. There is no room in such a world for the evil matter of the Cathars.[47]

Dominic and heresy in Languedoc

So far we have told the story of men's views about the natural world largely in terms of groups and their common beliefs. By far the biggest of these groups was the Catholic Church. Up to now its common knowledge had been determined largely by church councils. But the Pope who is so important to the story, Innocent III, had greatly strengthened the power of the papacy and as a result the Church became more centralized. This had two important results. The first was that now that doctrine was the property of the Pope and his advisers heresy could be identified more exactly and more rapidly than by a council of bishops. Second the Pope could sanction special groups within the Church to deal with things he thought important. One of the most important challenges facing him was the practice and beliefs of the Cathars. First we must look at the earlier attempts of the Church to deny the knowledge possessed by the Cathars.

The Cathar Church of Languedoc[48] threatened both the new unity of the Catholic Church and the doctrines that characterized that unity. At the Council of Tours in 1166 Pope Alexander III had hoped that ostracizing the heretics would be enough; at the Third Lateran Council of 1179 seculars were urged to take up arms against the Cathars. Alexander had dispatched Cistercian preaching missions in 1178 and 1180, and Innocent tried again in 1198–99. An apparent initial success in 1203, when the city of Toulouse agreed to fight the heresy, was short-lived. In 1204 the Cistercians engaged the Cathars in open debate, but failed to make much progress.

Preaching was at the centre of the matter. Catharism was spread not only by personal contacts of the cloth merchants, the doctors and the women moving from house to house, but also by Cathar missionaries, who preached to crowds. As for the Catholics, preaching was mainly a missionary activity, having now a new urgency.[49] Before this preaching had been the often neglected duty of the bishop, and the new preaching of both Cathars and Catholics was a novelty that surprised and interested the laity. There was a 'hunger to hear'[50] on the part of a populace largely ignorant of the details of the faith. In Italy Piacentino Salvo Burci heard the physician Andreas preaching of the two creations,[51] and was prompted to write a tract in reply.[52] The Cathars' readiness of speech recorded by their enemies included their preaching and missionary activity as well as joint disputations – a technique in which the Cathar priesthood had been trained. Bonacursus of Milan, a Catholic convert from the heresy, recorded that the same Italian Cathars were formidable in speech and dreadful in the heresy they spoke.[53] The 'new preaching' of the Catholics in the thirteenth century was largely in reaction to the Cathar threat and the Fourth Lateran Council of 1215, convened largely to find answers to the problem of the Cathar heresy, sought to control unauthorized preaching. According to Alain of Lille preaching was the final stage of a ladder climbed by good Catholics, rising through confession of faith, prayer, and the reading of, resolving the problems of, and exegesis of the Sacred Page.[54]

A few sermons against the Cathars survive. They antedate both the Cistercian mission and also the sermons of the Dominicans – the Preachers – but probably similar arguments were used by the friars, the Cistercians and the earlier clergy. One such series dates from 1165 to 1169, those of the Canon Egbert (or Eckbert),[55] in the diocese of Cologne, where the Cathar heresy survived down to the time of Albertus Magnus, about a century later. Egbert saw the Cathars in his own diocese as a danger. There was much in the Bible, he admitted, that appeared to support their case, and they were very quick and argumentative – *linguosi* – in using it against the Catholics. Egbert saw it as his task to show that they were using the Sacred Page in the wrong manner. He did so partly by using Augustine's arguments against the Manichees. The Cathar belief he describes agrees closely with what we can read in their surviving texts. Another text (which may represent sermons) from northern Italy, another place where the Cathars survived through the thirteenth century, is that of Bonacursus of Milan, whose conversion to Catholicism had occurred by 1190.[56] The argument is entirely from the Sacred Page.

This was the state of affairs when Dominic and Diego (Didacus), Bishop of Osma, travelled through Languedoc in 1203 and were distressed at the extent of the heresy. Dominic was a Spanish Augustinian canon, educated at Palencia, and he and Diego were on a mission to the borders of Christendom. Some say it was to non-Christian north-east Europe and others to the marches of a country closer to home. Dominic and Diego were then at all events used to travelling in spreading the faith and were equipped with learning to help them. What they saw in Languedoc, probably on their way home to Spain, worried them more than conditions further north.

Dominic in particular was determined to do something about it. So was Innocent III: by 1204 by means of the Fourth Crusade, he had brought the church of Constantinople under papal domination, and he had had some success in his dealings with the monarch of Bulgaria. He was thus in a position to combat the dualist, Cathar, heresy at its source and on its historical route to the West, and it may be, as Runciman suggests,[57] that he was all the more determined to stamp out the heresy in Languedoc. In 1205 Dominic and Diego joined the Cistercian mission. Diego persuaded the Cistercians, with some difficulty, that the best way of appealing to the Cathars was to adopt a lifestyle of poverty, humility and zeal. This matched the ascetiscism of the *perfecti* among the Cathars and gave them a sort of moral acceptability in the heretics' eyes.[58]

To the preaching of the Cistercians, Dominic and Diego added more public disputation, a form of argument at which Dominic was said to be very good and in which he had doubtless been trained in Palencia (and the development of which we have glanced at in the previous chapter). These disputations were important. In a dispute, particularly in one where the penalties for losing it are dire, each side naturally comes to emphasize its most successful arguments and to strengthen its weakest defences or to shift its ground. The Cathar texts were partly shaped by the dispute with the Catholics. In particular the extreme dualism that had always found a place in their beliefs now became more assertive.

General features of the Catholic Church's treatment of dissenting groups too big to be destroyed as quickly as those of David of Dinant and Amalric can be seen from a comparison between the Church's treatment of the Cathars and of the Jews. It seems likely that neither threat to the Church was urgently new, but rather that the Church, under a strong Pope and ruled by his councils, was newly in a position to react to any threat. The Catholics' treatment of the Jews, like that of the Cathars, changed from local coexistence to organized suppression. The era of liberal Jewish thought was typified by Maimonides, who introduced Aristotle and his Arabic commentators into Judaism.[59] He was part of a circle of Jews active in Spain and, like the Cathars, in Provence. His views increasingly came to be seen as suspect as persecution grew and orthodox principles came to be more pronounced. In a similar way the Cathars retreated to a defence of their own orthodox principles. Like the Cathars, the Jews defended themselves at first in

5.1 St Dominic's book leaps out of the flames

public disputation in which, again like the Cathars (for example at Toulouse), they generally ended up under some sort of condemnation unless they recanted.[60] And finally both Jews (after the Fourth Lateran Council) and Cathars were ultimately obliged to wear yellow marks on their clothes as a public identification.[61] Disputations were discontinued and force was used.

The early public debates with the Cathars would be arranged some days in advance, and attracted audiences from all levels of society. Even before Dominic and Diego arrived, Pedro II of Aragon had arranged a dispute between Cathars and Catholics at Carcassonne, so that he could learn about the heresy. For five years, from 1203, when Pierre de Castelnau and Raoul[62] began their campaign of preaching, until the crusade, there were 'conferences' between the two sides. It was Diego's innovation to propose free disputations, without threat. There were disputations at Pamiers, Lavaour, Montréal, and Fanjeax. Some extended to 'theological tournaments', lasting for eight days at Servian and 15 at Montréal, where Dominic and Diego took part. Among the topics disputed were the human (and thus the physical) nature of Christ and the supposed diabolic origin of the Catholic Church. Other topics are not known but these two suffice to show that their concerns were central to Cathar doctrine and scandalous to the Catholics. According to Jordanus of Saxony, Dominic's biographer, both sides in the disputes would prepare documents for their case, which was to be judged by three mutually agreed judges. At one such dispute, says Jordanus, the judges could not agree, and the documents from each side were thrown into the fire in the belief that the one representing the truth would not burn. Not once, but three times Dominic's paper leaped of its own accord from the flames.[63]

The preaching and disputations must often have been successful on both sides. The heretic Durand de Huesca was converted to Catholicism at the disputation at Pamiers in 1207, having heard Diego and perhaps Dominic.[64] Durand conceived a missionary zeal against his old religion. Going with his companions to Rome, he prevailed upon Innocent III to approve a new style of life for the group – poverty, common living and spreading the word. Innocent agreed in 1208 and the 'Poor Catholics' came into existence.[65] The oath Durand swore upon becoming a Catholic begins with the singleness of God as Trinity and as Creator, *ex nihilo*, of all things 'corporeal and spiritual, visible and invisible'.[66] Here then was a new group, of religious men, licensed and controlled by the Pope for the explicit purpose of attacking the group of heretics. In 1212 Innocent appointed a Cardinal Protector to ensure acceptance for the group and no doubt to keep an eye on its doctrines. Durand explained to Innocent that his group were for the most part clerics and almost all learned, and hence suited to tackle the heretics by 'reading, exhortation, teaching and disputation'. The study that made this preaching and disputation more effective was to an extent formalized, and Durand speaks of *schola nostra*,[67] which produced tracts against the Cathars. So like other agents of the 'new preaching' of the thirteenth century, Durand and his school were to be trained in the techniques of the schools, with their dialectic, their *distinctiones*, their theology and their ways – including the literal – of reading the Sacred Page. Durand's treatise against the Cathars survives, and we shall examine it later. Although they claimed for themselves the right of preaching against the Cathars, little seems to have become of his band of followers. Perhaps this was because the preaching missions were largely abandoned in 1207 and 1208, after the murder of the papal legate Pierre de Castelnau.

While Durand was preparing to secure recognition of his Order, or School, from the Pope, Dominic was in Toulouse, wondering what to do. Nothing seemed to have any effect on the obstinate heretics. As he pondered, kneeling on a hillside overlooking the Toulousain contryside and praying to Mary, the answer appeared to him in a suitably impressive way. On three successive nights a ball of fire descended from the sky and hovered above the little church of Prouille, rather like the star that had guided the Magi. Suddenly Dominic knew what he had to do. He had prayed to Mary the Mother of God on the day of Mary Magdalen. He knew from experience that the Cathar heresy was partly spread and at least partly maintained by the women of the region, who had charge of the children and guided their earliest learning. He knew that the women of the nobility were staunch defenders of the heresy. What he had to do was to attack the heresy by way of its female supporters. And he now knew that he had to begin at the church of Prouille.

He accordingly sought the advice of Foulques, his friend, an old Troubadour and now a Cistercian. Foulques was, on both these counts, a figure acceptable to the heretics, for the Troubadours shared a national feeling with those of the South, and the monkish image was sympathetic to the ascetic ideals of the *perfecti*: he was a useful man for Dominic to know. Foulques secured help from the patroness of the church and it became under Dominic's guidance part of his answer to the heresy. It was also the beginning of the story of the Dominicans as an Order of Friars and what is important about it at this early stage is that Dominic's plan was shaped by the nature of the challenge – the heresy of the Cathars – that he faced.

The church of Prouille was to be in the first place, a community of women who had been converted to Catholicism. It was in part a refuge, where converts could escape the disapproval of their families and friends.

Even this idea may have come to Dominic from the fact that the Cathars – and the Jews – provided similar refuges for their own converts. Naturally in such an environment could be developed an atmosphere that mutually supported the new converts and their new beliefs; and naturally Dominic expected that this atmosphere would lend itself to propagandizing purposes, both for visitors and by way of the school for children that was set up to match the extant Cathar schools. Indeed, the whole idea of Prouille, if not divinely suggested, probably came to Dominic from the Cathar convents which functioned as centres of dissemination for the heresy, and which often took the young daughters of impoverished Cathar families. Prouille women – it would be premature to call them nuns – were mostly from the noble families that were heretical because (as Dominic saw) part of the authority that helped spread Catharism derived from the social position of the women who defended and propagated the heresy. Dominic had clearly thought carefully about the nature of the heresy in order to enable him to combat it most effectively.

The Prouille model proved effective, and when Pope Honorius III decided in 1218 to tighten up on religious laxity in Rome, he employed a similar convent-based strategy and Dominic supervised it. The convents in Languedoc provided help. There was a similar exercise by Dominic in Madrid. There were also men at Prouille. Again, their organization, even in their earliest years, was shaped by the task Dominic saw they had to do. They were to be poor, to match the ascetic lifestyle of the *perfecti*. They were to be educated, to meet the arguments of the *perfecti*. Foulque agreed and in 1215 provided local church funds for those of Dominic's followers who were furthering their education in the school at Toulouse. Things seemed to be going well to Dominic and he applied to Innocent III for recognition of his religious house as a new form of religious organization. Innocent approved of the house at Prouille as a force against heresy, but could not accept what Dominic now revealed as radical new aims. Dominic saw his battle from now on, fired by the Languedoc heresy, as nothing less than a world-wide organization, mobile and controlled by a single centre, devoted to the destruction of heresy and paganism. Such a thing was unprecedented. When Foulque understood that this was not to be simply a local missionary base, he wanted his money back. It was unprecedented partly because the big religious houses were either autonomous or hierarchical, but stationary. Even Durand's school, which had aims in common with Dominic's proposed group, seems to have been conceived as a settled organization working with texts. Dominic had in mind the Templars and Hospitallers, which were mobile military orders, fighting for orthodoxy and Christendom itself by the most direct of physical means. Dominic did not object to these means. He was a particular friend of Simon de Montfort and accompanied him on most of the operations of the Albigensian crusade that sought to wipe out the Cathar heresy.

But Dominic's weapons were not to be the fire and the sword favoured by the later Dominicans and the crusaders. He foresaw their use when he quoted a Spanish proverb, 'where kindness fails, a man must try a stick'. But now his weapon was learning, for the Cathars with whom he had debated were learned men. This was an unusual feature of the Cathar heresy and the illiteracy of earlier heretics had become a commonplace within the Catholic Church. It was partly of course that 'illiteracy' could easily be invoked to describe other people's wrong ideas, but some heretics, like the Waldenses, contemporary with the Cathars, took pride in their illiteracy, claiming to live the true apostolic life. But the Cathars were committed to their books. Reading was seen as a characteristic action of the *perfecti*.[68] Italian Cathars at least sent their bright young men to study in Paris, and the Cathars of Languedoc were delighted when they recruited a Catholic canon with a Parisian education. When the recruitment was in the other direction and a Cathar was converted, the image it generated could be the confuted heretic tearing up his book: 'heresy with a book, a peril vanquished by St Dominic with a book' was a commonplace after the 'crisis of c.1200'.[69] The Inquisitors came to see carrying a book as a mark of Catharism, and among those they found were medical texts and calendar, and collections of sayings of philosophers and saints.[70] Durand de Huesca called the perfects *doctores*, reading to their followers in conventicles and writing books. Many Cathars were medical doctors, and when one Catholic bishop, disputing with his Cathar opposite number, insulted him with the observation that he was like a young doctor from Salerno, reading his books in reverse, it may have been a barb directed at the special nature of medical learning. Certainly medical knowledge often enough attracted the criticism that it gave too much attention to nature and not enough to God. Medicine was one of the first of the disciplines to use the physical doctrines of Aristotle, and this may be why such things came easily to the Cathars in argument. To Alain of Lille the Cathars' learning appeared in their dialectical arguments and Dominic knew that the Cathars were learned because one of his first encounters was when he sat up all night arguing with one of them. In the early days of his group at Toulouse he made sure that the group was to be learned by taking its members to lectures at the school in Toulouse.[71] Some of the first money secured by Foulques for the group was for books.[72] Dominic's express intention was to be able to preach more effectively against the heretics.[73] The passion for learning marked also the early years of the Order after its recognition by the Pope. 'The Lord hath given me the tongue of the learned' might have described the feelings of many, like Jordan of Saxony upon entering the Order. Jordan became its second Master General; and a later Master, Humbert of Romans, knew that many of the Order's large numbers of recruits were attracted by its learning.[74] The Constitutions of the Order urge the Brothers to snatch every moment of day or night in order to study, in their cells or on a journey. Because the same source prescribes that the Divine Office was to be said 'briskly and shortly, so that the brethren may not lose devotion nor their studies be impeded' some historians have concluded that for the Preachers learning was a kind of religious observance.[75]

Dominic succeeded in establishing his Order in 1216 when Innocent's successor, Honorius III, recognized Dominic's followers as canons regular with special duties of preaching. It was the formal beginning of the Order of Preachers. Like the followers of Durand, the Dominicans were trained in scholastic techniques, the better to preach against and dispute with the Cathars. Life for Dominic and his followers was to be a constant battle, against the 'old adversary', the Devil,[76] and he sent his followers, trained theologians, into towns all over Europe.

Thus the Preachers were to be a mobile Order, formed at a moment of crisis for the Catholic Church and for the purpose of fighting what the Church saw as a heresy. In practice the Brothers were often called from one of their *studia* to another. Matthew Paris, the chronicler, said of them, sarcastically, that the whole earth was their cell and the sea their cloister.[77] But so influential were they in the universities that this very mobility made for uniformity of doctrine, religious and philosophical. They came rapidly to be agents of the Pope in pursuit of the heresy, and their mobility and their learning helped to define a pan-European notion of what learning – including natural philosophy – was. An important part of their mobility derived from the fact that they were mendicant, in theory depending on local hospitality for their support. In practice the Pope dropped broad hints to the local bishops that the Preachers were to be supported. It was probably in this that Innocent's experiments with Durand's sedentary school were improved on by Honorius, as the Dominicans moved to where they were needed. Their weapons were at first arguments, in both preaching and disputation, and we can gain some idea of them from texts produced in refutation by the Cathars (we shall meet them below). All historians of the Preachers, whether themselves Domicans or not, have stressed their learning, sought primarily for the overcoming of the heresy and the resultant saving of souls. Preaching – we can insist again – was central to the issue at stake. We saw above that preaching became a renewed and necessary tool of the Church before Dominic established his Order, but to understand the hesitation of Innocent III, the eventual success of Dominic and the importance of learning to his Order we have to go back to the preaching immediately before his time. The Vaudois and the Humiliati had been groups who had hoped to contribute to the Church's purposes in preaching. But they were uneducated, preached badly and slid into heterodoxy and even heresy. Lucius III, before Innocent III, had controlled the situation by being careful to give the licence to preach to those of the uneducated who promised only to offer moral exhortations. No doubt this is why Durand and Dominic emphasized the (superior) learning of their followers and why Innocent was hesitant; and the important point is that preaching was a scholastic as well as a religious exercise. In the language of the time, a Preacher, *praedicator*, was the equivalent of *doctor*,[78] a man who could teach because he was learned. The Preacher in his sermon as often as not took a fragment of the Sacred Page and examined it as a scholastic commentator or a disputant would examine a lemma of a philosophical text. He needed to explain it, so he examined any obscurities it might contain by making *distinctiones*[79] of them. He located the passage in the Scriptures as a whole. Above all he drew out from the literal meaning of the words the higher meaning, the spiritual or moral[80] (our expression the 'moral' of a story is a survival of this). This is the essence of the Dominicans' strategy: to proceed to the spiritual and theological by way of the literal, the physical and the rational.

The Dominicans depended very largely on the reading of the Sacred Page that had been the mainstay of learning since the monastic schools and the purpose of education within the Order during Dominic's lifetime seems in this sense to have been wholly theological.[81] But at some stage Dominic or his followers found that the Cathars' main contention, that the natural world was the evil creation of an evil principle, was being supported by physical reasons drawn from an Aristotelian philosophy of nature. Like the other characteristics of the Cathar heresy, this one also shaped the nature of the Dominicans' response. Not only were they to be learned, they had to be learned also in Aristotle's philosophy of nature. We shall see that it was hence the Dominicans who really took Aristotle to heart and taught the natural works in their own *studia*.

Notes

1. *Chartularium Universitatis Parisiensis*, p. 70.
2. H. Rashdall, *The Universities of Europe in the Middle Ages*, 1936, repr. 1958, vol. I, p. 356 says the ban on the Aristotelian works was for three years only.
3. G. Théry, 'Autour du Décret de 1210', p. 7. E. Maccagnolo, 'David of Dinant and the Beginnings of Aristotelianism in Paris', in P. Dronke,

Twelfth-Century Western Philosophy, pp. 429–42, argues that David was the *translator* of the banned texts. He also argues that the banned texts were the commentaries by Averroes, although it is sometimes said that the first signs of Averroistic interpretation of Aristotle are to be found in the works of Philip the Chancellor and William of Auvergne, two Chancellors of Paris whom we shall meet below. The earlier commentaries were those of al Kindi, al Farabi, Avicenna and Algazel.

4. As we saw in the last chapter 'division' was the framing of dialectical *distinctiones*.
5. M-T. d'Alverny, 'Translations and Translators', p. 437. David's sources are not the usual ones noted by historians of 'transmission': he is an 'outsider'. See also Théry, 'Autour du Décret de 1210' and Birkenmajer, *Etudes d'Histoire des Sciences*. This contains Birkenmajer's 'Découverte de fragments manuscrits de David de Dinant'.
6. David did not at first seem to be offensive to the papacy, for he spent some time at the court of Innocent III in 1206, apparently without ideological friction. Nor was David condemned by the Fourth Lateran Council of 1215, although Amalric was. And Gregory IX, Innocent's nephew, was inclined to forgive those who had incurred the punishment of the Paris council.
7. Non legantur libri Aristotelis de methafisica et de naturali philosophia, nec summe de eiusdem, aut de doctrina magistri David de Dinant, aut Amalrici heretici, aut Maurici hyspani. Théry, 'Autour du Décret de 1210', p. 7.
8. See also *Chartularium*, vol. 1, p. 71.
9. On this region and its culture in precisely this period, see Linda M. Paterson, *The World of the Troubadours: Medieval Occitan Society, c.1100–c.1300*, Cambridge University Press, 1993.
10. See Peter Biller, 'Heresy and Literacy: Earlier History of the Theme', in Peter Biller and Anne Hudson, eds, *Heresy and Literacy, 1000–1530*, Cambridge University Press, 1994, p. 2.
11. S. Runciman, *The Medieval Manichee. A Study of the Christian Dualist Heresy*, Cambridge University Press, 1982, p. 167.
12. E. Gilson, *History of Christian Philosophy in the Middle Ages*, London, 1980, p. 172.
13. Gedaliahu G. Stroumsa, 'Anti-Cathar Polemics and the *Liber De Duobus Principiis*' in Bernard Lewis and Friedrich Niewöhner, eds, *Religionsgespräche im Mittelalter*, Wolfenbüttler Mittelalter-Studien, vol. 4, Wiesbaden, Harrossowitz, 1992, pp. 169–83. The relations between Christendom and Islam have of course a high historical profile, and no historian of 'science' is unaware of the translations from Greek to Arabic and Latin and the subsequent philosophical dialogue in Arabic and Latin culture. However, this is a different story from the one we are telling.
14. J.H. Mundy, 'Urban Society and Culture. Toulouse and Its Region', in Benson and Constable, *Renaissance and Renewal*, pp. 229–47; 230.
15. S. Runciman, *The Medieval Manichee. A Study of the Christian Dualist Heresy*, Cambridge University Press, 1982, p. 136.
16. According to Runciman, *The Medieval Manichee*, p. 18. An important stimulus for the Cathar heresy was the crusades and their contact with Constantinople. As early as 1119 there was a Church council of Toulouse which anathematized the local heretics.
17. Some sources attribute the spread of Catharism to weavers (Runciman,

The Medieval Manichee, p. 119), and in France the heretics were known as *texterant[es]*, meeting in weaving workshops and cellars. See Eckbert's sermons against them, Migne, *PL*, vol. 195, p. 11. Stock points out how the growth of the Lyons textile industry was coterminous with the Waldensian heresy, which flourished at the same time as Catharism. The economic conditions in both cases were important. See B. Stock, 'Science, Technology and Economic Progress in the Early Middle Ages', in D.C. Lindberg, *Science in the Middle Ages*, University of Chicago Press, 1978, pp. 1–51. In Montaillou, where Cathar missionaries in blue hoods spread the word, at least one sheep farmer became anti-Catholic because of the tithe on sheep; Ladurie, 1978, p. 243.

18. Runciman, *The Medieval Manichee*, pp. 123, 130; R. Brooke, *The Coming of the Friars*, London, 1975, pp. 72, 153. The authenticity of the documents on which the story of the council of St Félix is based has been questioned. See Bernard Hamilton, 'The Cathar Council of Saint-Felix Reconsidered', *Archivum Fratrum Praedicatorum*, **48**, (1978) pp. 23–53.
19. P. Schaff, ed., *A Select Library of the Nicene and Post Nicene Fathers of the Christian Church. Volume IV: St. Augustine: the Writings against the Manicheans and against the Donatists*, Michigan, 1887. Faustus denied the Old Testament and held that while God was the principle of all good things, *Hyle*, or the Devil of common speech, was the principle of all evil. See Augustine's *Contra Faustum Manichaeum*, this volume, p. 151. Augustine tried to counter the threat posed by Faustus by representing *Hyle* as prime matter. See his *De Natura Boni contra Manicheos*, p. 343.
20. Brooke, *The Coming of the Friars*, p. 175.
21. L. White, *Medieval Religion and Technology*, University of California Press, 1978, p. 34. For a pre-Aristotle discussion of the change that takes place in transubstantiation of bread see the disputations of Simon of Tournai (second half of twelfth century): J. Warichez, ed., *Les Disputationes de Simon de Tournai*, Louvain, 1932, p. 202. On transubstantiation see also M. Rubin, *Corpus Christi. The Eucharist in Late Medieval Culture*, Cambridge University Press, 1991.
22. A. Dondaine, *Un Traité Néo-Manichiéen du XIIIe Siècle: Le Liber de Duobus Principiis, suivi d'un Fragment de Rituel Cathare*, Rome, 1939, p. 65.
23. Alain of Lille, *The Complaint of Nature*, trans. D.M. Moffat, New York, 1908; S.C. Ferruolo, *Origins of the University*, Stanford University Press, 1985, p. 194.
24. J.W. Baldwin, 'Masters at Paris from 1179 to 1215. A Social Perspective', in Benson and Constable, *Renaissance and Renewal*, pp. 138–72; 147.
25. It is said that more than 5 000 lines of the *Roman de la Rose* are imitations of, or inspired by Alain's *Planctu*. See Moffat's edn of 1908, preface.
26. C.S. Lewis, *Allegory of Love*, Oxford, 1977, p. 87, argues that Thierry of Chartres was influential in this movement in reconciling Genesis with the *Timaeus*. See also G.B. Lardner, 'Terms and Ideas of Renewal', p. 15.
27. This concept of Nature is similar to that of Bernard Sylvestris (Sylvester); on Bernard see P. Dronke, ed., *Bernardus Sylvestris Cosmographia*, Leiden, 1978. Bernard's own well-known allegory, involving Natura, Nous, Silva and Chaos (including man's errant behaviour) would have made Alain's message unmistakable, and particularly pointed at the time of the Cathars' heresy.

28. Moffat's translation, pp. 30 ff.
29. For Alain's Platonism see also C.H. Lohr, 'The Pseudo Aristotelian Liber de Causis and Latin Theories of Science in the Twelfth and Thirteenth Centuries' in J. Kraye, W. Ryan and C. Schmitt, *Pseudo-Aristotle in the Middle Ages, The Theology and Other Texts*, London, 1986, pp. 53–62. Alain's *regulae* follow the technique of the *Liber de Causis*.
30. Alain's *planctus* is a word often used in the poems of the Troubadours (and was used also by Neckam for the loss of Jerusalem); see also R.W. Hunt, *The Schools and the Cloister. The Life and Writings of Alexander Nequam*, Oxford 1984, pp. 4 ff.
31. Alain of Lille, *Anticlaudianus*, J.P. Migne, *Patrologiae Cursus Completus* (*PL*), vol. 210, col. 491: 'Illic arma parat logico, logicaeque palaestram Pingit Aristoteles ... '.
32. *De Fide Catholica Contra Hereticos sui Temporis, Praesertim Albigenses*: Migne, *PL*, vol. 210, col. 305.
33. Gilson (1980) p. 172.
34. Alain records a Cathar argument that does not seem to be found elsewhere, namely that some animals – the small, noisome and dangerous – are without use and so most obviously the work of an evil creator: *PL* 210, 310. As a Catholic Alain was of course very concerned that the material sacraments were seen by the Cathars as evil, and he devotes much space to the question of transubstantiation: *PL*, vol. 210, p. 339.
35. The three levels of interpretation often gave rise to a threefold structure of sermons. See R.H. and M.A. Rouse, *Preachers, Florilegia and Sermons: Studies on the Manipulus Florum of Thomas of Ireland*, Toronto (Pontifical Institute) 1979.
36. Migne *PL*, vol. 210, 482.
37. Stock, *Myth and Science*, p. 31.
38. Lohr sees in the method an insight into 'scientific method' of the Middle Ages. See Lohr, 'Liber de Causis', note 29 above.
39. Migne *PL*, vol. 210, p. 622.
40. Tempora nostra carent laetis successibus, error
Praeceps pervertit dogmata, jura, fidem.
Gens quondam luce micans, cur tenebrosa perit?
Cur Fausti sequeris errores, cur Manichaei?
Nil creat obscurus Lucifer tuus.

Alexander Neckam, *De Naturis Rerum, De Laudibus Divinae Sapientie*, ed. T. Wright, London, 1863 (*Rerum Britannicarum Medii Aevi Scriptores*) p. 450: the verse *De Laudibus* (from which this is taken) is a paraphrase of the prose work; see preface, p. lxxv.
41. Alexander Neckam (Nequam) *Speculum Speculationum*, ed. Rodney M. Thomson, Oxford University Press (for the British Academy) 1988. The attack on the Cathars is concentrated in the first few chapters of book 1. Thereafter, having demonstrated that there is one God and not two, Alexander spends much space on showing how He consists of three persons.
42. When theology became dialectical it was seen that syllogisms about the Trinity could be based on sound premisses and have faultless logic but still produce false conclusions. Such reasoning was called 'paralogism' and was subject to intense debate because of the special nature of revealed

knowledge. Needless to say, other people's knowledge could never be paralogistic. See Michael H. Shank, *'Unless You Believe, You Shall Not Understand.' Logic, University, and Society in Late Medieval Vienna*, Princeton University Press, 1988.

43. 'What a defect, what weakness, if in this matter the Principle of things needed the help of another!', Alexander Neckam, *Speculum Speculationum*, p. 14.
44. For the *Liber de Causis* in Islam, see R.C. Taylor, 'The Kalam Fi Mahd al-Khair (*Liber de Causis*) in the Islamic Philosophical Milieu', in Kraye, *Pseudo-Aristotle*, pp. 37–52.
45. 235 mss survive and it had attracted 27 commentaries before 1500. See Taylor, note 44 above.
46. Dondaine, *Liber de Duobus Principiis*, pp. 81, 82.
47. See also Taylor, 'The Kalam ... ', note 44 above. For the geometrical method see C.H. Lohr, 'Liber de Causis', in the same volume, pp. 53–62.
48. The Cathar heresy has attracted a great deal of historical attention. Important in the large literature are C. Thouzellier, *Catharisme et Valdéisme en Languedoc à la Fin du XIIe et au Début de XIIIe Siècle*, Paris/ Louvain, 1969; J. Duvernoy, *Le Catharisme: l'Histoire des Cathares*, 2 vols, Toulouse, 1979; M. Roquebert, *L'Epopée Cathare 1198–1212: l'invasion*, Toulouse, 1970 followed by the second volume, ... *1213–1216: Muret ou la Dépossession*, Toulouse, 1977. Collections of documents in translation are presented by R.I. Moore, *The Birth of Popular Heresy*, London, 1975 and E. Peters, *Heresy and Authority in Medieval Europe*, London, 1980, and shorter accounts by, for example: J. Sumption, *The Albigensian Crusade*, London, 1978; J. Madaule, *The Albigensian Crusade. An Historical Essay*, London, 1967; and J.R. Strayer, *The Albigensian Crusade*, New York, 1971.
49. R.H. and M.A. Rouse, *Preachers, Florilegia and Sermons: Studies on the Manipulus Florum of Thomas of Ireland*, Toronto, (Pontifical Institute), 1979, pp. 43–6.
50. Rouse, *Preachers*, p. 55.
51. The 'two creations' seem to have been a feature of Italian Catharism, discussed in the next chapter. Andreas spoke of a carnal and a spiritual creation, but these were not the mundane and celestial worlds of the Provencal Cathars, but parallel worlds, each with its 'wives, sons, horses, arms and serpents'. See P. Ilarino da Milano, 'Il "Liber supra stella" de Piacentino Salvo Burci contro i Catari et altre correnti ereticali. 4 – le dottrine catare', *Aevum*, 1945, **19**, pp. 281–341.
52. Burci was a layman; his reply was written in 1235. See da Milano, note 51 above.
53. R. Manselli, 'Per la storia dell'eresia nel secolo XII', *Bullettino dell'Istituto Storico Italiano per il Medio Evo e Archivio Muratoriano*, 1955, **67**, pp. 189–264; 192. Bonacursus had himself been a Cathar, indeed, one of their 'masters' or 'bishops' in Milan. Tracts by converted heretics are a feature of the anti-Cathar literature; that of Bonacursus, the *Manifestatio Haresis Catharorum* treats of the evil creation of the Devil as a rearrangement of extant matter to make the material world. Bonacursus' *Vita Haereticorum* (Migne, *PL*, 204, p. 772) is a Sacred-Page refutation of the evil creation of the Devil. On Bonacursus see also P. Ilarino da Milano, 'La 'Manifestatio heresis catarorum quam fecit Bonacursus' secondo il cod. Otob. Lat.136

della biblioteca Vaticana', *Aevum*, 1938, **12**, pp. 281–333. The related Paterine heretics called the Devil the 'minor creator'. See Ilarino da Milano, 'Fr. Gregorio OP, Vescovo di Fano, et la "Disputatio inter Catholicum et Paterinum Hereticum"', *Aevum*, 1940, **14**, pp. 85–140.

54. Migne, *PL*, vol. 210, p. 113. We have seen how Alain's collection of *distinctiones* was compiled for use in preaching.
55. Migne, *PL*, vol. 195.
56. Migne, *PL*, vol. 204.
57. Runciman, *The Medieval Manichee ...* , p. 138.
58. The disputes between the Cistercians and Diego on the one hand and the 'Bulgarian' heretics on the other is described in the *chanson* of the Albigensian crusade.

    E l'ordres de Cistel, que n'ac la senhoria
    I trames de sos homes tropa mota vegia;
    Si que l'avesque d'Osma ne tenc cort aramia,
    E li autre legat, ab cels de Bolgaria,
    Lai dins e Carcassona, on mota gent avia.

59. F. Heer, *The Medieval World. Europe from 1100 to 1350*, Trans. J. Sondheimer, London, 1962, p. 310.
60. W.L. Wakefield, *Heresy, Crusade and Inquisition in Southern France*, London, 1974, p. 89.
61. The wearing of crosses on the clothes was enacted at the Council of Toulouse, 1229, as part of the Catholic attempt to deal with the heresy on a political, social and educational level. See Peters, *Heresy and Authority*, p. 194 and the section on re-education below.
62. Raoul (Ralph, Rudolphus) the legate and companion of Pierre de Castelnau was a learned master and at the time of the Cistercian mission he was a Cistercian, from Fontfroide (Thouzellier, *Catharisme*, pp. 184, 185, 196) and a canon of Narbonne. He died in July 1207. He seems after the mission to have become the Abbot of Candeil and may have been made the bishop of Arras by Innocent. If indeed this is the same man, then Innocent was unaware of his death when writing in April, 1208. (J. Duvernoy, *Le Catharisme: L'Histoire des Cathares*, Toulouse, 1979, vol. 2, pp. 132, 140, 247). There is a faint possibility that this Raoul is to be identified with the Raoul of Longchamps who made extensive use of the Aristotelian physical works in his commentary on Alain of Lille's *Anticlaudianus*; see A. Birkenemajer, 'La role jouée ... ', in *Études d'Histoire ...* , Warsaw, 1970, p. 8.
63. Brooke, *Friars*, pp. 89–93. For an account of Dominic's canonization miracles see also J. Guiraud, *Saint Dominic*, London, 1901.
64. A. Dondaine, 'Durand de Huesca et la polémique anticathare', *Archivum Fratrum Praedicatorum*, 1959, **29**, pp. 228–76.
65. The group did not survive the century. See Bede Jarret, OP, *Life of St Dominic (1170–1221)*, London, 1924, p. 29.
66. Quoted by E. Peters, *Heresy and Authority in Medieval Europe*, London, 1980, p. 184.
67. Dondaine, 'Durand', p. 237.
68. See P. Biller, 'The Cathars of Languedoc and Written Materials', in Biller and Hudson, 1994, pp. 61–82; 80.

69. Biller in Biller and Hudson, 1994, pp. 1–18; 8.
70. This was the *Perpendiculum Scientiarum*. See Biller, 1994, p. 69.
71. W.A. Hinnebusch, OP, *The Early English Friars Preachers*, Rome, 1951, p. 333. On Dominic's life see also P. Mandonnet OP, *Saint Dominique. L'Idée, l'Homme et l'Oeuvre*, with additions by M.H. Vicaire OP, 2 vols, Paris, 1938; and Bede Jarrett OP, *Life of St Dominic (1170–1221)*, London, 1924.
72. Bede Jarrett, 1924, p. 61.
73. ... *in partibus Tolosanis contra infideles*. See H.-M. Féret OP, 'Vie intellectuelle et vie scolaire dans l'ordre des prêcheurs', *Archives d'Histoire Dominicaine*, **1**, 1946, pp. 1–37.
74. Hinnebusch, 1951, p. 261.
75. See Hinnebusch, 1951, p. 335.
76. Brooke, *Friars*, p. 180.
77. Hinnebusch, 1951, p. 331.
78. As Mandonnet says, an *Ordo Praedicatorum* was the same thing as an *Ordo Doctorum*. Mandonnet, 1938, vol. 2, p. 84.
79. An example of distinctions made to explain a text is provided in an Oxford sermon by the Dominican Richard Fishacre (d. 1248). He takes as his lemma the simile of Mary as an olive tree, 'Ego autem, sicut oliva fructifera in domo Dei' and makes three distinctions: 'Tria hic videamus: primo, quare Maria comparatur arbori et tali, et hoc est "ego sicut olivia"; secundo, quia arborum quedam sunt steriles, quedam fructifere – quare fructifere et non sterili, et hoc est "fructifere"; tertio, quia fructiferarum quedam sunt domestice, quedam silvestres – quare domestice et non silvestri, et hoc est "in domo Dei".' See R. James Long, 'The Virgin as Olive-Tree: A Marian Sermon of Richard Fishacre and Science at Oxford', *Archivum Fratrum Praedicatorum*, **52**, 1982, pp. 77–87; 83. Fishacre, unusually, drew upon the pseudo-Aristotelian *De Plantis* which was probably already being taught in the arts course (as we surmise from later statutes).
80. An example may be given of a sermon by the Dominican Robert Kilwardby, who begins directly with a biblical prophecy as a lemma and distinguishes the literal from the moral reading: Expedit vobis ut unus moriatur homo pro populo, ut non tota gens pereat. Hec verba literaliter possunt intelligi et moraliter. Si literaliter ... See P. Osmund Lewry OP, 'A Passiontide Sermon of Robert Kilwardby O.P.', *Archivum Fratrum Praedicatorum*, **52**, 1982, pp. 89–113; 101.
81. See Féret, 1946.

CHAPTER SIX

The evil and good world

Cathar and Catholic texts

We saw in Chapter Four that the doctrine that nature was an autonomous principle, so readily found in Greek philosophy, caused trouble in twelfth-century Christian society. The problem reached a crisis at the end of the century when the Catholics fully understood the dualism of the Cathars. What was critical was the doctrine that the natural, physical, world had been made not merely by an autonomous principle that stood between God and His creation, but by an Evil Principle that rivalled the Catholic God in power and even eternity. A prime focus of the learned debates between the two sides had to be the physical world, its creator and governor, or in other words, 'nature' in one of the senses discussed above. One of these senses, we can recall, was nature as a generative and normative principle, outside the things she controlled. The other was the nature-of-the-thing, the Aristotelian final form of thing, which explained the processes that produced it. This was wholly internal, the very essence of the thing generated. The Dominicans found that by adopting Aristotle's doctrine they could show that the physical world was good, and had been created by the good God, without any second autonomous principle.

When the Catholics gave up disputing with the Cathars and began to burn them (as we shall see) they also burnt their books. Only a few survive, but enough to provide a picture of Cathar belief and the form that the disputations took. The most important surviving Cathar text is the sizeable *De Duobus Principiis* – that is, on the 'two principles', Good and Evil, and written most probably by John of Lugio, a Cathar bishop.[1] According to the ex-Cathar Rayner Sacconi, this book is an attempt to systematize Cathar belief in the face of Catholic attack.[2]

Second is a text written by Durand of Huesca, the heretic who was converted to Catholicism, and who became a keen inquisitor. His text takes the form of a commentary, written about 1223, that embodies, for refutation, parts of a Cathar text.[3] Third, another ex-Cathar turned inquisitor, Rayner Sacconi, wrote in about 1250 a short summary of Cathar belief for the same purpose.[4]

There are in contrast a large number of Catholic tracts against the Cathars, which help us follow the dispute. One of the earliest is the

Summa contra Haereticos ascribed to Praepositinus (Prévostin) of Cremona[5] and dating most likely from the end of the twelfth century and so predating the earliest surviving Cathar text, Durand's school and the Dominicans. Praepositinus had worked amongst the heretics of Lombardy from about 1185 to 1195 and was familiar with the beliefs and practices of Cathars of all kinds. As Chancellor of Paris from 1206 to 1210 he can hardly have been without influence in shaping the northern, French, reaction to heresy. Praepositinus' reply to the Cathar claim that the Devil created *hyle* and then the elements is taken entirely from the New Testament, which alone these Cathars accepted. He realized that to be effective, Sacred-Page arguments had to be taken from what both sides agreed was sacred. It was in turn in using the New Testament (Ephesians and John) that these Cathars argued that the rulers – *rectores* – of the world were demons and therefore the whole world was in a state of evil. The answer from Praepositinus was a scholastic-theological *distinctio* on 'world', *mundus*. What *mundus* really means, said Praepositinus, is God's upper world, so called on account of its purity, *mundiciam*. It was the upper world that was so often called 'nature' in the twelfth century, and Praepositinus is steering the reader away from the imperfect corruptible lower world, the 'works of nature'. Secure in his Christianity, Praepositinus argued that the pagan Greek philosophers did not know of the upper world, and concluded that the physical world (with its demons) contained everything. As in all Cathar-Catholic encounters, the nature of the physical world was central. However, unlike later Chancellors of Paris, Praepositinus did not find it useful to use, or did not know of,[6] the physical works of Aristotle, which were to be so useful to the Dominicans in rebutting the doctrine of the evilness of the physical world. Indeed, the thrust of his argument here is rather to group the Cathars, in their ignorance of the true faith, and in their learning, *together* with the pagan philosophers. This is an important point, for if the heretics were to be answered on their own terms (and we have seen that some common ground was necessary for an argument to be successful) then it was necessary to know some philosophy in order to refute them.

Durand on the Antifrasis: nature and evil

We saw in the last chapter that Durand's school was part of Innocent's strategy to deal with the Cathars. Durand undoubtedly knew of the Cistercian missions against the heresy and had been converted probably by Diego, so he was familiar with special initiatives of the Church in a time of special crisis. His own initiative was to write against the Cathars, and his text is perhaps the only surviving product of his school.

This is Durand's refutation of a Cathar text called *Antifrasis*. This term seems to mean 'the other world',[7] which again recalls the 'otherness' of the Cathars' 'world' in these texts and disputes. Parts of the *Antifrasis* are embedded in Durand's refutation of it, which he wrote sometime between 1223 and 1230. However, his knowledge of heretical doctrine included what he believed as a heretic (although not a strict Cathar) before he was converted in 1207. When he writes that it was in their secret meetings that the Cathars talked about diabolic creation of the physical world, it is clear that he believed that this was the central point of difference between the Cathars and Catholics. It is also clear that by the late 1220s it had become a position difficult to hold openly.[8] In doing so in his book, the Cathar author took the phrase 'God created the world' and used the *distinctio* of 'world' as 'the kingdom of heaven': God's only created 'world'. The Catholics, in contrast, distinguished the term 'world' of this sentence as 'this world and everything in it': the physical world. Similarly the Cathars quoted the biblical sentence 'God does not live in temples made by man' in order to prove that earthly, material churches are evil and that God's habitation is the kingdom of heaven, his own creation. Durand countered this by again applying a *distinctio* to the word 'habitation', that is, by showing that in the Scriptures it is meant in a number of ways, symbolic, allegorical, spiritual as well as literal. His argument was then that the Cathars had chosen the wrong *distinctio* from those available.[9]

Thus Durand's central argument concerned the evilness of the physical world. Durand treated this as the Cathars' inability to separate nature from evil, where 'nature' was the physical world (and where evil would have been man's turning from God). They forget the account in Genesis of the good God's creation, said Durand, and believe that the real world is limited to the incorruptible part of creation: God's kingdom. But for the Cathars the Old Testament, including Genesis, was the work of the devil and could not be believed. The *substance* of that real world, said the Cathars, is faith, a view they supported from Paul's letter to the Hebrews. To refute this, it was necessary for Durand and the Catholics to insist that nature, the real world, was good, as God's creation, and Durand speaks of the goodness of God's physical creatures, like sea animals. In arguing for a second time that the Cathars are unable to separate creatures (that is, created things) from evil, Durand explicitly employs Augustine's definition of evil as a human and voluntary turning away from God.

Yet again the argument returns to what is meant by 'world'. The Cathar author had pointed to a number of places in the New Testament where Christ and the apostles seem to show distaste for the evil world of men, and this is explained away by Durand's making a *distinctio* of the term 'seculum' for 'world'. *Seculum* he says, can mean the *machina mundi*, the physical world in which the heavens, earth, trees, seas, fish and beasts all venerate God. But it can also mean the scheming and evil world of men, and this is what was meant, says Durand, by Christ and the apostles. Durand's argument is that the Cathars did not make this distinction, and so confused the world of men with that of nature and creation. Durand goes into a more extensive *distinctio* in exploring the different levels of meaning of *mundus*, which can be material, spiritual, heavenly and infernal. The material world is partly the *machina mundi* and partly human nature. The spiritual world is partly the human intellectual world and partly composed of holy people. In turn, the heavenly world is triple, the creating wisdom of God, called the 'first world' by the philosophers, secondly the angels and thirdly eternal life. The infernal world is human injustice and ignorance of God.

Creation and evil

There is no doubt that the central question was the Cathars' belief in the evilness of the *physical* creation. Durand identifies this as the *maxima lis*, the 'great dispute', between the heretics and the *catholici*. He was writing at, or at least referring to, a time when the dispute was still in the open and his rebuttal takes the form of a commentary on the text, with built-in structures of argument for and against stated opinions, together with refutations and solutions of difficulties. The arguments are overwhelmingly interpretations of the Sacred Page, and directed to the underlying single insistence of the Cathars that the world is so obviously an evil place that it must have had an evil creator. At times this feeling overcomes the technicalities of argument: *O insensati literati*! exclaims the Cathar author at one point, directing his insult at the learned Catholics who had opposed the Cathars in disputation, 'O sons of the devil, why do you resist the truth?'[10] Durand's reply includes the doctrine that the physical creation is God's and is good. Durand differs from the Cathars (he says) in being able to separate nature from vice; the *machina mundi* knows that it is created by God, and adores him; God saw that what he had made was good; God made all things in number, weight and measure. Nor is it true, says Durand, that everything in the *machina mundi* is born of lust and so to be despised, for lust is a vice of the mind, and is not substantial within the creature: men, beasts and fish are thus not the results of lust, and still less are the other parts of God's good creation, the sky, sea, earth and its produce. And, adds Durand at a more prosaic level, the Cathars of Aquitaine and 'Gothie' are making a very good living from the fruits of the earth, the material things – largely the products of their prosperous agriculture – that they affect to despise. Durand is here trying to show to the Cathars the *reality* as well as the goodness of the physical creation. Durand has to provide a *distinctio* even for this, to show that God's kingdom *includes material parts*: the body of Christ (in the physical world, which some Cathars denied); the sacred scriptures (including the Old Testament, which most Cathars denied) and the Catholic Church (which all Cathars denied). For Durand, the Church is the *ecclesia militans:* the good, although militant, Church with its Christian soldiers marching onward. In short, what we have here is a Catholic report from a specialist opponent of heresy of the disputes that were waged with the Cathars. The central issue is the evilness of nature and Durand has to find what reasons and authority he can. About a half of the work is taken up with the question of the natural world, and the rest with other aspects of creation. Durand finds his reasons and authority almost entirely within the Sacred Page, but his argument is one in support of which Alain of Lille had already used dialectic. Although part of Durand's argument is natural, or physical, and is used to show that the physical world is good, he does not use Aristotle's nature books.

The Two Principles: introduction for beginners

The most important of the Cathar texts is the *De Duobis Principiis*, the book on the two principles. Dating from about 1230, this is the only Cathar text that survives in its original form. It is not, that is, a collection of fragments selected for refutation by the Catholics. We can guess that the Catholics were most likely Dominicans, or perhaps members of Durand's school.

We can most conveniently look first at that section of it that is addressed to beginners. This is concerned with what we might today call the metaphysics of an alternative theology. Its first concern is to disprove the Catholic attack directed at them, that is, that there is a single omnipotent God. The Cathars argued that God cannot be omnipotent because he cannot lie and cannot destroy himself. A good God cannot produce evil, yet the world abounds in evil; God cannot make another god who is equally eternal and uncreated. It follows, says our Cathar text, that there is another coeternal Principle which is the source of all evil in the world. This Principle is characterized as the power of darkness or the lord of the shadows. The evidence for these arguments is again almost entirely from the Scriptures, and the Old Testament is much used to show the evil characteristics of the prince of darkness. Three examples will do. One is the story in Samuel where God, to punish David's sins, takes away his wives and gives them to his neighbour to sleep with, in the sight of all Israel. Here, says our Cathar text, is a god who encourages adultery and fornication, and who cannot therefore be a single good God. Secondly, elsewhere in the Old Testament the Lord appears as a military strategist, advising Moses on the manner of taking cities by deceit and on the annihilation of their occupants. Third is the story of the 'Egyptian gold'. Our author holds this up as an example of the work of an evil principle, upon whose advice the Jews stole the valuables of their masters.[11] Ironically, 'Egyptian gold' – philosophy – was shortly to be used with great effect upon the Cathars.

The conclusion from a great mass of biblical evidence is that here there is another principle besides God, a principle of evil who like God is eternal. Neither can be seen directly and each is to be judged by his manifestations, the effects of a cause, on earth. The biblical evidence, for example Old Testament accounts of an eternal and diabolical fire, showed to the Cathars that evil has *always* been with us: it is eternal in being without beginning or end.[12] To such an assertion, Aristotle's eternal world could not provide an answer for Catholic use, for it seemed to support rather than deny the infinite pre-existence of the world as they knew it. Such an answer had to come from a Christianized Aristotelianism in which evil was the result of the action of man, a creature beginning and ending within time.

Causality

An examination of the way in which causes have their effects became an important part of the argument as the *only* means of knowing the two principles. 'It should be recognised that no one can show that the evil god or creator exists except from his evil works and his unsteady words' argued the Cathars.[13] The causality is double at a metaphysical level, the good God causing all that is good and the evil principle causing all evil. Evil is associated with darkness and shadows and with the material world and its despicable elements: *de infirmis et egenis elementis istius mundi*. In contrast, the creation of the good God, largely Christ and the New Testament, is characterized by light, the instrument of the true God's causality.

This argument for causality rests on a literal reading of the Sacred Page. It is a direct reading of the Old Testament that leads our Cathar author to deny its allegorical and spiritual meaning. Our author insists indeed that the literal is the reading given to it by the Catholics. As we have seen this is also the language of the commentators on the physical works and of the philosophers and medical men. The Cathars could use a literal reading also to show that the Old Testament God was vengeful. Both positions had counter-arguments, and what we see in the surviving texts is an argument which has been refined in disputation.

The main text of *The Two Principles* handles the argument in a rather different way. The existence of evil is again the central fact, and it is again argued that a purely good and omnipotent God would not generate evil. The Catholic position was that God gave his angels freedom of choice to do good or evil and that Lucifer chose evil. Our Cathar author, objects that, as omnipotent, God would have known from the moment of creating his angels how they would choose in the future, and the fact that one or more would choose evil meant therefore that God had made them imperfect to begin with.

It is again a question of cause and effect: if God is omnipotent then he is the cause of causes and foresees all effects of his causality, including the angels becoming demons. But the angels becoming demons was evil, argues our Cathar, and it follows that God must be the cause of evil. But God could not for the Cathars be the author of both good and evil, which were for them mutally exclusive. It followed that there must be, contending with God, a separate Principle of Evil, the second principle of Cathar dualism. The Catholic reply was that God did not necessarily make his angels choose evil, but gave them free will to serve him or not. The Cathar answer in turn to this was that if God wanted the angels to serve him freely, out of choice, then there was some imperfection, something incomplete in him which was satisfied by the angels doing this. But a cause of all good could not be imperfect, so, said the Cathars, God could not have acted like this in making his angels. The same argument applied to man, and our Cathars could point to texts in the Bible that seemed to prove that God regretted having made man, was grieved by man and so on, and the Cathars argued that God had thus deliberately made himself miserable through His creation. Even the idea that man can serve God for them implied some imperfection in God that man's actions could remedy. This was unthinkable, and the natural conclusion was that God was entirely good, but *limited in his powers*. He was opposed by the Principle of Evil, who tempted God's subjects away and battled against goodness by means of evil. Man's service to God, concluded our Cathar author, was to resist the temptation.

This text bears much evidence that at the time it was written (about 1230) the dispute between the Cathars and the Catholics was in full flow. We cannot be sure that the Catholic position was largely argued by Dominicans, but it seems reasonable to suppose so. The arguments of the Catholics are here put forward and resolved; objections are further raised and again solved: these are no doubt actual arguments that were put forward in public, and the author of this Cathar text complains of the loud behaviour of the opposing and surrounding Catholics: *nostri adversarii, dicentes ante et retro vociferantes, clamarent, dicentes* ... The subject is still the free will of the angels and the argument is all about causality: God as the cause of causes must have known what the angels would do, and they had no free will. Assume that God is omnipotent and good, then anyway the angels could not have chosen evil because evil did not exist, having no cause in God. But, continues the text, nothing can exist without a cause. Strikingly, this is illustrated by quotations from a non-Biblical source. Amongst the many hundreds of Sacred-Page readings used to support the Cathar arguments, here are quotations in technical language from another source. Here is the passage:

> But this [evil existing without a cause] would seem to be impossible, that is, that anything can begin without a cause, as it is written: 'For whatever happens, it is impossible for it not to have a cause'. And again: 'Everything that goes from potency to effect needs a cause by which it is drawn to the effect'. And even that which was, according to them [the Catholics] its cause, that is, good, needs it less than that which was not, that is, evil, as it is certainly written: 'It is necessary for something to be before it can act'. It must be clearly understood that if a cause remains in precisely the state it was before then nothing will emerge from it other than happened before; for every action which begins is because of the novelty of something, as it is written: 'For when something is acting that was not acting, this necessarily happens on account of the novelty of something'. It is therefore to be understood, because if the dispositions of the agent remain as they were and nothing new happens to the agent, either within or outside itself up to that point, then there will not be for the agent any 'action of being' more than any 'of not being', but Non-Being remains for ever. For just as something emerges from diversity, so the same thing endures by identity. Truly, even if without free-will none of the angels could have sinned....[14]

So in the middle of a series of heated exchanges between Cathars and (probably) Dominicans about God's causal relationships to his angels, one of the Cathars has seized upon what looks very much like a commentary on Aristotle's *Physics* or *Metaphysics* as an authority to match the Sacred Page.

This is very important. The learned heretic, perhaps John of Lugio, knew that peripatetic philosophy had an authority of its own, not, certainly, equal to that of the Sacred Page, but able to stand beside it and endorse it. He saw that 'natural reason' was common to all men and could not be refuted on the grounds that parts of the Scriptures could be – that they were not sacred and so revealed nothing. He also saw the power of 'reasons from nature' where nature was Aristotle's *physis* and part of a sophisticated treatment of causality and existence.

If one were to summarize Aristotle's philosophy of nature in a sentence, it would be 'a search for causes', and its power in argument was as clear to our Cathar author as it shortly came to be to the Dominicans. We shall see that their response centred on these points. The space devoted to the central topic of causality by our Cathar author and his frequent demolitions of opposing argument strongly suggest that this was a very hotly disputed point. In the text of the *Two Principles* the argument is slowly and systematically expounded, and our author has paused at the impossibility of an omnipotent God as the cause of causes causing evil. The disputation underlying the form of the treatise allows us to see that the noisy Catholic reply to this was to *reject* the argument, which was based partly at least on an Aristotelian view of causality, as the mere words of philosophers. From the words of St Paul the Catholics warned: 'Beware lest any man spoil you through philosophy and vain deceit, after the tradition of men, after the elements of the world, and not through Christ.' It was of course precisely with the 'elements of this world', *elementa istius mundi* that Aristotle's philosophy of nature and its causality was concerned. But as we have seen above, it was also to the 'elements of this world' that the Cathars' attention was drawn in trying to prove that the world had been made by the evil Principle. Here we see the learned Cathars using Aristotle's physical principles in their arguments. To the Catholic reader of the *Two Principles*, the Cathars seemed much too philosophical, as they had to Praepositinus. Clearly Aristotle's philosophy was available if wanted, but the Catholic argument as represented in this text – and thus from the Cathar's viewpoint – was apparently based wholly on readings of the Sacred Page that are higher than the literal.

Nature and learning

In the first place then, the Catholics used the same kind of Sacred Page arguments that had been employed by Durand. But they greatly extended their use of natural arguments. It seems likely that this at first was simply to counter the heretics' natural arguments, which so readily centred on the nature of the world. The friars' purposes after all were theological, and all arguments they employed were subordinate to the end of overcoming heresy and strengthening true doctrine.

The Cathar *perfecti* were, as we have seen, learned men. Perhaps this use of natural arguments was related to the special standing of the Sapiental books of the Old Testament on both sides. On the Catholic side, we have already noted first, a shift towards a literal reading of the Sacred Page within the schools (and literal readings moved easily to 'natural' readings), and secondly that monks and others made attempts to draw out a whole philosophy from the Bible, to counter the growing interest in pagan philosophy. In such schemes the Sapiental books, particularly Ecclesiastes, was held to be equivalent to *physica*, 'natural' philosophy.[15] (We have also seen that Alexander Neckam's book on the natures of things was an introduction to a commentary on Ecclesiastes.) The Dominicans paid special attention to the Sapientals as the source of true wisdom, the wisdom that saves. As for the Cathars, some of them rejected the Old Testament as the Devil's work *except* for the Sapiental books,[16] while others, still dualists, accepted the Old Testament and relied on the Sapientals for natural arguments. So there were biblical as well as physical reasons for the use of 'natural reasons'. Catholic opponents like Moneta of Cremona[17] and Peter the Martyr[18] make clear that arguments from nature were a sizeable part of the Cathars' armoury.

It is with Moneta that we are particularly concerned. He was a Dominican and felt a special spiritual commitment to Dominic and his fight against the Cathars, which he continued. He was also exposed to the 'natural reasons' of the Cathars and reacted in a characteristically Dominican fashion. His *Adversus Catharos et Valdenses libri quinque*, of about 1241, 'Five Books against the Cathars and Waldensians', is set out in disputation form, with passages of the Dominican view of Cathar belief and proof being followed by the Dominican *solutiones*. Although this is less direct evidence of a Cathar text than Durand's textual citations, it still preserves the for-and-against form of the disputations between the two sides. Important of course are the distinctions of 'world' – its meaning is limited, says Moneta (as Durand had also said) to 'the world of men' when the Bible appears to say that the world is evil. But Moneta does more than make Sacred-Page and dialectical *distinctiones* and draws special attention to the Cathars' use of natural reasons. Moreover, he replies in kind, arguing *naturaliter* and *physice*. One major Cathar tactic he has to rebut is their argument for the existence of the two principles *on the authority of Aristotle*. From Moneta's text we can see that the Cathars had taken the Aristotelian phrase 'contraries are the principles of contraries' as proof that good and evil, being contraries, must have contrary principles. Moneta's reply makes use of the Augustinian notion of evil, but he goes beyond Durand's use of it – that is, a human and voluntary turning away from God – and it is now expressed in terms of the Aristotelian notion of *privation*: evil is privation from God when people use their free will to turn away from Him. Moneta explicitly chooses Aristotle as his authority and expresses himself in Aristotelian terminology.[19] Anything with Form and Matter, argues Moneta, is composite, and single true principle must be unbounded by Form. For this reason it is infinite and necessarily single – there cannot be two separate principles. Moneta then, seems to have been drawn into using Aristotle because the Cathars were already using Aristotle in a development of the argument about causality.

The same may be said of our next Dominican, Peter the Martyr, if he indeed is the author of another *Summa*. His use of Aristotle is much greater than that of Moneta. Peter became a Preacher in Bologna (where he had studied) in 1220–21, before Dominic died, and devoted himself to the suppression of heresy. Like Moneta, he also had experience of the Italian version of the heresy; he was sent by Gregory IX on such errands to Milan and Como. His martyrdom was at the hands of the heretics in 1252. The *Summa* dates from about 1235 and employs some of the important Aristotelian *libri naturales*: *Physics, On Heaven and Earth, On the Soul.*[20] Like the work of Moneta, this text is set out in disputation form, with the opinions of the *respondens* (the Dominican) alternating with those of the *objiciens* (the Cathar). Again the form seems designed to meet actual points raised in the early days of open dispute between the two sides. During such disputations and the war of texts undoubtedly arguments were refined and new ones introduced. It was probably during the course of this that 'natural' and then Aristotelian arguments were first used in two stages. The first stage might well have been the use of what Peter calls *rationes naturales* during the use of the argument from causality: that created things could have only one ultimate cause. There is some evidence the argument that the physical world is *good* came later, a second stage. Peter, at all events, uses only the first, arguing in the first place for the singleness of God *per rationes naturales de uno principio*: every composite thing has a composer, every moved thing a mover, for which there can be only a single source. We shall meet below the argument about the goodness of the natural world.

Cathar learning

Having looked at some of the texts of the Cathars, how can we summarize their learning? This was not a peasants' heresy. The Cathars' leaders were learned men. They preached their mission abroad and defended their religion with the recognized and formal procedures of disputation. The grudging admission of their opponents that they were 'wordy' must mean that they were difficult to defeat in argument. (So difficult indeed that the Catholics ultimately turned to force.) In order to attack the heretics' learning and arguments the two new Orders of clergy designed specifically to campaign against the Cathars, Durand's and Dominic's, made learning their main weapon. Durand represented to the Pope that his group consisted mostly of learned clerics and would tackle the Cathars by 'reading, exhortation, teaching and disputation'.[21] There is evidence of tracts produced by his school. Dominic's diffused *studium* of Preachers fought their battle in a similar way and also by preaching.

The Cathars' learning was, like that of the Dominicans, very much concerned with their beliefs, and was similarly defended by use of the pages they regarded as sacred. But their traditions were different from those of the Dominicans and other Catholics of the West. The Cathars had historical links with Constantinople, and their famous council of St Félix (sometime between 1167 and 1177) was presided over by a 'pope' from Constantinople, Niquinta. Rayner Sacconi recorded that there was both a Latin and a Greek Cathar church in Constantinople, the former with about 50 active members; he reckoned that there might be a total of about 500 active members in Cathar churches in Greek areas.[22] Cathars were widespread in Italy, in parts of which Greek was spoken. The setting up of a Latin Empire in Byzantium in 1209 must have brought Greek philosophies to the attention of the West,[23] or the new Emperor and the Pope would not have found it desirable to set up a Latin *studium* in Constantinople. Moreover, theological disputes in Constantinople had already made the differences between the two sides evident early in the previous century.[24] In a word, the Cathars – the word itself is from Greek for 'pure' – had reason to be somewhat Greek in their beliefs. In the western world, where the newly uncovered philosophizing writings of the Greek Fathers contrasted somewhat uncomfortably with the traditional meditation and grace of the Latin cloister, this must have added to the suspicion with which the heretics were viewed.

Physicians were often seen as the main agents spreading the heresy.[25] We have seen that it was just this group who were interested in pagan philosophy. Often in the West they were at the forefront of mining this Egyptian gold from Arabic sources; but with Byzantine connnections Cathar doctors may well have been more aware than the men of the West of Aristotelian doctrines that could, additionally, support their religion. It looks possible that the Cathars' learning, like their Bibles, contained materials of eastern and heterodox origin. A natural, physical and 'literal' reading of the world, based on Aristotle, could readily be used to reinforce an understanding of causality that existed between the Evil Principle and the physical world. This is what the Cathars insisted on in their texts, before the Dominicans had thought of using Aristotle to show the goodness of the physical world. Indeed, the Cathars seem to have been doing this while the Dominicans were still arguing in tropological ways from the Sacred Page. Certainly, from the point of view of the Cathar author of the book on the Two Principles, the Catholic position was entirely based on the Sacred Page. This is why the Catholics' first reaction was to group the Cathars with the philosophers and regard them with the old western suspicion of 'the mere elements of this world' and of Greek philosophy. Moreover, in the 1230s, when the book on the Two Principles was being argued about and when the Dominicans we have discussed were meeting the Cathar's arguments from nature, there was a ban on reading Aristotle's nature books in force in Paris. For masters, scholars and others these books may well have been seen as unsuitable material from which to construct a reply to the heretics.

But Dominicans in Paris and more especially elsewhere were probably free to read the *libri naturales* of Aristotle. Moreover, philosophy, in being *dialectical*, had one considerable strategic advantage: it could overcome a stalemate in a battle where the weapons were otherwise Sacred-Page distinctions. The Cathars had little common ground with the Catholics in the case of Old Testament distinctions, and could not feel their force; and in any case the Sacred-Page method of making *distinctiones* could supply an indefinite number of examples and counter-examples with the result that neither side could convince the other. But dialectic (and, later, 'natural' arguments) relied on human reason and human authority which provided common ground to both sides; dialectical *distinctiones* could not be multiplied indefinitely and were a sharper if less weighty weapon.

In this way the first Catholic reaction to the Cathars – to classify them as pagan philosophers, like old Faustus – could not succeed in a newly dialectical age. It was necessary to examine and refute the arguments about causality on a shared ground of dialectical philosophy. The Dominicans did so, denying an evil chain of causality and denying on metaphysical grounds the possibility of two ultimate principles, before realizing that Aristotle's nature books could be used to show that the world was good.

Much the same story of a move away from Sacred-Page distinction to a philosophical consideration of causes and ultimately of the goodness of the physical world is clear from the near-contemporary text, T*he Art of the Catholic Faith*. This book has been attributed to Alain of Lille[26] and more recently to Nicholas of Amiens.[27] It opens with an explanation of the difficulties of meeting Sacred-Page *distinctiones* with others: the heretics reject or pervert them (that is, they use others). In place of this technique, the 'art' (the title is *De Arte seu Articulus Catholice Fidei*) of the Catholic faith is, like Alain of Lille's *Regulae de Sacra Theologia*, dialectical. Like Alain too, Nicholas can base his dialectical arguments on self-evident truths, agreed among all men, *communes animi conceptiones*.[28] But Nicholas' argument is also *physical*. The language is that of the nature books of Aristotle – matter, form, substance, accident, generation, corruption and above all, causality: nothing is its own cause; whatever is the cause of a cause is the cause of the caused; there is a supreme cause of all lesser causes; the supreme cause is not composed and has no form or properties. Ascending with Aristotelian language to the Christian image of God, the argument now descends to the goodness of creation, with an emphasis that can only be seen as another blow at Cathar dualism. As William of Auvergne said,[29] God does not have qualities and his essential goodness is an inseparable aspect of His existence. It follows for Nicholas that God as *summum bonum* made a good creation; everything – substance and accident alike – is *necessarily* good, if only in existing; the *machina mundi* loves its creator, and man has in addition a rational appreciation of His works.

Nature and creation: all things bright and beautiful

The Dominicans found a very simple way of proving that the material world was good: 'Nature' was equated with 'creation'.

The equation was a little time in forming. As we have seen, in the teaching of the twelfth-century schools the late-classical 'nature' as a generative principle (in authors like Pliny and Galen) could not of course be presented as having any degree of autonomy. Such 'nature' in a Christian world with an omnipotent Creator could only exist as allegory or in direct classical quotation. And at the same time most attention was given to the spiritual side of what the Creator had created. For both these reasons 'nature' often simply had its local meaning, the nature-of-things. But now two circumstances drew attention to the physical side of creation: the need to refute the Cathar belief that it was evil, and the new theology with its systematic exposition (including that of Genesis, the story of creation), its new dialectic and its need for literal exposition. Physical creation now became 'nature' in the sense of 'the natural world'. Mother Nature could now be 'distinguished' from the Nature of Things. The twelfth-century *distinctio* between 'nature' (the celestial regions) and 'the works of nature' (the sublunary world) was forgotten, and all became nature-creation. The new thirteenth-century distinction was between *natura naturans*, God, and *natura naturata*, creation. *Natura* as a whole was Aristotle's *physis*, Christianized. The equivalence extended even to Aristotle's description of the active and passive aspects of *physis*, form and matter: nature too was double.[30]

To put it another way, the single *scientia* that some twelfth-century men saw in the astrology-medicine-Plato amalgam described in Chapter 4, in which God's will for the sublunar world was achieved by the agency of the animated celestial bodies, gave way to a world in which God achieved His purposes throughout nature by Aristotelian causality.

To understand this properly, we need to look in some detail at how

Aristotle's *libri naturales* were used to combat Catharism and ultimately to provide the material for Dominican natural philosophy and for that of the schools. What was it in Aristotle's nature books that could be used as a resource for those who wished to demonstrate that nature was *good*? Aristotle's philosophy was characterized above as a search for causes. This was certainly how it was seen by people in the thirteenth century like Albertus Magnus, particularly when he was failing to live up to Aristotle's methods.[31] Aristotle held that in general natural change – the operation of these causes – was *good*, first in that the Potentiality of matter was being fulfilled by the Actuality of Form in the process of informing. The goodness of the process, according to Aristotle, was greater with the greater complexity of the form, so that there was a hierarchy of excellence from inorganic things and imperfect animals to man, whose soul was the most complex of natural forms.

Secondly, Aristotle had derived all motion in the sublunar sphere, all natural change, ultimately from a single unmoved mover in the heavens. This was readily adapted for Christian purposes: the unmoved mover became God, and his singleness provided the Dominicans with another weapon against the dualism of the Cathars. The chain of causality, by which all local changes are ultimately referred back to a single cause, was as we have seen already being used against the Cathar system of double causality (good and evil) and it was easily reinforced with the Aristotelian argument.

Thirdly, of the four Aristotelian causes it was necessary to emphasize the Final Cause, the purpose or goal of the natural change, and this was readily done by expressing it as ultimately God's will, which was necessarily good. Thus for example in medical commentaries we find the Aristotelian principle of the eternity of the world replaced by God the Creator who, however, although omnipotent and creating *ex nihilo*, nevertheless uses the Aristotelian material and formal causes to produce the four Aristotelian elements.[32] It will be recalled that one of the Cathar texts spoke disparagingly of the poor and contemptible elements of the physical and hence evil world. It is precisely the Aristotelian justification of the study of the less noble parts of the physical world that was used in the thirteenth century to defeat the Cathars and create natural philosophy.

Fourthly, the *certainty* of some knowledge made its possession a good thing. We quoted in Chapter 1 a well-known passage in the books about animals where Aristotle defends the study of even the insides of animals as being worthy of a philosopher, and part of the philosopher's task. The certainty of the knowledge so gained from its close-at-hand sources is its chief justification: it is *good* for the philosopher to know such things. There is, says Aristotle, something marvellous and beautiful in all natural things, even animals; did not Heraclitus think there were gods even in the kitchen? Writing about animals was important for Dominicans in the thirteenth century – for example to Albertus Magnus – to make the case that they were part of the single good God's good creation, nature.

In summary, let us return to this central point, that nature was identified with Creation. This is directly concerned with what the Catholics saw as the central issue between themselves and the Cathars: the existence of evil (and hence of an evil god). Durand de Huesca had said, as we have seen, that the Cathars could not separate nature from evil. As Durand was clearly aware, to make nature the creation of the one good God was to make it good itself. It was as necessary for Durand as for his fellows opposing John of Lugio and his *Two Principles* to prove that nature was good, but neither saw the usefulness of Aristotle for this. It did not take the Dominicans long to see Aristotle in this way. Apart from what we have already seen, most of our evidence for this comes in connection with evidence of education and re-education in the new *studia generalia* and in the *studia* of the friars themselves. These are examined in the next chapter.

Finally, we must make a 'distinction' between the forms of the heresy. We have noted that Catharism was widespread in Languedoc, and present also in Italy and Germany. It was not uniform in its beliefs and strict dualism seems to have been characteristic of the form in southern France, particularly after the Council of St Félix. From the attacks on it by the Catholics of Italy we can guess that the Italian heresy contained different emphases. In particular the 'world' of God and of the Evil Principle was often distinguished to mean 'alternative world', as if the Italian Cathars believed in the parallel existence of a good and an evil world containing the same kind of things, including the physical. Their opponents made much of the physical problems of dual worlds: is one contained inside the other? Are they contiguous? If so, is there space where such spheres cannot touch?[33] There were also differences of opinion on whether the Devil had created the evil world *ex nihilo* or had rearranged (into elements) the matter originally made by the good God, and had peopled his world with souls stolen from God's creation. Either of these views or a combination of them could not be opposed as effectively as Catharism in Provence and Languedoc by the use of Aristotle's natural works to show that the single physical world was good and could only have had a single, good, creator.[34] Our story of natural philosophy and the friars accordingly has its focus in Provence and Languedoc on the one hand and Paris on the other.

Notes

1. A. Dondaine, *Un Traité Néo-Manichéen du xiiiè Siècle: Le Liber De Duobus Principiis*, Rome (Institutum Historicum FF. Praedicatorium), 1939. This doctrinal exposition is matched by a surviving fragment of Cathar ritual, written in parallel columns of Latin and Provençale, for the use of the Cathars of Languedoc. We shall not be concerned with it here.
2. See also the discussion of the changes in Cathar belief from the twelfth to the thirteenth century by D. Radcliff-Umstead, 'The Catharists and the Failure of Community', *Mediaevalia*, **1**, 1975, pp. 64–87.
3. C. Thouzellier, ed., *Une Somme Anti-Cathare. Le Liber Contra Manicheos de Durand de Huesca*, Louvain, 1964. See also A. Dondaine, 'Durand de Huesca et la polémique anti-cathare', *Archivum Fratrum Praedicatorum*, (hereafter *AFP*), **29**, 1959, pp. 228-76.
4. F. Sanjek, 'Raynerius Sacconi O.P. Summa de Catharis', *AFP*, **44**, 1974, pp. 31–60 (with an improved text).
5. J. Garvin and J. Corbett, *The Summa Contra Haereticos Ascribed to Praepositinus of Cremona*, University of Notre Dame Press, 1985.
6. See D.A. Callus, 'Introduction of Aristotelian Learning to Oxford', *Proceedings of the British Academy*, 1943, pp. 229-81.
7. See the appendix to Garvin and Corbett, *Praepositinus*.
8. Thouzellier, *Durand*, p. 87.
9. Habitation, said Durand, could be related to grace (God be with you) and for example, God could be said to 'dwell' in Mary in three ways, essentially, by grace, and potentially.
10. O vos insensati litterati, quis vos fascinavit ista non intelligere? O pleni omni dolo et omni fallacia, filii diaboli, inimici crucis christi et omnis iusticie, cur non desistis veritati resistere? O ceci, duces cecorum ... . See A. Dondaine, 'Durand de Huesca et la polémique anti-cathare', *AFP*, **29**, 1959, pp. 228-–76; 246. Also Thouzellier, *Durand*, ch. 14 of the text.
11. Quod autem supradictus dominus et creator per vim fecisset rapere aliena et causa comoditatis thesauros Egyptiorum ... Dondaine, *Liber de Duobus Principiis*, p. 127.
12. Dondaine, *Liber de Duobus Principiis*, p. 124.
13. Quare sciendum est quod deum malum esse vel creatorem aliter ostendere nemo potest nisi ex operibus eius malis et ex instabilibus verbis suis. Sed dico creatorem illum non esse verum qui creavit et fecit visibilia istius mundi. Dondaine, *Liber de Duobus Principiis*, p. 125.
14. ... quamvis hoc videatur impossibile, scilicet quod aliquid possit incipere sine causa; sicut scriptum est: 'Quicquid enim cepit id non habere causam impossibile est'. Et iterum: 'Omne enim quod exit de potentia ad effectum eget causa qua trahatur ad effectum'. Et etiam id quod erat secundum illos eius causa, scilicet bonum, minus eget quam id quod non erat, idest malum, quamvis scriptum sit: 'Oportet aliquid prius esse quam agat'. Et etiam manifeste sciendum est, quod si causa permaneret in sua dispositione penitus sicut erat prius, quod non proveniret aliud ex ea quam fiebat prius; omnis enim actio que incipit est propter novitatem alicuius rei, sicut scriptum est: 'Cum enim quis sit agens qui non fuit agens, necesse est hoc fieri propter novitatem alicuius rei'. Quare sciendum est, quia si dispositiones agentis permanerent ita ut erant et non fieret agenti novum aliquid nec in se nec extra se usque tunc, profecto non esset agenti pocius

actio essendi quam non essendi, sed non esse permaneret incessabiliter. Nam sicut ex diversitate aliud provenit, ita ex identitate idem durat. Verum etsi absque libero arbitrio nullus angelorum peccare potuisset ... Dondaine, *Liber de Duobus Principiis*, p. 93. Dondaine was unable to find the precise source of these quotations and concluded they came from an Arabic commentary. Dondaine, *Liber de Duobus Principiis*, p. 17.

15. See for example B. Smalley, 'Some Thirteenth-Century Commentaries on the Sapiental Books', *Dominican Studies*, **2**, 1949, pp. 318–55; **3**, 1950, pp. 236–74.
16. See B. Smalley, 1949, p. 324.
17. Moneta of Cremona, *Adversus Catharos et Valdenses Libri Quinque*, Rome, 1743. The text has strong relationships to that of one Georgius' attack on the Paterines. See S. Wessley, 'The Composition of Georgius' Disputatio inter Catholicum et Paterinum Hereticum', *AFP*, 1978, pp. 55–61.
18. T. Kaeppelli, 'Une somme contra la hérétiques de Pierre Martyr(?)' *AFP*, **17**, 1947, pp. 295–335.
19. Moneta, *Adversus Catharos*, p. 24r.
20. Kaeppelli (note 18 above) pp. 301–3.
21. Dondaine, 'Durand de Huesca', p. 237. The *schola nostra* was composed *ex magna parte clerici et pene omnes literati.*
22. Dondaine, *Liber De Duobus Principiis*, p. 70.
23. Perhaps this is what is intended by Anselm of Alexandria in his brief history of the heresy, the *Tractatus De Hereticiis*, when he said that the heresy, reaching Constantinople from Bulgaria along trade routes, was spread to the *Francigenae* who had come to Constantinople 'to subdue land'. The resulting 'bishop of the Latins' and another of the Franks guided the growth of the Western form of the heresy. See A Dondaine, 'La hiérarchie Cathare en Italie', *AFP*, xx, 1950, pp. 234–324 and in the collection, *Les Hérésies et l'Inquisition, xiie-xiiie Siècles. Documents et Etudes*, ed. Y. Dossat, Aldershot, 1990.
24. See Chapter 4, note 1.
25. E. Peters, *Heresy and Authority in Medieval Europe*, London, 1980 p.195.
26. It is listed under Alain's name in Migne, *PL*, vol. 210, p. 594.
27. See C.H. Lohr, 'The pseudo-Aristotelian Liber de Causis ... ' in Kraye et al. *Pseudo Aristotle ...* , p. 53.
28. As pointed out by Lohr the taking of 'common conceptions of the soul' as a starting point in argument can be seen as a geometrical method. Lohr adds that Nicholas was addressing himself to Muslims as well as the heretics, in which case of course, Sacred Page *distinctiones* had no use at all. This is equally true of the *De Arte seu Articulis Catholice Fidei* of Alain, who discusses the 'ridiculous doctrines of Mohammed' in his prologue. Migne, *PL*, vol. 210, p. 594.
29. William of Auvergne is discussed below.
30. J.A. Weisheipl, 'Aristotle's Concept of Nature: Avicenna and Aquinas', in L.D. Roberts, ed., *Approaches to Nature in the Middle Ages*, New York, 1982, pp. 138 ff.
31. See below for Albertus' treatment of the Aristotelian text on animals.
32. See R.K. French, 'Gentile da Foligno and the via medicorum', in J.D. North and J.J. Roche, *The Light of Nature*, Dordrecht, 1985, pp. 21–34; 24.
33. For example, Moneta of Cremona, *Adversus Catharos*, p. 3. The 'double

world' form of Cathar dualism is also attacked by Praepositinus: see J. Garvin and J. Corbett, *The Summa Contra Haereticos Ascribed to Praepositinus of Cremona*, University of Notre Dame Press, 1985, p. 247.

34. Some Italian Cathars – and Paterines – believed like their Provencal counterparts in a strict division between the good and bad halves of a world, rather than in two parallel worlds. See P. Ilarino da Milano, 'Fr. Gregorio O.P., Vescovo di Fano et la "Disputatio inter Catholicum et Paterinum Hereticum"', *Aevum*, **14**, 1940, pp. 85–140. See also R. Manselli, 'Per la storia dell'eresia ... ', which is concerned with Bonacursus' *Manifestatio Haeresi Catharorum*, the text of which is given by P. Ilarino da Milano, 'La 'Manifestatio heresis catarorum quam fecit Bonacursus' secondo il cod. Otob. Lat.136 della biblioteca Vaticana', *Aevum*, **12**, 1938, pp. 281–333. See also P. Ilarino da Milano, 'Il "liber supra stella" del Piacentino Salvo Burci contro i catari e altre correnti ereticali', *Aevum*, **16**, 1942, pp. 272–319.

CHAPTER SEVEN

Conquest and re-education

In previous chapters we have looked at the beliefs and texts of the Cathars. We have also seen part of the reaction of the Catholics and particularly of the Dominicans to those texts and beliefs. But for the Dominicans and their view of the world – including the natural world – to prevail, more than argument was needed. We must return to the military events that enforced the Dominicans' arguments upon the doomed Troubadorean civilization.

The crusade

Raymond of Toulouse, Marquis of Provence, was being difficult. Under pressure from the Pope, he flirted with orthodoxy, heresy and excommunication.[1] He was held to be implicated in the ambush and murder (in 1207) of the papal legate, Pierre de Castlenau, who had been discussing the question with him.[2] Innocent III began to see that while the Cistercian campaign of preaching might bring back the poor to orthodoxy, it had little hope of reaching the aristocracy. The way to rescue them from heresy was by military force and politics. As early as 1204–05 Innocent reminded King Philip Augustus that he was entitled to deprive of their fiefs vassals who sheltered heretics. As the Inquisitors were to point out, heresy and Manicheeism in particular had their penalties already established in the legal codices.[3] But Philip was in no position to take the hint, because he was fighting the Plantagenets and needed the support of his vassals. But in 1207 Innocent was talking to the main feudatories of the north, that is, of feudal France: the Duke of Burgundy and the Counts of Bar, Dreux, Champagne and Blois.

The objective was nothing less than crushing the Cathar heresy by means of a fully blown crusade. The crusade was preached abroad by the Cistercians, and the same indulgences were offered as those on an oriental crusade. It was indeed a crusade that *replaced* one to the Holy Land, which gives some idea of the scale of the thing.[4] The crusade was preached especially in the north, and by 1208, despite some hesitation by Philip, their overlord, the combatants marched south under Simon de Montfort, Earl of Leicester. The objective of the Church in Rome was the defeat of the heresy, but the northern feudal barons were interested in territorial gains in the rich, commercial and independent south. The ultimate result was the disappearance of a medieval culture which had produced the Troubadours. This took about 20 years to happen, the political end of the Provençal culture coming in the Treaty of Paris in 1229, the year of the foundation of the ideologically correct university of Toulouse (which we shall meet below).

The course of the crusade itself did not run smoothly. The massacres inflicted by the over-anxious northern barons caused widespread reaction.

> Que lo coms de Montfort remas en Carcasses
> Per destruire los mals e que i mezes los bes,
> E casses les eretges els rotiers else Valdes
> E pobles los catolicos els Normands els Frances.[5]

sang the Troubadours mournfully of Simon de Montfort's destruction of the heretics in Carcassonne.

The southern lords temporized, Simon de Montfort died in 1218, and by 1220 the crusade seemed to be over, having caused little more than material destruction. By then too Innocent III was dead, and the new king of the north, Louis VIII invaded the territory of the new count of the south, Raymond VII. A Treaty of 1227 held unsatisfactorily for ten years. From about 1232 the castle of Montségur was the final refuge of the few heretics left.

> El pog de Montsegur fo per aital bastitz
> Qu'el les pogues defendre, els hi a cossentitz.[6]

Nevertheless, they were numerous enough to rebel in 1239. Their defeat led to further gains by the French king against Raymond of Toulouse. The last flourish of the Cathars was in 1242 when a group of inquisitors was ambushed and killed. The reaction by the French troops and the now orthodox Raymond was final. One of their weapons was a large new trebuchet – a catapult designed by Bishop Durand of Albi, apparently the same Durand whose verbal attacks against the Cathars we have examined. His trebuchet could throw missiles weighing 40 kilograms every 20 minutes and if necessary for weeks, its weighed stones always hitting the same spot.[7] It was known to the Troubadours as

> El trabuquet, que brize lo mur sarrasinor ...[8]

In 1244, with its help, the fortress of Montségur finally fell. When the beseiged Cathars saw that their defeat was inevitable, they all took the *consolamentum*, the final oath of commitment, even though they knew that in the eyes of the Inquisitors it made them irreclaimable and irrevocably condemned to the fire, into which they all calmly walked.

7.1 The trebuchet at the siege of Carcassonne

7.2 Montségur, last stronghold of the Cathars

The Inquisition

Physically, the heresy had been put down, but the Inquisitors remained fully occupied for another half century, determined that nothing like this should be allowed to recur. The early Inquisition provides some more evidence of Cathar beliefs and the Dominican reaction, and we need to examine it briefly. The Church's Inquisition had been set up by Lucius III in 1184.[9] Innocent III used it extensively in dealing with the Cathars, declaring in 1199 that heretics were the equivalent of traitors under Roman law. By the time of the crusade, he held that temporal rulers were under an obligation to root out heresy in their domains. The form of the Inquisition that dealt with the Cathars was originated by Cardinal Hugolino, friend of Dominic and later Pope Gregory IX; it remained an agent of the papal Curia. The threat of Catharism remained indeed up to and beyond the time of Gregory IX, who in 1231 enacted even more severe penalties for heretics and called upon the prior of the Dominican community of Regensberg to organize an inquisitorial tribunal that would be answerable to the Pope but *not* to the local bishops. That is, like the Dominicans themselves, it was to be a direct agent of the papacy.

Inquisitors were generally Dominicans, partly because of the stamp Dominic had put upon his Order, partly because the Dominicans were already the Pope's free-ranging agents, and partly because as they were learned they were in a position to question suspects effectively. Most of the questions routinely asked of suspects were about their associates and physical movements – did they attend secret meetings? were they befriended by the heretics? But when they were asked about belief a routine question was 'What do the heretics say about the creation of the visible world?'[10] Do you believe there are two eternal Gods, one good, the other evil? In Italy, in accordance with the local form of the heresy, they asked 'Do you believe that each of these has his own kingdom?'[11] Other questions were about the nature of Christ and the resurrection of the body. Very few verbatim reports of interrogation survive. One Peter Garcias of Toulouse was talking of his Cathar beliefs to two Catholics, but unknown to him Inquisitors were hidden in the room, and Peter's scathing remarks on the law of Moses, that is his contempt for the Old Testament, and his statements about the Two Principles and the evilness of creation led to his undoing.[12] 'Is this visible world', asked the Inquisitors of another Peter in 1266, 'the moon and the stars that are in it; and this earth likewise and the things that are on it, like food and wine, and human bodies and other animals that we see with our fleshly eyes: are all these of the kingdom of the omnipotent God, and made and created by the good God Himself?' The obstinate Peter replied 'All visible things are from the kingdom of the Devil, and all the foregoing have been made by the Devil'.[13] As late as 1307 one Stephen of Proaudo was caught by the Inquisitors denying creation.[14] Thus it is clear from the Inquisitors' questions that the central question for the Catholics was the singleness of God and the goodness of His creation. The same may be seen in the sacrament for those converting from the Cathar heresy, who had to swear by one God alone, one essence, virtue, power and majesty; one nature, one inseparable and discrete Person, the Creator of all Creatures, the unborn, uncreated Father, the Founder of everything visible and invisible, the Maker of heaven and earth, *celi et terre*.[15]

The Inquisition roused a great deal of resentment, not only for its excessive vigour against the heretics, but because it was seen in the more or less autonomous towns of Provence and Languedoc as an infringement of their liberties. As Inquisitors, the Dominicans too came to be recognized as agents of the Roman Curia, acting if necessary without the co-operation of the local bishops. Even as late as the 1270s the Inquisition was still fully occupied with heresy, and so savage was it 20 years later that the townspeople of Béziers and Carcassonne physically expelled the Inquisitors. Moreover, Cathar bishops took the opportunity to return, from Lombardy, and new gatherings of the heretics took place. The heresy was not finally suppressed by the French until about 1330.

Dominic and the universities

There was, then, a danger of the recrudescence of heresy throughout the thirteenth century, and the Inquisition and the Dominicans were not idle. The establishment of the university of Toulouse as an anti-Cathar seat of learning was the Church's attempt to correct the ideology of the region. It went hand in hand with military defeat of the heretics, just as more modern military conquests have been followed up by ideological correction in places of learning. The ideology was partly that of Aristotle. Very similar was the attempt by Innocent III to set up an ideologically correct school in Constantinople. Here again the Roman Church had guided a military crusade (Innocent had diverted the Fourth Crusade from its original objectives and had set up a Latin Empire in Byzantium) against a different and therefore threatening kind of Christianity; again, the ideology of the victors was to be imposed on the vanquished, and Innocent was quick, in 1205, to act in consort with the new Emperor, Balduinus, to ask some masters and scholars of Paris to go to Constantinople to reform the *studium*. This 're-education' was required in order to submit the original orthodoxy of the Eastern Church to a Roman orthodoxy;[16] ironically perhaps, the westerners wanted to re-educate the Greeks.

Toulouse was the centre of the Cathar heresy and the base of its aristocratic defenders, the counts of Toulouse. We have seen that Dominic had set up a house there even before his Order received papal recognition. We have seen too that Innocent at first kept Dominic to Augustinian rules, and that Dominic successfully prevailed in 1216 upon Innocent's successor, Honorius III, to recognize the 'house' in Toulouse as an order of canons regular with a special mission of preaching. So the Dominican Order was founded in a place of great significance in the story of the Cathar heresy. It took shape, as an Order of Preachers – *Praedicatores* – in two general chapters in 1220 and 1221 in Bologna. Dominic the Christian soldier strove to give his followers 'arms to fight the devil', the 'Old Adversary' as he told the nuns of Madrid.[17] Nowhere, of course, was the devil so obvious as in his embodiment in the evil Principle of Catharism. This is why Foulques, bishop of Toulouse, had been at first so supportive of the preaching of Dominic's group, directed against the heresy. But Dominic, like his biographers[18] saw that the forces at work in Toulouse were only an extreme form of those elsewhere. The people of the new towns could be readily reached by the heresy and were in a position to react in a way different from a dispersed rustic population. The danger was clear and prompted a reaction from the fourth Lateran Council of 1215, which referred to the laxity and ignorance of bishops in their duty of preaching and urged them to appoint men 'powerful in word and work'[19] to preach on their behalf. It is clear that Dominic's new Order supplied what Honorius wanted.

Dominic spread his followers across Europe from 1217. His intention was to set up Dominican centres in all towns where there were major schools or *studia*. The Preachers made for Paris at once, where with papal encouragement, the university granted them accommodation and recognition.[20] The first few to arrive completed their education there, just as Dominic and his early followers had attended lectures in Toulouse. Within two years, in 1219, the Dominicans had a house in Paris, 30 recruits and an internal teacher.[21] The Parisian masters understood what these Preachers were about and thus were very alive to the dangers of Catharism, no doubt also because some earlier Cathars had sought an education in Paris. When the Franciscans arrived (by 1219) the masters interrogated them to discover if they were Cathars. What, replied the Franciscans, are Cathars?[22] The Dominicans of course had no doubt at all about what Cathars were: they were their own *raison d'être*.

Dominic (who died in 1221) spent the last years of his life largely in Rome, at the papal curia, and was there perhaps better able to co-ordinate his own aims of suppression of the heresy with those of Honorius. At all events Honorius continued to show his concern that the

Dominicans should fight the heresy by addressing, or at least dedicating, some sermons to Dominic.[23] Honorius spoke of the Order of Preachers newly arising as from the sepulchre of Christ; he recalled Dominic's own Marian vision in saying that to preach the word of God is like carrying Christ. Preaching, he said, was like biting and he regretted the small number of Preachers. He pointed with dismay to the heretic's claim that Catholic preaching was, on the grounds of some Sacred Page citation, a sin, and was deeply concerned about the subtle deceptions, the sophisticated arguments and the rhetorical tricks whereby the Cathars perverted the Sacred Page, deceived the simple, enticed the vague and seduced the rash.

The Preachers' *studium* in Paris was St Jacques (hence they were often called Jacobins in later centuries) where they prepared their materials for the fight against heresy. Hugh of St Cher from 1230 led the Preachers' co-operative work on the Bible, writing 'postils' in the margin, that is, a commentary on important points (literally *post illa verba*).[24] It was important for the Dominicans to do well in Paris. It was the focus of European learning. So successful was it that those who wanted to learn and teach theology went to Paris, draining teachers away from other schools and towns. Once inserted into the university of Paris the Dominicans could spread their message the more effectively. By 1224 there were 120 Preachers reading theology at St Jacques.[25]

The Dominicans reached Oxford in 1221, just after the death of Dominic. It was four years after Dominic had 'dispersed' his followers and he had been able to plan more generously. Of his original 16 followers, seven had gone to Paris and the others in small groups to the other towns, hoping to make up their numbers by recruitment. But 13 Dominicans came to Oxford, one more than the number now laid down as the necessary minimum for a convent. Jordanus, the new Master hoped for a 'big catch'.[26] That is, the rapid spread of the Preachers was partly due to the attraction they exercised for young men with some education, readily to be found in a university like Oxford. They also educated their own novices of course, but their purposes were best served by men who had already demonstrated a competence in learning. Contemporaries saw them as attracting arts students (rather than theologians) with knowledge of the Sacred Page and of philosophy that would be so useful in meeting the challenge of the heresy. Some of their contemporaries indeed saw the Dominicans, particularly in England, as more concerned with natural philosophy than with preaching.[27] The Dominicans were soon too in Valencia and Bologna, where they had a *studium* by 1218; by 1248 it was one of the half-dozen that were second only to Paris in size and importance. They seem to have played an important role in bringing the study of Aristotle's nature books to

Bologna, and although the details are obscure, it has been said that the friars in Bologna had more philosophy at their disposal than the *studium* of the town.[28] The Dominicans' 'catch' in Bologna was extensively from among the lay masters,[29] and the friars accordingly gained considerable power within the town's *studium*. The point of establishing themselves in university towns was, of course, to instil the correct ideology where it most counted and from where it would most effectively be spread. If this was not 're-education' in the sense of Toulouse, it was nevertheless carefully selected education. And it depended partly on a carefully modified doctrine of nature, taken from Aristotle.

So, the Dominicans were to be learned, in the interests of defeating heresy, just as the Church had in its first centuries needed some carefully selected pagan philosophy to counter heresy: in fact as Augustine had used Plato to combat the dualism of the Manichees, so it was the Dominicans who now used a modified Aristotle to reject the dualism of the Cathars. The evidence is that they gave careful thought to the use of philosophy and who among them was to use it. The major distinction here was between the Brothers who had joined the Order after an arts education that included philosophy and the novices whom the Order educated itself. The Brothers who had been through a secular arts course now saw that the philosophies of the 'gentiles and philosophers', in which they had demonstrated their competence, had a purpose only in serving theology. The novices were to be educated to see this too, and only those who were apt enough for learning were allowed to proceed through philosophy. It was, after all, a sharp and double-sided weapon, and the Brothers carefully selected from among their own students the *fratres docibiles* who could handle the secular arts and philosophy. Such youths, *iuvenes*, says the Constitution of the Order, should read primarily theology: it is at the discretion of the Master of the Order or of a Chapter to allow some students for a time to inspect the secular knowledge of the 'gentiles and philosophers' and the liberal arts.[30] Particularly as the Order grew a little older, the *frater docibilis*[31] would be expected to read logic and philosophy and indeed while the threat of heresy was still real the Preachers set up special schools of arts and as (we shall see) of natural philosophy.

The Dominicans educated their own students both at their local houses and at houses in the university towns. The arrangements there too were evidence of the care given to what was taught and learned. When they first set up their own *studia* in the university towns, they were not part of the secular *studia generalia* that had been incorporated as the first universities, and while it seems that the town students could go to Dominican teaching, the Dominicans carefully controlled what their own students heard.[32] Provision was made for studies in the monastic cells and administrative duties were not expected of students.

Other sources suggest that novices were encouraged to read in a non-Dominican *studium* anything that would improve their preaching; they were however in the charge of a brother who guided their reading.[33] When they had been initiated into the Order they were allowed to read the liberal arts, and in any case, as we have seen, it was common for university men already trained in the arts to become Preachers (more common than for canonists or theologians). Learning was by lectures (where the student's notes were carefully corrected by the master) and by disputation. These are the regular features that we associate with *studia generalia* but which here are clearly designed as a training for preaching against the heretics. In short, suitable students from among the novice Preachers would be selected for a training in philosophy, after which they could join the Brothers who had had an external arts education[34] in the characteristic activity of the Order.

Contemporaries saw the Dominicans as the agents of the papacy[35] against heresy, constantly studying, collaborating in drawing up elaborate indices and concordances to the Bible (for the ready identification of telling passages)[36] and lists of variant readings that were also useful in argument.[37] The Dominican way of reading the Bible was now very different from that of the monks. Monastic authors quoted the Bible spontaneously in passages of reflective piety; the Dominicans wanted precise wording for dialectical treatment as a weapon in argument. They carried pocket Bibles ready indexed for useful arguments against the Cathars, *summa breviata ... contra Manicheos*.[38] So important did preaching become that the Paris masters developed preaching as a part of teaching. Teaching was the lecture, the disputation and preaching: *lectio*, *disputatio* and *praedicatio*,[39] of which the last was increasingly turned towards the laity. It was the practical part of school theology; in the phrase of Peter the Chanter, it was the roof of the house of theology whose walls are disputation and whose floor is the Sacred Page. A better metaphor perhaps is that used (before 1197) by Peter for the 'fighting church': the front teeth of theology are the apostles, the modern masters are the molars and the canines are the expositors who 'bark against the heretics'. From metaphor to pun: the Dominicans were known as *Domini canes*, 'the dogs of the Lord', the new teeth of the *ecclesia militans* of Peter and Durand. While disputation had been the method to engage and defeat the Cathars in open conflict, it was preaching[40] that came to the fore in the re-education programme.

Despite the military success of the crusade, the danger of a new growth of the Cathar heresy remained real to the Catholics. In 1227 the Dominicans decided to intensify their education programme. The 'Constitutions' of 1228 specify that every new priory was to have a

7.3 St Dominic and 'the dogs of the Lord' preaching against the Cathars

lector, every province a *schola provincialis*. In addition there were *studia generalia* at centres such as Paris, which the Dominicans opened in 1228.[41] The Dominicans saw their Order as a university spread through its *studia*. But above all, it was Dominican, not secular, and the loyalties of its brothers were to the order, not to lay institutions. We shall see that this was of particular significance for the story of natural philosophy in the secular *studia*.

The school and *studium* of Toulouse

After Dominic's activities in Toulouse, the first direct papal move against the heresy there was made in 1217 by Honorius III, who encouraged masters and scholars of Paris to go to the Cathedral school of Toulouse to help render the population acceptable to God.[42] The Pope's letter speaks of the area around Toulouse as an abode of dragons and thorns, needing to be ploughed afresh as virgin soil, lest the roots of the extirpated heresy shoot again. The masters are urged to 'read, preach and exhort' to lead the populace away from their indulgence and perversity.[43] It was expected then that the school would not only turn out a supply of appropriately educated graduates but that its teachers would actively proselytize in the city and its environs.

For the same purposes of education and re-education, in 1229, after the fighting was over, Gregory IX recognized the anti-Cathar school at Toulouse as a *studium generale*.[44] By the terms of a treaty[45] between Raymond and the pious and orthodox Louis IX, the reluctantly orthodox count was obliged to provide – he did so reluctantly – salaries for some of the masters and he and the citizens were to swear to provide the same privileges for the masters and scholars as they enjoyed in Paris. The purpose of the King's and Pope's move was indeed to attract the masters and scholars at that time dispersing from Paris to a *studium* of the Pope's creating which, no doubt, he hoped the better to control. Its 'protector' in its early years was the papal legate to France, Cardinal Romano.[46] In this way too, the military business of the crusade and its aftermath gave way to re-education. The new *studium* had, in accordance with its doctrinal purposes, a much greater weighting towards theology than there was in Paris. The four teachers of theology were to be maintained by Raymond at an annual salary – 50 marks – five times that of the two grammarians. There were to be only six artists, at less than half the salary of the theologians (and two canonists at 30 marks). The structure imposed upon the Toulouse *studium* was then, very top-heavy with theologians and church lawyers in comparison to Paris, where organic growth by student demand had created a very sizeable arts faculty.

About a month after it became a *studium*, that is, in May 1229, the masters of Toulouse wrote a circular letter to other *studia* in the hope of attracting more students and masters. The masters' rhetoric spells out the purposes of the *studium* at Toulouse. All the faithful are asked to come to the 'new root' of learning which, like all new enterprises, needs a firm base in Christ and the mother church. It is *for this reason* that the masters have already established a firm basis of philosophical study – *studii philosophici fundamentum stabile* – for others to now build on. So philosophy is a basis for further studies which themselves lead on to 'holy works'. The overall purpose of the *studium* was the religious one of suppression of heresy by promoting orthodoxy, *including philosophy* at the very centre of a province-wide dissent. It was Cardinal Romano, the agent of the Pope, who was 'our Moses', the law-giver of the new *studium*. It was he who supplied indulgences to relieve the first masters and students of their sins. As Cardinal Protector he controlled the doctrine of the school, just as Durand's Protector had controlled the doctrine of Durand's school.

'Where you once fought a way with a sword', said the masters, referring to the crusade against the Cathars,

> You can now fight with the sharpness of your tongue [in disputation]; where the catastrophe of war appeared, you may now fight by means of a peaceful doctrine; where the depravity of heresy grew like thorns in a wood, we shall through you raise up to the stars the cedar of catholic faith.[47]

The masters make much of the attractions of Toulouse, in a land of milk and honey, fat cattle and laden vines and apple trees. The academic attraction was partly that the spadework had been done and the students prepared, 'so that you do not have to bring a mattock to uncultivated fields'. So what was this preliminary work, that removed 'plebian ignorance'? What was it they regarded as a firm philosophical foundation? Grammar is mentioned; Aristotle's logic was taught to those beginning the arts; the theologian preaches to his students; the organist makes music; the canonist extols his Justinian, and the medical man his Galen. This is hardly philosophy; but the masters continue, without a break and implying that it was the duty of the medical teacher, to say that 'The *libri naturales* which have been prohibited in Paris can be heard by those wishing to scrutinize the inmost parts of nature'.[48]

If it was indeed the duty of the medical men in Toulouse to teach Aristotle, then it seems to be the continuation of an older story. We have already seen that in the pre-*studia* period medicine provided the vehicle for the physical works of Aristotle, and the medical men seem to have introduced their subject into the new institutions by linking it to the physical works of Aristotle. In the Italian universities, such as Bologna, students of arts and medicine composed a *universitas* of their own, distinct from that of the lawyers, and it had been the medical men who introduced the natural books to these universities.[49] We should also note that the *Canon* of Avicenna came to be an important medical text. Avicenna as an Aristotelian commentator was as much philosopher of nature as physician and many Aristotelian doctrines are carried in his work. It was not until well into the thirteenth century that texts from the *Canon* were used in medical teaching[50] but the text had been known since it was translated by Gerard of Cremona, and their study of this text is another reason why medical men should have been amongst the first to be aware of the Aristotelian physical works. Roland of Cremona for example, although not a physician, was well aware of the use of medicine as a part of philosophy and well aware of Avicenna. His early years in Bologna no doubt account for this.

So the philosophical foundation for the Church's purposes – the suppression of heresy – was to be Aristotle's physical works, a re-education already under way by the time the masters wrote. Perhaps it was intended as in the Italian universities that arts and medicine should be taught together, or at least that the natural philosophy component of arts should be taught by the medical teacher. It is clear that Aristotle was as acceptable to the theologians as to the masters in general, especially of arts and medicine. It is also clear that Aristotle had a considered part in the overall purpose of this *studium* in the seedbed of heresy, Toulouse.

In this way, said the optimistic masters, the *studium* of the militant would give way to the *studium* of philosophy, under the protection and with the support of the count and population. The situation also reflects the fact that in Paris the local heresy – Amalric's and David's – was of a kind that could be *supported* by the use of the *libri naturales*. In Toulouse, in contrast, the heresy was very different, asserting not (as in Paris) that the physical world was identifiable with the one good God, but that it was the work of the Evil Principle. Here Aristotle was more useful than dangerous, and the *libri naturales* accordingly were not prohibited. What else do you require? ask the Toulouse masters rhetorically, priding themselves on their scholastic freedom.[51]

The principal theology teacher (in 1230) was the Dominican Roland of Cremona. Roland had become a Preacher in 1219 after taking the arts degree at Bologna and was from the first active against the Cathars. It was probably for this reason and perhaps in reply to the circular letter of the Toulouse masters that after a year in Paris he gave up his theology post to Hugh of St Cher (his pupil and another Dominican) and moved to Toulouse. He regarded Toulouse and Albi (and 'almost all of Italy') as troublesome refuges of the Cathars – indeed, he says, they live in underground caves[52] – from which they had to be flushed out. Perhaps he thought he was successful, for in 1233 he returned to Italy to preach against the heretics there and to teach theology at Bologna and Cremona. It seems to have been Roland, as a Dominican in active pursuit of the Cathars, who was referred to by one of the Toulouse grammarians, John of Garland, when he said that 'fire, the sword and the teacher root out the depraved', *Pravos extirpat et doctor et ignis et ensis.*[53] We can discover a little of Roland's reaction to the Cathars from his commentary on Job. Its prologue begins with the story of the 'Egyptian gold', symbolizing the philosophy that was acquired before the law of Moses: philosophy has its place, and although subordinate to faith is extremely useful in its defence. Philosophy for Roland is largely Aristotelian, and it is clear from the teaching arrangements of Toulouse that he saw the value of it being taught in the arts course.[54] Thus it is clear that for Roland philosophy had a role in the extirpation of heresy, if only in revealing further meanings in the Scriptures. Philosophy helps to demonstrate the singleness of God (he says) and the brief life span of the earth. (The seven liberal arts, he adds, serve theology, medicine supplies allegories and moralities from the nature of things and astrology is also useful in biblical reading.) Roland's position is that the theologian must be familiar with pagan philosophy to be aware of its dangers and the dangers of those who practice it. By all this he can only be referring to the Cathars, and Roland's purpose in selectively using the *libri naturales* of Aristotle is to obey, like others we have met before, the biblical command 'Beware lest you be deceived by philosophy and empty fallacies'. This adds a little evidence to the picture we have formed of the Cathars being the first to use Aristotle's philosophy of nature, forcing the Dominicans to reply in kind. That Roland did so with obvious reluctance[55] is evidence of the necessity of refuting the Cathars, not of the simple diffusion of Aristotelianism. While in Toulouse Roland composed a commentary on the *Sentences* in which he characteristically used *De Caelo* but rebukes Aristotle for not knowing of the waters above the firmament. He was inclined to a cosmology based on light rather than on Aristotelian principles, but it seems likely that he was obliged to return to Aristotle for the purpose of answering the heretics. In the different circumstances of Paris, his commentary was ignored.[56]

The ideological purposes of the *studium*, its re-education programme, were clearly perceived by the folk of the town. Local resentment in Toulouse against the prominent members of the *studium* was such that despite more papal privileges in 1233, it began to wither. Raymond did not pay the salaries, and the 'consuls' of the city thought themselves autonomous enough to expel prominent Dominicans. Yet the university survived, largely because a newly vigorous Inquisition in 1236 succeeded in overcoming both these obstacles. The Order of Preachers remained, and when the university came to draw up statutes for the faculty of arts in 1311, it was to the friars that they went for advice.[57]

William of Auvergne

The third decade of the thirteenth century was significant for the friars' natural philosophy, particularly in its relationship to the *studia* and the friars' re-education policy. By 1220 the military campaign was petering out; in 1221 the Preachers sent more Brothers to Paris and established a new settlement in Oxford. In 1227 peace between the heretical south and orthodox north of France was governed by a less than satisfactory treaty; in 1228 the Dominicans opened a new house in Paris. In the same year a powerful ally, William of Auvergne, became Bishop of Paris. In 1229 the Treaty of Paris stopped the war; and a church council convened in Toulouse to try to silence the heretics permanently. In the same year the Dominicans opened a *studium* in Oxford, William of Auvergne began to favour Dominicans for teaching posts in Paris, the question of the use of Aristotle had been reopened at the highest level of the Church and, most important of all, the teaching masters of Paris went on strike.

While Gregory IX was considering what to do with the texts of Aristotle, and arranging other aspects of education to his satisfaction, the Dominicans were also taking advantage of the fact that little teaching was going on in Paris. It was Gregory[58] who had made William of Auvergne Bishop of Paris in 1228 and in fact rebuked him for his inactivity during the period of the masters' cessation of lectures. But from our point of view, William had been far from idle. He has been called the first great theoretical theologian; we shall see that he used Aristotle against the Cathars. It was also he who in 1229 had given Roland of Cremona, then a recent master and Dominican, his teaching position in theology. In the next year a secular master holding another such post, John of St Giles, became a Dominican and in practice two of the theology teaching positions were thus appropriated to the Dominicans. Well done, said Gregory in effect to William, you have cultivated the Order as one would a vine.[59] But these two successes for the Order of Preachers were achieved when the *consortium* of masters was in abeyance and could not incept – that is, admit – those of their students who were bachelors hoping for the master's degree. Moreover, the teaching of John of St Giles took place within the Dominican *studium*, outside the control of the Chancellor.[60] The Dominicans did not answer the masters' call to stop teaching, and did not stop their teaching when the secular masters returned. This may have been to avoid offending their patron, Louis IX,[61] but certainly their allegiance to the Pope and to the teaching of the Order gave them loyalties different from those of the masters. There were also economic reasons that allowed the Dominicans to act independently: as mendicants, they did not rely on salaries (as did for example the masters of Toulouse) or students' fees (as in arts in Paris). They could therefore survive and teach in economic circumstances that would not support secular teachers. The seeds of future conflict between secular and regular education had been sown. We shall examine it later.

William of Auvergne is an important figure in the story of the Dominicans' natural philosophy. He had studied arts and theology at Paris. As Bishop of Paris, he had not inconsiderable powers in a major centre of education and indeed of re-education. As Chancellor of the university he had the secular powers of a judge or magistrate,[62] and could commit people to his own prison; he convened the masters in 1241 to condemn the heretical propositions, including that which asserted that the evil angels had been created evil; in 1238 he had advised Gregory IX to take strong action against the Jews, which resulted in 1242 in a public burning of the Talmud. He insisted that heresy must be exterminated with the sword and fire, and when in 1234 the Dominicans of Sens stopped supplying Inquisitors, he gladly took up their duties.[63] He was explicitly and devotedly opposed to the Cathars.

So although not a Dominican, William clearly sympathized with the aims and methods of the Order and was in a position to help them. What he thought and wrote about heresy and the natural part of Aristotle's philosophy, because it agreed with Dominican opinion and because he was a powerful figure who encouraged the order within the university of which he was chancellor, is part of the Dominican story.

The foundation of his work *On Faith* is that the single good God is Creator.[64] Without this (and this is very telling) there would be total destruction of religion and of the worship of God, he said: that is, of civilization as William knew it. But this very thing was threatened by the 'modern Manicheans' and their terrible dichotomies of Good/Evil and Light/Dark. William seems to be specifically rejecting the terminology of the *Two Principles* when he denies that anything can be a principle unless it is absolute, without a partner: a genuine and ultimate source is single. This argument was most strongly set out in his *De Principio et Principe Universitatis*, a title that again seems specifically directed against *De Duobus Principiis*.[65] And this title also seems to be reflected in his major work, an important source for the invention of natural philosophy. This is *De Universo*, which was completed about 1240, after he had taken on the duties of an Inquisitor.[66] From its subject-matter we might have expected a *De Mundo*, 'The World', or something similar. But no, it is about the *single*, uni-creation of a single good God. Quite explicitly, it is a work conceived and executed in opposition to the Cathars' notion of two principles. The *uni*verse is the totality of everything that exists.[67] What William is pursuing is no longer *sapientia*, but *scientia*, and for a very practical purpose. Unlike Alexander Neckam's *philosophia*, William's *scientia* is distinctly physical and philosophical: the *scientia* of the universe is a philosophy composed of all the individual philosophical *scientiae* (which relate to the parts of the universe) and a study of the universe as a single *esse*, a Being capable of demonstration (in the Aristotelian sense of proof).

So, says William, the universe is the single universalness of *creatures*, that is, of created things. The recognition of this is the second part of the 'first sapiental and divine magisterium', with which words William signifies the development of the monastic *sapientia* into the school *scientia*. He also justifies it as the true philosophy, that is, to magnify God by investigating the 'great and wonderful things' of His creation. Now, such an activity on its own, says William, is not enough; not by this alone will we live good lives, perfect our souls and thereby protect them in eternity; but this activity as truth and sincerity are due to God on account of His supereminence. This expresses with great clarity the fact that the new natural philosophy (which William is about to embark upon) still had the ultimate aim of perfecting the soul by the living of the good life on earth.

Indeed, William characterizes philosophers precisely as failing in this undertaking. As philosophers, he says, they fail – indeed they sin – in a number of ways. Their major failing is to ignore the glory of the creator: a sin that is easily attributed to Aristotle, whose world was uncreated, eternal and determinist. But more than that, says William, the philosophers make philosophy sterile by ignoring the whole point of doing it, which is to prepare for eternal happiness. Such a sterile philsophy is like a peacock without its tail and worse, for it is impious in the face of God, and the philosophers glorify it rather than God.

So here we have in a nutshell the early thirteenth-century use of the physical and other works of Aristotle. William has to use Aristotle as the most effective weapon available against the Cathars, but there are grave disadvantages in doing so. For not only are major parts of the philosophy wrong (like the eternity of world) but the philosophers have misconceived the very purpose of practising philosophy. The *true philosophy* has the same subject-matter but different goals. The first of these goals, that is, the first reason for examining the universe, is to glorify the creator; the second is to destroy errors which would prevent one from following the true philosophy. These errors diminish God by half, denying his perfection and omnipotence and claiming that he does not care for man. These, in short, are the errors of the Cathars. William's programme – set out here in the first chapter – is explicitly and primarily to destroy this modern Manicheism. He takes up the cudgels directly in the following chapter, explaining the pagan roots of the modern sect and how its modern perniciousness must be destroyed with fire and with the sword. His present business is to destroy it with arguments, first at a level as low (he says) as that of the heretics themselves (assertion and counter-assertion) and then by metaphysical arguments. Again the weapon William uses is Aristotle, here the *Metaphysics*. He argues that the universe is a diverse whole that is in a technical sense caused by its parts. Any composite whole is a potential Being, not a Necessary Being. That is, the parts must be prior to the whole they cause and must ultimately be caused by Being that is simple, undivided and Necessary. A First Principle must always be single and undivided. Necessarily then, concludes William, there cannot be Two Principles, coeternal and independent.[68] While pure Evil and pure Good are indeed genuine contraries, says William, yet all true contraries have some common subject in which they inhere, like black and white on a surface, or health and illness in a body. The argument is again Aristotle's and is the same as that which the unfortunate David of Dinant had used to demonstrate the divinity of the material world. So we see once more that there were dangers in using Aristotle, and the construction of a Christian natural philosophy called for careful handling. The care with which William handles it is shown in his move to the next argument. He has shown that two principles cannot be true ultimate causes because they have something in common – substance – and so are composite. He now has to demonstrate that the evil principle is composite in being a substance in which a quality or accident – evil – inheres, *without* allowing the same argument to apply to the good principle. Above all (and it was the same with Dominican philosophy of nature) he must show that God is *single* (not a substance with an attribute) and good, the Creator of a good creation. William uses the *Metaphysics*[69] to show that what is primary, eternal and self-sufficient is for these reasons, good. In this text Aristotle himself is dealing with earlier philosophers who thought that contrariety between elements or principles (including good and evil) was fundamental to Being: a reason no doubt for William, fighting Cathar dualism, to find the argument attractive. Aristotle continues in the *Metaphysics* (particularly in book N) with the argument about true opposites (black and white on a surface), the argument indeed that William used. Aristotle's other arguments here were also attractive to a Christian who was fighting such a heresy as the Cathars': what is eternal, said Aristotle, is Actual and Substantial and single (in orthodox Christian terms, there is not a rival eternal evil principle); the ultimate final cause of physical motion is the Good of the unmoved mover, a Good that is desired by the moved (for the Christians, evil does not cause motion in the physical world); the unmoved mover is Necessary and therefore good (there is no Necessity in two principles, argued William); the unmoved mover has no parts, no size and is indivisible (there are not two principles); and most important, Aristotle argues that a Potentiality for good and bad is in most things, but Actual contrarieties cannot coexist: a surface cannot be black and white nor a man healthy and ill at the same time; nor, William argued, could a single God be good and evil, nor a double God exist. It followed for Aristotle that Actual good like the unmoved mover (or God, said William) was superior to potential good; Actual evil, continued Aristotle, is posterior to potential evil and so does not exist as a separate (or eternal and causal, said William) evilness: so eternal things contain no evil and are not peverse or defective.

William's language on concluding his metaphysical arguments is so impatient that it seems to reflect actual argument with the Cathars. He says their words have meanings that are not available to the intellect of others, and that they are equivocal about the word 'Being' (*ens* – William always uses *esse*).[70] It seems clear, at all events, that he and they had not agreed that their differences were resolvable by the terminology and techniques of Aristotle's *Metaphysics*. With its help William could also answer another Cathar assertion, that the material world was a world of shadows, evil like its creator. The Cathars argued that there were two separate chains of causality, running back from actual evil and good, to autonomous, self-sufficient but opposed principles. William's answer is that anything that is truly self-sufficient cannot have an opposite, and that an ultimate cause must be simply Being, which has no opposite except non-Being. It follows that evil is not a form of Being but merely of Privation. So the world of shadows is simply deprived of divine light.

The arguments of the Cathars determine the shape of these early chapters of William's *De Universo*, the eighth of which is given over to the chain-of-causality argument. 'First Evil' (argues William) the source of all subsequent evil, arises from privation of the first natural Good, or Being, and its true opposite is First Grace. First Grace among the intelligences is their natural recognition of God, but this grace has to be taught to men; it is, indeed, the very basis of true religion: in other words, Catholic and not Cathar. William continues by arguing that subsequent evils may come of good in an unnatural way. The evil of drunkenness may arise from good wine; from excessive sanctity may come the sin of pride. In these examples it is the nature of man that has become unnatural; but William also uses 'nature' as 'the natural world', that is, just what his new philosophy was dealing with. The elements of fire and water, says William, are in a sense good and bad: fire burns and destroys, but it also cooks; water both drowns and relieves thirst. But more generally, Nature cannot take the blame, because it acts necessarily, not voluntarily: fire does not intend to destroy, but to multiply its species; dangerous animals like lions do not intend harm, but only to nourish or defend themselves.

Having employed the first tract of the work in destroying the Cathars' view of the two principles, William devotes the second to demonstrating that there is only one world, one creation, and that it is good. God is the *artifex* and the universe a *universitas* of creatures (created things), an overflowing of the first and universal Goodness: *Neque enim aliud est mundus, vel creaturae universitas, quam redundantia quaedam primi et universalis fontis bonitatis, qui est creator benedictus, et sublimis*: 'The world, or universe of created things, is nothing else than an overflowing of the first and universal fount of goodness, which is the blessed and sublime Creator'.[71] Such a definition of the world and its goodness and singleness was also programmatic for the new Dominican philosophy of nature.

William is not content (as Alexander Neckam had been) to draw moral and allegorical contemplation from the natural world. It is in the very workings of nature that the wisdom, skill and immensity of its Creator are to be seen; in nature there are signs pointing to the One. So nature leads to God, continues William, but not directly. God speaks in his natural creation, but not fully, for it is impossible for creatures to hear and to understand the full word of God. What is needed to hear Him is not only nature, but philosophy. Man's unaided intellect can never grasp all of the particulars of the natural world, nor arrive at the truest universals, but with the true philosophy man can understand the Word that was in the beginning, and the word written in nature. Here is the new philosophy of nature; William summarizes: 'one skill, or work, one discourse or meaning, one sign or designation of Himself, one book or scripture, placed in the sight of the human intellect so that, reading, it may become wise in it and as far as possible learn about its creator ... '.[72] William's insistence on the singleness of the world leads him to emphasize the relatedness of its parts. Thus *every* part of the world shows some indication of its Creator, even if only in being an integrated part of the whole. This integration, according to William, primarily shows through the interdependence of the parts of the world. This is chiefly expressed as the great hierarchy of creation. It is the very expression of God's will and power that the world is ruled by God's law in descending stages, from God himself down through the heavens, heavenly bodies, the meteorological regions (as one may read in Aristotle, says William), man and the lower world, including animals (the old philosophers were wrong, says William, in not giving any role to animals in the unity of the world). A city is a single city, in William's analogy, even though it contains slaves, free men, women, and men of different callings. This version of God's law, of course, has no room for men – the heretics – who stand outside the hierarchy. William's description of the heavenly bodies and of the divine law which passes down through them is explicitly written to oppose the heresy, and the philosophy of nature which includes the divine law applies equally to the lowly animals under man's vicarious law.

William's philosophy of nature, the modification of Aristotle to defeat the Cathars, is equally evident in his pursuit of the theoretical question of the plurality of worlds. (He may here be facing the doctrines of the Italian rather than the Cathars of Provence and Languedoc.) Here he is opposed to the Cathar notion of the two creations of the Two Principles: if there are two such worlds, how can they relate to each other? His notion of 'world' is Aristotelian, so it is a sphere. Is then the 'other' world outside this one – that is, enclosing it? (In which case it is little more than another outer sphere to add to those described by Aristotle.) Or do they imagine it is juxtaposed? But two spherical worlds could touch only at a point, and there would be a vacuum elsewhere, and Aristotle is very firm that there is no such thing as a vacuum. Again, William writes in the present tense about the difficulties his opponents, the heretics, have in answering these questions, which suggests that he himself had disputed with them, and still felt the threat their belief offered. And again, his opponents did not use the terms and principles of Aristotelian philosophy.

> However, with these people, who do not know, or who cannot know, what it is that is said, the path of philosophising or even of disputing is entirely closed, since the knowledge of this, that it is, what it is, what it is said to be, is one of the principles of investigation or philosophising, as you have learned elsewhere.[73]

So, for William, rationality itself, the techniques and substance of arguing, is Aristotelian. And he knows that by now his readers will have been taught it. The heretics were external to the group to which William and his similarly educated readers belonged, and could not, in their perversity, even argue properly. There was nothing for it; it was a case of the fire and the sword.

So for William the philosophy of the natural world, based on an Aristotelian dialectic, physics and metaphysics, was something that was within *his* church, and of which the heretics were incapable of knowing. Men who are unable to understand what is said, or unable to understand themselves, are not to be consulted in philosophy, says William. (By this we may reasonably understand him to be referring to men who did not admit his premisses and who consequently found his conclusions to be false.) William adopts the Aristotelian view that philosophy is a way of reaching the unknown by way of the known (and so is closed to the heretics, who do not know). It is clear that this process is for him the same as the rational process of reaching the invisible (God) through the visible (the physical creation), and that the Aristotelian method of proof, demonstration, is available in this philosophy of nature, common to both divine and natural, physical, things.[74] Moreover, the making visible is the throwing of [divine] light into the shadows of the Prince of Darkness, his race of demons of evil – *cacodaemones* – and their shadowy physical world. No one within the shadows, says William, can see more shadows – within the shadows nothing is visible, nothing known, and so there can be no philosophical or divine reaching of the unknown from the known. This illumination can only come from outside and it shows that the world is single and finite: 'I believe you will recall proofs and natural declarations by which certainty has been established, as much by Aristotle as by others, about the body of the heavens, that is, how in the book *On Heaven and Earth*, he makes it known that it is finite.'[75] But as in some other particulars, when William turns his philosophy to nature, the result is not simply the philosophy of Aristotle for William was obliged to correct some of its objectional features, such as the eternity of the heavenly bodies.

In the third tract of *De Universo* William describes the creation of the world. He has not forgotten the Cathars, but having already defeated them in proving the unity of the Creator and of his Creation, his chief enemy, at least at the outset, is the Platonist. It is probable here that he is comparing his own philosophy of nature – about which this tract tells us more – with that of men who had retained an older tradition based on neo-Platonism and St Augustine.[76] In the beginning was the Word, says William the Dominican. 'God said "Let there be light",' said his opponents. William opposed the neo-Platonic theory of creation by emanation (of which light was an example), by saying that what pours out of a spring or fountain is simply what was in there before it came out; no, God *makes* things.

In creating the world, according to William, God used Word in a spiritual or intellectual sense and, in William's philosophy of nature, it is the intellectual operations of man that can approach God's creation. This Creation was Act in ultimate Actuality, William tells his readers; only in human actions is act preceded by potency. Both divine and human creations are accounted for in Aristotelian terms by William; and in both of them Word – discourse or speech – is an instrument of creation and a component of the natural philosophy that makes creation intelligible to man.

So William's philosophy of nature is more than simply an Aristotelian weapon against the Cathars. It is, rather, a weapon designed to minimize self-inflicted damage, for Aristotle in his completeness could be dangerous to true belief. Moreover, the Arabic commentators, particularly Avicenna, presented a development of Aristotle's views that was almost as bad as the heresy that William was still fighting. He now had to turn his philosophy of nature against the Arabs, and use his Christianized Aristotle against the Islamic God who in the hands of the commentators was obliged to make the world as He did; who in fact made only the outermost sphere, or intelligence, which then created the next, which created the third, and so on until the tenth, which was the active intelligence of men. William, of course, can have none of this, because his natural philosophy rests on the intelligible signs of God's direct action in making the physical world, and on an intellect that is connected to God's through the Word. Indeed, God created the world, says William, in such a way that man can see and understand these signs. In an extended metaphor William says that we can follow these signs as hunters follow footprints to their quarry: God wishes to be found and helps those who are trying to find Him by leaving signs in the natural world.

In summary, to discover more of God by hunting down the natural signs of His action, goodness and unicity in the physical world is the programme of William's philosophy of nature. This philosophy was created to crush the Cathars. It came in very useful to deal with other variants from what William saw as orthodoxy, like the neo-Platonic version of creation by emanation, and also to deal with the non-Christian beliefs about God and the world held by the Arabs and Jews.

Notes

1. S. Runciman, *The Medieval Manichee. A Study of the Christian Dualist Heresy*, Cambridge University Press, 1982 (reissue) p. 138.
2. The author of the *Chanson* describes the Cistercians' disputes with the Cathars and the murder of Pierre de Castlenau:

   E l'Abas de Cistels, cui Dieus amava tant,
   Que ac nom fraire Arnaut, primier el cap denant,
   A pe et a caval anavan disputant
   Contre 'ls felos eretges, qui erant mescrezant;
   E'ls van de lors paraulas mot fortment encusant,
   Mans eli no n'an cura ni no'ls prezo niant.
   Peyre del Castelnou es vengutz ab aitant
   Vez Rozer en Proensa ab so mulet amblant:

Lo comte de Toloza anet escumenjant,
Car mante les roters qe'l pais van raubant.
An tant us escudiers, qui fo de mal talant
Per so qu'el agues grat del comte an avant
L'aucis en traicio dereire en trespassant,
E'l ferit per la equina am son espeut trencant ...

(Martin-Chabot, E., ed., *Les Classiques d'Histoire de France au Moyen Age*, vol. 21: *La Chanson de la Croisade Albigeoise*, Paris, 1931, vol. 1, p. 12.)

3. The Inquisitors were still active into the fourteenth century. About 1315 they were told not to accept ignorance of the law as an excuse in their suspects, on the grounds that the Decalogue was based on natural law, the first rule of which is that we seek good and flee from evil. This was considered a *ius naturale* because what God had given to man is 'natural' to him. It was also 'natural' because as Aristotle says, man 'naturally' desires to know, here that God is the governor of the world and equally naturally avoids evil. Thus was Aristotle used to confirm the legal status of heresy. See A. Dondaine, 'Le manuel de l'inquisiteur (1230–1330)', *Archivum Fratrum Praedicatorum*, **17**, 1947, pp. 85–194; 119.
4. R. Brooke, *The Coming of the Friars*, London, 1975, p. 73.
5. (Le comte de Montfort est resté en Carcassès pour y anéantir les méchants et y introduire les bons; il en a chassé les hérétiques, les routiers, les Vaudois et y a installé des catholiques, des Normands et des Français.) *La Chanson* (note 8 below), vol. 2, p. 70.
6. Que le pic de Montségur a été précisément pour servire à leur défence et qu'il les y a tolérés. *La Chanson* (note 8 below), vol. 2, p. 49.
7. L. White, *Medieval Religion and Technology*, University of California Press, 1978, p. 268.
8. The troubadours' lament for the damage caused by the crusade is given in *Les Classiques d'Histoire de France au Moyen Age*, vol. 24: *La Chanson de la Croisade Albigeoise*, vol. 2 (part 1), ed. E. Martin-Chabot, Paris, 1957 and vol. 25: *La Chanson ...* , vol. 3 (part 2), Paris, 1961.
9. E. Peters, *Heresy and Authority in Medieval Europe*, London, 1980, p. 189.
10. W.L. Wakefield, *Heresy, Crusade and Inquisition in Southern France*, London, 1974, p. 177.
11. A. Dondaine, 'La Hiérarchie Cathare en Italie, II: Le tractatus de hereticis d'Anselme d'Alexandrie OP', *Archivum Fratrum Praedicatorum*, **20**, 1950, pp. 234–324; 320.
12. Wakefield, *Heresy*, p. 242.
13. A. Dondaine, 'La Hiérarchie Cathare en Italie, II: Le tractatus de hereticis d'Anselme d'Alexandrie OP', *Archivum Fratrum Praedicatorum*, **20**, 1950, pp. 234–324.
14. P. von Limborch, *The History of the Inquisition*, trans. S. Chandler, 2 vols, London, 1731; vol. 1, p. 46.
15. R. Manselli, 'Per la storia dell'eresia nel secolo xii', *Bullettino dell'Istituto Italiano per il Medio Evo e Archivio Muratoriano*, **67**, 1955, pp. 189–264; 232.
16. *Chartularium*, p. 62.
17. Brooke, *Friars*, p. 180.

18. For example W.A. Hinnebusch OP, *The Early English Friars Preachers*, Rome, 1951, p. 279
19. Hinnebusch, (1951) p. 280.
20. *Chartularium*, p. 95.
21. Bede Jarrett, OP, *Life of St Dominic (1170–1221)*, London, 1924, p. 84.
22. John C. Murphy OFM, 'The Early Franciscan Studium at the University of Paris', in Leslie S. Domonkos and Robert J. Schneider, *Studium Generale. Studies Offered to Astrik L. Gabriel*, Notre Dame, 1967, pp. 159–203.
23. V. J. Koudelka, OP, 'Notes pour servir à l'histoire de saint Dominique II', *Archivum Fratrum Praedicatorum*, **43**, 1973, pp. 5–27.
24. B. Smalley, *The Study of the Bible in the Middle Ages*, Oxford, Blackwell, third edn, 1984, p. 286.
25. Wakefield, 1974, p. 139.
26. Brooke, *Friars*, p. 188.
27. Smalley, *The Study of the Bible*, p. 309.
28. N. Siraisi, *Taddeo Alderotti and his Pupils. Two Generations of Italian Medical Learning*, Princeton University Press, 1981, p. 10.
29. Bede Jarrett, 1924, p. 85.
30. In libris gentilium et philosophorum non studeant et si ad horam inspiciant seculares scientias non addiscant nec eciam artes quam liberales vocant nisi aliquando circa aliquos magister ordinis vel capitulum voluerit aliter dispensare. Quoted by Hinnebusch, 1951, p. 295.
31. See A.G. Little, 'Educational Organisation of the Mendicant Friars in England (Dominicans and Franciscans)', *Transactions of the Royal Historical Society*, New Series, **8**, 1894, pp. 49–70; 53.
32. R. Creytens, 'Les constitutions des frères prêcheurs dans les rédactions de S Raymond de Peñafort (1241)', *Archivum Fratrum Praedicatorum*, **18**, 1948, pp. 5–68; 65. The text of the 'old' or 'primitive' constitution under Jordanus of Saxony is given by H.C. Scheeben in 'Die Konstitutionen des Predigerordens unter Jordan von Sachsen, *Quellen und Forschungen zur Geschichte des Dominikanerordens in Deutschland*, vol. 38, Cologne/Leipzig, 1939; the text is pp. 48–70.
33. R. Creytens, 'L'instruction des novices Dominicains au xiiiè siècle d'après le ms Toulouse 418', *Archivum Fratrum Praedicatorum*, **20**, 1950, pp. 114–93.
34. See also A. Dondaine, 'Un commentaire scripturaire de Roland de Crémone "le livre de Job"', *Archivum Fratrum Praedicatorum*, **11**, 1941, pp. 109–37; 116.
35. Dominic spent much of his later years in Rome and may well have continued to shape his Order in line with papal strategies.
36. Brooke, *Friars*, p. 201.
37. Smalley, *The Study of the Bible*, p. 268.
38. R.H. and M.A. Rouse, 'Statim invenire. Schools, Preachers and New Attitudes to the Page', Benson and Constable, *Renaissance and Renewal*, pp. 201–25; 221.
39. S.C. Ferruolo, *Origin of the University*, Stanford University Press, 1985, p. 198.
40. We shall see below that some of the works by Dominicans nowadays seen as examples of medieval 'science' are in fact collections of snippets from the authors about the natural world from which to compose sermons.
41. The Preachers had been extending their power in Paris for some time.

There had been a 'new plantation' of the friars in 1219, to which the Paris chapter objected, and again in 1221. A big campaign by Jordanus in 1223 resulted in about 40 Paris scholars becoming Preachers between Advent and Easter 1224. In 1226 (when the friars acquired more land) there were 21 new novices, including 6 MAs in March alone. *Chartularium*, pp. 99, 101, 104, 108.

42. P. Kibre, *Scholarly Privileges in the Middle Ages*, London, 1961, p. 93.
43. *Chartularium*, p. 83.
44. R. Gadave, *Les Documents sur l'Histoire de l'Université de Toulouse*, Toulouse, 1910.
45. Raymond was obliged to pay 400 marks yearly. H. Rashdall, *The Universities of Europe in the Middle Ages*, eds Powicke and Emden, Oxford University Press, 3 vols, 1936, **II**, p. 163.
46. J. van Steenbergen, *Aristotle in the West. The Origins of Latin Aristotelianism*, Louvain, 1970, p. 82.
47. *Chartularium*, vol. 1, p. 130.
48. Ibid., p. 131.
49. A. Birkenmajer, 'La rôle jouée par les médecins ... ', in *Etudes d'Histoire ...* , Warsaw, 1970. See also N. Siraisi, *Arts and Sciences at Padua: The Studium of Padua before 1350*, Toronto, 1973; and P.O. Kristeller, 'Bartholomaeus, Musandinus and Maurus of Salerno ... ', *Italia Medioevale e Umanistica*, 1976, **19**, pp. 57–87.
50. N. Siraisi, *Avicenna in Renaissance Italy. The Canon and Medical Teaching in Italian Universities after 1500*, Princeton University Press, 1987.
51. *Chartularium*, p. 131.
52. On Roland, see A. Dondaine, 'Un commentaire scripturaire de Roland de Crémone "Le livre de Job"', *Archivum Fratrum Praedicatorum*, **11**, 1941, pp. 109–37; W. Breuning, *Die hypostatische Union in der Theologie Wilhems von Auxerre, Hugos von St. Cher und Rolands von Cremona*, Trier, 1962.
53. Pravos extirpat et doctor et ignis et ensis. Rashdall, *Universities*, vol. 2, p. 163.
54. Roland accepts that one of the drawbacks of this kind of 'Egyptian gold' was Aristotle's belief that the earth was eternal. Roland attributes this to Aristotle's 'jealousy' of Plato and the created world he had described in the *Timaeus*.
55. See R.S. Avi-Yonah,'The Aristotelian Revolution: A Study of the Transformation of Medieval Cosmology, 1150–1250', Harvard Ph.D. diss., 1986, p. 100.
56. Avi-Yonah, 1986, p. 106.
57. J. Vaissette, *Histoire Générale de Languedoc*, Toulouse, 1872–92, 15 vols; vol. 7, p. 442 (part 2).
58. S.P. Marrone, *William of Auvergne and Robert Grosseteste: New Ideas of Truth in the Early Thirteenth Century*, Princeton University Press, 1983, p. 27.
59. *Chartularium*, p. 126.
60. Rashdall, *Universities*, **I**, p. 375.
61. J.C. Murphy 'The Early Franciscan Studium at the University of Paris', in Domonkos and Schneider, eds, *Studium Generale ...* , Notre Dame, The Medieval Institute, 1967, p. 191.

62. See E.A. Moody, *Studies in Medieval Philosophy, Science and Logic*, University of California Press, 1975: 'William of Auvergne and His Treatise De Anima', pp. 1–109; 3.
63. N. Valois, *Guillaume d'Auvergne Evêque de Paris (1228–1249). Sa Vie et ses Ouvrages*, Paris, 1880, p. 25.
64. William of Auvergne (G Alvernus), *Opera Omnia*, Rouen, 1674.
65. It does not appear to have been published. William discusses it in the *De Fide*, ch. 3 (included in the *Opera Omnia*).
66. See Marrone, *William of Auvergne*, p. 28.
67. The tract is in the *Opera Omnia*, p. 593.
68. For these points chapters 3 and 4 depend on *Metaphysics*, 10.
69. *Metaphysics*, 1091b.
70. The point seems to be that *ens* is merely an existing thing, while *esse* relates to the nature of existence itself.
71. Tract II, chapter 11: *Opera Omnia*, p. 605.
72. quemadmodum praedixi, ut unum artificium, vel fabrica, una locutio, vel innuitio, unum signum, vel designatio ipsius, unus liber, vel scriptura coram posita humano intellectui, ut erudiatur legens in ea, et addiscit, prout possibile est, ipsum creatore. *Opera Omnia* p. 606, our translation.
73. Cum his autem, qui non sciunt, aut non possunt scire, quid est, quod dicitur, praeclusa est omnino via philosophandi, et etiam disputandi, cum scientia ejus, quod est, quid est, quod dicitur, unum sit de principiis investigandi, et philosophandi, sicut alibi didicisti. *Opera Omnia*, p. 609, our translation.
74. *Opera Omnia*, p. 609.
75. Credo autem te reminisci probationum, et declarationum naturalium, per quas facta est certitudo tam ab Aristotele, quam ab aliis de corpore coeli, qualiter scilicet in libro coeli, et mundi scire fecit ipsum esse finitum. *Opera Omnia*, p. 609, our translation.
76. For an indication of who these people might have been, see Chapter 9.

CHAPTER EIGHT

Dominican education

Vincent of Beauvais

In the last chapter we looked at William of Auvergne as Bishop of Paris, as chancellor of its university and above all as a figure assisting in the formation of Dominican natural philosophy. Here we continue the story of Dominican natural philosophy with the brothers of the Order working more as members of a team.

The purpose of the Dominican education programme was to ensure the continuation of true doctrine, and it was informed, as we have seen, by the need to show that the natural world was, as God's handiwork, good. This in turn required the further refining of the 'Egyptian gold' of pagan philosophy. The Brothers worked together, some acting as scribes, excerpting from the authors, others as compilers. They served the Dominican cause by providing materials for teaching and preaching, both within and outside the Order.[1]

The first of them is Vincent of Burgundy, later Bishop of Beauvais (and hence generally known as Vincent of Beauvais), who went to Paris to study with the Dominicans in about 1220. His later contributions to the collaborative Dominican education programme were no doubt shaped by his introduction to it in Paris, and he wanted them to be judged by the bishop (William of Auvergne from 1229) and masters of Paris.[2] Vincent was also called upon to preach at the court of, and to teach the children of, the 'holy king', Louis IXth, who as we have seen was a patron of the Preachers. Vincent's position as royal teacher no doubt added authority to his views and to the Dominican view of nature. Moreover, royal assent to his views was active rather than merely passive, and Louis undertook to pay at least a part of the expenses incurred in the production of Vincent's *Speculum Majus*, the book we are about to examine. Patronage of this kind also indicates the approval with which the royal saint viewed the Dominicans' religious purposes in looking at nature.

This *speculum*, 'mirror', is divided into three, a *speculum naturale*, followed by a *speculum doctrinale* (originally an appendix to the first) and a *speculum historiale*. The latter extended at first to 1244, later to 1250; the whole was published in about 1256–59 and was a major source for later commentators on natural philosophy.[3] In other words, in the part that is of most interest to us, Vincent was holding up a mirror to nature, and examining the images he found there.

The chief part of his purpose was to provide materials for preaching, reading, disputing and the solving of difficult questions: that is, the Dominican education programme itself.[4] The 'teachers, preachers and exegetes' whom he exhorts to learn about God from nature,[5] are the Brothers at work in their own *studia* and in the university towns. Vincent's *Speculum* expresses this overall purpose, common to the four parts of the book, as his dealing with those things that strengthened[6] 'the dogma of our faith'. (Secondary considerations were the practical aims of instructing morals and awakening charity.) These aims were to be achieved by a consideration of nature, as creation, in the natural part of the book (and equally by morals, by doctrine and by history in the other parts). Vincent provides abundant evidence of the collaborative nature of the programme he was engaged in and the common utility within the Order of the results. He begins his general prologue by modestly claiming that he was not the most learned of the Brothers, but that it fell to him to select and gather the 'flowers' of the authors for this *florilegium*. He recognized that there had been a great increase in both secular and sacred learning: in particular 'our brothers' had been very diligent in pursuing literal and mystical meanings of the Sacred Page. In defending his use of paraphrases rather than quotations from Aristotle, Vincent makes clear again that not all of the business of excerpting from the authors was his own work, for some of the paraphrases had been passed to him by other Brothers.

> In this work I hear the souls of several readers opposing me, in that I have quoted certain *flosculi* of Aristotle, chiefly his physical and mathematical books (which in fact I have never excerpted from, but took the excerpts from several brothers) but not in precisely the same order of words as in the original, but in a changed order, sometimes too changing a little the form of the words, but preserving the meaning of the author.[7]

In the common programme of the Dominicans Vincent collected material from some of the Brothers and in turn served their needs by meeting their request and organizing his subject-matter into the four *specula*, natural, doctrinal, moral and historical, like a manual to the Bible.[8] Even the subject-matter of Vincent's text was affected by the Dominican programme, for he deals less with God and the angels than he might have done because, he says, so much had already been written by the Brothers on these subjects. Indeed, in responding to the requests of the Brothers for *natural* knowledge, Vincent later came to think he had strayed too far into mere curiosity:[9] although the results had pleased the Brothers as being useful in instruction of morals, Vincent, now a bishop, saw his own role rather differently.

The techniques and the materials used by Vincent in achieving this end can be considered together. The true faith of course is Catholic, and it is to be strengthened in a particularly Dominican way. It is again a question of mining and refining the 'Egyptian gold' in order to show that the physical world is good. Vincent reassures the reader that when God instructed the Israelites to take the treasure from the Egyptians, He was acting morally (and not inciting them to theft): He was causing them to be enriched with the gold of wisdom and the silver of eloquence. A morally proper way of holding such treasure was not to derive pleasure from it, but to use it, in overcoming ignorance and in knowing what to reject. Secular knowledge, says Vincent, is gained for erudition, not for joy.[10] 'Egyptian gold', the books of the gentiles, pagan philosophy could all be used to complement the Sacred Page, the Fathers, papal utterances and recent approved authors. These are Vincent's authorities in preferred order. To them he adds that credence should be given to the secular liberal arts as taught in the schools: all have the overall purpose of explaining the Sacred Page, of serving *divina scientia* as a queen.[11]

What is particularly Dominican in this is that Vincent gives so much space to evidence from all these sources of the goodness of the natural world. He is not content, like Alexander Neckam, to allow the mind to rise from general statements about the natural world to God, without the aid of philosophy or the consideration of particulars. His emphasis, by contrast, is on the works of God rather than on His nature, or the nature of the angels or the sacraments. 'This sensible world is like a book, written by the finger of God' he says.[12] Indeed, the organizing principle of the book is to follow, like a hexameron, the six days of God's creation, by considering what was created. This gives the work a strong historical slant, not only in the sequence of creation but also in the subsequent events in the created world. Indeed, part of his purpose in writing was to provide a new style of exposition, an historical account of the Church, to correct – he said – the lamentable ignorance of many of the Brothers.[13] Vincent discusses the rise of secular empires, wars, and the growth of the Church. He can in this way introduce the opinions of the philosophers, take what is of value from them, but not be committed to them. (We have seen Hugh of St Victor use the same technique.) It is amongst the opinions of the philosophers that he says he has searched diligently for the natures of things, and it is in the richness of such descriptions that his readers will find (he hopes) the book of creatures, that is, the physical world of created things, the book in which one may read the power, wisdom and goodness of God.[14] Although the philosophers and gentiles were ignorant of the Catholic faith, yet, says Vincent, they said many wonderful things about the Creator and creation, which are true both to human reason and to Catholic faith.[15]

Vincent's historical method then, enables him to present what he chooses from the philosophers and leave the remainder: he is refining the 'Egyptian gold'. He knows that the philosophers disagree. He is careful to point out that he is not writing as an author, an authority, an *auctor* having *auctoritas*, but as an excerptor: it is not his job to reconcile the philosophers, but to leave his reader with the eye of faith, and a notion of history, so that his reader can choose between them. The philosophers contributed insights to true knowledge, particularly from the natural world, said Vincent, but they lacked revelation. The philosophers had reason, and God is partly knowable through reason: philosophy is useful.

Vincent does not, then, present a system of natural philosophy, and does not write synthetically. His purpose in providing materials for preaching and teaching was not to offer a systematic exposition of Aristotle's works on the physical world and the heavens. Such was the devotion to Aristotle shown by some scholars that some of them, as Vincent says, treated Aristotle's text with exaggerated care, never changing so much as an iota:

> There are even some (to speak with feeling), who are very faithful and cautious observers of words, and thus wish to excerpt notable opinions from any books so faithfully and sincerely that they will not suffer to be changed even the smallest iota of the words of this author, or even the order of words; but I have not seen that our learned Catholic doctors have held to the restriction of such caution, either in picking the flowers of the ancients or in borrowing from the books of others.[16]

William of Auvergne would have agreed, for he knew of many masters and students in Paris who thought Aristotle's text was as true as revealed knowledge.[17] Almost certainly Vincent too was referring to secular masters, for the literal text of Aristotle was of less use than an interpretation of his ideas, moulded gently but firmly to Christian doctrine. Nor was a textual exposition of Aristotle among Vincent's purposes in providing snippets of philosophy for Dominican consumption. (This purpose meant too that he could give space, amongst the excerpts from Aristotle, to Platonic modes of causation[18] that involved forms becoming real by the agency of light.)[19]

Clearly he found that his purposes could be better served by collecting his *flosculi* in a bigger field of philosophers. Like other authors we have met, he gave a considered analysis of the parts of philosophy, and his historical treatment is like that of his fellow Dominican Kilwardby. The purpose of course is to show that Truth in philosophy has emerged as part of the historical process, until it has reached the point where it can complement the Truth of the Sacred Page. The need itself for philosophy is historical, argues Vincent, having arisen only after the Fall, as a need to remedy man's fallen status. Thus Vincent's arguments about the purposes of philosophy are similar to those of Gundislavi and Hugh of St Victor, more than a century before. God, he says,[20] gave man three internal gifts, a similarity to Himself in terms of knowledge, of virtue and of immortality. But there are three vices, ignorance, lust and weakness, that tend to destroy these gifts. The three remedies are wisdom (knowledge of all things), virtue (accommodating life to nature) and necessity (material provision). These in turn have given rise to the *scientiae*, of which the most recent is logic, which with grammar and rhetoric, is the science of communication. So philosophy as a whole is composed for Vincent of these four *scientiae* and its purpose is the religious one of perfecting the man and allowing him to lead the good life.

To strengthen the truth of his own philosophy, Vincent gives a brief history of philosophies that have enquired into nature. He points out that the earliest philosophers (the people whom we nowadays call the Presocratics) were looking for the principles of things and the gods. This is followed by an account of Socrates who desired to know how to live well. So, Pythagoras among the Presocratics was contemplative, Socrates active; the two philosophies were combined by Plato, said Vincent, who thus produced a better, tripartite philosophy: natural (contemplation), moral (active) and rational (distinguishing truth from error). So by degrees philosophy has improved, adopting what was good and rejecting what was wrong and finally presenting that which Vincent offers to his readers.

If we had to choose between the many examples of classifications of the arts and *scientiae* that Vincent cites, in order to identify what is the philosophy that describes his own *Speculum Naturale*, it would be the *Scientia de natura*.[21] The subject-matter of this was the upper, celestial world. This leads directly to the divine *scientia*, the perfection of them all, the subject of which was God as *natura naturans*.[22] Knowledge of the lower world, in which we live and about which we must take action, is *scientia naturalis*, subordinate to the knowledge of the higher (it was in a very similar way that the twelfth-century philosophers had distinguished upper 'nature' from the lower 'the works of nature'). In Vincent's treatment all three are so connected as to form a single philosophy of God-and-His-world, a Dominican successor to the twelfth-century single philosophy of God-and-his-world.

Thomas of Cantimpré and Albertus Magnus

The Dominican education programme was serviced by collections of materials that could be used as examples in teaching and preaching. That these were largely collections of fragments of writings about the natural world points to the direction which the Dominican answer to heresy had taken.[23] These could be used also in later compilations having the same purpose, producing a Dominican 'library'. Thus Thomas of Cantimpré's book on the natures of things, *De Natura Rerum*,[24] was used by Albertus Magnus in writing for the Dominican *studia* of Germany. Thomas tells the reader he has been collecting material from the authors for 15 years. Perhaps he started after he became a Dominican in 1232, which would put his book at about 1250. His main source was Aristotle, followed by Pliny and Solinus, two patristic hexamerons and so recent an author as Jacques of Vitry (*Oriental History*). The 'things', *res*, of the title of the work are created things, creatures, and it is his purpose to provide examples and *flosculi* for use in preaching, in correction of morals and in arguing for the faith. The appetite of the Order of Preachers for material for sermons seems to have been great: Thomas assures his readers, as Vincent had done, that he is providing a new collection and there are surviving manuscript excerpts from Thomas's book that seem designed for use in the pulpit.[25] The price of copies of the book was controlled by the university regulations in Paris. To make the book more convenient for the preachers and teachers who would dip into it, Thomas arranged his text in a way that did not preserve Aristotle's arguments, and we may consider this as another way in which his philosophy of nature was modified for Dominican purposes.

Thomas says that he began the work some 15 years earlier, 'having had for a long time before my eyes that saying of the most blessed father Augustine in his book *On Christian Doctrine*, where he says how very useful it would be if someone took up the work of assembling into one volume the natures of things and especially of animals'.[26] Unable to find such a work amongst the Latins, Thomas had therefore set out to create it. By the time he finished he became aware that the accounts of the natures and habits of animals and effects of herbs he had excerpted from the philosophers applied to eastern animals and plants, where the philosophers had lived, rather than western ones. Nevertheless, he wrote in his Prologus:

> Anyone who applies himself to these writings will find plenty of material for arguments of faith and corrections of morals by allegorical means, so that for the preacher who finds the eloquence of the prophets failing to awake the minds of brutes, and has thus rightly moved away from following the very footprints of the

> scriptures, he may adduce the witnesses of created things to the eye of faith, so that if things heard frequently and inculcated from the scriptures do not move someone, yet new things in the mouth of the preacher may attract the ears of the sluggish.[27]

Hence Thomas's sequence: it is alphabetical, so that one can the more easily find 'material for arguments of faith and corrections of morals'. He begins with the anatomy (*anatomia*) of man who, 'created mortal amongst the mortals, in dignity of mind has been made superior to all the immortals'. Then he goes on to: the soul (*anima*), monstrous men, and animals (*animalia*): quadruped animals, birds, marine monsters, serpents, insects, and thence on to trees, plants, springs, stones, metals, the air, the sphere of the earth and the seven planets and their virtues, and finally the elements.

In reading and excerpting his Aristotle, Thomas was much taken with the passage in the animal books in which Aristotle justifies the study of the structure of animals.[28] Aristotle's message is that although the subject-matter of such knowledge is ignoble and even disgusting, yet the certainty of such knowledge, derived from the very proximity of the subject-matter to the observer, makes it worthy of the philosopher's attention. This passage could well be taken as programmatic for the Dominicans' task: they had turned to a study of the natural world because their opponents had despised it and when their predecessors had ignored it. Like Aristotle they studied it not for itself but because knowledge of it had significance in a higher realm of thought. Thomas indeed seems to identify with the Aristotelian position, and in doing so paraphrases Aristotle in a Christian way: 'Because of this we must consider the forms of creatures and delight in the artifex who made them.'[29] Again, believing himself to be paraphrasing Aristotle, Thomas holds that nothing has been *created* useless or without purpose: in all natural things, even in vile animals, there is something noble and wonderful.

The most luminous figure in the Dominican education programme was Albertus Magnus. He was persuaded to join the Dominicans by Jordanus of Saxony in Padua in 1223,[30] and may have made the acquaintance of Aristotle's natural works here or in Bologna, in the previous year. He returned to Germany for nearly 20 years, having become a lektor in 1228, and from this period dates his *De Natura Boni*, 'On the Nature of Good', which makes use of some of the *libri naturales* (the *Physics*, *Metaphysics*, *On the Soul* and *On the Heaven*). The Master-General of the Order sent him to Paris to study, in the early 1240s. For two years he lectured on the *Sentences* as a bachelor and from 1242 to 1248 he was a regent master in one of the two Dominican chairs. He was thus in Paris with William of Auvergne and the artists' proctor, William of St Amour, all important figures in the story of natural philosophy.[31] As we have seen, it was unusual for Dominicans to study at a secular *studium* (it required the permission of the Master-General) but not so unusual for Dominicans to fill positions as teachers.[32] Thomas Aquinas arrived, as Albertus' Dominican pupil in theology, in 1245.

So Albertus and Aquinas were in Paris on the theological business of the Order. Despite the apparent rejection of the Aristotelian physical works in Paris, it may have been the case that Albertus and his pupil studied them there. In 1248 they were both sent by the Order to set up a Dominican *studium* in Cologne. A great deal of Albertus' written output from about 1250 was a paraphrase of Aristotle's natural works modified for use in the new Dominican *studia*. It was again the Dominican education programme in action: Albertus says that the whole of his *scientia naturalis* was an attempt to satisfy the demands of the Brothers, who for many years had asked him for a physics (which in Aristotelian fashion, was the basis of the whole *scientia*).[33] Albertus replied to their prayers (in about 1249)[34] in a characteristically Dominican fashion, beginning with God as the Creator and governor of the natural world and taking it for granted that Aristotle's business had been to describe the Creation. Albertus' own business (he says) was then to follow Aristotle's order and opinions and give an explanation of them. To achieve the latter he has to offer proofs and other things that Aristotle did not include in his text – that is, Albertus' devices to Christianize Aristotle. In this way Albertus contrives to be in a position where he is expanding and completing Aristotle's enterprise, and in doing so making it seem natural that it is a Christian enterprise. By such means Albertus hoped to bring clarity to Aristotle's famous 'obscurity'.[35] His mode of presentation was adapted for teaching in the *studia*, for it includes the treatment of disputed questions and digressions.

Albertus called his philosophy of nature *philosophia realis*, the term used in the *studium* of Toulouse. The term meant philosophy 'about the things [*res*] themselves', that is, about their natures, where 'nature' was still the nature-of-a-thing. The term included Aristotle's physical subjects, but *also* mathematics: its three parts were physics, metaphysics and mathematics. It was Albertus' intention to make these thoroughly intelligible to his Latin audience, that is, in the Dominican *studia*. In doing so he equates metaphysics with theology and makes it the principal subject of study, the *philosophia prima*. In a very unAristotelian way, mathematics is then the second subject in order, being concerned with matter and perceptible motion. Here is another major way in which Aristotle's physical philosophy, which did not include mathematics, was modified for Dominican purposes within the *studium*. In this sequence of topics, physics is last. For the purposes of *teaching* however, Albertus worked in essentially the other direction. His teaching began with Aristotle's *Physics* as a general study of simple and mixed mobiles. This was followed by a study of their form in *De Generatione et Corruptione* and of their motion from place to place in *De Caelo*. After this motions of actual mixed bodies were examined in the *Meteorologia*. Albertus divided mixed bodies into two categories, of which the first was composed of bodies without souls. These were held to be dealt with by the text called *De Mineralibus*, then attributed to Aristotle, but now to Avicenna. Ensouled bodies were, said Albertus, treated of in a series of works, beginning with that on the soul itself, *De Anima*. For Albertus of course the soul was not only the Aristotelian principle of animal life, but the vehicle of Christian immortality. For both reasons it took precedence[36] in this sequence of the Aristotelian *libri naturales*, and was followed by those works in which were described the actions of the soul and its parts in the living body: the texts on life and death, length of life, sleeping and waking, memory and reminiscence, sense and the sensed, respiration and the motion of animals. Here Albertus added the little book by Costa ben Lucca on the difference between soul and spirit (it explains in simple terms what classical authors like Galen meant by 'spirit'). Lastly in the whole sequence of Albertus' *philosophia naturalis* come the works on animals and plants.[37]

Although his basic technique was to paraphrase the Aristotelian works, Albertus also drew on his immediate predecessors, like Vincent of Beauvais and the English translator and commentator Alfred of Shareshill, whose work on the pseudo-Aristotelian *De Plantis* was in use in Oxford.[38] Albertus also used an Oxford model in dividing the text of *De Anima* for commentary. He also used some of the Salernitan questions.[39] The technique of paraphrase-plus-new material is in the style of Avicenna, whose expositions of Aristotle came to be eclipsed by adoption of the analytical and rational commentaries of Averroes by the mid-thirteenth century.[40] To this method Albertus often adds formal lists of objects or qualities, sometimes alphabetical.[41]

Thus his *De Animalibus* (early 1260s) is derived from Aristotle's works on animals. But it is modified for its immediate and for its ultimate purpose in the new Dominican *studia*. First, it is constructed partly on material that had been used in disputations, and its purpose was partly to provide material for later disputations, a circumstance that undoubtedly helped to shape the work. Secondly, Albertus recognizes and attempts to follow Aristotle's practice by treating the *scientia* of the body as double: first to know the differences in the parts of animals and secondly to discover 'true and natural causes' of the parts and their differences.[42] But Albertus cannot fully carry out what he took to be

Aristotle's programme. In the first place he recognizes that his audience is less sophisticated (unwise and rustic, he says) than the Greek philosophers whom he took Aristotle to be addressing. Because of this, he has to do what Aristotle expressly rejected, that is, to repeat many of the details of structure when describing related species. In his own words, he was 'adding seven books to what Aristotle has done so well in this *scientia*'.[43] Part of this addition is a series of alphabetical lists of names, which although not, as he says, *proprium* to philosophy is useful because animals are handled (in a *scientia*) by their names; and of course, unlike Aristotle, he had Arabic and Latin names to handle, too. His alphabetical list begins to take on the function of an index to the literature. The form adopted by Albertus would render the great bulk of the work readily accessible to students who wanted topics to defend or attack a thesis in a disputation, or Preachers who wanted examples of God's creation to use in preaching or teaching. Aristotle's books on animals, particularly the *Historia Animalium* contains for example, accounts of their 'personalities' (foxes are sly) that would have been entirely sympathetic to the views of the Church Fathers. It is in these ways that Albertus adapts Aristotle to the new circumstances of teaching within a *studium*.

Moreover, Aristotle had to be squeezed into a *studium* that was Christian, and this meant in fact modifying Aristotle's argument. Aristotle's procedure in the *Historia Animalium* was to compare the parts of animals first, and to consider the causes of the differences and similarities later (in the *De Partibus Animalium*). Important among the causes so discovered were the formal and final, both of which, in different ways, involved the soul.[44] Thus in some sense for Aristotle the nature of the soul was inferred from the nature of animals, of whose life it was the essence. On the other hand *De Anima* starts[45] with the notion of the soul as the principle of animal life and seeks to explain its working in the body.

Of these two modes of procedure, the latter was much more congenial to Albertus. As a learned Dominican he knew all about the soul, and had already dealt with it when coming to compose the books on animals.[46] So the books on animals now become an account of what the soul does in life: its state, its generation, and its part in the generation of animals.[47] That is to say, he *begins* with the human soul of Christian doctrine. This soul is the vehicle of Christian immortality and its perfection, which had been the goal of the philosophies of the twelfth century by means of living the good life. But Albertus also treats of it in a Greek philosophical way and proceeds to explore those components of it that had in fact come into Christian belief from Greek philosophy: the vital and nutritive faculties, by which the soul gives the body its heat and powers of motion and generation. Albertus is effectively treating the animal body as a manifestation of the soul, not deriving a knowledge of the soul from an inspection of animals. For this reason too his sequence of exposition is different from Aristotle's. He begins with perfectly general accounts of how animals differ from man, then moves on to causes of the parts, then to generation as the way the soul organizes the developing body and finally to descriptions of individual animals. Albertus' treatment of animals is just one example of his philosophy as it touched upon nature, but it exemplifies well the Dominican position that the natural world was good and was evidence of the work of a single good Creator, and should therefore be studied.

Kilwardby

Robert Kilwardby came from Paris to Oxford during the time when Albertus was continuing the Dominican programme in Germany. He seems to have been in Paris for about eight years, from 1237 to 1245, covering his arts course during a period in which natural philosophy was about to be taught again after the cessation of lectures of 1229 and which reached into the period of Albertus' stay in Paris. His book on the history and types of knowledge, *De Ortu Scientiarum* gives another view of Dominican natural philosophy.[48] It was written about 1250, after Robert had become a Dominican, but before he had finished his theological studies. What is interesting about Robert is that he, even more than Vincent, makes a serious attempt to give a history of the branches of knowledge, rather than a historicized ideal curriculum, as Hugh of St Victor had done in the previous century (although Robert borrows from Hugh). To give a history of something is often to defend its apparent novelty with the dignity of age. Robert is defending Dominican philosophy of nature, and the history he constructs for it is a nice blend of pagan philosophy and Christian doctrine, which is what we might expect in view of the reasons behind the Dominican philosophy of nature.

Robert's history of philosophy-as-it-looked-at-nature begins with an opinion of Aristotle's (in the *Metaphysics*) that men first began to philosophize in their admiration for wonderful things. This was a starting point natural to an Order of Preachers whose own origin and philosophy were events designed to deny the evilness of natural things. From this beginning, says Robert, men slowly began to recognize the enduring constants in an ever-changing world of appearance. The Aristotelian qualities constitute such a reality: they are the causes of generation and corruption and as *naturales* are basic to all change

(Robert has in mind Aristotle's account in the books *On Life and Death*, and *On Sense*.) The next stage in the slow and painful growth of the philosophy of nature, says Robert, was the recognition that the changes, particularly annual, of the lower world were caused by the unceasing circular motions of the heavens. The moving forces, above and below, were called *natura* and each of the moving bodies was a *naturale*: it follows, concludes Robert, that the knowledge of mobiles is *scientia naturalis*. The purpose of Robert's 'natural knowledge' is to satisfy the desire of the soul to know things; 'All men by nature desire to know', says Aristotle in the *Metaphysics*. According to Robert the Dominican, the natural object of man's desire to know is all knowable nature, that is, God and his Creation. So the *scienta* of mobiles combined with that of God produces *philosophia*. Robert is careful to call this catholic knowledge, to be sharply distinguished from knowledge of malign spirits and their operations, which he calls magic. (Neither are judicial astrology or the theatre good for *catholici*.) Useful, catholic philosophy (it is called 'theoretical' when not concerned with such human matters as ethics) is divine and 'perfective': it not only satisfies the desire to know, and so improves the soul, but teaches how to live well. (In this it is like Robert's divine science, or theology, which is not theoretical philosophy but a 'necessary science' that shows how to live and what to believe in order to achieve salvation.) This practical and religious aim of philosophy is achieved in an Aristotelian way in Robert's account: the intellectual desire of the soul to know depends upon the sensitive appetite and must rely on the senses. As Aristotle said, there is nothing in the mind that was not first in the senses; but nothing of God is directly perceptible, so how does philosophy achieve its aim? Robert's answer is to borrow from Augustine's literal interpretation of *Genesis* and declare that a *cognitio scientifica* (God is to be known intellectually) can be achieved in a corporeal, spiritual and intellectual way, and that the latter two correspond to Aristotle's 'intellectual cognition'.

Robert also gives a firmly catholic cast to his metaphysics, as part of philosophy, by giving it a historical treatment. Men first, he says, admired Substance as matter and form. But then they began to consider spiritual substance, that is, substance as prior to and without matter and form. Finally they saw that this caused substance could not be understood fully without reference to its creator, the creative eternal substance.

To summarize, Robert is to a certain extent suggesting an ideal basic education for a Dominican. Aristotle is its centre, but as we have seen, has had to be modified in accordance with catholic principles. Nor is Aristotle complete, and Robert has to give the reader an account of the origin and nature of geometry and perspective. What binds them all together as philosophy is that they are – and Robert is very clear on this – all divine, in that they concern parts of the Creation.

The difficulties in an Aristotelianism that was providing the basis for a Dominican philosophy of nature were probably seen more acutely by Dominican theologians than artists. Kilwardby's book on the *scientiae* as we have seen dates from before he began to read theology. As a master of theology (1256), Prior Provincial of the English Dominicans (1261) and Archbishop of Canterbury (1272) he may well have felt (as Vincent of Beauvais did on becoming a bishop) some hesitation about Aristotle's curiosity about the natural world. Kilwardby the Archbishop banned some Aristotelian propositions in Oxford as Bishop Tempier was banning more in Paris.

The Dominican educational curriculum was reorganized in 1259 at a General Chapter of the Order in Valenciennes. Albertus, Aquinas and Pietro di Tarantasia (later Pope Innocent V) were members of a committee that drew up a new course of study. This paralleled what was going on in the universities, and the Brothers moved up in their *studia* through grades of bachelor and master.[49] Their course of study included a philosophy of nature, which was to be served by new translations of Aristotle. More translation seems to have begun in 1262 in Orvieto, where Pope Urban IV had his court and apparently displayed an interest in philosophy. In that year not only Aquinas and Albertus Magnus, but the translator William of Moerbeke were also in Orvieto, and it has been said that Aquinas 'was at the centre of an organized attempt to make Aristotle available to the world of western scholarship'.[50] But of course Aristotle had been available for two generations or so for those who found him useful. For the Dominicans, who found him very useful, this was the last stage of their thirteenth-century education programme. By now the Dominican schools included *studia naturalia* with curricula which that of the arts course of the universities closely resembled.[51]

Aquinas

Aquinas is easily the central figure in Dominican natural philosophy. Canonized in 1323, his influence was immense and he is commonly accepted as the architect of the medieval reconciliation of Aristotelian philosophy and Christianity.

He learned his liberal arts at Naples (from 1239) before becoming a Dominican in 1244 and from 1245 until 1248 he was in Paris as a pupil of Albertus Magnus. He had then undoubtedly made the acquaintance of Aristotle's physical works before coming to Paris, where they were still banned, and as a Preacher inside the Dominican *studium* it is unlikely that the ban applied to him; it may in any case have been intended only for the artists. After three or four years in Cologne with Albertus, Aquinas returned to Paris in 1252. He arrived at a critical time. The artists were beginning to frame their first statutes, in part against the encroachments made on teaching positions by the friars. Aquinas entered the battle and wrote extensively on why members of the religious orders should be allowed to join the secular *consortium* of the teaching masters, the group they had formed for promoting their own interests and which formed the essence of the university.

Bowing to papal pressure the masters admitted Aquinas and the Franciscan Bonaventure to their group. They had already admitted another two friars and both Dominicans and Franciscans became very powerful groups in the university, doing the Pope's business and dominating the teaching of theology. The secular masters complained loudly of being constrained to remain as regents in arts. What they taught were the liberal arts, now in an almost completely Aristotelian form. Natural philosophy, derived from the *libri naturales* and adapted to Christianity in the Dominican fashion, was what was read by the bachelor who intended to become a master: it was this knowledge that was a criterion used by the masters in incepting the candidate. This is at least what the statutes and the manuscript texts and notes of the students bear witness to, and there is little reason to doubt that this was the actual practice. In addition, the chancellor required evidence that the student had a wide range of knowledge in other and more traditional fields before awarding the licence to teach, the *ius ubique docendi*.

In short Aquinas typifies the influence of the friars. They were the Pope's agents and he actively promoted them. The Dominicans had conceived of a particular use of Aristotle's physical works in fighting heresy and to spread their message by preaching and teaching they inserted themselves into the secular *studia* to secure as wide an audience and as many new members as possible. Their education and re-education programme was to be grafted on to systems already constructed by secular masters.

Having played a major part in this task in Paris, and having taken the master's degree in theology, Aquinas spent the years 1259 to 1268 at the papal Curia in Rome. Here he wrote one of the greatest books of his life and of the whole Trobadourean period, the *Summa Contra Gentiles*. It sets out with clarity and authority the Dominican position on heresy, natural philosophy and learning, the three things that had forged the Order of Preachers and taken Aquinas himself to Paris. The book is second only to, and was written shortly before, the great *Summa Theologica*, which was intended to set out the whole of Christian thinking. Clearly, the culmination of his life's work could be attempted only after the final removal of the objections, difficulties and errors of the *gentiles*: infidels, apostates and above all, heretics. The book was intended as a guide to Dominican missionaries spreading the word of true Catholic orthodoxy among such mistaken people.

In the *Summa Contra Gentiles* Aquinas sets out his position with a claim of authority, and in an entirely characteristic way, by relying on complementary quotations from the Bible and Aristotle. His claim is derived from Aristotle's remark in the *Topics* that they who direct and guide things well are said to be wise, and asserts that wisdom is to govern things well (he cites the *Metaphysics*). Wisdom of course is religious ('For my mouth will speak truth; and wickedness is an abomination to my lips'[52]) and Aquinas' claim is essentially that the Wise have the right to govern things. It is the wise who see that the correct ordering of things – all things – is done in view of their end or purpose. And the purpose of things – everything – is the Good.

So Aquinas' very notion of wisdom excludes our heretics' view of the natural world and its evil. Not only that, but Aquinas uses wisdom of this sort to defend the hierarchical structure of knowledge of arts and society. Knowledge of the purpose of things, he says, involves knowledge of how some things are subordinate to others, as the art of making pigments (as components of medicines) is subordinate to health, the goal of the art of medicine in which the pigments are used. Similarly subordinate to the overall military purpose are the 'knights and all the apparatus of war'.[53] The purpose behind such things is the business of the 'principal arts' and of their architectonic practitioners, who alone can be called wise. Again, the Wise are as Christian as they are Aristotelian and Aquinas is ready with appropriate quotations: 'According to the grace of God which is given unto me, as a wise masterbuilder, I have laid the foundation ... '[54] and 'to be wise is to consider the highest causes'.[55]

The 'highest causes' that Aquinas derives from Aristotle are for him identifiable with the purposes of things because they both unite in the purpose of the Creator in making them. Aquinas argues that the purpose of the whole universe is 'the good of the intellect'.[56] Many a Greek philosopher would have agreed, and agreed too with Aquinas' equation of 'the good of the intellect' with 'truth'. It is equally philosophical for Aquinas to assert that wisdom takes such truth as its subject-matter, but he leaves the philosophers behind in arguing that divine wisdom clothed in flesh was Christ, come into the world as a witness to the truth.

In arguing thus Aquinas is doing what many others (as we have seen) had done and making philosophy the intellectual arm of Christianity. But he is also reinforcing the claim of Christians of his kind to 'order' or control others. It was not only that his conception of wisdom excluded the heretics from the start, it was that wisdom as a knowledge of purpose put some some actions or arts and their practitioners above others, and that the ultimate wisdom was Christ as seen by the Catholic Church. In this way the Church of Christ had both philosophical and revealed authority. Its duty with relation to truth was not only to reveal it, but to supress falsity. Just as medicine in seeking health has to oppose illness, so the Wise have a double duty in speaking the truth ('For my mouth will speak truth') and in the suppression of falsity ('and wickedness is an abomination to my lips').[57]

In setting out how he intends to suppress the falsity of the *gentiles*, Aquinas shows himself aware of the problem that we saw others had in promoting their form of Christianity. It is necessary, says Aquinas,[58] to choose one's weapons appropriately. Against Jews, use the Old Testament, for they accept its authority. Against heretics, use the New Testament, for they accept only this (we have seen how the Cathars rejected the Old Testament as the work of the Evil Principle). But against the pagans, who accept neither, 'it is necessary to return to natural reason, with which all are compelled to agree'.[59]

We have seen indeed that it was on the New Testament that the Catholics concentrated when attacking the Cathars. We have also seen that when counter-example and the drawing of different *distinctiones* made a clear-cut victory difficult on either side, 'natural' reasons were employed. The Catholics using natural reasons against the Cathars were essentially in the same position as Aquinas against the pagans, because the New Testament was for one or other reason no longer effective. While the Catholics at first (because the heretics had begun to do so) used Aristotle's 'nature books' to supply 'natural reasons', Aquinas' use of 'natural reason' is wider. He sets out that at a fundamental level there are two ways of knowing truth – that is, God – revelation and philosophy. Revelation gives what is above and beyond reason, while philosophy supplies demonstrative proofs 'in the light of natural reason'.[60] Of this 'double approach to truth' Aquinas here uses only the philosophical, since his concern is with those who cannot accept the Sacred Page and its revealed word and so who present no common ground for argument.

Historians of theology have often taken this 'natural reason' of Aquinas to have belonged to, or even to have begun, a Catholic tradition of 'natural theology'. The argument is that it represents an approach to God based on the power of reason 'natural' to man, that is, what God supplied him with at Creation (subject to the effects of the fall). But reason is 'natural' for Aquinas also because it is taken from, or indeed includes, natural philosophy, and here we are closer to the earlier Catholic use of natural reasons against the Cathars. Thus at one level 'natural reason' for Aquinas means demonstrative argument, taken from

Aristotle's logical works and applicable within natural philosophy. The principal use of demonstration for Aquinas was not to reach a high level of truth but to destroy the arguments of the *gentiles*.[61] Demonstrative reasoning was 'natural' for Aquinas because it was innate in intelligent men and had simply been codified by Aristotle. We have seen that this was the case for William of Auvergne too, for when his opponents did not use Aristotelian dialectic, he saw them as devoid of the power of reason. For Aquinas, since 'natural reason cannot oppose the truth of faith'[62] the fact that his opponents and especially the heretics had the wrong faith was to be explained by their having little natural reason.

In these ways Aquinas discussed God in terms that were equally suitable for the Christian society in which he lived and the natural philosophy that the Dominicans had derived so largely from Aristotle. In proving the existence and eternity of God from natural reasons, Aquinas makes abundant use of the principles of motion in the *Physics*: act, potency, the unmoved mover and so on. The *Metaphysics* as a study of Being was also of great use to him. The same may be said of his demonstration of the singleness and immateriality of God, in the course of which he attacks the Cathars who believed that [the good] God was 'a certain infinite substance of light distended through an infinite space'.[63] In these proofs of God's attributes natural reason is both the reason that is innate and natural to man and the reasons drawn from nature in the Aristotelian *libri naturales*, including *De Caelo et Mundo* and the *Meteorologica*. His proof that God is single is directed primarily at the Cathars.[64]

An important doctrine that Aquinas had to overcome in his natural reasoning about God was that God had no knowledge of particulars. Some men of Aquinas' time were arguing that the myriad of details that made up man's daily experience were too numerous, accidental, insignificant, transient or disgusting to be worthy of God's interest. Aquinas sets out systematically to prove that on the contrary God knew of these things, not only in the past but in the future, and also of man's every whim and use of particulars. It is a major task that he had to undertake, not only because of the influence of these dangerous opinions but because the whole scheme of Dominican natural philosophy rested its Christianized Aristotle on God as the First Cause of everything, on the physical world as the effects of God's causality and on the duty of looking at particulars of the physical world in the light of their relation to the First Cause. Here Aquinas is almost certainly (he is not explicit) attacking the Averroistic Aristotelians in the universities, probably Paris, who argued that God was separated from the physical world by a hierarchy of generative Intelligences. He is also implicitly attacking the Cathars, who maintained that the good God did not know of the particulars of the evil physical world. He argued, as the Catholics had now been arguing against the Cathars for some time, that God knows evil and its particulars as a human and voluntary turning away – privation – from Him.[65]

It is because Dominican natural philosophy had this nature that Aquinas devotes the later books of the *Summa Contra Gentiles* to natural reasons taken from the things that God had created. By thinking upon created things, says the Angelic Doctor, we can admire the divine wisdom, power, goodness and perfection.[66] And by the same means, he adds, we can destroy the erroneous opinions of others, like those who think that there are two principles of things, or that things happen by necessity of nature rather than by divine will.[67] So Dominican natural philosophy for Aquinas as for William of Auvergne could be used against both those who in their dualism denied the goodness of nature and those who made it too autonomous. Again the enemies are the Cathars and the Averroists.

The problem of evil, including the perceived evilness of the physical world, which we saw was so central to the Cathars' beliefs, forms a major part of Aquinas' *Summa*. The book is organized so that 'natural reasoning' about God and His attributes logically takes precedence and occupies the first book. The remaining three books are given over to a consideration of God's creatures – His creation – by means of 'natural reasons' in the sense of being taken from nature. The question of evil in the physical world takes up the first 15 chapters of the third book[68] and so is a major plank of Aquinas' argument. It is expressly directed at the Cathars, the modern Manichees.

We must therefore give some attention to Aquinas' argument about evil. He handles the problem in a characteristic way, supporting the Sacred Page with a judicious selection of Aristotelian arguments. All things, he says, act for an end and for Good, which is ultimately God's will, but which is also expressed in Aristotle's *Ethics*. It is not only that Aquinas in a Dominican way has identified Creation with 'nature' in the general sense of the word and is demonstrating that both are good, but also that the natures-of-things are also good in an Aristotelian sense of fulfilment; that is that they reach their goal of full development, that their forms fully inform their matter. When Aquinas says evil is not 'a nature'[69] he means it is not a nature of a thing in this Aristotelian sense: it has no existence of its own, but is simply privation of good. This is perhaps a patristic commonplace, but with Aquinas is thoroughly Aristotelian. To the *Ethics* and the Sacred Page Aquinas adds natural-philosophy arguments about causality that the Catholics had been obliged to use in their direct confrontations with the Cathars and which Aquinas now essentially codifies. His argument is that evil is secondary to good; indeed, good produces evil by privation. The whole system of causality for Aquinas is a single one based on the uncaused Highest Good, *summum bonum*. Good is the *only* source of evil, for evil does not beget evil. There is then for Aquinas no *summum malum* as a source for all evil, as there was for the Cathars. He assembles the arguments with relentless patience: things that happen not from their essences but, in an Ariostotelian sense, Accidentally, like evil, are posterior to things that happen *per se* and cannot be a principle of other things; evil has no essence; it cannot give rise to good; it is always caused, never a cause; the *summum bonum* is entirely without evil: 'by this is removed the error of the Manichees, who suppose a certain Evil Principle which is the source of all evils'.[70]

In Aquinas' arguments against the heretics, natural reason, reasons taken from Aristotle's nature book and those from the Sacred Page are hardly to be separated: it is a synthesis of elements whose earlier separate stories we have now become familiar with. When he says that every agent works for good and thus also that all things have a good purpose (*finis*); that all things desire the good, whether they know it or not (and that if they do not know it they are moved by something else); that the ultimate good and end or *finis* is God, his story is a seamless garment. God is the cause of all causes, just as fire is the cause of all heat, for in any hierarchy or category of causes the first is the greatest; in the category of final causes God is the ultimate. In medicine (continues Aquinas) where a potion is the cause of purging, purging the cause of reduction, and reduction the cause of health, health is the superior final cause; so in the physical world God is not only the source of all things but their goal, their final cause, the reason for them to tend to assimilate themselves to Him. Nowhere is this more true and important than in the case of intellectual substances, whose *finis* is to know God. Here Aquinas is combining the traditional role of philosophy in a Christian world (which we met in the twelfth century) with an Aristotelian physics and ethics working in a spiritual way, together with a notion of Being in a hierarchy derived from the *Metaphysics* and from Dionysius' work on the celestial hierarchy: all presented with a remorseless Natural Reason 'with which all are compelled to agree', as he said at the outset.[71]

Dominican natural philosophy in Aquinas' hands was partly shaped by the use it had been put to in defending the faith. This included developing the arguments about the nature of the physical world in order to rebut other views. The greatest of these, we have seen, was Catharism, but Aquinas also dealt with David of Dinant, whose views we have also met. He also had to deal with those who said that all natural change was due to God's direct action, and that natural things were otherwise inert. Such a view (Aquinas cites Avicebron)[72] was entirely inconsistent with the teleological Aristotelian doctrine of the natures of things fulfilling themselves, and to counter it Aquinas had to stress that God did indeed work through secondary causes, that is, that He had given things natures and powers with which to act.[73] In developing this answer Aquinas is able to strengthen his earlier view about the nature of evil, so important for the first appearance of Dominican natural philosophy. He now argues that, in the chain of causality from God to material things, it is in the operation of secondary causes that evil arises, which, therefore, is not directly caused by God. Aquinas can now directly answer a question of Boethius: If there is a God, whence comes evil? Aquinas confidently replies that the existence of evil is a *proof* of God's existence, for without evil, which is a privation of good, there would be no chain of good – *ordo boni* – and no God at its head. Developing the argument further, Aquinas can add further reasons from nature to return to attack the Cathars. These are the people, says Aquinas,[74] who see evil in material corruption which they saw as the creation of the devil and which Aristotle saw as a species of natural change. They accordingly denied that the good God's actions reached the earth, being restricted to the incorruptible celestial bodies. Aquinas' answer is his usual authoritative fusion of physics and faith: God's power reaches down even to the corruption of material bodies, but through secondary causes; evil, whether physical or moral, is at one and the same time a privation and a proof of good, operating in secondary causes and showing that the only ultimate chain of causality is from a single good God. Thus 'is destroyed the error of the Manichees, who have proposed two prime principles, good and evil, as if evil could not find a place under the good God's providence'.[75]

Another reason for Aquinas to insist that God's providence reached all matter and particulars, even corruption, was that the Cathars had denied that Christ had a material body. That is, they accepted Christ as a creation of the good God, but could not allow that he had a body of matter, the creation of the Evil Principle. Aquinas attacks the Cathars' notion of Christ's 'fantasm' of a body with a barrage of quotations from the Sacred Page,[76] but his fundamental position is that he prefers a literal, rationalistic reading of the events and particulars of the life of Christ. This is entirely in line with the literal and rationalistic reading of the natural world and its particulars that the Dominicans used in their natural philosophy. It is quite opposed to the other-worldly spirituality of the Cathars, who mocked the rituals of the Catholics as empty procedures carried out with evil matter. Aquinas has to defend Catholic ritual involving sensible particulars as serving human, not divine needs.[77] It is natural, says Aquinas, for man to recognize things by the senses, and it is difficult to rise above them. It is for these reasons, he says, echoing

William of Auvergne, that God has left signs of Himself in the particulars of the sensible world, so that man's attention should be recalled to the divine, even though he is not able to bear the full illumination of God.

In these ways Aquinas defended Dominican natural philosophy against those who gave God too intimate a contact with the physical world (Avicebron and David of Dinant) and those who allowed Him too little (the Averroists and the Cathars). His arguments against the Cathars led him into another set of doctrines from which he had to defend his philosophy, those of magic. The angels who became evil, so important in the Cathars' arguments about the nature of evil, were treated by Aquinas as the 'demons' or 'devils' of common speech.[78] He does not answer some of the Cathars' penetrating questions on the relationship between God as omniscient and omnipotent and angels choosing to obey Him or not, and treats the evil angels as the demons that can be summoned in magic. He discusses them in Aristotelian terms as intellectual substances and argues that they are not evil in nature.[79]

Finally we must look at Aquinas' greatest work, the *Summa Theologica* itself.[80] It would be difficult to exaggerate the importance of this work in the Western intellectual tradition. Yet its authority and the influence it has had on so many subsequent theologians and philosophers can obscure its historical causes. Centuries of commentary do not always make it easy to see the work for what it is – a Dominican document, shaped by the concerns of a thirteenth-century Dominican friar. These concerns include those we have already met and are part of the account we are giving of natural philosophy.

With the masterly clarity of the disposition of his arguments and mode of expression, Aquinas first sets up two matters on which his whole case must rest.[81] They are that God exists; and that we can have valid thoughts about Him. For Aquinas of course it is the second of these that could be the more problematic, and so he deals with it first, for the whole of what follows depends upon its truth. So in the first place Aquinas wants to know what kind of a study theology is, and how far we as imperfect beings can come to be aware of God. From what we have seen of the difference between monastic contemplation and dialectical school theology, it is no surprise to find that Aquinas decides that theology is a *scientia* rather than simply a *sapientia*. The difference is that Aquinas' *sacra scientia*, theology, is overwhelmingly an *argument*. His *Summa* of theology is the text of a Preacher whose Order had been founded to argue against the heretics. Aquinas was aware that the essence of Christianity, belief in the Articles of Faith, was not itself rational, being beyond the powers of reason. He knew that the monks knew God by contemplation and that the Franciscans knew Him in related ways, without argument. But he also knew that defence and propagation of the faith necessarily involved reasoning, as we saw in the *Summa contra Gentiles*. He knew too that it was the duty of the bishops (and of course of his own Order) to preach sound doctrine and to be ready to argue (he says)[82] against those who contradict them. Of all the people who needed reason within the faith, the Preachers needed it most.

Accordingly Aquinas sets out what 'reason' is and produces a characteristic mesh of Christian and Aristotelian thought: arguments are of two kinds (he says), from authority and from reason. While those from authority are in general weak (as Aquinas knew that Aristotle had said) in the *sacra doctrina* they are strong because the authority is Revealed. Likewise, the *scientia* that is produced is also double for Aquinas, reaching into both the rational and the religious: one kind of *scientia* comes from principles known to natural reason, like arithmetic and geometry, while another comes from principles known in a superior *scientia*, as perspective comes through geometry and music from arithmetic. In just the same way, says Aquinas,[83] the *sacra doctrina* comes from the principles of a higher knowledge, that of God and the saints.

The point, then, is both Aristotelian and religious: no branch of knowledge rationally proves its own principles, for they are taken from elsewhere. Ultimately the articles of faith are beyond reason because they cannot be proved by their consequences; and to try to do so would destroy the very merit of faith. Instead, the articles of faith can rationally explain the principles of subalternated fields of knowledge, as when the Apostle derived a general resurrection from the resurrection of Christ. The parallel in the field of reason, continues Aquinas, is metaphysics, the ultimate source of principles that are used in the lower *scientiae*. Again, this question of first principles is equally Aristotelian as Christian, and again formed by the particular circumstances of the Preachers as an Order. Aquinas argues that in metaphysics, it is possible to argue about its first principles against a sceptic as long as he concedes something. Likewise in *sacra scriptura* it is possible to argue about first principles with a sceptic as long as he concedes something of divine revelation, 'just as we dispute against the heretics by the authority of the sacred doctrine', *Sicut per auctoritates sacrae doctrinae disputamus contra haereticos*.[84] Not only does this remind us that in disputing with the Cathars the Catholics had to find some common ground, including natural reasons, but even that the whole mode of argument and its perceived validity was formed among the Preachers by their fight with the Cathars. Rationality itself, as we have seen with William of Auvergne, was Aristotelian dialectic used for Christian purposes.

To summarize to this point, Aquinas is setting out quite briefly and in a tightly organized way why it is that human reason can give us some knowledge of God. That the heretics should occupy space here, in

Aquinas' most general work, and likewise that he should give room here to the discussion about arguments in the defence of the faith, both powerfully suggest that Aquinas' theology was formed primarily in the fight against heresy.

The same may be said of Aquinas' second major proposition, that God exists.[85] Here too the confident use of human reason reflects the early disputations with the heretics. Here too the use of 'natural reason' and 'reasons from nature' is an extension of techniques used previously by both sides. To be sure, says Aquinas, natural reasons and reasons from nature cannot take us all the way to God, but there is no clash between them and faith, 'For since Grace does not destroy nature, but perfects it, it is necessary that natural reason subserves faith'.[86] Nevertheless Aquinas argues that we can actually *demonstrate* the existence of God. He does so in his characteristic way, using a spiritualized Aristotle. Demonstration is double, he declarès; it is by cause, and by effect; it is *propter quid* 'on account of which' and *quia*, simple demonstration 'that'.[87] These are the words of Aristotle's logic, in their Latin versions. In other words, a rational demonstration of God's existence proceeds by an analysis of the causes by which God created the world. It is primarily a question of taking the natural world as evidence of its causes, that could only have come from God. It is of course precisely the argument that the heretics had used to argue the existence of an evil Principle from the nature of the physical world, and precisely the argument used by the Catholics to rebut the Cathars.

Aquinas extends the argument. His technique with such a disputable question as *utrum Deus sit* is the scholastic one of setting up first the opposing proposition and then basing his own on its destruction. The proposition he chooses is surely a Cathar one, namely that if of a pair of 'opposites' one should be infinite, the other could not exist. But if God were infinitely good, says Aquinas as the Devil's advocate, there would be no evil; but there is evil, so there cannot be a God as we know him, as purely good. This argument from the proposition is undoubtedly that used by the Cathars.

In formally proving the existence of God Aquinas calls on arguments from natural reasons and reasons of nature that equally reflect the crisis faced by the Catholic Church as it faced the disruptions of heresy. The first of them is the chain of motion, where every moving thing is said to be moved by something else and all is ultimately derived from a single unmoved mover. This is another Christian use of Aristotle, and a very deliberate choice on Aquinas' part. That everything is moved by something could be seen as fundamental to Aristotle's philosophy of nature, but was not necessary to Christianity, for it was often said that God gave self-active powers to things. Moreover, it would have been entirely possible to emphasize another of Aristotle's principles, the self-fulfillment of every 'nature', as equally Christian but not at first sight concordant with the chain of motion argument. It was not to Aquinas' purposes to do this.

The second of Aquinas' arguments is from the chain of causes. Nothing, he says, can be an efficient cause of itself, because it would have to be prior to itself. Each efficient cause must rely on the action of a higher cause and this upon another: ultimately all must be derived from a single uncaused cause, God. It was of course precisely in disussing hierarchies of causes, the good and the evil, that the Cathars used Aristotelian arguments and prompted the Catholics to reply in kind.

Aquinas' third argument is about Necessity and Possibility of things. That is, some things in an Aristotelian way come into being and pass away, and so are not necessary or eternal and are merely possible beings. But if all the *possibilia esse* were *non esse*, nothing would exist or could begin to exist. There must be necessary things of God's creation. Then by a version of the chain of causality argument Aquinas demonstrates that necessary things have causes, which can only be ultimately referred to God.

Fourthly, Aquinas argues from the hierarchy of Good. There are gradations of things in the world, he says,[88] for things are more, or less, good, noble, true and so on. Mostly such gradations are seen in respect of some maximum. So there must be something which is the hottest, the truest, the best and the most noble. Each of these is a *maxime ens*, the highest thing in that category. Aquinas is using the *Metaphysics* and argues that the *maxime ens* of each category is the *cause* of the lesser grades, as fire is the cause of all heat. Aquinas concludes that for all these there is a single cause of 'all being, good and perfection; and this we call God'.[89]

Lastly, Aquinas argues 'from the governance of things'. Natural bodies without cognition act towards an end, *finis*. They do so always or at least most often, and it is good, the best way for them to act. But this cannot happen by chance, and so they must be directed by God, who knows the purpose, like an archer directing an arrow. There must be something intelligent 'by which all natural things are guided to a purpose; and this we call God'.[90]

Thus *all* of Aquinas' reasons for the existence of God are taken from natural reason and the reasons of nature. It is 'natural reason' because that is what God gave to man's nature; but it is also Aristotle's dialectic. They are 'reasons of nature' because drawn from the natural part of God's creation; but they are also Aristotle's arguments about *physis*. They are reasons appropriate for use against an enemy that does not believe that all of the Sacred Page is sacred and against whom as a consequence the authority of Revelation is a limited weapon. They are reasons appropriate for use by a group formed for the purpose of defending the Catholic view of God and the world against another group who with vigour and learning defended their own belief in the Two Principles. But Aquinas' proofs of God's existence are more than merely appropriate: they are *all* in some way concerned with causality, as were the Cathars' arguments when they turned to natural reason and reasons from nature. And Aquinas, like the Cathars, is trying to prove something very precise about how that causality relates to the goodness of God and the physical world, and to the existence of evil.[91]

Notes

1. Some of the works examined in this section provided material for preaching, that is, the Brothers' preferred form of interaction with the outside world. Others must have provided materials for the education of the novice brothers themselves, and perhaps were directed also at the secular students to whom the Order opened its doors. But we cannot always tell at what audience Dominican texts were aimed, for the range was enormous, from the arts students who heard, without writing, the statutory texts, to the audience, perhaps theological, of Aquinas' huge and sophisticated commentary on Aristotle. According to J.A. Weisheipl, ('The Life and Works of St Albert the Great', in Weisheipl, ed., *Albertus Magnus and the Sciences. Commemorative Essays 1980*, Toronto, Pontifical Institute, 1980, p. 40), the equally large paraphrases of Albertus Magnus were intended not for classroom teaching but as extra-curricular reading for those Brothers preparing for theology.
2. Astrik L. Gabriel, *The Educational Ideas of Vincent of Beauvais*, Notre Dame, Indiana, 1956 (*Texts and Studies in the History of Medieval Education, IV*, ed. A.L. Gabriel and J.N. Garvin), p. 11.
3. B. Smalley, *The Study of the Bible in the Middle Ages*, Oxford, Blackwell, third edn, 1984, p. 310.
4. Vincentius Burgundus, *Bibliotheca Mundi, Speculum Quadruplex, Naturale, Doctrinale, Morale, Historiale*, Douai, 1624. Book I, ch. 4. The *Morale* was completed after Vincent's death.
5. Ibid., 'Doctores, Praedicatores, Expositores': book I, ch. 6.
6. Ibid., astructio: prologue.
7. Ego autem in hoc opere quorundam legentium animos refragari audio, quod nonnullos Aristotelis flosculos, praecipueque ex libris eiusdem Physicis et Mathematicis (quos nequaquam, ego ipse excerpseram, sed a quibusdam fratris excerpta susceperam,) non eodem paenitus verborum schemate, quo in originalibus suis jacent, sed ordinem plerumque transposito; nonnumquam etiam mutata perpaululum ipsorum verborum forma, manente tamen auctoris sententia ... Ibid., prologue, ch. 10, our translation.
8. Ibid., book I, ch. 16.
9. Ibid., book I, ch. 18. See also the *Speculum Doctrinale*, book 1, ch. 26, on the difference between study and curiosity. Historians of science, of course,

have grasped at Vincent's curiosity about natural particulars as evidence of 'medieval science'. In such a view Vincent's very purposes in writing, the goal which determined everything he wrote, become merely obfuscating habits. Thorndike says Vincent 'cannot keep his mind off' religious topics; Vincent has 'excessive theological bias' which 'makes his compilation, extensive as it is, scarcely representative of medieval natural science at its best'; L. Thorndike, *A History of Magic and Experimental Science*, New York, Macmillan, 1923–58, vol. 2, p. 466.

10. *Speculum Quadruplex* ... , book III, ch. 35.
11. Ibid., book I, ch. 11 (the sources); book I, ch. 7 (the queen of the *scientiae*).
12. Mundus iste sensibilis, quasi quidam liber est scriptus digito Dei. Ibid., book I, ch. 10.
13. Ibid., prologue; book I, ch. 2.
14. Ibid., book I, ch. 6.
15. Ibid., book I, ch. 11.
16. Quidam etiam (ut cum stomacho loquor) tam fideles et cauti verborum observatores existunt, adeoque fideliter, ac syncere de quibuslibet libris sententias notabiles excerpi volunt, ut nec minimum iota de verbis ipsius auctoris, sive etiam de verborum ordine patiantur immutari; huiusmodi tamen cautelae districtionem patros nostros Doctores catholicos, nec in antiquorum flosculis excerpendis, nec in libris aliorum transferendis omnino tenuisse cognovi. Ibid., prologue, ch. 10, our translation.
17. Quoted by E.A. Moody, 'William of Auvergne and his Treatise "De Anima"', in his *Studies in Medieval Philosophy, Science and Logic*, University of California Press, 1975, pp. 12 ff.
18. *Speculum Quadruplex* ... , book I, ch. 21.
19. Ibid., book II, chs 12, pp. 35–41.
20. *Speculum Doctrinale*, book 1, ch. 9
21. *Speculum Doctrinale*, book 1, chs 14–18.
22. On *natura naturans* and *naturata*, see O. Weijers, *Pseudo-Boèce: De Disciplina Scolarium*, Leiden, 1976, esp. p. 169.
23. It also explains why they have been taken by historians of science, erroneously, as medieval scientific encyclopedias.
24. Thomas of Cantimpré, *Liber de Natura Rerum*: edn of Berlin and New York, 1973. Bartholomew of England's near contemporary book, with a very similar title, played a complementary but different role in Franciscan natural philosophy (for which see Chapter 9).
25. Thorndike, vol. 2, p. 376.
26. Thomas of Cantimpré, *Liber De Natura Rerum*, pp. 313–14. What St Augustine wrote (Book II, c. 39, para. 59) was this: 'What some men have done in regard to all words found in Scripture, in the Hebrew, and Syriac, and Egyptian, and other tongues, taking up and interpreting separately such as were left in Scripture without interpretation ... making it unnecessary for the Christian to spend his strength on many subjects for the sake of a few items of knowledge, the same, I think, might be done in regard to other matters, if any competent man were willing in a spirit of benevolence to undertake the labour for the advantage of his fellow brethren. In this way he might arrange in their several classes, and give an account of the unknown places, and animals, and plants, and trees, and stones, and metals, and other species of things that are mentioned in Scripture, taking up these only, and committing his account to writing'.

Augustine, *On Christine Doctrine*, translated by J.F. Shaw, Edinburgh, Clark, 1873, p. 75. It is ironical that this passage is part of an attack by Augustine on the importance of secular learning!

27. Hiis ergo scriptis si quis studium adhibuerit, ad argumenta fidei et correctiones morum integumentis mediis sufficientiam reperiet, ut interdum predicatore quasi e vestigio scriptuarum apte digresso cessantibus eloquiis prophetarum ad evigilationem brutarum mentium oculata fide creaturarum adducat testes, ut si quem saepius audita de scripturis et inculcata non movent, saltem nova in ore suo pigritantium aures demulceant. Thomas of Cantimpré, *Liber De Natura Rerum*, p. 5, our translation.
28. We quote it *in extenso* in Chapter 1, pp. 10–11.
29. Propter hoc igitur debemeus considerare formas creaturarum et delectari in artifice qui fecit illas; Thomas, *Liber De Natura Rerum*, prologue, p. 4.
30. See Weisheipl, 'The Life and Works of St Albert the Great'; J. van Steenbergen, *Aristotle in the West. The Origins of Latin Aristotelianism*, Louvain, 1970, p. 121.
31. Albertus represented the interests of the friars in Paris to the Pope, just as William of St Amour represented the very different interests (which also included natural philosophy) of the artists. See also Thorndike, *Magic and Experimental Science*, vol. II, p. 525 who says that while in Italy Albertus discovered the text of Aristotle's book on the motions of animals.
32. Weisheipl, 'The Life and Works of St Albert the Great' pp. 13–25.
33. Albertus Magnus, *De Vegetabilibus libri VII. Historiae Naturalis Pars XVIII*, ed. E. Meyer and C. Jessen, Berlin, 1867, p. xxv.
34. Weisheipl, 'The Life and Works of St Albert the Great', p. 30.
35. For centuries the Aristotelian commentators (especially in Alexandria) had asked a rote of formal questions in teaching Aristotle's texts. One of them was: Why is Aristotle's work so difficult? See R.K. French, 'A Note on the Anatomical Accessus of the Middle Ages', *Medical History*, **23**, 1979, pp. 461–8. Of course the light that Albertus was able to bring to Aristotle's obscurity was Christian.
36. See also K. Park, 'Albert's Influence on Late Medieval Psychology', in Weisheipl, *Albertus Magnus and the Sciences*, p. 504.
37. In his work on plants (Book III, chs 3 to 9) Albertus relies partly on a translation and commentary made by Alfred of Shareshill, and probably used in Oxford. It is possible that the study of the banned *libri naturales* was reintroduced to Paris from Oxford.
38. Alfred's circle seems to have included David of Dinant, some of whose heretical fragments are preserved where Albertus refutes them in his commentaries on the physical works of Aristotle. G. Théry, 'Autour du Décret du 1210' ... , *Bibliothèque Thomiste*, **VI**, 1925, pp. 13, 120. See also D.A. Callus, 'Introduction of Aristotelian Learning to Oxford' *Proceedings of the British Academy*, 1943, p. 2.
39. B. Lawn, *The Prose Salernitan Questions*, London, 1979, p. xviii.
40. Callus, 'Introduction of Aristotelian Learning to Oxford', p. 265.
41. See also K. Reeds, 'Albert on the Natural Philosophy of Plant Life', in Weisheipl, *Albertus Magnus and the Sciences*, p. 341.
42. Albertus Magnus, *De Animalibus Libri XXVI*, ed. H. Stadler, 2 vols, Münster, 1916–21, vol. 1, p. 2 (book 1, ch. 1 where *veras et physicas causas* is the quivalent of *causas naturales et veras*: p. 761 (book 11, ch. 1).

43. Addentes hiis quae ab Aristotele de hac scientia bene digesta sunt, libros septem. Albertus, *De Animalibus*, book 1, ch. 1, p. 4.
44. 639a–641a.
45. 402a.
46. Albertus, *De Animalibus*, book 1, ch. 1, p. 2.
47. See also B.M. Ashley, 'St Albert and the Nature of Natural Science', in Weisheipl, *Albertus Magnus and the Sciences*, p. 94, who points out that Avicenna also dealt with the soul before the combined 'animal book' in his own paraphrase of Aristotle.
48. Robert Kilwardby, *De Ortu Scientiarum*, ed. A.G. Judy, Toronto (British Academy/Pontifical Institute), 1976, p. xii.
49. Weisheipl, 'Life and Works', p. 39.
50. Thomas Aquinas, *Commentary on Aristotle's Physics*, trans. R.J. Blackwell, R.J. Spath and W.E. Thirlkel, London, 1963, p. xix.
51. H. Rashdall, *The Universities of Europe in the Middle Ages*, eds Powicke and Emden, Oxford University Press, 3 vols, 1936, vol. 1, p. 371.
52. Veritatem meditabitur guttur meum, et labia mea detestabuntur impium. These are the words, Proverbs VIII,7, with which Aquinas opens his first book: *Summae Contra Gentiles Libri Quatuor*. We have used the edition of Rome, 1924.
53. Et in militari, respectu equestris et omnis bellici apparatus. Que quidem artes, aliis principantes, architectonicae nominantur, quasi principales artes; unde et earum artifices, qui architectones vocantur, nomen sibi vindicant sapientum. Aquinas, ibid., book 1, proem (p. 1).
54. Ut sapiens architecton fundamentum posui (1 Corinthians III.10): ibid., p. 1.
55. Unde, secundum Philosophum (ut supra) [Metaphysics] sapientis est causas altissimas considerare. Ibid., book 1, proem (p. 1).
56. Oportet ergo ultimum finem universi esse bonum intellectus. Ibid., book 1, proem, (p. 2).
57. As a good scholastic, Aquinas uses this quotation of Proverbs as a proposition, opening his proem as with a lemma from the Bible. The ensuing discussion is then a determination of the proposition, to which he returns as the proem closes. He has 'proved' it in the manner of the schools and so added authority to his already powerful Christianized Aristotle.
58. *Summa Contra Gentiles*, book 1, ch. 2 (p. 3).
59. ... quia quidam eorum, ut Machomestite et Pagani, non conveniunt nobiscum in auctoritate alicujus scriturae, per quam possint convinci; sicut contra Judaeos disputare possumus per Vetus Testamentum; contra haereticos, per Novum. Hi vero neutrum recipiunt. Unde necesse est ad naturalem rationem recurrere, cui omnes assentire coguntur; ... Ibid., book 1, ch. 2 (p. 3).
60. Est autem in his, que de Deo confitemur, duplex veritatis modus. Quaedam namque vera sunt de Deo, quae omnem facultatem humanae rationis excedunt ... Quaedam vero sunt, ad quae etiam ratio naturalis pertingere potest ... quae etiam philosophi demonstrative de Deo probaverunt, ducti naturalis lumine rationis. Ibid., book 1, ch. 3 (p. 3).
61. Ad primae igitur veritatis manifestionem per rationes demonstrativas, quibus adversarius convinci possit, procedendum est. Sed quia tales rationes ad secundam veritatem haberi non possunt, non debet esse ad hoc intentio, at adversarius rationibus convincatur, sed ut ejus rationes, quas

contra veritatem habet, solvantur. Ibid., book 1, ch. 9, p. 10.

62. ... quum veritati fidei ratio naturalis contraria esse non possit, ut ostensum est. Ibid., book 1, ch. 9, p. 10.
63. Ibid., book 1, ch. 20, p. 28.
64. Ibid., book 1, ch. 42, p. 51.
65. Ibid., book 1, ch. 71, p. 87.
66. Ibid., book 2, ch. 2, p. 120.
67. Ibid., book 2, ch. 3, p. 121.
68. Ibid., p. 286 ff.
69. Ibid., p. 295.
70. Per hoc excluditur error Manicheorum ponentium aliquod summum malum quod est principium primum omnium malorum. Ibid., p. 305.
71. Aquinas carries this part of the argument from Chapter 17 of Book 3 to Chapter 25, p. 318. On Dionysius, see Chapter 9 this book.
72. Ibid., book 3, ch. 69, p. 383.
73. Ibid., book 3, ch. 71, p. 388.
74. Ibid., p. 390.
75. Ibid., p. 390.
76. Ibid., book 4, ch. 29.
77. Propter hoc non est mirari, si haeretici, qui corporis nostri Deum esse auctorem negant, haec corporalia obsequia exhibita reprehendant. Ibid., ch. 86, p. 415.
78. Ibid., book 4, ch. 107. Aquinas does not seem to face the important question of why the angels chose to become evil.
79. Ibid., book 4 ch. 92 (p. 452) is 'That an intellectual substance, by the help of which the magic arts are employed, is not evil in its nature'.
80. Thomas Aquinas, *Summa Theologica*, 4 vols, Rome, 1925.
81. Ibid., questions 1 and 2 of the first part of the work (vol. 1, pp. 15–31).
82. Ibid., question 1, article VIII, p. 22.
83. Ibid., question 1, article II, p. 17.
84. Ibid., question 1, article VIII, p. 22.
85. Ibid., question 2.
86. Cum igitur gratia non tollat naturam, sed perficiat, oportet, quod naturalis ratio subserviet fidei. Ibid., question 1, article VIII, p. 23.
87. Ibid., question 2, article II, p. 29.
88. Quarta via sumitur ex gradibus, qui in rebus inveniuntur. Ibid., question 2, article II, p. 30.
89. Ergo est aliud, quod omnibus entibus est causa esse, et bonitatis, et cujuslibet perfectionis, et hoc dicimus Deum. Ibid., question 2, article II, p. 31.
90. a quo omnes res naturales ordinantur ad finem, et hoc dicimus Deum. Ibid., question 2, article II, p. 31.
91. To complete the question Aquinas returns to Augustine's explanation of evil; and makes it clear that 'nature' is simply the operation of God's secondary causes.

CHAPTER NINE

Fiat lux! Let there be light!

Greyfriars

To this point we have seen how, as a consequence of the power struggles and politics of twelfth- and thirteenth-century Europe, interest in and discussion of nature was promoted as part of a major campaign to keep the intellectual and physical peace and retain the *status quo*. In their *studia*, shadowing the secular *studia*, the Dominicans created a Christianized version of Aristotelian teaching in order to fight a very particular foe. The message was that God is good, His creation is good, the goodness and the causality of the Creation are evidence of the goodness of God. At its inception this new concern with nature was thus God-centred, and the point of it was to convey a certain message about God. Nature was to be studied, discussed, disputed about and even observed and investigated, not primarily for itself nor for the sake of disinterested knowledge but for what it said about God its creator.

This attitude to nature was a Dominican innovation and it was made in the context of their *studia* where they learnt to fight heresy. But this particular concern with nature was also spread beyond their *studia*, for the Order of Preachers used the evidence thus found in nature about God in their preaching, preaching which the friars aimed at the urban population of Europe. According to an enormous treatise 'On the formation of preachers' by the fourth Master of the Order, Humbert of Romans (Master 1254–63), 'there are many kinds of knowledge necessary for preachers. One is knowledge of the holy scripture'; the second kind of essential knowledge is knowledge of creatures. God has poured out his wisdom over all his works, and that is why St Anthony said that creation is a book. Those who know how to read this book will draw from it many things which are serviceable for helping people to grow. The Lord made use of this kind of knowledge in his preaching, when he said, 'Consider the birds of the air' and 'Consider the lilies of the field'.[1] And writing about the use of *exempla* in preaching, Humbert says that 'no *exemplum* should be included [in a sermon] which does not have a sufficient weight of authority behind it ... the best thing of all is to take material from the Bible. But the books of well-known philosophers can also count as having sufficient authority, as can the book of creation.'[2] Thus, although historical study of Dominican sermons is still at an early stage, we can see that their concern with nature had an important function for the Dominicans in their primary role, that of preaching.

But our story so far, of the creation of their natural philosophy by the dogs of the Lord, does not exhaust the story of new concern with nature by friars in the thirteenth century. For there was another approach to nature created now, and which was also to be influential on the structure and contents of natural philosophy in the secular *studia*. It was an approach obsessed with something which the Dominicans, basing themselves on the works of Aristotle and the rationality of argument to be found in Aristotle, almost totally neglected: mathematics, and especially geometry. The friars who created the alternative concern with nature were the grey friars, the Friars Minor, the followers of St Francis.

Francis (*c*.1182–1226) was the son of a prosperous cloth merchant in a prosperous Italian hilltown, Assisi. His life has been gloriously painted round the walls of the upper basilica at Assisi, in frescos which have traditionally, though probably erroneously, been attributed to Giotto.[3] According to the familiar story, Francis heard the call when he was about 26 years old, the call to live like Christ and be an example to others.[4] To live like Christ meant to marry Lady Poverty and to live in poverty, begging for one's daily subsistence. Innocent III is said to have dreamt that the Lateran basilica – the whole Church of Rome, that is – was tottering and that a man was holding it up on his shoulder. When he then saw Francis in person Innocent said, 'This is certainly the man. By his work and teaching he will uphold Christ's Church'.[5] So Innocent allowed Francis in 1210 to form a brotherhood to preach repentance, confirming this at the Lateran Council in 1215. The revised Rule for the brothers received papal approval in 1223.

Francis called his Order the 'Friars Minor' to stress the humbleness which he wished to be typical of them (there are no 'Friars Major'). Many joined to serve God's Poor and the order rapidly spread, and Francis organized it on a system of provinces, with the brothers going out in twos and threes across the world, taking nothing for their journey, 'neither scrip, nor purse, nor bread, nor money, nor staff. And into whatsoever house they shall enter, they shall first say "Pax et Bonum"' (as Francis instructed in his Rule of 1210)[6] and attempt to draw the souls of the people away from the vanities of the world. In 1224 Francis, long obsessed by and weeping for the Passion of Christ, while reportedly in a state of ecstatic contemplation on Mount Alverna, saw a seraph in a vision. St Bonaventure, a follower of Francis, described the memorable event in these words, which he presumably had from an earlier follower of Francis himself:

> Francis saw a Seraph with six fiery wings coming down from the highest point in the heavens. The vision descended swiftly to rest in the air near him. Then he [Francis] saw the image of a Man crucified in the midst of the wings, with his hands and feet stretched out and nailed to a cross ... He was overjoyed at the way Christ regarded him so graciously under the appearance of a Seraph ... [7]

In the course of this vision Francis received from the seraph the *stigmata*, the wounds and nails in his hands and feet and side like Christ. He died two years later, and was canonized within just two more years by that great friend of the Franciscans, Pope Gregory IX.[8]

There were many similarities between the Dominicans and the Franciscans. Both orders took the world as their parish. Both were, ultimately, under the control of the Pope – and hence they were both potentially (and often in practice) at odds with the bishops and parish clergy where they worked. Both were town orders, and both were initially mendicant: they lived in and off the thriving towns, and for both of them their primary audience were urban folk. And both orders gathered an extraordinary number of followers in their early years.

But the two orders also had many differences. Poverty, for instance, was much more basic to the Franciscan way of life than it was for that of the Dominicans.[9] Again, the two orders had different aims. The Dominicans saw preaching as their main activity, preaching against heresy and to prevent heresy; they were the Champions of the Faith. The Franciscans saw their primary role as being examples to others in their piety, devotion and way of life: living like the Apostles, they were the Friends of the Poor. Indeed, the Franciscans saw themselves as called to promote greater spirituality in a world which they regarded as one of excess wealth and materialism. They were themselves poor in order to keep their own spiritual lives free from material encumbrances. They preached against the dangers of wealth and in favour of the virtues of poverty and self-denial. They were the spiritual consciences of the age, in the service of the Roman Catholic Church. As we shall see, their own spiritual practices were very other-worldly, and it was such practices that they wished to inspire in others.

But, distinctive as the Franciscans and Dominicans were, they were from the very first in rivalry, and this was to continue for centuries and to be very bitter at times. In the early years this rivalry showed itself most clearly in the fact that everywhere the Dominicans went, the Franciscans were sure to go. When the Dominicans went to a particular town and took up residence, the Franciscans went to the same town and began settling in. When the Dominicans built large preaching churches, with the pulpit half-way down the nave so as to be in the centre of the gathered congregation, the Franciscans also built great preaching churches,[10] even though preaching played a relatively smaller role in their activities. When the Dominicans went to *studium* towns and inserted themselves into the life of the *studium*, the Franciscans went there too. And when Dominicans moved into the theology faculties, the Franciscans followed them in the race for theology chairs. There were theology faculties only at Paris, Oxford and (from about 1250) Cambridge. At the Paris *studium* the Dominicans arrived in 1217; the Franciscans were there by 1219. The Dominicans had reached Oxford by 1221; the Franciscans arrived hotfoot in 1224. The Dominicans were barely established at Cambridge (building on the site of what is now Emmanuel College) before the Franciscans, breathless, turned up in 1225 and took up residence in the former house of Benjamin the Jew.[11] As usual, and as befitted their missions, both orders settled at the boundary of the existing town.

Within all the *studia* that they reached the friars of both orders came to be equally resented by the secular masters, who were quick to realize that they were being colonized. But both orders continued to concentrate on the most important faculty, that of theology. The permanence of the orders in the *studia* towns, with their own houses, gave them the advantage in the long term over the secular masters in such matters.

The Franciscans, like the Dominicans, flourished in the *studia* towns for centuries. In the case of the Dominicans the grounds for their interest in learning is obvious, for they saw it as fundamental to their role as preachers, and from an early date (before 1236) their constitutions insisted that all preaching friars should have studied theology for a year and preacher generals for three years.[12] But it was far less obvious that learning had any role in the life of Franciscan friars. Indeed they would appear to have entered the *studia* against the wishes of Francis himself. 'Friars of mine who are seduced by a desire for learning will find their hands empty in the day of trouble', Francis is reported to have said, 'for a troublous time is coming when books will be no good for anything, and will be cast aside in windows and corners'.[13] A Franciscan reported that after a consultation with Francis a learned Dominican went back to his brethren and said 'My brothers, this man's theology is grounded on purity and contemplation, and resembles a flying eagle; but our knowledge (*scientia*) crawls along the ground on its belly'.[14] And Francis is said to have reproached his followers at Paris who had appointed a teacher of theology as their Master: 'I am afraid, Brothers, that such men will end by killing my little plant'.[15] In Bologna Francis is said to have personally closed a Franciscan house which had been opened to teach the brothers law (like the Dominicans were currently doing), and laid a curse upon the brother responsible. Eventually he seems to have relented a little, at least over the teaching of theology by St Anthony to the brothers at Bologna 'as long as they do not extinguish the spirit of prayer and devotedness over this study, as is contained in the Rule'.[16]

None of these reports of Francis' attitude to learning can be taken at face value, for the very existence of such reports derives from the early conflicts within the Order over what kind of life the Rule imposed upon Franciscans. Was it to be ascetic and contemplative, lived far from the habitations of men; or was it to be active, with preaching and teaching – and hence including the pursuit of learning – and based in the towns? Initially the Franciscans did both: as Jacques de Vitry wrote in 1216 about them, 'During the day they go into the cities and villages giving themselves over to the active life of the apostolate; at night, they return to their hermitage or withdraw into solitude to live the life of contemplation'.[17] The reports of Francis' hostility to learning tend to come from those hostile to the active life, in order to illustrate that a better kind of fruit was to be obtained (as one of them wrote) 'by the holy simplicity of those friars who did not preach about Aristotle or philosophy, but briefly about the pains of hell and the glories of Paradise, as is written in the holy Rule'.[18]

There are similar ambiguities about the attitude to nature of St Francis, and again they came to be intimately bound up with representations of Francis himself, both verbal and pictorial. On the one hand, that Francis loved the beauty of the Creation and every created thing has long been legendary, and the accumulation of myths and legends about Francis' devotion to nature have led, in the twentieth century, to him being made the patron saint of ecology. Early accounts say Francis preached to the birds, urging them to praise their Creator.[19] He also preached to the flowers, cornfields and vineyards, stones and forests and to 'all the beautiful things of the fields, fountains of water and the green things of the gardens, earth and fire, air and wind, to love God and serve him willingly'.[20] Celano recorded of Francis that

> In every work of the artist he praised the Artist; whatever he found in the things made he referred to the Maker. He rejoiced in all the works of the hands of the Lord and saw behind all things pleasant to behold their life-giving reason and cause. In beautiful things he saw Beauty itself; all things were to him good. 'He who made us is the best', they cried out to him.[21]

Most famous of all in this respect is the Canticle of the Creatures that Francis himself is reported to have composed in the Umbrian vernacular in 1225, saying 'For His glory, for my own consolation, and the edification of my neighbour, I wish to compose a new *Praises of the Lord* for His creatures. These creatures minister to our needs every day; without them we could not live, and through [our treatment of] them the human race greatly offends the Creator'.[22]

Most high all powerful, all good, Lord!
All praise is yours, all glory, all honour
And all blessing.
To you, alone, Most High, do they belong.
No mortal lips are worthy
To pronounce your name.
All praise be yours, my lord, through all that you have made,
And first my lord Brother Sun,
Who brings the day; and light you give to us through him.
How beautiful he is, how radiant in all his splendour!
All praise be yours, my Lord, through Sister Moon and Stars;
In the heavens you have made them, bright
And precious and fair.

Praise be also from Brothers Wind and Air, Sister Water, Brother Fire and Sister Earth. All creatures should 'Praise and bless my Lord, and give him thanks, And serve him with great humility'.[23]

But on the other hand, reports such as these reveal, of course, more about the attitudes of the reporters than they do about the attitudes of St Francis himself. Indeed it is impossible now to be certain what, if any, attitudes to nature Francis had. For all reports of Francis' attitude to, and use of, nature were produced to promote certain spiritual practices and attitudes within the Order — that is, they were part of propaganda campaigns and power struggles within the Order. The first of the various attitudes to nature ascribed to Francis was one dear to the Spiritualist and Joachimist Franciscans of the next century, and was that of seeing Francis as being a new Adam, and thus having the renewed powers of Adam over the creatures, and hence fulfilling prophecy.[24] The second was the spiritual practice of seeing every part and feature of creation as symbolic and allegorical. Hence St Francis was portrayed as loving lambs as representing the Lamb of God, water as symbolic of baptism and repentence, stones as Christ the keystone, trees as the Cross. Everything had a symbolic signficance; and for the spiritually aware, of course, the symbolic meaning is the actual, higher, meaning. In this way Francis was portrayed as living (in Gilson's phrase) 'in the midst of a forest of symbols'.[25]

The third of these spiritual practices and attitudes being promoted via nature is the most important for our purposes. It is the practice of ecstatic contemplation. For Franciscans the act of looking at and meditating upon visible created nature was the essential first step on the ladder of practical and regular mystical and ecstatic contemplation. Thus contemplation of Nature and of God's creatures was regularly represented by the saint's early biographers as a means Francis himself used to go into ecstatic trances.[26] As Bonaventure wrote about Francis:

So that he might be excited to love God in everything, Francis

> delighted in all the works of God's hands and from the vision of joy on earth his mind soared aloft to the life-giving source and cause of all. In everything beautiful, he saw Him who is beauty itself, and he followed his Beloved everywhere by His likeness imprinted on creation; of all creation he made a ladder by which he might mount up and embrace Him who is all-desirable. By the power of his extraordinary faith he tasted the Goodness which is the source of all in each and every created thing, as in so many rivulets.[27]

Amongst the early followers of St Francis who had visions or ecstasies, a certain Brother John of Alverna is reported to have gone into what we might call 'nature trances' and once 'saw all created things in a vision'. As the Spiritualist writer of *Little Flowers of Saint Francis* put it:

> One night he was raised to such a marvellous light in God that he saw in the Creator all created things, both in Heaven and on earth, all disposed in their various realms, for instance how the choirs of blessed spirits are disposed under God – and also the earthly paradise and the Blessed Humanity of Christ. And he likewise perceived the lower realms. And he saw and felt how all created things are related to the Creator, and how God is above and within and without and around all created things. Afterward God raised him above every creature so that his soul was absorbed and assumed into the abyss of the Divinity and Light, and it was buried in the ocean of God's Eternity and Infinity.[28]

That is to say, the contemplative Franciscan thought that an efficacious way of achieving trance-like ecstatic spiritual states was by making (in St Bonaventure's phrase) of all creation 'a ladder by which one might mount up and embrace Him who is all-desirable'.

Thus in their universal song of praise for God through His creatures, or for God's creatures,[29] Francis and the Franciscans were not saying the same thing about nature as their fellow friars the Dominicans were saying. The Dominicans claimed that Nature is good and is the evidence of the goodness of God its creator, and this is why it should be studied, and with the aid of reason. The Franciscans were saying something much more mystical: that God should be praised through his creation (and that all creation should praise God), and that contemplation of creation is a route to ecstatic communion with God. It is indeed the needs of the contemplative life – a life which the Franciscans were bringing out of the cloister and into the lives of urban folk – which is the source of the Franciscan attitude to nature.

Hence it can be seen that although the creation is paid at least as much attention by the Franciscans as by the Dominicans, the grounds of their attention was different, and this affected both *how* they saw nature and *what* they saw there. But we should note that the Franciscan interest in nature was as totally God-oriented as that of the Dominicans, though in a different way. The spirituality that the Franciscans practised assiduously, and which they wished to inspire in others, had a key role for nature – a role of a very particular kind. It was the pursuit of the inner spiritual life which led the Franciscans to look outwards to nature.

The mind's road to God

In order to understand the distinctive nature and goals of the highly influential Franciscan concern with nature, it is essential for us to understand something of the mind's road to God, since it was in pursuit of the spiritual journey to God that the Franciscans became concerned with nature. Perhaps the most famous exponent of this contemplative journey is St Bonaventure. The title that Bonaventure gave to his guide to ecstatic contemplation of 1259 was 'The mind's road to God' (*Itinerarium Mentis in Deum*).[30]

We can take Bonaventure as speaking with great authority and as fully representative of orthodox Franciscan teaching of his generation, for he was Minister-General of the Order for almost 20 years, from 1257 to 1274. He played a most important role in settling the divisions within the Order and in defending it against the attacks of the secular masters at Paris. As Minister-General he also produced an extensive and authoritative Exposition of the Rule, and he produced two new accounts of the life of the founder which helped define what Francis' sympathies, attitudes and opinions must have been, and which were meant to replace all previous accounts of Francis. All this earned for him the title of Second Founder of the Order. Bonaventure himself was trained as a young man under the first Franciscan to hold a chair of theology at Paris, Alexander Hales, and then was himself master of the Franciscan school at Paris. It is not surprising therefore that while Bonaventure's accounts of Francis show that Francis was an ecstatic contemplative, they do not indicate that Francis was opposed to learning. What Bonaventure does is to claim that learning – the active life – is essential for the contemplative life: that the active life should *serve* the contemplative life (*activa debet deservire contemplativae*).[31] Thus for Bonaventure learning was highly desirable for the promotion and pursuit of the central spiritual activity of the Franciscan friar.

In 'The mind's road to God' St Bonaventure claims to be expounding thoughts that occurred to him when he was on the very same mountain, Mount Alverna (La Verna), where St Francis 33 years earlier had received the stigmata from the six-winged seraph. Bonaventure had come here in pursuit of that highest peace which is the goal of contemplation, and (he says) he immediately recognized that the six wings of the seraph represent 'the six stages of the illuminations by which the soul, as if by certain steps or journeys, is disposed to pass into peace by ecstatic elevations of Christian wisdom'.[32] His reflections (*speculationes*) here are addressed to 'the lovers of divine wisdom' who wish to engage in contemplation.

The key Biblical text for understanding what Bonaventure is talking about is one he himself quotes, Romans 1.20:

> For the invisible things of Him from the creation of the world are clearly seen, being understood by the things that are made, even His eternal power and Godhead.
> In the Vulgate version: *Invisibilia enim ipsius, a creatura mundi, per ea quae facta sunt, intellecta, conspiciuntur: sempiterna quoque eius virtus, et divinitas.*

The invisible things of God can be grasped intellectually (*intellecta*) because they can be approached via the visible. Thus the role of contemplation of the visible (created things) by the contemplative, is to mount through them to the true reward: the invisible things of God.

In the first stage of illumination we should, says Bonaventure, consider created things in a seven-fold condition (*conditio*): according to their (1) origin, (2) magnitude, (3) multitude, (4) beauty, (5) plenitude, (6) operation, and (7) order. Each of these properties of things is testimony to a particular aspect of God. For instance the *magnitude* of (particular) created things indicates the immensity of the power, wisdom and goodness of the triune God; similarly the *operation* of created things 'by its very variety shows the immensity of that power, art and goodness which indeed are in all things the cause of their being',[33] and so on. In other words, the inspection and consideration of each and every created thing can tell us something about the characteristics of God their creator, and thus serves as the first stage of our mental journey.

> He who is not illumined by such great splendour of created things is blind; he who is not awakened by such great clamour is deaf; he who does not praise God because of all these effects is dumb; he who does not note the First Principle from such great signs is foolish. Open your eyes therefore, prick up your spiritual ears, open your lips, and apply your heart, that you may see your God in all creatures, may hear Him, praise Him, love and adore Him, magnify and honour Him, lest the whole world rise against you.[34]

We shall come back to this first stage in the next chapter to see how it could be and was translated into something like a programme of research into nature, and thus see how (in the words of George Boas) 'the impetus to the study of the natural world through empirical methods came from the Franciscans'.[35] But before that, the other stages claim our attention.

The second stage concerns the way in which 'the whole world can enter into the human soul through the doors of the senses'.[36] Bonaventure says that each object in creation throws off a likeness of itself – a *species* – into the medium surrounding it (usually the air); this impression in the medium then impinges on the outside of our sense-organs and generates a likeness of itself in the sense-organ; this likeness or species is then conveyed inwards to the interior of the organ, and thence to the faculty of apprehension and then to the faculty of judgement.[37] It is in this way that our reason is able to abstract 'from place, time, and motion'[38] and thus have abstract concepts.

The third stage is to move from these lights given from outside, to the mirror of our own minds, where the divine image shines.[39] Bonaventure here deals with the operation of memory and intellect, and very briefly with the role of the different *scientiae*, which 'have certain and infallible rules, like lights and rays descending from the eternal law into our minds'.[40] Thus *Philosophy* is the special support for this stage of contemplation. He also claims that 'our intellect cannot reach the point of fully revealing the intellect of any of the created beings unless it be assisted by the intellect of the purest, most actual, most complete and absolute Being, which is Being simply and eternal, and in which are the principles (*rationes*) of all things in their purity'.[41]

At the fourth stage, with our 'inner senses renewed to sense the highest beauty, to hear the highest harmony, smell the highest fragrance, taste the highest delicacy, apprehend the highest delight',[42] now our soul is caught up in wonder. For this reparation of the inner senses, the *Holy Scripture* is our special support, which deals especially with charity, by which the soul is reformed. Perfect charity resides in Christ, who is 'at once king and friend, at once Word uncreated and incarnate, our maker and remaker, the alpha and omega. He is the highest hierarch, *purifying* and *illuminating* and *perfecting* His spouse – the whole Church and each holy soul.'[43]

With the fifth stage we are ready to turn from the visible to the invisible, and to contemplate the invisible and eternal traits of God. The primary way of doing this is to look to His essential attributes. And this way

> first and foremost signifies Him in Being itself, saying *He Who Is* is the primary name of God ... If you wish to contemplate the invisible traits of God in so far as they belong to the unity of His essence, fix your eyes upon Being itself ... Being which is pure Being and most simply Being and absolutely Being, is Being primary, eternal, most simple, most actual, most perfect, and one [i.e. unity] to the highest degree ... Because Being is most pure and absolute, that which is simply Being is first and last and, therefore, the origin and end of all. Because eternal and most present, therefore it encompasses and

> penetrates all durations, being their centre and circumference. Because most simple and greatest, therefore it is entirely within and entirely without all things and consequently is an intelligible sphere whose centre is everywhere and whose circumference nowhere.[44]

To contemplate Being is to contemplate God, as God is unity.

The sixth stage turns us from Being to The Good, for 'just as Being is the root and name of the vision of the essential traits ... so the Good is the principal foundation of our contemplation of the divine emanations'.[45] The divine emanations are the 'outflowings' from the divine. Bonaventure then indicates how the Trinity is the exemplification of the highest Good. With this, one has mounted 'the six steps of the throne of the true Solomon by which one ascends to peace, where the truly peaceful man reposes in peaceful mind as if in the inner Jerusalem'.[46] There is one higher stage, which is only very rarely reached: St Francis did so when he received the stigmata and 'passed over into God through an ecstasy of contemplation'.[47]

The invisible through the visible

One kind of writing promoted by this Franciscan desire to mount the steps of contemplation was the compilation of certain enormous works. To our modern eyes they look like encyclopaedias, but they were not of course intended as encyclopaedias. Perhaps the most famous of these is by the Franciscan friar Bartholomew the Englishman, composed probably around 1230–50 after many years' work. Bartholomew called his volume 'On the properties of things' (*De Proprietatibus Rerum*), and it was in 19 'books' or sections.[48] It is a quite different kind of work from the works 'On the natures of things' (*De Natura Rerum*) produced by some Dominicans (as discussed previously in Chapter 8).

When Bartholomew talks of the *properties* of things, he means the same kind of characteristics which Bonaventure said one should consider about all created things, since each and every such characteristic displays a particular aspect of God. Bonaventure's list (the seven-fold condition of things) consisted of origin, magnitude, multitude, beauty, plenitude, operation and order, while Bartholomew's list of properties of things included substance, quality, content, beauty.[49] And in his preface to his work Bartholomew makes it quite clear that its ultimate purpose is to provide spiritual help and to assist in contemplation:

> This work is useful to me, and perhaps to other people who are not familiar with [the accounts of] the nature and properties of things dispersed through the books of the saints and of the philosophers, for understanding the enigmas of the Scriptures which are revealed

> and veiled by the Holy Spirit under symbols and figures of the properties of natural things and of things made by art; as the blessed Dionysius shows in *The Angelic Hierarchy*, saying 'It is not possible for the divine ray to illuminate us except veiled mysteriously in variegated sacred veils; how impossible it is for our mind to ascend to the immaterial contemplation of the celestial hierarchies unless it uses for material the guidance which is suitable for it, etcetera'; these things says Dionysius. It is not possible for our mind to ascend to the contemplation of the invisibles except it is guided via consideration of the visibles. For the invisible things of God are clearly seen, being understood by the things that are made, as the Apostle says.[50]

It is that same passage from Romans: the invisible things of God that the contemplative seeks, can be intellectually grasped via the visible things He has made.

As for the sequence of the work, this is tightly planned. As Bartholomew says in the opening sentence, 'Since the properties of things follow from their substances, the order and distinction of the properties – about which this present work is with God's help compiled – will be according to the distinction and order of their substances'. He will therefore start from the purest, simplest substance – 'from Him who is Alpha and Omega, the Beginning and End of all good things, in the beginning the Father of Lights' – for God, both as One and as Three-in-One, is one essence entirely simple. Book 1 thus starts with the official statement of this: the opening words of Innocent III's definition of the Catholic faith at the Lateran Council of 1215. We believe and confess 'the true God is one alone, eternal, immense and unchangeable, omnipotent and ineffable, Father, Son and Holy Spirit; indeed three Persons but one essence, substance or nature entirely simple'.[51] But as God is thus not knowable directly in His essence, in book one Bartholomew deals with the divine names used of God,[52] as expressing different aspects of His essence; in other words, expressing different properties of God.

Bartholomew then begins to move down the hierarchy of substances, with their respective properties. Next in order therefore come the properties of *incorporeal* substance, beginning with those not united to body, 'such as the angels. And of the angels some are good, others bad. The order amongst the good angels is according to the three-fold multiplication of the trinity. Hence three celestial hierarchies are distinguished by the blessed Dionysius, each of which contains the dispositions of three orders.'[53] So book 2 deals with the properties of the angels, in all their nine orders, and good and bad angels alike.

Then Bartholomew deals with the properties of incorporeal substance which *is* united to body, in other words he deals with the soul and its three powers: rational, sensible and vegetative. Hence book 3 deals with the soul of man and its properties, including its operations in the body, the five senses, and the pulse as the operation of the vital spirit.

With book 4 he reaches the properties of *corporeal* substance: 'someone setting out to deal with the properties of man's body and of its parts, should first begin from the elementary qualities and humours of which the body is made' (that is, the so-called 'naturals').[54] Book 5 brings him thus to the parts of the human body, made up of the elements and humours, and their properties. His attention here is particularly on those parts which are mentioned in Scripture. Book 6 deals with the properties of the different ages, conditions and roles of man and woman, and with the non-naturals. Book 7 deals with the contra-naturals, that is to say, with diseases and poisons affecting the body of man, and with the properties (that is, the role) of a good physician.

By book 8, Bartholomew believes it is time

> that we put our hand to the properties of the sensible world ... that we may elicit from the properties of things matter for divine praise, and the working of the Creator. For the unseen things of God are clearly seen, being understood by the things that are made, as the Apostle says. And thus we intend to introduce into this little work, as into a compendium, the properties of any thing of this world or of its contents, so that through the similitude of corporeal properties, we may be able more easily to understand the spiritual and mystical meaning in the Holy Scriptures.[55]

The heavenly bodies and their properties, and light and its properties, are therefore the subject of book eight. Book 9 deals with the effects and actions of the heavens: in other words, with time and its measures such as the times of the year, the months and the week, and the annual church festivals.

In book 10 Bartholomew turns to matter and form and their properties, and fire; then (in book 11) to air and its properties or *passiones*, such as the winds and other meteorological happenings. Then he turns to the creatures which add ornament to the earth, 'that in them as in other created things the great deeds of the Creator may be praised' (fol. c): birds, which ornament the air (book 12); the third element, water and the inhabitants of the waters, the fish (book 13). Books 14 and 15 deal with the fourth and last of the elements, the earth and its parts (especially the mountains mentioned in the Bible), and with the regions and countries of the earth. The final books deal with things engendered in the earth: precious stones and minerals (book 16); things engendered on the earth: the herbs and plants mentioned in the Bible or Gloss (book 17); things which have life and feeling: animals (book 18); and accidental properties of things ('accidents') such as colours, smell, taste, and the properties of fluids such as milk, and of number, weight and music (book

19). All these last books are arranged in alphabetical order.

Bartholomew made this enormous compilation for two main purposes, both of them spiritual. First to see and understand the symbolic role of created things, and thus help people to reach the allegorical meaning of things, especially when reading the Bible or the Gloss. If some thing or person or heavenly being is described as a lion or like a lion, consultation of 'lion' (*leo*) in book 18 will reveal the properties of the lion, and hence the allegorical or figurative meaning the Scripture intends. This is why Bartholomew's things are mostly limited to those mentioned in the Bible or the Gloss. Second, familiarity with the *properties* of natural things puts one in the position of being able to begin the contemplative ascent to God, for it is the properties of things that one first contemplates and at which one experiences wonder. As Bartholomew constantly repeats, from St Paul, the invisible things of God are understood through the visible.

Not a word of Bartholomew's work is original (so he vigorously and repeatedly claims) and hence it hardly yet merits Boas's compliment that the Franciscans were highly instrumental in furthering empirical research into nature. Yet it is a programme of work with a very precise goal: it turned Bartholomew's attention to discovering what the saints and philosophers had said about the natural world, and it led him to record it for other people's spiritual use. It was the Franciscan route of the mind to God which gave Bartholomew this programme of work about the natural world.

Bartholomew is not the only Franciscan friar who wrote such a work. We can briefly look at another such project, a *Historia Naturalis* by Johannes Aegidius of Zamora in Spain, written sometime around 1300.[56] This one is entirely in alphabetical order, though Aegidius did not get very far through the alphabet. Again, like Bartholomew's, it is compiled from the writings of the saints and philosophers. It begins thus:

> *Natura naturans*,[57] most high and eternal God, the most-powerful creator of all natural things, most-wise arranger and most-merciful observer, produced the most-secret causes of nature 'naturally' for this reason amongst others: so that in them His insuperable power, His unmistakable wisdom and His untiring goodness might shine forth. For the good Word and wise Life who made the world, may be seen when the world is contemplated. Though the Word itself cannot be seen, It is seen through that which It has made. For the invisible things of Him from the creation of the world are clearly seen, being understood by the things that are made.

After citation of confirmatory sayings from philosophers and saints, Aegidius claims:

> There are three invisible things of God: Power, Wisdom and

> Benevolence. From these three things, all things proceed, in these three things all things consist, and through these three all things are ruled. Power creates, Wisdom governs, Benevolence preserves. These three, as in God they are ineffably one, so they can in no way be separated in operation. Power creates wisely through Benevolence. Wisdom rules benignly through Power. Benevolence firmly conserves through Wisdom. The *immensity* of created things manifests Power, their *beauty* manifests Wisdom, their *utility* manifests Benevolence.
>
> The *immensity* of created things consists in multitude and magnitude. For who could number the very great multitude of created things, viz. the stars of the heavens, the sands of the sea, the dust of the earth, the drops of the rain, the feathers of the birds of the air, the scales of the fish, the hairs of the animals, the grass of the fields, the roots, trunks, branches, leaves and fruit of the trees, and the innumerable multitude of similarities of innumerable other things, such as man and man, and of dissimilarities, such as man and lion, and of mixtures, such as all these considered together?

And just as the immensity of created things manifests the Power of God, so the *beauty* of created things manifests the Wisdom of God, which beauty is considered in *location* and *motion*, in *species* and in *quality*. If we take *motion* as our example, then

> Raised aloft in admiration is the mind of someone contemplating the circular motion in the heavens, the rectilinear motion in the elements, the motion from the middle to the circumference in plants, the contracting and extending motion in insects, the progressing motion in animals, the rational motion in man (that is, in deeds and deliberation).

As St Paul wrote, through the visible things in the world are manifested the invisible things in God, and since through their magnitude and multitude the visible things in the world are not easily grasped, 'for this reason I have compiled the properties and natures of the visible created things in this book, which is "On Natural History, or On the Natures of Things", in alphabetical order ... so that anyone may find more easily, in such a variety of things, what he wants to use for himself in contemplation'. In other words, this is intended as a guide and resource, in the form of a book, for people wishing to engage in ecstatic contemplation. And indeed, as Aegidius says, each letter of the alphabet is itself also a ladder for contemplation:

> In this first ladder (letter A) there are many stages by which, both through the qualities of things and their colours and flavours and fragrances and powers and virtues, the wise person will be able to contemplate the Most High. If anything is lacking, it will be supplied in general treatises on animals and on birds and on trees and on fish and on metals and on stones and the like.

Aegidius could hardly be more explicit about his intentions: this whole work on Natural History or The Natures of Things, is composed to assist the contemplative. This is what makes it a typically Franciscan enterprise.

But there were of course other large works composed in this period on the nature of things, and which again strike us as being 'encyclopaedias', and which were composed by members of the rival Order of friars, the Dominicans. Most famous amongst these are the giant *Speculum Naturae* of Vincent of Beauvais, completed around 1245, and the book of Thomas of Cantimpré: his *On the Nature of Things, According to Various Philosophers* of perhaps 1250, both of which we have already encountered (Chapter 8).[58] If we take the Dominican Thomas as our example, in what ways does his compilation differ from those of the two Franciscans we have been discussing? In the first place Thomas' aim is different. He makes no claim about the potential or prospective use of his work for spiritual exercises or contemplation. That verse from Romans which runs like a refrain through the writing of Bartholomew and of Aegidius – the invisible things of God can be known through the visible things He has made – never appears. Nor is there any indication that Thomas intended his work to assist one in the symbolic interpretation of the Bible and the world. Nor does he set out particularly to discover what the saints have said about created things. No; by contrast Thomas' authorities are philosophers, including Pliny, Galen and others, but above all Aristotle. The work thus has nothing to do with contemplation. Instead it is intended as a resource for preachers – which of course is what the Dominicans were – and to oppose the heretics.[59] And its dialectical rationality and literal level of reading of the natures of things are typically Dominican. Of course, Franciscan works on the properties of things, such as that by Bartholomew the Englishman, could also be used as resources for sermons, for Franciscans also preached, and Bartholomew's work seems to have been used extensively in this way, as a source of *exempla*. But this was a use secondary to Bartholomew's intended one, which was to provide (like a good Franciscan would) materials to assist the spiritual exercises. The Dominicans, on the other hand, saw the natures of things primarily as material for preaching, to show that God is good and His creation is good. As Thomas of Cantimpré wrote about his own book: 'I think that only he to whom divine wisdom has given an understanding in lower matters can fully appreciate how much use this work will be and how much value it will have for those who want to pursue the word of preaching. For Aristotle says in book xi of 'On animals': Although a thing is most noble as it is to do with the heavens, and ignoble as it is to do with animal creation, yet animal creation will be a cause of greater delight to those who are able to get to know it'.[60] Aristotle of course was the Dominicans' favourite author, and citing him came as second nature to them.

Dionysian contemplation

If for the Dominicans the philosopher Aristotle was the most favoured author, the one whose teachings could be best fitted to their purposes, and who thus in turn came to provide the primary model for the Dominican attitude to nature, who was by contrast the most favoured author of the Franciscans, the one whose teachings could be best fitted to their purposes and who thus in turn came to provide the primary model for the Franciscan attitude to nature? We have already heard his name mentioned several times by our Franciscans: it was the blessed Dionysius. They adopted him because his were the main works in the tradition of ecstatic mysticism of which they were making themselves the heirs and the chief practitioners.[61] In turn their adoption of him for contemplation led certain Franciscans to be concerned with and to investigate some very particular features of nature, and hence – unlike their fellow Franciscan compilers of works 'On the properties of things' – to actually engage in innovative and constructive investigation into nature, some of it even empirical. This particular and distinctive turning of the thousand-year tradition of Christian ecstatic mysticism to new interests and achievements derived from the Franciscans' particular and distinctive role in thirteenth-century society.

Dionysius was a Christian writer. The Franciscans (like everyone else at the time, except Peter Abelard) thought he was Dionysius the Areopagite who had become a disciple of St Paul on Mars' Hill in Athens (as we saw in Chapter 1). Doubts about this identification were to be raised in the fifteenth and sixteenth centuries, and now historians recognize this author to have been alive at some date between about AD 130 and AD 500, and have thus dubbed him (or her) 'Pseudo-Dionysius'. A copy of the Greek text of Dionysius' writings was sent as a gift from the Pope to the King of the Franks in 785, and another was sent from the Greek Emperor to the Roman one in 807.[62] The Greek text was translated painfully into Latin by Abbot Hilduin (*c.*832), and more perfectly a few years later by John Scotus Eriguena who also added a commentary, and then again in the 1160s by Sarracinus.[63] Hilduin, Scotus and Sarracinus were each associated in their time with the church of St-Denis near Paris, and it was natural for them to treat these as writings by that church's patron saint, who was also the patron saint of France. And St-Denis is also where the Franciscans of Paris had their first home, until they moved into the city in 1231.[64]

For Dionysius contemplation is the central pursuit of the proper Christian. It involves initiation and practice, and its higher mysteries are necessarily restricted to an élite. The point of Dionysian contemplation is to become 'deified': assimilated to God, and thus like God, to the extent appropriate to one's status amongst the initiated, and thereby possessing 'the knowledge of things as they are in themselves'.[65] The work of Dionysius is neo-Platonic, especially in that it is concerned with the journey and well-being of the soul, and with the soul reaching, and being fulfilled by, *the unchangeable*, beyond matter and form.[66] As a neo-Platonic work it thus stands in complete contrast to the Aristotelian tradition adopted by the Dominicans.

Of the writings attributed to this Dionysius, two have been referred to explicitly or implicitly in the passages we have already quoted from our Franciscans: *The Celestial* (or *Angelic*) *Hierarchy* and *On the Divine Names*. The other surviving works attributed to Dionysius are *Mystical Theology*, *The Ecclesiastical Hierarchy*, and some *Letters*.[67] *The Ecclesiastical Hierarchy* describes the hierarchy which obtains amongst earthly contemplatives; the lowest rank is Leitourgoi, then Priests, and the highest is that of Hierarchs. Those in a higher rank possess all the sacred knowledge available to the lower ranks and more, and impart to the lower ranks their sacred knowledge in due amount. These ranks within the hierarchy also represent the mystic rites that the contemplative regularly goes through: *purifying* (the Leitourgoi rank), *illumination* (the Priest rank) and *perfecting* (the Hierarch rank). Through membership of this Divine Priesthood, and exercise of priestly functions 'we ourselves become nearer to the Beings above us, by assimilation, according to our power, to their abiding and unchangeable holy steadfastness ... and each [of us], as far as may be, participates in the truly Beautiful, and Wise and Good'.[68] Dionysius describes also certain rituals of Christian worship (baptism, the eucharist, the sacred oil) and the inner, contemplative, meaning of these rituals.

This hierarchy of initiates is the earthly mirror of the hierarchy which exists amongst the heavenly beings, and this is described by Dionysius in *The Celestial Hierarchy*. The purpose of this hierarchy, like the earthly one, 'is the assimilation and union, as far as attainable, with God ... by perfecting its own followers as Divine images, mirrors most luminous and without flaw, receptive of the primal light and the supremely Divine ray ... and spreading this radiance ungrudgingly to those after it'.[69] The angelic beings are in three ranks. Those closest to God are the order of Seraphim and Cherubim (also known as the Holy Thrones); second come the Authorities and Lordships and Powers, and the outermost order are the Angels and Archangels and Principalities. This 'most reverend Order of the Minds around God, ministered by the perfecting illumination

9.1 St Francis receiving the stigmata from the seraph

through its immediate elevation to it, is purified, and illuminated, and perfected by a gift of light from the Godhead'.[70] The Seraphim and Cherubim are most deified as nearest God, enjoying 'first participation of the knowledge of His deifying illuminations'[71] and 'the imitation of God is given to them in the highest degree'.[72] In their turn the Seraphim and Cherubim transmit the divine ray, which illuminates and enlightens, through their own selves to the next order, who in turn transmit it to the outermost order. Thus each order participates in the divine emanations in the manner and to the extent appropriate to its position. To be filled with divine light, to participate in the divine emanations to the highest appropriate degree, and thus to possess the knowledge of things as they are in themselves is what it is to be deified, and is the goal of contemplation.

The Divine Names celebrates the names or epithets used in the (Greek) Bible of God as Father, Son and Holy Ghost, and which set forth His providence:[73] The Good, The Beautiful, Being, Life, Wisdom, Reason (*Logos*), Truth, Faith, and so on. It also deals quite extensively with the distinction between the sensibles (perceived by the senses) and the intelligibles (grasped through the mind), and with how one can ascend through the sensibles – the created things of this world – to the intelligibles. We must ask, writes Dionysius, how we know God; we know Him

> not from His own nature (for that is unknown and surpasses all reason and mind), but from the ordering of all existing things, as projected from Himself, and containing a sort of images and similitudes of His Divine exemplars, we ascend, as far as we have the power, to that which is beyond all, by method and order in the abstraction and pre-eminence of all, and in the Cause of all.[74]

Such discussion of the way we ascend to God from created things, and of how the intelligible is veiled within the visible (that is, within the sensible) occurs also in *The Ecclesiastical Hierarchy*[75] and *The Celestial Hierarchy*.[76] Dionysius also says one can find within each of the parts of the human body 'harmonious images of the Heavenly Powers',[77] and discusses the representation of the Heavenly Minds through animals, rivers and other features of the natural world.[78]

In all these respects – aims, concepts, vocabulary – it can be seen that the Dionysian works underlie those of St Bonaventure and other Franciscans. Dionysian attitudes permeate every aspect of Franciscan thinking. The centrality of Dionysius to Franciscan thinking can perhaps best be appreciated by us looking again at the most important and distinctive feature of the St Francis legend – the stigmatization of the saint – and seeing how Dionysian it is through and through. St Francis was the first person to receive the stigmata since Christ Himself, and the meaning that the Franciscans intended by reporting this story, as also the meaning which people understood from it, was that Francis, the founder of the Order, was literally *next to God* – a Second Christ.[79] It was a seraph who appeared to Francis, and the seraphs (according to Dionysius) are in the heavenly hierarchy closest to God, where (he says) they enjoy first participation in the knowledge of God's deifying illuminations. The divine light flows from God first through this rank, and only thence to the other ranks of the hierarchy; the seraph thus enjoys the divine light in its fullest and purest and brightest. It is this purest possible divine light that Francis received from the seraph and, as all pictures of the stigmatization correctly show, the wounds were made by rays of light – the purest possible divine light. In *The Celestial Hierarchy* Dionysius discusses the vision that the prophet Isaiah had of the seraphs with their six-fold wings (Isaiah 6), proclaiming the glory of the Lord, and giving Isaiah his mission. Dionysius claims that through seeing them Isaiah

> was brought to the intelligible knowledge of the things seen, since there was manifested to him the power of the most exalted minds [i.e. of the seraphs] for deep penetration and contemplation, and the sacred reverence which they have, supermundanely, for the bold and courageous and unattainable scrutiny into higher and deeper mysteries.[80]

In other words, his vision of the seraphs made Isaiah like a seraph and thus gave him the reward of contemplation: knowledge of things as they are in themselves, intelligible knowledge of the things seen. In the Latin versions of Dionysius available to the followers of Francis, this is expressed as '*scientia exsistentium aut quae sunt*', '*intelligibilis visorum ... scientia*'.[81] Isaiah is the only person in the Bible known to have seen a seraph, and thus by reporting that Francis too had seen a seraph, Francis' biographers intended that what had happened to Isaiah was to be read also as applying to Francis: that Francis too had entered the higher and deeper mysteries and thus had acquired knowledge of things as they are in themselves, intelligible knowledge of the things seen. Now, when Francis saw the seraph, Francis of course was actually engaged in contemplation. The point of contemplation, as Dionysius says, is *to become deified*. And this is just what the stigmata prove that Francis did: he became like God by receiving the stigmata in the same form as God Himself – as Christ – had received them, as wounds in hands, feet and side! And he received the stigmata *from* God/Christ Himself, for Christ is the mystic centre round which the hierarchy of Seraphim and Cherubim are arranged and whose bidding they do. Moreover, the seraph figure, as described by Bonaventure, was ambiguously both a seraph with wings *and* a man whose hands and feet were nailed to a cross.[82] God/Christ thus personally deified Francis the ecstatic contemplative.

But more than this: in receiving the stigmata Francis achieved

> the most Divine Knowledge of Almighty God, which is known through not knowing (*agnosia*) during the union above mind; when the mind, having stood apart from all existing things, then having dismissed also itself, has been made one with the super-luminous rays, thence and there being illuminated by the unsearchable depth of wisdom.[83]

'Made one with the super-luminous rays': the above description comes from Dionysius but it applies equally well to Francis, for light, rays, emanations, illuminations, were all considered, both by Dionysius and by the Franciscans, as being *God in action*. For light is The Good, is God, is Christ. Light is God's means of operation (it is what He emanates). Light gives being to – it is the cause of being of – all things that have being. The intellect grasps the intelligibles through the action of light: he who has received Divine Wisdom is, quite literally, enlightened and illuminated. That is to say, the light itself, which performed the stigmatization of St Francis, *was the emanation of God Himself*. In receiving this light in his own flesh, St Francis 'passed over into God through an ecstasy of contemplation' as St Bonaventure described it: Francis achieved the seventh and highest stage of contemplation – deification – and the stigmata proved it.[84]

Here is Dionysius in *The Divine Names* talking about 'The Good' as an epithet applied to God, a Goodness which is extended to all things which exist, and he is comparing it to the sun:

> For as our sun, through no choice or deliberation, but by the very fact of its existence, gives light to all those things which have any inherent power of sharing its illumination, even so the Good (which is above the sun, as the transcendent archetype by the very mode of its existence is above its faded image) sends forth upon all things according to their receptive powers, the rays of Its undivided Goodness[85]
>
> ... And what shall I say concerning the sun's rays considered in themselves? From the Good comes the light which is an image of Goodness; wherefore the Good is described by the name of 'Light', being the archetype thereof which is revealed in that image ... as the Goodness of the all-transcendent Godhead reaches from the highest and most perfect forms of being unto the lowest ... and gives light to all things that can receive It, and creates and vitalizes and maintains and perfects them, and is the Measure of the Universe and its Eternity, its Numerical Principle, its Order, its Embracing Power, its Cause and its End.[86]
>
> ... And so that Good which is above all light is called a Spiritual

> Light because It is an Originating Beam and an Overflowing Radiance, illuminating with its fullness every Mind above the world, around it, or within it, and renewing all their spiritual powers, embracing them all by Its transcendent elevation. And It contains within Itself, in a simple form, the entire ultimate principle of light; and is the Transcendent Archetype of Light ... the presence of Spiritual Light joins and unites together those that are being illuminated, and perfects them and converts them toward that which truly Is – yea, converts them from their manifold false opinions and unites their different perceptions, or rather fancies, into one true, pure and coherent knowledge, and fills them with one unifying light.[87]

That is to say, *visible* light is the visible, earthly counterpart of *spiritual* Light. Spiritual Light is what God is, and which acts on the level of the intelligible. Visible light is what He uses to carry out His purposes in the sensible world. Study of visible light therefore tells one most directly about God and His actions.[88] This is what the Franciscans believed.

All this shows why certain Franciscans chose, out of all possible things in nature, to study and investigate light above all. Their approach to nature was about light, where that of the Dominicans was about causality. For us to separate any Franciscan study of light from its motive in the pursuit of contemplation and deification, is therefore for us to misrepresent it and to mistake its identity.

The blessed Dionysius was (with St Augustine, of course) the Franciscans' favourite writer. But they did not have a monopoly of his texts.[89] The Dominicans too read him. But they made something different of him. Albert the Great gave lectures on *The Divine Names* at Paris (*c.*1250), for instance, and St Thomas Aquinas made many, many references to the Dionysian writings, and he too wrote a commentary on *The Divine Names* (*c.*1256–*c.*1260); commentaries on the other Dionysian writings have also been attributed to St Thomas. But though St Thomas used Dionysius as a resource (especially for his knowledge of angels, as we saw in Chapter 8), yet ultimately he parted ways with Dionysius over the significance of studying the sensible things of this world and the whole mystical approach.[90] He preferred to see sensible, created, things as evidence of the Creator and His goodness, rather than as stepping-stones to mystical experience of the Creator. In other words, he preferred Aristotle to (neo-) Plato. And Chenu has shown how in the very act of giving exegesis of Dionysius, St Thomas could and did reverse the whole Dionysian doctrine![91] Tugwell has put it appropriately, when he said that the achievement here of the Dominicans (particularly Aquinas and Albertus Magnus) was to have made 'an *intellectualist* interpretation of the works of the pseudo-Dionysius'.[92] To a Franciscan, that was to miss the point.

Notes

1. Simon Tugwell, OP, *Early Dominicans: Selected Writings*, London, SPCK (Classics of Western Spirituality), 1982, gives this translation, working from the manuscript; see pp. 216–17.
2. Ibid., p. 376.
3. See Alastair Smart, *The Assisi Problem and the Art of Giotto*, Oxford, Clarendon, 1971.
4. All the early writings on St Francis have been conveniently collected together, in English translation, in Marion A. Habig (ed.), *St Francis of Assisi: Writings and Early Biographies. English Omnibus of the Sources for the Life of St Francis*, 3rd edn, Chicago, Franciscan Herald Press, 1973. Hereafter cited as *Omnibus*. See p. 377 from Celano's Second Life of Francis.
5. So claimed Bonaventure; see *Omnibus*, p. 653. A similar story is also told about St Dominic.
6. John R.H. Moorman, *The Sources for the Life of S. Francis of Assisi*, Manchester, University Press, 1940, p. 53.
7. Bonaventure, 'Major Life'; see *Omnibus*, p. 730.
8. See Michael Goodich, 'The Politics of Canonization in the Thirteenth Century: Lay and Mendicant Saints', *Church History*, 1975, **44**, pp. 294–307; reprinted in Stephen Wilson (ed.), *Saints and Their Cults: Studies in Religious Sociology, Folklore and History*, Cambridge University Press, 1983, pp. 169–87.
9. According to R.F. Bennett, *The Early Dominicans: Studies in Thirteenth-Century Dominican History*, Cambridge University Press, 1937, p. 49, Dominic 'subordinated poverty to preaching – or better expressed, used poverty as an adjunct to preaching'.
10. See the Dominican and Franciscan churches in Florence, for instance, (S. Maria Novella, Dominican; S. Croce, Franciscan) both of which have the pulpit in the nave.
11. They began building on the site of what is now Sidney Sussex College only in 1238. On the Franciscans in Cambridge see J.R.H. Moorman, *The Grey Friars in Cambridge 1225–1538*, Cambridge University Press, 1952; A.G. Little, 'The Friars and the Foundation of the Faculty of Theology in the University of Cambridge', *Bibliothèque Thomiste*, 1930, **14**, pp. 389–401. On them in Oxford, see A.G. Little, *The Grey Friars in Oxford*, Oxford Historical Society, Oxford, 1892; A.G. Little, 'The Franciscan School at Oxford in the Thirteenth Century', *Archivum Franciscanum Historicum*, 1926, **19**, pp. 803–74. For the Dominicans at Oxford see W.G. Dimock Fletcher, *The Black Friars of Oxford*, Oxford, privately printed, 1882; and at Cambridge, see Walter Gumbley, OP, *The Cambridge Dominicans*, Oxford, privately printed, 1938. See also the valuable essays in *Le Scuole degli Ordini Mendicamenti (secoli XIII–XIV), Convegni del Centro di Studi sulla Spiritualita Medievale XVII*, Todi, Presso L'Accademia Tudertina, 1978, esp. the 'Panorama' of the studia of the mendicants (Joanna Cannon writes that on England), and Jacques Verger's essay on 'Studia et Universités'.
12. Tugwell, *Early Dominicans*, p. 467; H.-M. Féret, OP, 'Vie intellectuelle et vie scolaire dans l'Ordre des Prêcheurs', *Archives d'Histoire Dominicaine*, 1946, **1**, pp. 5–37. Bennett, *Early Dominicans*, quotes Humbert de Romans, Master-General of the Order 1254–63 as saying that those

brothers with learning should be preferred over those who only had sanctity: 'ita et ordo cum scientia non immerito praefertur illis in quibus est sola sanctitas'.

13. The 'Mirror of Perfection', printed in *Omnibus*; see p. 1198.
14. Ibid., p. 1176; Celano, Second Life (*Omnibus* p. 477); Bonaventure, Major Life of Francis, cap. xi (*Omnibus* p. 712).
15. *Omnibus* p. 1840.
16. Ibid., p. 164.
17. Ibid., p. 1608.
18. 'Little Flowers of St Francis', a document of the spiritualists; see *Omnibus* p. 1492. For a brief discussion of this great dispute within the Order, see the Introduction by Raphael Brown to the version of the 'Little Flowers of St Francis', printed in *Omnibus*, pp. 1269–93. See also M.D. Lambert, *Franciscan Poverty. The Doctrine of the Absolute Poverty of Christ and the Apostles in the Franciscan Order 1210–1323*, London: SPCK, 1961. Umberto Eco's celebrated novel, *The Name of the Rose* (originally published in Italian in 1980), London, Secker and Warburg, 1983, deals with a later stage of the dispute. For the later history of the Franciscans, see John Moorman, *A History of the Franciscan Order from its Origins to the Year 1517*, Oxford, Clarendon, 1968.
19. Celano's First Life of Francis, *Omnibus*, p. 278.
20. Ibid., *Omnibus*, p. 297.
21. Celano's Second Life of Francis, *Omnibus*, pp. 494–5.
22. The Legend of Perugia, section 43; *Omnibus*, p. 1021.
23. *Omnibus*, pp. 130–1.
24. John V. Fleming, *An Introduction to the Franciscan Literature of the Middle Ages*, Chicago, Franciscan Herald Press, 1977, p. 70.
25. Etienne Gilson, *The Philosophy of St Bonaventure*, translated by Dom I. Trethowan and F.J. Sheed, London, Sheed and Ward, 1938, p. 72.
26. There seems to be no significant work on this most important topic, but see Edward A. Armstrong, *Saint Francis, Nature Mystic. The Derivation and Significance of the Nature Stories in the Franciscan Legend*, University of California Press, 1973; and Roger D. Sorrell, *St Francis of Assisi and Nature. Tradition and Innovation in Western Christian Attitudes toward the Environment*, Oxford University Press, 1988.
27. Bonaventure, Major Life cap. ix, in vol. 8 of the *Opera* (Quaracchi edition, 1937), p. 530 (the translation is taken from *Omnibus* p. 698): Ut autem ex omnibus excitaretur ad amorem divinum, *exsultabat in cunctis operibus* [= Psalm 91.5] manuum Domini et per iucunditas spectacula in vivificam consurgebat rationem et causam. Contuebatur in pulchris pulcherrimum et per impressa rebus vestigia prosequebatur ubique dilectum, de omnibus sibi scalam faciens, per quam conscenderet ad apprehendendum eum qui est *desiderabilis totus* [= Cant. 5.16]. Inauditae namque devotionis affectu fontalem illam bonitatem in creaturis singulis tanquam in rivulis degustabat ...
28. *Omnibus*, p. 1424.
29. Armstrong, *St Francis, Nature Mystic*, p. 229, points out the ambiguity of the preposition *per*.
30. Printed in volume 8 of the *Opera Omnia* in the Quaracchi edition (1937). There is a reliable English translation by George Boas, *The Mind's Road to God: Saint Bonaventura* [*sic*], Library of Liberal Arts, New York,

Bobbs-Merrill Company, 1953. We use Boas' translation, with modifications.

31. Bonaventure, *Epistola de Tribus Quaestionibus*, in *Opera* vol. 8, p. 334; see Gilson, *The Philosophy of St Bonaventure*, pp. 50–1.
32. Boas, *The Mind's Road*, p. 4; *Opera*, vol. 8, p. 295.
33. Boas, *The Mind's Road*, p. 13; *Opera*, vol. 8, p. 299.
34. Boas, *The Mind's Road*, p. 13; *Opera*, vol. 8, p. 299.
35. Boas, *The Mind's Road*, Introduction, p. xix.
36. Boas, *The Mind's Road*, p. 17; *Opera*, vol. 8, p. 301.
37. The distinctively Franciscan features of this otherwise partly Aristotelian account of perception will be touched on in a later section in this chapter.
38. Boas, *The Mind's Road*, p. 17; *Opera*, vol. 8, p. 301.
39. Boas, *The Mind's Road*, p. 21; *Opera*, vol. 8, p. 303.
40. Boas, *The Mind's Road*, p. 27; *Opera*, vol. 8, p. 305.
41. That is to say, we can never understand the natures of things until we understand Being itself. Boas, *The Mind's Road*, p. 24; *Opera* vol. 8, p. 304.
42. Boas, *The Mind's Road*, p. 29; *Opera*, vol. 8, p. 306.
43. Boas, *The Mind's Road*, p. 31; *Opera*, vol. 8, p. 307.
44. Boas, *The Mind's Road*, pp. 38–9; *Opera*, vol. 8, p. 308–10.
45. Boas, *The Mind's Road*, p. 39; *Opera*, vol. 8, p. 310.
46. Boas, *The Mind's Road*, p. 43; *Opera*, vol. 8, p. 312.
47. Boas, *The Mind's Road*, p. 44; *Opera*, vol. 8, p. 312.
48. Our translations are from the Latin text as printed in the 1472 Cologne and 1515 Strasburg editions. There is a convenient critical edition of the *c.*1394–98 English translation as edited in M.C. Seymour et al., *On the Properties of Things: John Trevisa's Translation of Bartholomaeus Anglicus De Proprietatibus Rerum*, Oxford, Clarendon Press, 3 vols, 1975–88. On Bartholomew and his book see Fleming, *Introduction to Franciscan Literature*, pp. 161–5, and the Introduction to R. James Long (ed.), *Bartholomaeus Anglicus On the Properties of Soul and Body: De Proprietatibus Rerum Libri III et IV*, Toronto, Pontifical Institute of Medieval Studies, 1979, and the references there given.
49. 1472 Cologne edition, folio cxv verso: *substantia*, *qualitas*, *contentium*, *ornamentum*.
50. Ibid., folio i.
51. Ibid. For the full text see Henry Denzinger, *The Sources of Catholic Dogma*, translated by Roy J. Deferrari, St Louis, B. Herder Book Co., 1957, pp. 168–9.
52. On the significance of this discussion of the divine names, see the next section below.
53. Prohemium.
54. 1472 Cologne edition, folio xvi. On the 'naturals', 'non-naturals' and 'counter-naturals', see Chapter 4.
55. Ibid., folio lxxiii.
56. Printed as Johannis Aegidius Zamorensis (Juan Gil de Zamora), *Historia Naturalis*, critical edition by Avelino Domínguez García and Luis García Ballester, Barcelona: Junta de Castilla y León, 3 vols, 1994, vol. 1, quotations are from pp. 105–10. We are most grateful to Professor García Ballester for letting us see and use the text before publication. The translations are our own.

57. On this term to refer to God as Creator, see Chapter 4 and Henry A. Lucks, 'Natura naturans – Natura naturata', *The New Scholasticism*, 1935, 9, 1–24.
58. For the text see H. Boese (ed.), *Thomas Cantimpratensis, Liber De Natura Rerum,* Berlin, De Gruyter, 1973. The translations are our own; on Thomas see Chapter 8.
59. *Thomas Cantimpratensis, Liber De Natura Rerum*, see p. 82.
60. Ibid., p. 4.
61. St Bonaventure, for instance, was a devoted follower of Dionysius: 'Bonaventure, comme l'écrivait le P. Y.M. Congar, s'il utilise Aristote et Averroès, il le fait "dans un esprit dionysien, peut-être l'un des plus authentiquement dionysiens qu'on rencontre en Occident"', Jacques Guy Bougerol, *Saint Bonaventure: Études sur les Sources de sa Pensée*, London, Variorum, 1989, I 'Saint Bonaventure et le Pseudo-Denys l'Aréopagite' (1968), p. 113.
62. Georges Duby, *The Age of the Cathedrals: Art and Society, 980–1420* (first published in French, 1976), translated by Eleanor Levieux and Barbara Thompson, Chicago University Press, 1981, p. 99.
63. P. Chevallier, *Dionysiaca, Recueil donnant l'Ensemble des Traductions Latines des Ouvrages Attribués au Denys de l'Aréopage*, Paris, 2 vols, 1937, 1950, gives the Greek text and nine Latin translations, including those by Hilduin, Sarracinus and Eriguena (Scotus), of everything except the *Letters*. Ceslai Pera, OP (ed.), *S. Thomae Aquinatis In Librum Beati Dionysii de Divinis Nominibus Expositio*, Rome, Marietti, 1950, conveniently gives a Greek and Latin text of the 'Divine names'.
64. John C. Murphy, OFM, 'The Early Franciscan Studium at the University of Paris', in Leslie S. Domonkos and Robert J. Schneider, eds, *Studium Generale: Studies Offered to Astrik L. Gabriel*, Notre Dame: The Medieval Institute, 1967, pp. 159–203.
65. From the 'Ecclesiastical Hierarchy', as translated by John Parker, as *The Works of Dionysius the Areopagite*, 2 vols, London, James Parker and Co., 1897–99, vol. 2, p. 71.
66. See the 'Divine Names', in Parker *The Works of Dionysius the Areopagite*, vol. 1, pp. 33, 35, 42.
67. For the texts see note 63 above. The translation by Parker (*The Works of Dionysius the Areopagite*) is the only complete one into English. *The Divine Names* and *Mystical Theology* have both been translated into English also by C.E. Rolt (London, SPCK, 1920) and John D. Jones (Milwaukee, Marquette University Press, 1980).
68. *The Works of Dionysius*, vol. 2, p. 68–9.
69. Ibid., vol. 2, p. 14.
70. Ibid., vol. 2, p. 41.
71. Ibid., vol. 2, p. 27.
72. Ibid., vol. 2, p. 27.
73. Ibid., vol. 1, p. 73.
74. Ibid., vol. 1, p. 91; see also p. 46.
75. See for example *The Works of Dionysius*, vol. 2, pp. 70, 81, 124.
76. Ibid., vol. 2, pp. 3–4.
77. Ibid., vol. 2, p. 58.
78. Ibid., vol. 2, pp. 62–6.
79. The attempt to show St Francis as a second Christ culminated in

Bartholomew of Pisa's work, written *c.*1385–95 and first printed in 1510. It is known under various titles; the 1590 Bologna edition is called *Liber Aureus. Inscriptus Liber Conformitatum Vitae Beati ac Seraphici Patris Francisci ad Vitam Jesu Christi Domini Nostri* (The Golden Book. The Book of the Conformities of the Life of the Blessed and Seraphic Father Francis, to the Life of Our Lord Jesus Christ). The Franciscan devotion to Christ is paralleled by the Dominican devotion to Mary, their special protector.

80. *The Works of Dionysius*, vol. 2, pp. 50–1.
81. This is the version of Hilduin; for this and the other medieval translations, and the Greek text, see Chevallier, *Dionysiaca*, vol. 2, pp. 1091, 966.
82. Francis saw 'that the Seraph was nailed to a cross although he had wings. His hands and feet were stretched out and nailed to the Cross, while the wings were arranged about him wonderfully'. Bonaventure, 'Minor Life'; see *Omnibus*, p. 821. For the account in Bonaventure, 'Major Life' (*Omnibus*, p. 730), see above page 204.
83. *The Works of Dionysius*, vol.1, pp. 91–2.
84. Boas, *The Mind's Road*, p. 44, *Opera* (of Bonaventure) vol. 8, p. 312.
85. *The Divine Names*, tr. Rolt, p. 87.
86. Ibid., tr. Rolt, pp. 91–2.
87. Ibid., tr. Rolt, pp. 94–5, slightly modified.
88. See in general the excellent article by James McEvoy, 'The Metaphysics of Light in the Middle Ages', *Philosophical Studies* [the journal of that title published by the National University of Ireland], 1979, **26**, pp. 126–45.
89. On the availability of the several Latin translations and of a working edition of the Dionysian corpus, see H.F. Dondaine, OP, *Le Corpus Dionysien de l'Université de Paris au XIIIè Siècle*, Rome, Edizioni di Storia e Letteratura, 1953.
90. This is the conclusion of J. Durantel, *Saint Thomas et le Pseudo-Denis* (Thèse pour le Doctorat à la Faculté des Lettres de l'Université de Paris), Paris, Libraire Felix Alcan, 1919. For the text of St Thomas' commentary, see Pera op. cit.; on Albertus' pro-Aristotle (and anti-Plato) attitude which affected his view of Dionysius, see J.A. Weisheipl, 'Albertus Magnus and the Oxford Platonists' *Proceedings of the American Catholic Philosophical Association*, 1958, **32**, pp. 124–39.
91. M.-D. Chenu, OP, *Toward Understanding St. Thomas* (published in French 1950), translated by A.-M. Landry, OP and D. Hughes, OP, Chicago, Henry Regnery Company, 1964; see pp. 228–9, esp. n. 51.
92. Tugwell, *Early Dominicans*, p. 26; our emphasis. 'Intellectualist' here is being used by Tugwell in a modern sense, and not in the sense of 'intelligible' (in contrast to 'sensible'). It is ironical that in the Apostolic Letter of Pope Pius XII (1941), which made Albert the Great retrospectively the patron of students of the natural sciences, Albert is accidentally made into an honorary Franciscan by his concern with nature being characterized as inspired by that passage from Romans, I.20! See for the English text James A. Weisheipl, OP, *Albertus Magnus and the Sciences, Commemorative Essays, 1980*, Toronto, Pontifical Institute of Medieval Studies, 1980, p. 578. Such a mistake would not have been made by the papal office in the thirteenth century.

CHAPTER TEN

Et facta est lux! And there was light!

Dominus illuminatio mea

Thus when our Franciscans were studying light, they were studying God Himself, or the emanations of God, or the agency of God for the whole of creation.[1] Light was God in operation: the visible universe was light or the product of light; it was visible through the operation of light; it was intellectually graspable because the intellect too operated through light, and proper knowledge was illumination. And light was 'The Good': hence created nature was good. 'All the bodies of the universe are products of radiating light ... Light is the universal agent of causation ... it gives active powers to substances'.[2]

This view of what light is, and this attitude to its importance in God's universe, were of course strikingly confirmed by the very opening verses of the Bible:

> In the beginning God created the heaven and the earth. And the earth was without form and void: and darkness was upon the face of the deep. ... And God said, Let there be light: and there was light. And God saw the light, that it was good: and God divided the light from the darkness.

It was light, therefore, which brought *form* to heaven and earth. Light was brought into existence on the very first day of creation. And light was created by direct fiat of God, without intermediary: as He said in the Latin Bible, *Fiat lux*, Let there be light. And there was light! What Dionysius said about the equivalence of the Good and Light is here confirmed: *And God saw the light, that it was good*. There are many other references in the Bible to the importance of light, to God as Light and as Father of Lights from whom comes 'every good gift and every perfect gift' (Epistle of James 1.17) and to Christ as 'the true Light, which lighteth every man that cometh into the world' (the opening chapter of John's Gospel); followers of Christ are also called lights (Matthew 5.14–15). So when our Franciscans studied light they were engaged in the most important possible study, and in the study of the most important possible thing.

We can see from this that the reason that Franciscans turned to the study of light with such intensity lies beyond questions of the accessibility (or otherwise) of Greek and Arab works on 'perspective'.[3] If anyone had the motivation to pursue it, the study of light was possible without access to such ancient books; and, on the other hand, the availability of particular books is in itself not a sufficient reason for anyone at all ever to pursue the study of anything. But as the Franciscans were indeed motivated in the way we have been describing, then it is obvious that they would have used such books as were available, and sought out ones they had heard of but never seen. This is how they came across what we sometimes term the 'legacy' of previous writings on or related to what we call 'optics' but they called 'perspective'.

The Franciscans and Franciscan sympathizers we shall deal with here who pursued the study of light are all familiar in the story conventionally told these days of 'the development of optics'. They come from three successive generations. Our first is Robert Grosseteste (*c.*1168–1253) of England. He was of poor parentage, but acquired for himself an education in the Schools. His name ('Big-head') was probably a nickname; a contemporary, Herman the German, called him 'Robert of the big head but subtle intellect'.[4] In his youth, it was said, 'he knew all the natures (*omnes naturas*) of beasts and of every reptile and creeping thing'.[5] Grosseteste was not actually a Franciscan by profession – he apparently did not like the stress on begging[6] – but he was the next best thing: someone who sympathized greatly with their mystical contemplative outlook and practices. He had much intimate contact with Franciscans, being appointed lecturer in theology to their house at Oxford, 1229–35.[7] At some point he was Chancellor of Oxford – that is, the agent of the Bishop of Lincoln overseeing the *studium*. And eventually in 1235 he became Bishop of Lincoln himself, where he set himself vigorously to reform the behaviour of the priests in their parishes, and oversaw some of the rebuilding (which took place 1186–1280) of the splendid cathedral. In his episcopal court he is known to have favoured Franciscans highly. His final gesture to his friends the Franciscans was to bequeath his library to their house at Oxford.

Grosseteste's written output was very large,[8] but even within such a large corpus of writings it is clear that he had, to put it mildly, an obsession with the Dionysian writings and with light. He taught himself Greek in his old age and promoted and participated in a revision, from the Greek, of the existing translations of the works of the most blessed Dionysius, and made a commentary on them (*c.*1239–43).[9] Amongst other works he wrote *De Luce* (On Light), *De Colore* (On Colour), *De Iride* (On the Rainbow), *De Calore Solis* (On the Heat of the Sun),[10] in which he claims that its heat comes from the scattering of its light rays, and a *Hexemeron* (On the Six Days of Creation) in which light of course figures largely. As Southern has described it, light was 'an ever-recurring subject of his thought in every branch of knowledge'.[11] Indeed Grosseteste had a dominating interest in light and its operations.[12] Crombie has summed it up quite nicely, when he writes that Grosseteste 'held that the fundamental physical substance, the ultimate identity persisting through all change and the original physical cause of all change, was light'.[13]

Grosseteste was also very interested in mathematics (geometry), writing 'On Lines, Angles and Figures'.[14] But although the opening lines of this work have been greeted as 'the first statement of a claim which was to prove fundamental to the metaphysics of early modern science',[15] viz. that mathematics is fundamental to the enquiry into nature, yet the full or alternative title of the treatise reveals Grosseteste's own obsessions: 'On Lines, Angles and Figures, or On the Refractions and Reflections of Rays'. Grosseteste is here interested in the way that all natural effects – for instance, the functioning of the senses, and the operation of heat and cold – either are produced by, or in the same way as, light rays. It is in this sense, concerned with light as the model of the 'universal action' of natural effects, that Grosseteste writes:

> The utility of a consideration of lines, angles and figures is the very greatest, since it is impossible that natural philosophy be known without them. They obtain absolutely in the whole universe and in its parts. They obtain also in related properties, such as in straight and circular motion. They obtain too in action and being-acted-upon, and this whether it be in matter or in the sense ... For all causes of natural effects must be given through lines, angles and figures. For otherwise it is not possible to know 'propter quid' with respect to them.[16]

'Propter quid' means the reason *on account of which* things are as they are. In every case Grosseteste is concerned with tracing, in lines, angles and figures, the route of the *virtus* which is bringing about change through 'multiplying its virtue' from itself into whatever it acts upon. 'Virtue' operates most strongly in straight lines, for they are the shortest distance between agent and acted-upon, and particularly when it falls on the acted-upon at equal rather than unequal angles – 'Therefore when virtue falls at angles not only equal but completely right [i.e. right angles], it can be seen that its action is most strong, since it is in every way an equality and a completed uniformity'.[17] When refracted or reflected, the virtue is weakened. Thus Grosseteste's interest in geometry with respect to nature is not in measuring and calculating, but in generalizing and extending his neo-Platonic and Dionysian understanding of the behaviour of the virtue of light – which travels in straight lines and multiplies its 'virtue' in whatever it encounters – to the understanding of all natural effects or change. Light is for him the paradigm of natural action.

In the short treatise 'On the Nature of Places' Grosseteste gives an instance of this geometric approach to nature in action:

> With these rules and bases and fundamentals given of the power of geometry, the diligent observer of natural things can give the causes of all natural effects through this means ... The first and greatest variety of nature is in the places of the world, and this is especially to be considered by the natural philosopher, since according to the varied natures of places, there is a variety of locations.[18]

Following Grosseteste's first rule of geometry – that the shorter the straight line the more it promotes action (*linea recta brevior magis facit ad actionem*) – one can work out why different regions of the earth have different climates, i.e. according to the different angles at which, and longer distances from which, they receive the rays of the sun.

Grosseteste's most famous application of geometry (at least in the eyes of modern historians of science) was to the rainbow, which is of course again a phenomenon of light. Speculation on the rainbow pertains, Grosseteste writes, both to the *perspectivus* (the student of perspective) and to the *physicus*: to know the 'what' (*quid*) is for the *physicus*, but to know the 'reason on account of which' (*propter quid*) is for the *perspectivus*. Perspective is a *scientia* which deals with visual figures, and has three parts, according to the three ways in which the rays from the eye of the observer reach the thing seen: first, *sight*, where it travels direct; second, *mirrors*, where it has been reflected; and third, where it has been refracted. This third (unnamed) part has been unknown to our day, writes Grosseteste, and to it belongs the study of the rainbow:

> This part of Perspective, when perfectly known, shows us the means whereby we may make things most distant appear placed very close, and by which we may make great nearby things appear very small, and by which we may make small things placed far away appear as large as we like, so that it would be possible for us to read the smallest letters at an incredible distance, or to count sand or grains or blades of grass or any other minute things.[19]

Grosseteste claimed this because he believed that 'the size, position and arrangement according to which a thing is seen depends on the size of the angle through which it is seen and the position and arrangement of the rays, and that a thing is made invisible not by great distance, except by accident, but by the smallness of the angle of vision'.[20] Grosseteste's particular explanation of the formation of the rainbow need not detain us here, but in brief 'Grosseteste thinks the colours of a rainbow are caused by the weakening of white light, and both reflection and refraction, he feels, do this'.[21] It is the 'virtue' of light, its capacity to 'multiply its virtue', which is weakened by reflection and refraction.

It can be seen from all this that Grosseteste, taking his own starting-point in the special Franciscan interest in light, was definitely and explicitly promoting certain new fields of study for the philosopher to engage in (the nature of places and perspective, are the ones we have just touched on). We have also seen that the kind of thing he sees, i.e. the multiplication of 'virtue' and the weakening of 'virtue', are so typically Dionysian. This call of Grosseteste's to institute a new approach to nature had some effect in his own time, in that some of the books the Franciscans favoured did become basic texts of natural philosophy in the *studia*, and it also encouraged other Franciscans to engage in similar enquiries.

'The knowledge of things as they are in themselves'

One of Grosseteste's grounds for promoting an interest in geometry lay, as we have seen, in his concern with the operation of *virtus* in the created universe. But there was another reason for his strong interest, and this he held in common with others of his generation who had Franciscan sympathies. Again it has to do with the mystic and ecstatic experiences central to Franciscan spiritual practice. We recall what St Bonaventure wrote: that it is both desirable and possible for a Christian to take the spiritual journey which involves travelling mentally from the *sensibles* (the things accessible to the senses), to the *intelligibles* (the things accessible only to the intelligence). And this is the mind's road to God, God being accessible as fully as possible only to the intelligence. In attacking the Aristotelian view Grosseteste wrote that full knowledge is accessible without the aid of the senses:

> the highest part of the human soul, called the intelligence ... would have full knowledge without the aid of the senses through the irradiation received from the higher light if it were not clouded and weighed down with the weight of the corrupt body. It will have that knowledge when it has laid the body aside, and some may, perchance, already have it – namely, those who through love have been completely freed from the phantasms of their corporeal bodies.[22]

Full knowledge (*completa scientia*) is available to those who in a state of ecstatic contemplation can free themselves from the body, and it is knowledge separate from and superior to that obtainable via the senses. The sensibles are, by definition, the things of this world; the intelligibles, on the other hand, are things in a form which is not strictly of this world. For the sorts of thing that the intellect grasps are ones separate from matter: abstractions, ideas, and essences – 'the knowledge of things as they are in themselves' (as Dionysius described essences).[23] Such intelligibles all treat things as separate or freed from their matter. They deal in pure form. And geometrical figures – more, perhaps, than anything else – are archetypical 'ideas'. For geometrical figures are pure abstractions, pure form, form without matter. The circle, the triangle, the square are form without matter, and so are lines and angles. To deal in geometry is to deal in pure form, in pure intelligibles. They are the currency of the intelligence loosed from the phantasms of the body. This is why geometry is so important to Grosseteste.

We will recall that the point of engaging in contemplation, in which the intelligence is loosed from the phantasms of the body and deals in the intelligibles, was to become 'deified', to become like God. The intelligibles were, for Grosseteste and others in the Franciscan tradition, the divine ideas themselves (that is, the ideas in the mind of God Himself). Thus to understand geometry was to understand the ideas and operations of God in the world.[24] Such a view could be powerfully supported by a celebrated sentence from the Bible: *thou hast ordered all things in measure and number and weight.*[25] Neo-Platonic Christians often favoured this sentence to justify their approach to nature. It is noteworthy that it occurs in the book of *The Wisdom of Solomon*, which was composed in the Greek period of Hebrew history: that is to say it was neo-Platonic by original sentiment and inspiration, and hence its suitability for later neo-Platonic uses is understandable.[26] This neo-Platonic tradition, as we have been showing, was, in the person and works of Dionysius, the source also of the mystical interest in light shown by the Franciscans and their sympathizers.

Because geometry was the key to the ideas of God, we can appreciate why Grosseteste saw geometry as giving *causes*. We have already quoted him as writing 'all causes of natural effects must be given through lines, angles and figures. For otherwise it is not possible to know *propter quid* with respect to them'.[27] Roger Bacon was later to say of Grosseteste that he 'knew how, through the power of mathematics, to explain the *causes* of all things'.[28] The divine ideas are geometrical, God operates through geometry; hence to understand the operations of things geometrically is to understand them in terms of their causes (or *propter quid*).[29] 'In mathematics alone', as Grosseteste wrote, 'is there knowledge (*scientia*) and demonstration, properly and particularly called'.[30] This brings us back once again to light. For light was God in operation and, as we have seen, Grosseteste believed that light functioned geometrically, and should therefore be studied geometrically. But light was also, for Grosseteste, pure form: that is to say, light is an intelligible. Light is the form which gives form to everything else. This is what Genesis says, the earth was without form and God said let there be light – and then there was form. Light is not a form separated from matter; it is, instead, a form which gives form to formless matter. It is therefore a *corporeal* (or *substantial*) *form*: the form which first comes to matter to constitute body, and which gives form to formless matter; it is the form of corporeity. This concept of 'corporeal form' was very important to the enterprise of Grosseteste and others in the Franciscan tradition. Grosseteste's work *On Light, or The Beginning of Forms* applies this concept to explaining the formation of the universe. As Crombie has summarized it, Grosseteste here describes how 'in the beginning of time God created unformed matter and a point of light, which, propagating itself into a sphere, produced the dimensions of space and, subsequently, all other physical beings. By its expansion light gave corporeal form to the unformed primitive matter.'[31] Light is the first form which gives form to all other things. Light should be studied geometrically because it operates geometrically. And God is light.

Finally it needs to be noticed that Grosseteste worked on the assumption that all objects throw off a sort of image of themselves – a *species* – and that it is this which is perceived by the sense (the eye) in the act of sight. Historians of optics have called this his 'theory of species' and seen it as a new development in optical theory by Grosseteste.[32] However, the thing that an object thus throws off, the *species*, is nothing other than an image or *material form* of the object, and 'form' or 'appearance' are among the conventional meanings of the term 'species'. That is to say, Grosseteste's understanding of what is happening in the acts of vision and perception, is exactly of a piece with his view of the importance of 'forms': 'forms' are what the intellect can grasp, 'forms' (as *species*) are what objects throw off, and light itself is a 'form'.

All this is contrary to what Aristotle wrote. It is contrary to the Aristotelian world-view which was being concurrently promoted by the Dominicans. For instance, to Aristotelians light was not a form at all.[33] To Aristotelians light was therefore not primary, and certainly not the basic thing an investigator of nature should be studying. Grosseteste, by contrast, shows in *On Light, or The Beginning of Forms* how the spheres of the universe and the four elements, as described by Aristotle and Ptolemy, came into existence naturally through the action of light: Aristotle gave an Aristotelian account of these phenomena; Grosseteste is giving a *non*-Aristotelian explanation of these same 'Aristotelian' phenomena. Similarly, Grosseteste sees light as fundamental to knowing, to being, to the angels (or intelligences), to creation, to the Word of God, and to how God is first form and the form of all things. Here again, although some of the same phenomena are being accounted for here as Aristotle accounts for (e.g. how we know), it is by a non-Aristotelian explanation.[34] Again, a Christian Aristotelian (following Aristotle himself) did not see the universe as constructed geometrically: his God was not a geometer, except in a trivial sense; instead He was a craftsman, shaping the matter of the world to match the ends He had in mind for it. For a Christian Aristotelian, geometry most certainly did not give the *causes* of things, but only relationships between things: causes were given from analysis by means of the so-called 'four causes' and especially the final cause, the 'that-for-the-sake-of-which' a thing is as it is – the purpose the Creator designed it to fulfil. For an Aristotelian, although the mind necessarily deals in abstractions and forms and essences, these have no real, no substantial, existence: essences, ideas and forms for an Aristotelian can not exist separately from their embodiment in things, except as mere concepts. For Aristotle and Aristotelians, the 'real' things (from *res*, a thing) are substantial: a combination of form and matter. For someone with Platonic inspiration, such as Grosseteste, the 'real' things (if one can use this vocabulary) — the 'things as they are in themselves' — are forms *without* matter.

Such radical differences in doctrine from the Aristotelians were not unconscious mistakes or misunderstandings on the part of Grosseteste and others in the Franciscan tradition, such as Bonaventure.[35] They were perfectly well aware of how their accounts of the universe and their approach to nature differed from those being promoted by their brothers the Dominicans. The difference was deliberate. And yet historians have hitherto considered Grosseteste to be one of the leading figures in the assimilation of the new learning of Aristotle,[36] and have treated him as an Aristotelian, even if one with some strange views.[37] It is certainly the case that Grosseteste spent much time in translating and commenting on Aristotle, including the *Physics* and the *Posterior Analytics*. But this did not make him an Aristotelian. For, as Lynch has shown by his analysis of Grosseteste on divine ideas, when Grosseteste comments on Aristotle he makes Aristotle speak like (neo-) Plato.[38] Grosseteste uses the vocabulary of Aristotle, but to ends which are opposed to those of Aristotle. It is the exact parallel to the case of St Thomas Aquinas and Albertus Magnus when they commented on Dionysius: their Dionysius speaks like Aristotle, Grosseteste's Aristotle speaks like Dionysius. That is to say, there are two traditions here, two different approaches to nature, not one, and they have different – sometimes opposing – concerns.[39]

Mathematics and light: Roger Bacon

The second of our early investigators of nature in the Franciscan tradition, now the most famous of them all, is Roger Bacon (*c.*1219–92).

He is famous today, and has been now for a century and a half, for having been an early 'scientist', for practising magic and for projecting flying machines; more recently he has been credited, along with Grosseteste, with creating early 'experimental science'. Bacon could not of course have been a 'scientist' because he lived in the wrong age for this.[40] So we, by contrast, shall be looking at Bacon as a man of the thirteenth century, and therefore at the major part he played in trying to develop a specifically Franciscan approach to nature – one based, that is, on *perspectiva*, on the *virtus* and 'species' of light, and on geometry – and pointing out that he did so because he was a Franciscan friar. This approach to nature, as in the case of Grosseteste, was the outcome of the contemplative mystical approach typical of Franciscans, and it was concerned with grasping the 'intelligibles' and their nearest equivalents in sensation, and with light as God at work in the world.

Given the enormous mass of writings that he left, surprisingly little is known about Bacon's life. He is believed to have been born in England and to have spent much of his adult life in the Franciscan houses associated with Paris and Oxford, lecturing on Aristotle's books at Paris (some of these lectures survive).[41] But it is an open question when he became a Franciscan (the conventional date is 1247), and which particular periods he was in Paris or Oxford. His works are, for the most part, very difficult to date with any precision,[42] though Lindberg says that 'it appears safe to conclude that all of Bacon's optical works were written after he had entered the Franciscan Order'.[43] He probably had sympathies with the Joachimite branch of the Franciscans, who were highly mystical in their outlook, and he may have been punished for this.[44] At some point he became familiar with the work of Grosseteste, whom he thenceforth viewed with great admiration.

What we shall do here is simply look at the argument of Bacon's largest work, the one he himself called his 'Larger Work' (*Opus Majus*),[45] and treat this as being representative of his attitudes, obsessions and general approach, and to see from this something of what his goals were, why and how he promoted a particular approach to nature, what that was like, and what role in it was to be played by *perspectiva*.

The *Opus Majus* was one of a whole package of writings that Bacon wrote and sent to the pope at Viterbo in about 1267–68. For some reason the pope, when still a cardinal, had asked Bacon to send him his 'composition about good letters' and, as secretly as possible, his remedies for the dangerous matter Bacon had spoken to him about.[46] What Bacon eventually sent was 'The Larger Work' (the *Opus Majus*), 'The Smaller Work' (the *Opus Minus*), and three versions of 'On the Multiplication of Species' (the *De Multiplicatione Speciarum*); he also wrote, but probably did not send, 'The Third Work' (the *Opus Tertium*). All of these works are considered by historians to be attempts to cover similar ground in somewhat different ways. The works Bacon sent did arrive at the papal court, but the pope in question, Clement IV, was then dead, and no subsequent pope is known to have read or profited from them. But that they were intended for the attention of the pope is very important, for Bacon wanted the pope to take certain action on the basis of them: nothing less than acting to ensure the preservation of Christendom and fighting Antichrist – this seems to be the dangerous matter Bacon had spoken about.[47] The friars saw themselves as the direct agents of the pope in maintaining orthodoxy, preserving true Christianity, and promoting spirituality, so it was perfectly appropriate for Bacon to send his thoughts on such matters directly to the pope.

The means of saving Christendom that Bacon advocated was primarily the cultivation of mathematics (geometry) and *perspectiva*. That is how important these subjects were to Bacon, and this is for him their true purpose and proper use. For wisdom, to which geometry and *perspectiva* are central, will save Christianity. 'The perfect consideration of wisdom (*sapientiae perfecta consideratio*)', Bacon begins,

> consists in looking at two things: what is required to obtain it, and how it may be applied to everything. For by the light of wisdom (*lumen sapientiae*) the Church of God is ordered, the commonwealth of the faithful is governed, the conversion of unbelievers is secured, and those who persist in evil may be restrained through the power of wisdom, so that they may be driven off from the boundaries of the Church in a better way than through the shedding of Christian blood.[48]

These are the declared aims of the whole of the work: wisdom should be pursued not for its own sake, not for the advancement of the material state of mankind, but for the promotion of the proper government of the Church and the conversion of unbelievers. Everything else Bacon writes in this work needs to be seen in this Roman Christian context with its Roman Christian goals. 'Everything which requires the guidance of wisdom comes down to these four goals, and no more.'[49]

In everything he writes about the acquisition of wisdom, Bacon is calling on what is sometimes called an 'illuminationist' understanding of how knowledge and wisdom are acquired: they are acts quite literally of 'illumination'. Light is thus completely central to Bacon's view of what wisdom is and how it is acquired. In this he is at one with other Franciscan-oriented people writing about knowledge and wisdom, such as Grosseteste, and like them he is a Dionysian.[50] And, again like Grosseteste, Bacon takes the Aristotelian account of how perception and understanding work and transforms it, without comment, into an essentially neo-Platonist one.[51] Here in the *Opus Majus* Bacon speaks of philosophy being acquired through the influence of divine illumination, and calls to his support both Socrates and Augustine to the effect that man cannot know the causes of things except in the divine light and by its gift.[52] Like others in the Franciscan tradition, for Bacon true wisdom, acquired by illumination, meant one could 'see God Himself and contemplate the causes and reasons for things, and *scientiae*, truly in Him'.[53]

There are four causes of error which inhibit us from grasping true wisdom, Bacon writes, and hence inhibit us from achieving the larger goals of the development of Christianity under the Church. The first part of the *Opus Majus* deals with these causes of error, which are (i) too much respect for authority, (ii) custom, (iii) popular prejudice, and (iv) presumption of wisdom before we have actually achieved it. These need to be recognized and rejected before we can proceed in our pursuit of true wisdom.

At the beginning of the second part Bacon announces that there is only one perfect wisdom, and it is contained wholly in the Scriptures: the truth of Jesus Christ is that wisdom. Hence theology is the most important *scientia*, and theology is to be explicated by canon law and philosophy. Then Bacon argues that philosophy is not alien to the wisdom of God, but contained within it; all true wisdom will be in accord with the Bible and theology. Philosophy is like the 'Egyptian gold', Bacon says, using a metaphor now familiar to us.[54]

> Now, the point of the whole of philosophy is that the Creator may be known through the knowledge of His creation (*suae creaturae*). Service is due to Him in honorable worship and in the harmony of morals and the honesty of useful laws, because of the reverence due to His majesty and the benefits of the creation, its preservation and of future happiness, so that men may live in peace and justice in this life. For speculative philosophy flows right through to the knowledge of the Creator from the things He has made. And moral philosophy establishes standards of morals, just laws, and the worship of God, and it teaches usefully and excellently about the happiness to come, insofar as lies within the power of philosophy. These things are known for certain by those running over all parts of philosophy, as the following pages will teach. Since therefore these things are in every way necessary for Christians, and in every way consonant with the wisdom of God, it is obvious that philosophy is necessary to divine law and to the faithful who glory in it.[55]

As with other Franciscan writers, we find Bacon here specifying the point of philosophy as being 'that the Creator may be known through the knowledge of His creation' (*ut per cognitionem suae creaturae cognoscatur creator*). Moreover, he says that such knowledge of the

Creator can be acquired from the things that He has made. This is of course an echo of that same passage from Romans so dear to Franciscans: 'the invisible things of Him from the creation of the world are clearly seen, being understood by the things that are made, even His eternal power and Godhead'.[56]

Thus pagan philosophy is essential for the true Christian seeking knowledge of God. There are five parts of philosophy most valuable for the exposition of the sacred wisdom of the Scriptures, Bacon writes. The first is Grammar, the study of language and languages, which Bacon deals with in Part Three. But the most important of all parts of pagan philosophy, Bacon quotes Cassiodorus as saying, are the *mathematical sciences*:

> These four sciences, geometry, arithmetic, astronomy and music, when we consider them with an attentive mind, they sharpen the sense, they wipe away the mire of ignorance and, by God's help, they lead us to that divine contemplation; the holy fathers rightly insisted they were to be read since through them the appetite may in great part be drawn away from carnal things, and they make us desire those things which we can view in the heart alone.[57]

To Mathematics Bacon devotes most of the *Opus Majus* – Parts Four, Five and Six. Indeed, Mathematics is one of four great sciences without which the other sciences cannot be known (we shall come to the other three great sciences shortly). If these mathematical sciences are known, Bacon says, then

> any one can make glorious progress in the power of knowledge without difficulty and labour, not only in human sciences, but in that which is divine ... Of these sciences the gate and the key is mathematics, which the saints discovered at the beginning of the world, as I shall show, and which has always been used by all the saints and sages more than all other sciences. Neglect of this branch now for thirty or forty years has destroyed the whole system of study of the Latins. Since he who is ignorant of this cannot know the other sciences nor the affairs of this world, as I shall prove.[58]

Bacon argues the importance of mathematics for knowing anything at all about the operations of the heavens and the earth, and he does so along lines similar to those we have met with already in Grosseteste's writings. He claims that all 'efficient causes' – an Aristotelian concept of explanation – require geometry for their proper comprehension, and thus he quietly turns a potentially Aristotelian account of the universe and its operations into an actually Neo-Platonic account:

> For every natural thing in nature is brought into being by an efficient cause and the material on which it works ... But the *virtus* of the efficient cause and of the material cannot be known without the great power of mathematics even as the effects it produces cannot be

> known without it.[59]

A species (as will be recalled from the discussion of Grosseteste) is the thing thrown off by any object, and through which the power (*virtus*) of the object is exercised and multiplied:

> Every multiplication of species is either with respect to lines, or angles, or figures. While the species travels in a medium of one rarity, as in what is wholly sky, and wholly fire, and wholly air, or wholly water, it is propagated in straight paths, because Aristotle says in the fifth book of the Metaphysics that nature works in the shorter way possible, and the straight line is the shortest of all.[60]

When it passes into denser or rarer media, the direction of the species is changed: the more perpendicular it remains, the stronger its *virtus* and its capacity to multiply its power. Virtually everything Bacon writes about the power of mathematics, about its centrality to the operations of nature, and of its indispensability in understanding nature, dwells on the operations of *species*. Lindberg has rightly written that 'Bacon regarded the doctrine of species as central to his natural philosophy ... Bacon attributes all natural causation to the multiplication of species'.[61] Understanding the operation of species enables us to understand geography, the tides, health and weakness in the human body, theology and biblical history, and Bacon goes on about these applications of geometry for hundreds of pages.

Light is of course the paradigm example of the operations of *virtus*. And the Fifth Part of Bacon's plea to the Pope, the *Opus Majus*, is duly on the operations of light: it is the *Perspectiva*.[62] 'It is possible that some other science may be more useful', Bacon writes, 'but no other science has so much sweetness and beauty of utility. Therefore it is the flower of the whole of philosophy and through it, and not without it, can the other sciences be known'.[63] Historians generally applaud Bacon for opting in this Fifth Part of the *Opus Majus* for an 'intromission' rather than an 'extramission' theory of vision – that is, for claiming that nothing comes out from the eye to the object in the act of sight (as for instance Ptolemy had thought) but that the whole action is accomplished by something coming *into* the eye from the object outside it – and especially for his geometrical analysis of the mode of sight. The reason why Bacon actually uses geometry to investigate the mode of sight lies, however, in the fact that he is investigating the action of the *virtus* of objects, both on each other and on our senses, and light and sight is of course the great exemplar of the action of *virtus*.

How then does the *species* of an object (through which its *virtus* is exercised) arrive at our eye, given that the pupil of the eye is so small? Bacon asks. The answer for Bacon has to be in terms of *straight lines* since, like Grosseteste, he believed that *virtus* operates most strongly in straight (perpendicular) lines. Hence he embraced the theory of so many geometrical 'pyramids', with their base in the thing seen and their vertex in the eye of the beholder:

> We must recognise then, as was verified in what precedes, that [all] natural action is carried out by a pyramid whose vertex is the patient [the object passively receiving the action] and whose base is the surface of the agent [the object actively giving off the *species*]. For this is how the *virtus* comes from the whole agent to the patient, as has been stated before, so that the action may be strong and complete.
>
> In vision therefore it is necessary that the *species* should come from the whole surface of the agent. But although in the natural alteration of patients [the objects acted upon] it is necessary that separate pyramids come to each part of the patient, because every point of the patient must be affected, yet in the natural alteration that happens in vision this is not required, so long as one pyramid comes from the agent, and the vertex fall on the eye; this pyramid falls perpendicularly on the eye, so that all of its lines are perpendicular to the eye.[64]

From such discussion we can see that Bacon's concern is constantly with the *virtus* emitted by all objects, and by the geometrical analysis of *species*, especially with respect to vision.[65] To trace this is to trace the means by which God acts in this world. He takes these attitudes because he is first a Franciscan, with all the devotion to the operation of virtus, light and sight that that involved. Only if we remember that he is a Franciscan will we appreciate why Bacon was so interested in light and sight in the first place, and why his treatment of it is in the terms that it is. Similarly we shall come to a new understanding of Bacon's famed promotion of 'experiment' in 'the experimental science' which he had advocated: the mystical intellectual grasp of things and their causes is best; only *failing* that do we use the regulated experience of the senses, which is experiment.

John Pecham and Witelo

Our next perspectivist is John Pecham (*c.*1230–92), again a Franciscan friar who, like Roger Bacon, also appears to have studied at Paris and Oxford, entering the Order, and then gaining a degree in theology and becoming Lector to the Oxford Franciscans, *c.*1272. Ultimately he received one of the highest accolades and succeeded the Dominican Robert Kilwardby as Archbishop of Canterbury in 1279 – the first and last Franciscan to hold this post. Like Bonaventure, Pecham defended the mendicant orders against the attacks of the Paris secular masters. But he also fought against the 'new' Aristotelianism being introduced at Paris and elsewhere, especially by the Dominicans, and above all by Aquinas. In the late 1270s he said about the teaching at Oxford:

> we are far from condemning philosophy, in so far as it serves the cause of theology; what we condemn are the unsanctified and novel terms that have these last twenty years been introduced into the treatment of high theology, to the manifest contempt and rejection of the saints of old. Which of these two doctrines, we ask, is more sound and solid, that of the sons of St Francis, Alexander of Hales and Bonaventura [*sic*] of blessed memory and their like, who in their treatises take for authorities saints and philosophers above criticism, or that newfangled system opposed to this at all points, which strains every nerve to demolish the teaching of Augustine on the eternal prototypes, on the divine illumination of the intellect, on the faculties of the soul, on the radical potentialities of matter, and on numberless other points, thus filling the whole world with the strife of words? Let the doctors of old, the truly wise, regard this; let God in heaven regard it and punish it![66]

This placing of himself firmly in the Franciscan tradition of thinking, from St Francis, through Alexander of Hales, Bonaventure and others, extended also to Pecham's concern with light and *perspectiva*, in which he was as interested as Grosseteste and Bacon had been. He wrote at least two treatises on *perspectiva*: a 'Tractatus de perspectiva', and a 'Perspectiva' which is sometimes known as the 'Perspectiva communis'.[67] Moreover, Pecham wrote on other mathematical themes, such as on the sphere, and a 'mystical' work on numbers.[68] Like Grosseteste, Pecham is concerned with the multiplication of species, and his debt to the writings of Roger Bacon is evident everywhere.

The *Tractatus de perspectiva* was written around 1277–79. Its opening words are Dionysian in theme. The point of pursuing *perspectiva* is to use number and light in order to ascend to the Divine:

> Augustine says in book I of *De libero arbitrio* that 'the further the learned and the scholarly are removed from earthly sin, the better are they able to contemplate both Number and Wisdom in very truth'. But since we are not equipped to gaze on Divine Number (I mean the number which is without number) nor on Wisdom (of which there is no number, according to the Psalmist) in their fullness, since according to the Apostle they dwell in the light which no man can approach, it is necessary for us to seek out their footprints in the mirrors of created things, so that through created number we may ascend to uncreated Number, and through created light to the uncreated Light of Wisdom. For light is the purer in essence and the more efficacious in operation between bodily created things, and in this is more like the eternal Light ... I do not speak of light metaphorically but most truly and in itself ... Therefore beginning

> from light, seeking to be like Wisdom, the author of everything, and calling on her for help, I will attempt this work on light and number as well as I can, in order to be of use to the less educated brothers [of the Order], trusting that they will be more ready to hear than jeer.
>
> You should know therefore that geometry considers line insofar as it is mathematical, but *perspectiva* considers line not only insofar as it is mathematical, but also insofar as it is natural. Hence it has for its subject-matter radiating line, and is thus far subalternated to geometry, but more to physics, since it is more 'natural' than 'mathematical' ... [69]

The science of *perspectiva* is 'natural' because it deals with the action of natural species or forms. The *Perspectiva* was a revised version of the *Tractatus*, and can be taken therefore to have had the same point and aims. And it too deals in terms of the multiplication of species, and it deals with light as the exemplar of the action of natural bodies:

> Every natural body, visible or invisible, diffuses its power (*virtus*) radiantly into other bodies. The proof of this is by a natural cause, for a natural body acts outside itself through the multiplication of its form. Therefore the nobler it is, the more strongly it acts. And since action in a straight line is easier and stronger for nature, every natural body, whether visible or not, must multiply its species in a continuous straight line; and this is to radiate.[70]

Such statements clearly put Pecham's *Perspectiva* in the same Franciscan tradition we have been looking at. Pecham's work was of the greatest practical consequence of all the works on *perspectiva*, for it seems to have been a fundamental work in the arts course at many universities in the next (fourteenth) century, as one of the works read for the quadrivium.

Our last famous perspectivist of the thirteenth century is Witelo. We know only a little for certain about Witelo (and indeed only this one name for him), and the direct information does not reveal whether he was a Franciscan or not. We know that he was 'a son of Thuringians and Poles' and was at Paris University in the early 1250s; later, in the next decade, he was at Padua, and for the years 1268–70 he was at the papal court at Viterbo, where he became closely acquainted with William of Moerbeke, and where it seems he wrote his *Perspectiva* (*c.*1270–73).[71] The *Perspectiva* shows significant signs that Witelo was familiar with the *Opus Majus* of Roger Bacon, especially in his discussion of the rainbow. Although it had been sent too late to be read by the Pope it was intended for, this great work of Bacon's was at the papal court, and this is presumably where Witelo came across it.[72]

When we turn to the *Perspectiva*, we find that, like all the other works under that name we have been looking at, it too has Dionysian inspiration. The Dedication is pure Dionysius. And it is within this Dionysian context that Witelo composed the rest of the work, which, taken alone, might otherwise seem to be simply a technical work on 'optics'. Dionysius' lyrical account of how divine light flows out from the divine centre through the ranks of Seraphims, Powers and Angels, conveying to them in due measure the divine ray to allow them to participate in the divine virtues as far as befits their station, is all reflected here. So too is the Dionysian discussion of how earthly light is the earthly counterpart of divine light, and how it too is the means or medium by which the *virtus* of superior entities is conveyed to inferior beings. Here for instance is Witelo writing in his *Perspectiva* about the project; he is addressing William of Moerbeke and describing the project as Moerbeke had conceived it for himself (Witelo) to take up:

> While you were mentally making causal links between intelligible being coming-to-be from its first beginnings, and individual sensible beings, it occurred to you, as to a sedulous observer of all being, that the influence of the divine virtues on inferior corporeal things is brought about through superior virtues in an amazing way. For corporeal things, inferior in the universal order of parts, are not participants incorporeally in divine virtue, but they participate in and are capable of the virtues contracted through those things of an order superior to their own, just as in the other order of intellective substances the inferiors participate in and are capable of substantiality through illumination by those superior to their own order, illumination derived from the fount of divine goodness. You realized through the sharpness of your mind that the nature of everything is borne to it through the medium of intelligible influences; just as every entity of things flows out from the divine entity, and every intelligible flows out from the divine intelligence, and every life from the divine life. Of these influences the divine light (*divinum lumen*), working through the intelligible mode, is the principle, the medium, and the end by which, through which, and toward which all things are disposed. But of corporeal influences perceivable light (*lumen sensibile*) is the medium, miraculously assimilating the lower bodies, which are varied according to their forms and their location, to the perpetual superior bodies according to their substance, and alone linking them in power, from wherever they are, to the lower bodies. Light is the diffusion of the supreme corporeal forms, applying itself through the nature of corporeal form to the matter of inferior bodies and impressing the descended forms of the divine and indivisible artificers along with itself on perishable bodies in a divisible manner, and ever producing by its incorporation in them new specific or individual forms, in which there results through the actuality of light the divine formation of both the moved orbs and the moving powers. Therefore because light has the actuality of corporeal form it makes itself equal to the corporeal dimensions of the bodies into which it flows and extends itself to the limits of capacious bodies, and nonetheless since it

> always contemplates the source from which it flows according to the origin of its power, it assumes *per accidens* the dimension of distance, which is a straight line, and thus it acquires the name 'ray'. And since the natural straight line always exists in any natural surface, what happens to surfaces [i.e. what they undergo, their 'passion'], which happens to them through terminating lines, is an angle.[73]

Here Witelo reveals that not only is he interested in *perspectiva*, like our Franciscans, but also that he is absolutely obsessed by the same concerns with *virtus*, light and geometry as was typical of the Franciscans, and that he shares with them his understanding of what light is, how it functions, and its central importance in understanding God's relation to nature.[74] Moreover, Witelo also wrote a *Philosophia naturalis*, though no copy of it now survives; he refers to a chapter in it as showing that 'all diffusion of forms', of which the multiplication of forms at the surface of mirrors is one kind, occurs 'by the work of nature' and is therefore natural.[75]

His text reveals that Witelo was a 'Franciscan' at least in his interests. But it would perhaps be going too far beyond the strict evidence to infer from this that Witelo was actually a Franciscan by profession, even though everyone else we have found in the thirteenth century who wrote on *perspectiva* did so because they were Franciscans or sympathizers with the Franciscans and held Dionysian views on the nature and importance of light as God in operation in the world. Moreover, Witelo consorted with an important Dominican, William of Moerbeke, who (according to Witelo) thought similarly about light, urged Witelo to undertake the work, and was the dedicatee of the completed book. Moerbeke was of course highly active in these very years in translating from Greek to Latin in order to help the Dominican programme of 're-education' (see Chapters 7 and 8).

To this list of people writing about light and *virtus* in the thirteenth century we could add Alexander of Hales, and his pupil St Bonaventure, both of them again Franciscans. The Franciscan (Dionysian) motivation for them to write on light would seem to be vital,[76] since beyond these no one in the thirteenth century seems to have written extensively on light or perspective – except for some Dominicans, whose treatment of such issues was, as we might by now expect, quite different. Lindberg has shown that Albertus Magnus, for instance, with access to a far greater range of relevant writings than Grosseteste had had, deploys them not to develop *perspectiva* in the manner we have been seeing, but to defend the views of Aristotle and criticize all other approaches: he was, according to Lindberg, 'a loyal defender of Aristotle on the subject of vision'.[77]

Perspectiva or optics?

We have been speaking here of a thirteenth-century *scientia* of *perspectiva* practised, it would seem, exclusively or at least primarily by Franciscans. Yet historians of science conventionally place all this work within a history of *optics*. What, if anything, is the difference between these two *scientiae*, and what relationship does our story here bear to the more usual one that is told of the history of medieval 'optics'? Both the terms 'optics' from the Greek and 'perspective' from the Latin are related to 'seeing': but were the *scientiae* of *optics* and *perspectiva* different in any substantial way? It would seem that in Antiquity (and then possibly in the Arab world) there may indeed have been a *scientia* of optics developed, that is a geometrical treatment of vision, and important works within this *scientia* included the *Optics* of Euclid and the *Optics* of Ptolemy and (presumably) the *Optics* of Al-Haytham (Alhazen). This *scientia* may have been revived in the Renaissance.[78] But in our Troubadourean period, the High Middle Ages, there does not seem to have been a *scientia* of optics – but only a *scientia* of *perspectiva*. Every thirteenth-century person who wrote on *perspectiva* that we have looked at in the present chapter was concerned with treating the operations of nature as being brought about by the propagation of the *virtus* of objects through their emanation of *species* (or forms); they were concerned with the importance of the straight line for the propagation of *virtus* in its strongest form, and thus with the mathematical analysis of the path of the *virtus*. Light was for them the pre-eminent and most studyable form of such *virtus*, and light was also for them God's mode of creative action in the world: *perspectiva* was a whole aspect of natural philosophy for them. Such concerns do not seem to be central, let alone basic, to the *scientia* of optics, at least as it had been practised by Euclid, Ptolemy or Al-Haytham, which seems to have been limited to the mathematical analysis of rays, whether projected out from the eye, or into the eye, or both at once. It looks as if historians of optics may have run these two *scientiae* together, and thus represented our Franciscan concern with light and sight as being a continuation of the classical tradition of optics, and indeed they have for the most part translated the medieval term '*perspectiva*' as 'optics' in the histories they have written.[79] They have then had a problem, which has taken up much time and ink, over the seemingly peculiar way in which these medievals developed the *scientia* of optics, introducing into it what seem like unnecessary and discordant traditions from Antiquity, such as the multiplication of species. The effect of this approach by historians has been that while we have a history of 'optics' from Antiquity on, in which the medieval period provides a highly tortuous and confusing moment, simultaneously offering both 'contributions' to the development of the *scientia* of optics and also regressions from its advance, yet we still lack a history of that medieval *scientia*: *perspectiva*.

The sources of this problem about the missing history of *perspectiva* seem to be threefold. First there has been the determination of historians of science to write a history of *optics*, even where the historical actors claimed they were pursuing *perspectiva*. Second, there was an actual technical hiccough in the so-called 'transmission' of Greek and Arabic authorities to the West: sections of both Ptolemy's *Optics* and Al-Haytham's *Optics* were either missing from the texts used for translation into Latin, or were deliberately omitted from the Latin translations of these works. The omitted passages were in the case of Al-Haytham (and probably in the case of Ptolemy – only the Latin translation now survives) highly important discussions of the nature and mode of transmission of light – in an *optical* (that is, purely mathematical) mode. One might conclude (as some historians have done) that as the medieval Latins therefore did not have such a theory available, they had to work one out from such other texts as they did have available to them, and hence made something of a shambles out of what had been a respectable science. As A.I. Sabra has recently put it:

> These two historical accidents [the non-translation of the pertinent passages in Ptolemy and Ibn-Haytham] constituted the occasion for the choice of the metaphysical doctrine of multiplication of species as a basis for optical theory in the Latin Middle Ages. The result of this choice was a hybrid theory combining heterogeneous elements that ill-suited one another, and the Latin medieval 'synthesis' was thus fated to bring about a serious weakening of the empirical logic rigorously adhered to in Ibn Al-Haytham's *Optics*.[80]

Thus *perspectiva*, the particular approach to light and sight, to *virtus* and *species*, that we have been discussing in this chapter, as developed by Grosseteste, Roger Bacon, and others in the thirteenth century, can look to modern eyes like a random mishmash, or even a bastard science, which was due to a simple lack of decent Greek and Arabic texts in the thirteenth century.[81] But the third source of this problem takes us beyond such judgements, and it lies, we would suggest, in an unwillingness on the part of historians to look at thirteenth-century discussions of *perspectiva* as just that: *thirteenth*-century discussions of a thirteenth-century science, *perpectiva*. In our discussion here of Grosseteste, Bacon et al., we hope we have at least begun the exploration of *perspectiva* as a thirteenth-century science, created by thirteenth-century men for thirteenth-century purposes. And it is here that the Franciscan commitments or sympathies of the 'perspectivists' we have looked at are so important: for this is what gave these people their motive, ground and reason for investigating light and sight at all, and also for doing so in this particular way which put *virtus* and the multiplication of species at the heart of the science.[82] Hence we can begin to understand why they were interested in Greek and Arabic texts which dealt with *optics* and how and why they applied them to the creation of their own science of *perspectiva*, whose subject-matter was 'the action of natural forms' or 'species'.[83] We can also see that it would have been natural enough for the perspectivists themselves to have read works in the ancient *optical* tradition, including that of Al-Haytham (Alhazen), and assume that they were works in their own (new) science of *perspectiva*.[84]

Divine light

Such are the grounds of Franciscan interest in light and its behaviour and properties, for by studying light they were studying God and were engaged in the highest possible activity: the mystical attempt to become deified. This desire on their part led them to study perspective and the rainbow; it led them to study how the eye works, and to trace the paths of rays of light. And it led them to study these things geometrically, for mathematical ideas are 'intelligibles' par excellence and their God was a geometer who had arranged all things in number, weight and measure. It led them to create a new approach to nature. The account we have given of them in this chapter has tried to account for their motivations, for why they were interested in the study of light and mathematics at all, and hence why they studied them in the particular way they did and as the particular things that they believed them to be; our account has therefore deliberately steered clear of looking at their work as simply the spontaneous consequence of the existence and availability of Aristotelian and Platonic 'traditions' and texts in the study of geometry or light or vision or optics or optical theory. We hope that we have by contrast shown the striking fact that the promotion of *perspectiva* and geometry, which we today associate with precision and exactness, was made at this period by people seeking a mystical understanding of God and his universe – and it was made by them *because* they were seeking a mystical understanding of God, rather than *in spite of* the fact that they were seeking a mystical understanding of God.

Like the Order of Preachers, the Franciscans too saw one of their roles as preaching. Franciscan sermons, like those of the Dominicans, regularly reached an audience in the universities. At Oxford in the 1290s, for instance, the Dominicans preached on Sundays in their own church, and the Franciscans on other holy days in their own church, and the audience for them appears to have consisted of all members of the faculty of theology.[85] But usually, like the Dominicans, the Franciscans took as the primary audience for their sermons the townsfolk, including what has been termed the 'upper bourgeoisie', attacking the accumulation of material riches, but seeking to provide this bourgeoisie with 'a spirituality adapted to their way of life'.[86] The particular interests of the Franciscans in nature found a role in their sermons, just as the particular interests in nature of the Order of Preachers found expression in the sermons of the Dominicans. It has been shown recently, for instance, how the *De oculo morali* (On the moral eye), a book of *exempla* for sermons, by the Franciscan Peter of Limoges uses concepts and explanations from the domain of *perspectiva* which (as we have seen) was of such central concern to Franciscans. Peter discusses the anatomy of the eye, the eye as receiver of forms and species of visible things, how vision works, optical illusions, the operations of the 'internal sense', perception by the mind of things seen by the eye, and the superior virtue of light rays which have been neither refracted nor reflected. This is taken from the writings of his fellow Franciscans, and also from one of their favourite texts, the *Perspectiva* of Al-Haytham (Alhazen). All of it is put at the service of expounding morality, in particular the need to promote the role of the internal sense in censoring species received by the eye, filtering out immoral stimulation, and enabling desirable sensations to affect the will.[87] The Franciscan interest in light and its operation was thus not simply either a mystical or an academic study, but one of very practical value to help the townsfolk live good Christian lives. We see here the Franciscans in their role as the upholders of the spiritual dimensions of Roman Catholicism in a world which threatened to be overwhelmed by materialism: unlike some heretics and other extremists calling for the renunciation of the material world, the Franciscan message found a compromise with materialism in its defence of Roman Catholic belief.

The preoccupations of those in the Franciscan tradition in their concern with nature were reflected (the metaphor is exact) also in other areas, particularly in respect of the eucharist or mass. From the fourth Lateran Council of 1215 it was official doctrine of the Church that the bread and wine were *transubstantiated* into the body and blood of Christ. Aquinas, later in the century, was to give an account of this in fully Aristotelian terms. The substance of the bread and wine (that is, their form and matter combined) was changed by the act of the priest consecrating them, changed into the body and blood of Christ. But the accidents (the look, feel, texture, taste etc.) of bread and wine remained; this combination of accidents was sometimes referred to as the 'species' or appearance. Thus the miracle of the mass was that it was the great exception to the usual Aristotelian relation of substance, form, matter and accidents. For, as Aquinas put it, in the mass 'God, who is the first cause of substance and accident, is able, through His infinite power, to keep the accident in being, even after the removal of the substance through which it was kept in being ... '[88] It still *looks like* bread (or wine), but it is now *really* Christ's body (or blood). The Franciscans, with their obsession with light, prompted a different kind of explanation of the miracle of the mass, and it has been shown recently for instance that Wyclif's heretical views on this in the next century owed a great deal to the writings of Grosseteste and others like him on *perspectiva*, light and mathematics.[89] In particular Wyclif, who had Franciscans as friends, denied that transubstantiation takes place. Instead, he claimed, the eucharist is a mirror (*speculum*): 'Christ is present in the eucharist, he held, as an image is present in a mirror';[90] in other words in the consecrated bread and wine are the multiplied emanated 'species' of the body of Christ, though invisible to the bodily eye.

To drive home the mystical importance of light – the fact that light was made into and then continued as an important object of study *because* it was thought of as divine – we can look finally at the way in which this same tradition lies behind the greatest physical legacy of the Troubadorean period, the cathedrals. Cathedrals were being built or rebuilt everywhere now: in France alone some eighty were built in this period. The creation of cathedrals, and of ever larger ones at that, is an integral part of the extension all over Europe of papal power to the diocese, and of diocesan power to the parish. The cathedral is where the bishop had his chair (*cathedra*) of office; it was the church to which all the Christians in the diocese were supposed to look. Until the creation of the Orders of friars, it was the centre of preaching in the diocese, for preaching was the responsibility of the bishop. To fulfil these purposes effectively the cathedral had to be large, even though, unlike a parish church, it had no body of local worshippers to fill it regularly. Bishops and their chapters were often in rivalry with one another to put up the largest, grandest and richest cathedral. Hence the enormous numbers of these enormous buildings erected in this period – all in addition to the other great building programmes of towns, castles, palaces and monasteries.

The cathedrals which date from the early Troubadourean days are now referred to as 'Romanesque' in style; the later ones are now called 'Gothic'. Neither term, of course, was used at the time. The 'Gothic' cathedrals are the ones of concern to us here. In their own time they were called 'Frankish work' (*opus francigenum*), for they were originated in the lands of the Franks, and they were spread to other areas by Frankish or Norman masons. It all started with Abbot Suger (1081–1151), Abbot of St Denis (near Paris) in the years 1122 to 1151. St Denis was of course

10.1 The first 'Gothic' windows: the chevet windows of St Denis, Paris, installed by Abbot Suger

where the works of Dionysius were kept, and Suger was a fervent follower of Dionysius. Suger was therefore fascinated by light (as emanation of God) and by precious stones, which appeared to him to glow from within with a light of their own. Suger deliberately set out to rebuild the church of St Denis in order to let the light flood in. The pinnacle of his achievement was the rebuilding of the upper choir in the years 1140–44. In beginning the rebuilding of St Denis he began the whole tradition of 'Gothic' building. God as light had to be brought into God's church.[91]

As this obsession with bringing light into the church continued, so the masons found new ways of building which would allow the church to be filled with light. They tried to maximize the window space – best shown by their invention of the rose window, which involved narrowing the masonry support both within the window itself, and in the walls. As the walls were now made less solidly, this in turn meant that the downward pressure of the roof made the walls bow outwards; so the walls had to be buttressed. And to make these buttresses as open to the light as possible, they had to be 'flying' buttresses. In this sort of way, the demands of Suger and the bishops who tried to emulate him, led the masons to create all those features we regard as typical of 'Gothic architecture'. Most important to the promotors and builders of these cathedrals was that the light flooding into the building should be coloured. In other words, the glass had to be painted or stained, and this is the beginning of the widespread use of stained glass.[92]

These grand, glorious buildings, colour-ful in every sense of the term, were created all over Europe. In their principles of construction they were realizations of a commitment to that same neo-Platonic and Dionysian tradition of light mysticism which the Franciscans too represented in their explorations of nature. The churches of the Franciscans themselves however, though often large, were not 'Gothic' in structure or ornament, for such riches and display would have ill-befitted a mendicant order.[93] By a nice irony, the *outside* of the 'Gothic' cathedrals came to be a monument to the attitudes of the rival Order of friars, the Dominicans. For, as Emile Mâle showed many years ago,[94] the plants and animals carved in such profusion on the outside of these cathedrals are in many cases representations of descriptions given in the *Speculum Naturae* of the Dominican, Vincent of Beauvais. Hence a 'Gothic' cathedral was the complement of 'Franciscan and Dominican interest in nature' both inside and out, inside for the light, outside for the creatures made by God. The 'Gothic' cathedral was ecstatic contemplation and union with God put into light; and it was the goodness, powerfulness and causality of God, as expressed in His creatures, put into stone. The term 'Gothic' for this form of building was first used, and in a pejorative sense, in the fifteenth and sixteenth centuries, and then in a positive sense in the 'Gothic revival' of the eighteenth and nineteenth centuries.[95] As a term and category, however, it simply ignores the intentions of their mason builders and episcopal promoters, and the obsession with light which these buildings were meant to express: instead it treats them simply as instances of a style of 'architecture' in its modern sense – that is, as if designed by architects. 'Gothic' is thus an inappropriate term for them – at least if we want to recapture anything of their original role, purpose and point. Originally they were monuments to light as the emanation of God, and in this they were just like the nature interests of the Franciscans, as created and practised in the thirteenth century, and which came to constitute an important strand of natural philosophy in the *studia*.

Notes

1. On the importance of light see in general Klaus Hedwig, *Sphaera Lucis: Studien zur Intelligibilität des Seienden im Kontext der mittelalterlichen Lichtspekulation*, Münster, Aschendorff (Beiträge zur Geschichte der Philosophie und Theologie des Mittelalters, Neue Folge, Band 18), 1980.
2. Grosseteste *De Luce*, as cited in David C. Lindberg, 'The Genesis of Kepler's Theory of Light: Light Metaphysics from Plotinus to Kepler' *Osiris* 2nd series, 1986, **2**, pp. 5–42, 16.
3. It should be noted that the Franciscan interest in the writings of the Arab, Alhazen, comes from the fact that he was the first to distinguish *light* from *vision* (unlike the Greeks). This is just the distinction the Franciscans needed (as will be shown below). See A.C. Crombie, 'Expectation, Modelling and Assent in the History of Optics: Part I. Alhazen and the Medieval Tradition', *Studies in the History and Philosophy of Science* 1990, **21**, pp. 605–32. On the meaning of 'perspective' see later in the present chapter.
4. 'Robertus grossi capitis sed subtilis intellectus'; cited in F.M. Powicke 'Robert Grosseteste and the Nichomachean Ethics' *Proceedings of the British Academy*, 1930, **16**, pp. 85–104, see 88. On the name as nickname, see Appendix I in Samuel Pegge, *The Life of Robert Grosseteste the Celebrated Bishop of Lincoln*, London, John Nichols for the Society of Antiquaries, 1793.
5. According to Richard of Bardney, a very late account (1502), cited in R.W. Southern, *Robert Grosseteste, The Growth of an English Mind in Medieval Europe*, Oxford, Clarendon, 1992 (first edn 1986), p. 78.
6. James McEvoy, *The Philosophy of Robert Grosseteste*, Oxford, Clarendon, 1982, 46, quoting Eccleston's early history of the Franciscans in England.
7. Grosseteste's early life and career is impossible to date with exactitude; for a recent attempt to resolve the problems, see Southern, *Robert Grosseteste*.
8. For a list see S. Harrison Thomson, *The Writings of Robert Grosseteste, Bishop of Lincoln 1235–1253*, Cambridge University Press, 1940;

Appendix A of McEvoy's volume (*The Philosophy of Robert Grosseteste*) brings this listing up to 1980. Some of the works have been conveniently printed in Latin in Ludwig Baur, *Die philosophischen Werke des Robert Grosseteste, Bischofs von Lincoln*, Münster, 1912. Amongst modern critical editions there are Richard C. Dales and Servus Gieben OFM Cap., *Robert Grosseteste: Hexaemeron*, London, British Academy, 1982; Richard C. Dales, *Roberti Grosseteste Episcopi Lincolniensis Commentarius in VIII Libros Physicorum Aristotelis*, Boulder, University of Colorado Press, 1963.

9. On Grosseteste's use of and acquaintance with the works of Dionysius. The date of his first acquaintance is not known, only the (late) date when he translated and commented on them. An early date has been generally ruled out by historians' views on Grosseteste's intellectual development and on the dates of his works. But their views and disagreements here, as over the authenticity of some of the works ascribed to him, are mainly concerned with whether Grosseteste's interests in 'science' came before, during or after his 'theology': McEvoy, for instance (*The Philosophy of Robert Grosseteste*), claims the 'science' came first; Southern says 'that Grosseteste was a scientist before he was a theologian scarcely needs to be argued', and the 'science' continued after Grosseteste took up theology, and the theology fed his 'science' (*Robert Grosseteste*, pp. 120–3, 135; quotation from p. 120). We regard the 'science' category as misapplied here, and thus unhelpful to decide anything about the dating or order of Grosseteste's works; similarly, we regard the use of the label 'scientist' for Grosseteste as simply begging the question. It should be noted that the dates of virtually none of Grosseteste's writings is known with certainty. We assume that, as he was definitely intimate with Franciscans from at least 1229, he was acquainted with Dionysian teaching from at least that date. His enthusiasm, by 1239, to translate the Dionysian works was strong enough for him to have had the lengthy texts copied out for him at Paris by this time. Historians have usually seen Grosseteste (as they have seen other Franciscan-oriented people) primarily as an Augustinian, who was led to the study of light and of Dionysius by the neo-Platonic teaching he found in the works of St Augustine. We, by contrast, have assumed that he became interested in light and Dionysius through his Franciscan sympathies, and hence came to give special attention to the passages in Augustine where the Saint too writes about light. St Augustine's vast works, it should be noted, are and in practice actually were as susceptible of different interpretations of their meaning and emphasis as was the Bible itself. Thus the fact that Augustine writes about light is not, in our eyes, sufficient reason for Grosseteste to have taken up its study from there, for Augustine writes about so much else too. But that Grosseteste was a Dionysian by conviction first is indeed, in our eyes, sufficient reason for him then to see the pertinence of St Augustine's neo-Platonic writing on light for his purposes. On the translation of Dionysius and on Grosseteste's commentary, see McEvoy, *The Philosophy of Robert Grosseteste*, chs 2 and 3; on the actual manuscript see Ruth Barbour, 'A Manuscript of Ps.-Dionysius Areopagita Copied for Robert Grosseteste', *Bodleian Library Record*, 1957–61, 6, pp. 401–16. Grosseteste's own Latin translation is given in P. Chevallier, *Dionysiaca ...* , Paris, 2 vols, 1937. See also A.C. Dionisotti, 'On the Greek Studies of Robert Grosseteste', in A.C.

Dionisotti, Anthony Grafton and Jill Kraye, *The Uses of Greek and Latin: Historical Essays*, London: Warburg Institute, 1988, pp. 19–39. The modern scholarly editions of Grosseteste's versions are listed in McEvoy, *The Philosophy of Robert Grosseteste*, pp. 466–71.

10. Translated by A.C. Crombie in D.A. Callus, ed., *Robert Grosseteste: Scholar and Bishop*, Oxford, 1955, pp. 116–20.
11. Southern, *Robert Grosseteste*, p. 218.
12. Clare C. Riedl calls it a 'light metaphysics', see her *Robert Grosseteste On Light (De Luce), Translated from the Latin with an Introduction*, Milwaukee, Marquette University Press, 1942, p. 3. Lindberg calls it Grosseteste's 'philosophy of light', see David C. Lindberg, *Theories of Vision from Al-Kindi to Kepler*, University of Chicago Press, 1976, p. 95. Other historians have given it other titles. We have reservations about using any of these titles, especially as Grosseteste does not use any of them.
13. Crombie in D.A. Callus, op. cit, p. 111.
14. The Latin text is in Baur, *Die philosophischen Werke des Robert Grosseteste*, pp. 51–9; it is translated into English by Riedl, *Robert Grosseteste On Light.*
15. McEvoy, *The Philosophy of Robert Grosseteste*, pp. 168–9. The opening lines are quoted below.
16. Utilitas considerationis linearum, angulorum et figurarum est maxima, quoniam impossibile est sciri naturalem philosophiam sine illis. Valent autem in toto universo et partibus eius absolute. Valent etiam in proprietatibus relatis, sicut in motu recto et circulari. Valent quidem in actione et passione, et hoc sive sit in materiam sive in sensum; ... Omnes enim causae effectum naturalium habent dari per lineas, angulos et figuras. Aliter enim impossibile est sciri 'propter quid' in illis. Baur, *Die philosophischen Werke des Robert Grosseteste*, pp. 59–60; our translation.
17. Quando ergo cadit virtus ad angulos non solum aequales, sed omnino rectos, tunc videtur esse actio fortissima, quoniam omnino est aequalitas et uniformitas completa. Ibid., p. 61; our translation.
18. His igitur regulis et radicibus et fundamentis datis ex potestate geometriae, diligens inspector in rebus naturalibus potest dare causas omnium effectuum naturalium per hanc viam ... Prima autem et maxima variatio naturae est in locis mundi, et maxime consideranda est a naturali philosopho, quoniam secundum varias naturas locorum est varietas locatorum. Ibid., pp. 65–6; our translation.
19. Haec namque pars Perspectivae perfecte cognita ostendit nobis modum, quo res longissime distantes faciamus apparere propinquissime positas et quo res magnas propinquas faciamus apparere brevissimas et quo res longe positas parvas faciamus apparere quantum volumus magnas, ita ut possibile sit nobis et incredibili distantia litteras minimas legere, aut arenam, aut gramina, aut quaevis minuta numerare. Ibid., p. 74; our translation. Compare the translation by David C. Lindberg in Edward Grant, ed., *A Source Book in Medieval Science*, Cambridge, Mass., Harvard University Press, 1974, pp. 388–91, see 389.
20. As translated by A.C. Crombie, *Robert Grosseteste and the Origins of Experimental Science 1000–1700*, Oxford, Clarendon, 1953. p. 120.
21. Bruce S. Eastwood, 'Robert Grosseteste's Theory of the Rainbow: A Chapter in the History of Non-Experimental Science', *Archives*

Internationales d'Histoire des Sciences, 1966, **19**, 313–32, which gives a good account of Grosseteste on the rainbow; the quotation is from p. 329.

22. Grosseteste, *Commentarius in Posteriorum Analyticorum Libros*, ed. Pietro Rossi, Florence: Olschki, 1981; book I, c. 14, p. 213: 'si pars suprema anime humane, que vocatur intellectiva ... non esset mole corporis corrupti obnubilata et aggravata, ipsa per irradiationem acceptam a lumine superiori haberet completam scientiam absque sensus adminiculo, sicut habebit cum anima erit exuta a corpore et sicut forte habent aliqui penitus absoluti ab amore et phantasmatibus rerum corporalium'. Lawrence E. Lynch, 'The Doctrine of Divine Ideas and Illumination in Robert Grosseteste, Bishop of Lincoln', *Mediaeval Studies*, 1941, **3**, pp. 161–73, p. 168, thinks this last passage should be translated as above; on the role of love (*amor*) in freeing the intellect, see McEvoy, *The Philosophy of Robert Grosseteste*, pp. 307–8 and 335. Crombie, however, believes it should be translated 'those people who are free from the love and the imaginings of corporeal things'; see his translation of this extended passage in Crombie, *Robert Grosseteste and the Origins of Experimental Science 1000–1700*, pp. 72–4. Grosseteste of course (like Bonaventure, Bartholomew the Englishman, Aegidius of Zamora and others in the Franciscan tradition) believed that the invisible things of God are accessible through the things He has made (*per creaturas potest conspicere invisibilia dei*), as for instance through the structure of the human body; quoted in McEvoy, *The Philosophy of Robert Grosseteste*, p. 393–4, n. 87, from one of Grosseteste's sermons.
23. In Grosseteste's own Latin translation: *cognitio entium secundum quod entia sunt*. Printed in Chevallier, *Dionysiaca*, vol. 2, p. 1091. See p. 219 above.
24. See Crombie, *Robert Grosseteste and the Origins of Experimental Science 1000–1700*, pp. 128–31, and the passages from Grosseteste translated there.
25. This is the translation in the Authorized version; the Latin of the Vulgate is: *Omnia in mensura, et numero, et pondere disposuisti*. It comes from the book of *Wisdom*, XI, v. 20. Grosseteste cites it (for instance) in *Omnia Creatura Speculum Est*, see S. Gieben, 'Traces of God in Nature According to Robert Grosseteste' *Franciscan Studies*, 1964, **24**, pp. 144–58, esp. p. 153. Bonaventure also cites it; see (for instance) *The Mind's Road to God*: 'The view of someone contemplating in the first mode, considering things in themselves, sees them in weight, number and measure', (our translation from *Opera*, vol. 8, p. 298). 'That the Creator was a mathematician was Grosseteste's own original idea', according to McEvoy, *The Philosophy of Robert Grosseteste*, pp. 175 and 450.
26. G.H. Box, *Judaism in the Greek Period*, Oxford, Clarendon Press, 1932 (*The Clarendon Bible*, Old Testament, vol. 5), esp. pp. 172–4.
27. See note 16 above.
28. Quoted in D.E. Sharp, *Franciscan Philosophy at Oxford in the Thirteenth Century*, Oxford University Press, 1930, p. 9, from Bacon's *Opus Maius* i 108; our emphasis.
29. This sense of *propter quid*, knowing things through their causes, is quite different from the Aristotelian mode adopted by the Dominicans. For Aristotelians, knowing by causes meant knowing the *final cause*. For a neo-Platonist such as Grosseteste, it means knowing by its properties,

completely abstracted from matter, and (as here) preferably in geometric manner.

30. 'In solis enim mathematicis est scientia et demonstratio maxime et particulariter dicta', *Commentary on the Posterior Analytics*, i, 11, as quoted by Crombie, *Robert Grosseteste and the Origins of Experimental Science 1000–1700*, p. 59.
31. Crombie in Callus (ed.), *Robert Grosseteste: Scholar and Bishop*, p. 111. See also Lynch, 'The Doctrine of Divine Ideas and Illumination in Robert Grosseteste', p. 164.
32. See David C. Lindberg, 'Laying the Foundations of Geometrical Optics: Maurolico, Kepler, and the Medieval Tradition', in R.S. Westman (ed.) *The Discourse of Light from the Middle Ages to the Enlightenment*, William Andrews Clark Memorial Library, University of California, Los Angeles, 1985, p. 11. Best of all is Lindberg, 'Genesis of Kepler's Theory of Light', pp. 5–23, see esp. p. 19.
33. To Aristotle light was 'the instantaneous actualisation of a transparent medium – the process of its becoming actually transparent – owing to the presence of a luminous body', i.e. 'light (and colour) are *qualities* of visible objects imparted to, and thus propagated through, suitable media'; see Lindberg ('Laying the Foundations') pp. 5, 11. But in the same work, p. 65, n. 115, Lindberg says medievals stoutly maintain the *corporeality* of light, and he instances Roger Bacon. If we can begin to separate Aristotelians from neo-Platonists (Dionysians) in the medieval period we will be able to appreciate how both these views could be held in the period, but presumably not by one and the same person.
34. As has been shown by Lynch, 'The Doctrine of Divine Ideas and Illumination in Robert Grosseteste', pp. 172–3.
35. On Bonavenure against Aristotle, see E. Gilson, *The Philosophy of St Bonaventure*, translated by Dom I. Trethowan and F.J. Sheed, London, Sheed and Ward, 1938, *passim*.
36. See for example Sharp, *Franciscan Philosophy at Oxford*, p. 10, 'in him the Augustinian thought first encounters the philosophy of Aristotle ... Grosseteste is the first Englishman to assimilate the new learning of Aristotle and the Arabians'; McEvoy, *The Philosophy of Robert Grosseteste*, p. 26: Grosseteste was 'in the van of the new philosophical thinking of his time, the Aristotelian movement'.
37. Riedl, *Robert Grosseteste On Light*, p. 3, says of Grosseteste that 'while his terminology is Aristotelian, the ideas [on light] which he expresses in that terminology are often decidedly unAristotelian in content'; McEvoy, *The Philosophy of Robert Grosseteste*, p. 8: Grosseteste took up 'the study of Aristotle's physical treatises with an enthusiasm which was at no stage uncritical'. After pointing out (contrary to what Roger Bacon claimed) how very interested Grosseteste was in Aristotle, D.A. Callus remarks, 'On the other hand, in his original writings the trend of Grosseteste's thought was too much influenced by Neo-Platonic writers, such as the *Liber De Causis* and the *Fons Vitae* of Avicebron, to be purely Aristotelian', 'Introduction of Aristotelian Learning to Oxford', *Proceedings of the British Academy*, 1943, pp. 229–81, see p. 254. Grosseteste's differences from Aristotle were also recognized by someone like Wyclif in the next century; see Southern, *Robert Grosseteste*, pp. 298–307.
38. Lynch, 'The Doctrine of Divine Ideas and Illumination in Robert Grosseteste'.

39. Indeed, as is well known, by the end of the thirteenth century the Franciscans were trying to get the Pope to ban the writings of the Dominican St Thomas Aquinas, the great follower of Aristotle, as heretical.
40. Roger Bacon appears to have acquired his early reputation as a 'scientist' in the mid-nineteenth century, which is when the word 'scientist' was coined and the category was created. One of the important sources of the modern myth is E. Charles, *Roger Bacon, Sa Vie, Ses Ouvrages, et Ses Doctrines*, Paris, 1861. For the origins of Bacon's reputation as a magician, see 'Roger Bacon in English Literature', by Sir J.E. Sandys, in A.G. Little, ed., *Roger Bacon: Essays Contributed by Various Writers on the Occasion of the Commemoration of the Seventh Centenary of his Birth*, Oxford, Clarendon Press, 1914. It has become a commonplace of historical analysis of Bacon (as with so many medievals) to separate his interests into religious/mystical on the one hand and 'scientific' on the other, and then to contrast them; this approach is exemplified particularly clearly by two works by Raoul Carton, *L'Expérience Physique chez Roger Bacon: Contribution à l'Etude de la Méthode et de la Science Expérimentales au XIII*[e] *Siècle*, and *L'Expérience Mystique de l'Illumination Intérieure chez Roger Bacon*, Études de philosophie médiévale, nos II and III, Paris, Vrin, 1924.
41. Robert Steele, ed., *Opera Hactenus Inedita Rogeri Bacon.*, 16 fascs, Oxford, Clarendon, ?1905–41; see fascs 7–8 and 10–13.
42. Easton, one of the most sophisticated of the historians to work on Bacon, has produced a chronology for the writings. But this is highly speculative, and moreover it deals in the category 'science' and 'scientist' to construct the dating. See Stewart C. Easton, *Roger Bacon and his Search for a Universal Science: A Reconsideration of the Life and Work of Roger Bacon in the Light of his Own Stated Purposes*, Oxford, Blackwell, 1952, ch. 6.
43. D.C. Lindberg, 'Lines of Influence in Thirteenth-Century Optics: Bacon, Witelo and Pecham', *Speculum*, 1971, **46**, p. 71.
44. See Easton, pp. 126–40.
45. We are using the Latin text as printed by John Henry Bridges, *The 'Opus Majus' of Roger Bacon*, 2 vols, Oxford, Clarendon, 1897, (with parts one to three in revised form in his Supplementary Volume, London, Williams and Norgate, 1900); translation by Robert Belle Burke, *The Opus Majus of Roger Bacon*, New York, Russell and Russell, 2 vols, 1962; here and henceforth our translations are based on those of Burke, modified as we think appropriate. Unfortunately Burke tends to translate *sapientia* as 'science', which is misleading; the different meanings of *sapientia* and *scientia* for Bacon need to be kept distinguished. Burke even regularly translates *sapientes* as 'scientists', which is to unwittingly transform thirteenth-century philosophers into twentieth-century scientists.
46. Request, dated 1266, printed in *Opera Inedita* p.1: volumus ... opus illud ... scriptum de bona littera quam citius nobis mittere poteris non omittas; et per tuas nobis declares litteras quae tibi videntur adhibenda remedia circa illa, quae nuper occasione tanti discriminis intimasti: et hoc quanto secretius poteris facias indilate. *Fr. Rogeri Bacon Opera Quaedam Hactenus Inedita, vol. 1 Containing I – Opus Tertium, II – Opus Minus, III – Compendium Philosophiae*, [only one volume published], ed. J.S.

Brewer, London, Rolls Series, 1859.

47. See Brewer, pp. 3–4.

48. Pars Prima, capitulum I; Bridges vol. 1, p. 1; Burke vol. 1, p. 3. 'Sapientiae perfecta consideratio consistit in duobus, videlicet, ut videatur quid ad eam requiritur, quatenus optime sciatur; deinde quomodo ad omnia comparetur, ut per eam modis congruis dirigantur. Nam per lumen sapientiae ordinatur Ecclesia Dei, Respublica fidelium disponitur, infidelium conversio procuratur; et illi, qui in malitia obstinati sunt, valent per virtutem sapientiae reprimi, ut melius a finibus Ecclesiae longius pellantur quam per effusionem sanguinis Christiani'.

49. Ibid.; Omnia vero quae indigent regimine sapientiae ad haec quatuor reducuntur; nec pluribus potest comparari.

50. As in the case of Grosseteste and others who promoted the study of light, *perspectiva* and geometry, Bacon is usually considered by historians to be an 'Augustinian' rather than a 'Dionysian'; for our views on this assumption see note 9 above in this chapter.

51. As with Grosseteste and others in the Franciscan tradition (see above, note 37), Bacon is customarily treated by historians of science today as having been an Aristotelian, but one with odd views. Lindberg for instance says of him that 'Bacon was, first of all, an Aristotelian ... But Bacon's Aristotelianism was heavily Neoplatonized', David C. Lindberg, *Roger Bacon's Philosophy of Nature: A Critical Edition, with English Translation, Introduction and Notes, of 'De Multiplicatione Specierum' and 'De Speculis Comburentibus*', p. liv. As the argument of the present chapter indicates, we think it is more helpful to see Bacon firstly as a Franciscan, making choices amongst authors available to him on the basis of his Franciscan outlook and interests.

52. ' ... ostenditur quod philosophia sit per influentiam divinae illuminationis', Pars secunda, cap. V, Bridges vol. 1, p. 39; tr. Burke, vol. 1, p. 44. 'Et Augustinus octavo de Civitate Dei docet et approbat quod Socrates pater philosophorum firmavit, quod non potest homo causas rerum scire, nisi in luce divina, et per donum ejus', Pars secunda, cap. VI, Bridges, vol. 1, pp. 41–2; tr. Burke, vol. 1, p. 48.

53. This is particularly evident from the *Compendium Studii Philosophiae*, where Bacon writes: 'When therefore anyone from his youth falls into mortal sin, his soul is corrupted by a new corruption beyond what he has from original sin; and so he has in himself causes of many kinds of infinite depravity, so that he cannot behold the light of wisdom (*lumen sapientiae*), nor does he wish to see it, nor could he if it were not for the grace of God [...] For this reason the Scripture says [Book of Wisdom I 4] "Wisdom will not enter into the wicked soul, nor will it dwell in the body given over to sins". And this is not to be understood only of divine wisdom, but of wisdom of any kind. As Algazel says in his *Logic* that the soul is disordered by sins as a rusty mirror, old and dirty, in which the images of things cannot appear, and so no impression of anything can be made in such a soul. And he adds that a soul adorned with virtue is like a clean new mirror in which the *species* [of things appear best. Hence in such a soul the light (*fulgor*) of wisdom] shines, for which reason Socrates, the father of philosophers, when he was asked why he did not [in his earliest youth want to] study the speculative rather than the moral sciences, said that he could not perceive the light of wisdom unless his soul had been cultivated

by virtue — and then he would see God Himself and contemplate the causes and reasons for things, and sciences, truly in Him (*tunc Deum ipsum videret, et causas et rationes rerum et scientiarum in eo veraciter contemplaretur*) [just like blessed Augustine wished to do, in book eight of the *City of God*, and others too]', as translated by Easton, p. 125, from Brewer pp. 407–8, [omissions by Easton have been resupplied by us, and are placed in square brackets].

54. Pars Secunda, cap. III.
55. 'Caeterum totius philosophiae decursus, consistit in eo, ut per cognitionem suae creaturae cognoscatur creator, cui propter reverentiam majestatis et beneficium creationis et conservationis et futurae felicitatis serviatur in culto honorifico et morum pulchritudine et legum utilium honestate; ut in pace et honestate [justitia] vivant homines in hac vita. Philosophia enim speculativa decurrit usque ad cognitionem creatoris per creaturas. Et moralis philosophia morum honestatem, legas justas, et cultum Dei statuit, et persuadet de futura felicitate utiliter et magnifice secundum quod possibile est philosophiae. Haec sunt certa discurrenibus per omnes partes philosophiae principales, sicut sequentia docebunt. Cum igitur haec sint omnino necessaria christianis, et omnino consona sapientiae Dei, manifestum est quod philosophia necessaria est legi divinae et fidelibus in ea gloriantibus'. Pars Secunda, cap. VII (complete); Bridges vol. 1, pp. 42–3; Burke, vol. 1, pp. 49–50; Bridges, Supplementary Volume for the reading given here in square brackets.
56. See p. 210 above.
57. 'De mathematicis dicit Cassiodorus, Geometriam, arithmeticam, astroniam, musicam cum sollicita mente revolvimus, sensum acuunt, limamque ignorantiae detergunt, et ad illam divinam contemplationem, Deo largiente, perducunt; quas merito sancti patres legendas persuadent, quoniam ex magna parte appetitus a carnalibus rebus extrahitur, et faciunt desiderare quae solo corde possumus respicere'. Bridges, vol. 1, pp. 36–7; Burke, vol. 1, pp. 40–1. The Latin text in Bridges, Supplementary Volume, pp. 41–2 has 'ad illam speculativam contemplationem' for 'ad illam divinam contemplationem'.
58. 'quibus scitis, potest quilibet gloriose proficere in sapientiae potestate sine difficultate et labore, non solum in scientiis humanis, sed divina. Et cujuslibet istarum tangetur virtus non solum propter sapientiam absolute, sed respectu caeterorum praedictorum. Et harum scientiarum porta et clavis est mathematica, quam sancti a principio mundi invenerunt, ut ostendam, et quae semper fuit in usu omnium sanctorum et sapientum prae omnibus aliis scientiis. Cujus negligentia jam per triginta vel quadraginta annos destruxit totum studium Latinorum. Quoniam qui ignorat eam non potest scire caeteras scientias nec res hujus mundi, ut probabo'. Pars Quarta, Distinctio prima, cap. 1; Bridges, vol. 1, p. 97; Burke, vol. 1, p. 116. It is not known what Bacon was referring to in saying that mathematics had been neglected for the last thirty or forty years, which neglect had 'destroyed the whole system of study of the Latins'. Possibly he is harkening back to some (?imagined) time before the quadrivium and philosophy was dominated by logic: after all, his call here is for philosophy to be identified with mathematics (rather than with logic, as it was on the Abelardian model; see Chapter 3).
59. 'Nam omnis res naturalis producitur in esse per efficiens et materiam in

quam operatur ... Sed virtus efficientis et materiae sciri non potest sine magna mathematicae potestate, sicut nec ipsi effectus producti'. Pars Quarta, Distinctio secunda, cap. I, Bridges, vol. 1, p. 110; Burke, vol. 1, p. 129.

60. 'Omnia autem multiplicatio vel est secundum lineas, vel angulos, vel figuras. Dum vero species in medio raritatis unius incedit, ut in toto coelo, et in toto igne, et in toto aere, vel in tota aqua, semper tenet vias rectas, quia Aristoteles dicit quinto Metaphysicae quod natura operatur breviori modo quo potest, et linea recta est omnium brevissima'. Pars Quarta, Distinctio secunda, cap. II, Bridges, vol. 1, p. 112; Burke, vol. 1, p. 131.
61. David C. Lindberg, *Roger Bacon's Philosophy of Nature*, pp. xxix, lvi.
62. Although *perspectiva* is commonly translated as 'optics' these days, optics in the modern sense was not the subject of Bacon's writing. We discuss this issue further below. Unfortunately Burke in his translation consistently gives 'optics' for '*perspectiva*', and 'impression' for *species*. The *Perspectiva* is not only Part V of the *Opus Majus* but also circulated separately; David C. Lindberg, 'Lines of Influence', pp. 66–83, see p. 69.
63. 'Potest vero aliqua scientia esse utilior, sed nulla tantam suavitatem et pulchritudinem utilitatis habet. [Et ideo est flos philosophiae totius et per quam, nec sine qua, aliae scientiae sciri possunt]'. Pars Quinta, Distinction prima, cap. I; Bridges, vol. 2, p. 3; Burke, vol. 2, p. 420; the passage in square brackets only in one manuscript.
64. Considerandum ergo est, ut in superioribus verificatum est, actio naturalis completur per pyramidem, cujus conus est in patiente, et basis est superficies agentis. Nam sic virtus venit a toto agente objecto patienti, ut prius declaratum est, quatenus actio fortis sit et completa; et ideo in visu sic exigitur, ut a tota superficie agentis veniat species. Sed licet in alteratione naturali patientium exigatur quod singulae pyramides veniant ad singulas partes patientis, propter hoc quod quilibet punctus patientis debet alterari, tamen in alteratione visus principaliter non exigitur nisi quod una pyramis veniat ab agente, et conus cadat in oculum, quae pyramis cadid perpendiculariter super oculum, ita quod omnes ejus lineae sint perpendiculares super ipsum. Bridges, vol. 2, p. 35; translation by Burke, vol. 2, p. 454, modified.
65. This is all strikingly confirmed by another work attributed to him, and known as *Communia Naturalium*, where Bacon terms the subject-area '*Naturalia*', and discusses the sciences which pertain to it (Steele, fasc. II-V). He claims that *perspectiva* is the first of the sciences of *Naturalia*: 'Nam cum Perspectiva sit de visu, que res naturalis est, oportet ut hec sit scientia naturalis, et quoniam visus ostendit nobis rerum differencias secundum Aristotelem primo *Metaphisice* et libro *De sensu et sensato*, et scimus hoc per experienciam quoniam cecus nichil dignum scire potest de hoc mundo; oportet quod Perspectiva sit prima specialis sciencia inter sciencias naturales. Deinde per ordinem sequntur alie secundum seriem rerum naturalium, ut Astronomia de celestibus ... ', fasc. II, pp. 5–6. He says that he wishes here to compose a treatise on Perspectiva, and therefore will start with the fundamental topics: matter and form (pp. 15–16). But he uses *species* as his model of what constitutes form, and of how form is related to matter: form (*species*) is what, coming to unformed matter, makes matter like itself, as fire makes wood into fire. Hence he deals with light primarily, and its action through the operation of *species*, yet

discusses these *as the answer to* Aristotelian-type questions about form, matter, substance and causality, and in this sense gives Dionysian answers to Aristotelian questions.

66. As quoted by David Lindberg, *John Pecham and the Science of Optics: Perspectiva Communis*, University of Wisconsin Press, 1970, p. 8, quoting the translation by M.D. Knowles in 'Some Aspects of the Career of Archbishop Pecham', *English Historical Review*, 1942, 57, pp. 1–18, 178–201, see p. 189. The enemy for Pecham seems to be Dominican Averroistic Aristotelianism.
67. Both have been critically edited by David Lindberg: (1) *John Pecham: Tractatus de Perspectiva*, New York, The Franciscan Institute, 1972; (2) *John Pecham and the Science of Optics: Perspectiva Communis* (see note 66 above).
68. Of this last treatise, Lindberg has written, 'the *Tractatus de Numeris* is not what would today be classified as pure mathematics. It consists of arithmetic and number theory accompanied by a heavy dose of theology and number mysticism'; *John Pecham and the Science of Optics: Perspectiva Communis*, p. 9, n. 31.
69. *John Pecham: Tractatus de Perspectiva*, pp. 23–4, our translation. The last two sentences are referring to distinctions made in Aristotle's *Physics*, 194a, 10–11.
70. *John Pecham and the Science of Optics: Perspectiva Communis*, pp. 36, 109, as translated by Lindberg.
71. For Witelo's origins, see his own Preface to his Perspectiva, as printed in a critical edition in Clemens Baeumker, *Witelo, ein Philosoph und Naturforscher des XIII. Jahrhunderts*, Münster, 1908 (*Beiträge zur Geschichte der Philosophie des Mittelalters*, vol. 3, part 2), pp. 127–31, see p. 127. The preface has never been translated as a whole into English. For English translations of parts of the Perspectiva see Sabetai Unguru, *Witelonis Perspectivae Liber Primus: Book One of Witelo's Perspectiva; An English Translation with Introduction and Commentary and Latin Edition of The Mathematical Book of Witelo's Perspectiva*, Warsaw, Studia Copernicana XV, Polish Academy of Sciences, 1977; A. Mark Smith, *Witelonis Perspectivae Liber Quintus: Book V of Witelo's Perspectiva; An English Translation with Introduction and Commentary and Latin Edition of the First Catoptrical Book of Witelo's Perspectiva*, Warsaw, Studia Copernicana XXIII, Polish Academy of Sciences, 1983.
72. Lindberg, 'Lines of Influence', pp. 72–5.
73. Translated by us from the text given by Baeumker; part of the passage is as translated by David C. Lindberg, *Theories of Vision from Al-Kindi to Kepler*, University of Chicago Press, 1976, pp. 118–19; also in his article 'The Genesis of Kepler's Theory of Light: Light Metaphysics from Plotinus to Kepler', *Osiris*, 1986, second series, **2**, pp. 5–42, see p. 22.
74. Lindberg (following Birkenmajer) points out that while Witelo never uses the Baconian term *species*, yet *forma* is exactly equivalent for him. See D.C. Lindberg, 'Alhazen's Theory of Vision', *Isis*, 1967, **58**, pp. 321–41.
75. *Perspectiva*, Book 5, c. 18; 'multiplicatio vero formarum ad superficies speculorum est naturalis, quoniam est opere naturae, sicut et omnis alia diffusio formarum, ut in Philosophia naturali capitulo de naturali actione ostendimus'. See the edition of the work edited by Friedrich Risner as 'Opticae libri decem', in *Opticae Thesaurus*, Basle, Officina Episcopiana,

1572, p. 198, which also contains the Latin translation of Al-Haytham's work.

76. In the extensive sections on the 'history of optics' in E. Grant, *A Source Book*, the 'Revival of optics in the West' and the 'Late thirteenth century synthesis in optics', *all* the work on 'optics' is ascribed to (only) Grosseteste, Bacon, Pecham and Witelo, with Al-Haytham (Alhazen) being treated as a common source for these writers.

77. Lindberg in *Theories of Vision*, pp. 104–7, see p. 106. Lindberg concludes, somewhat oddly, that 'Grosseteste could not see beyond the Platonic theory; Albert, on the other hand, recognized other schools of thought and the need to arbitrate among them' (p. 107); yet he had been showing that Albert does not 'arbitrate' at all – but that he begins and ends by preferring Aristotle.

78. Gérard Simon has recently claimed that the Ancient science of optics was not the same as the one we pursue in the modern world, and should not be seen as its ancestor: Ancient optics dealt with lines of sight, he claims, not lines of light. It is therefore not at all clear whether it was Ancient optics which was revived in the Renaissance, or whether a new science was then created. See Simon's *Le Regard, l'Etre et l'Apparence dans l'Optique de l'Antiquité*, Paris, 1988, and the review of it by A. Mark Smith in *Isis*, 1992, **83**, pp. 118–19.

79. Exceptionally Lindberg has actually offered a definition of the practitioner of *perspectiva*, the 'perspectivist', but in the following way: 'I will mean by it precisely what late medieval writers meant by the term *perspectivus*, namely, a member of the mathematical tradition in optics, which included Euclid, Ptolemy, al-Kindi, Alhazen, Roger Bacon, Witelo, John Pecham, and others.' This definition differs from our own (above) and would seem to be so general as to include pretty well everyone from Antiquity on. In the chapter to which this definition is appended, Lindberg persistently translates *perspectiva* as 'optics'. See *Theories of Vision*, p. 251, n. 1., and ch. 6. Elsewhere Lindberg has attempted another definition of *perspectiva*, but again he appears to conclude that it was optics merely under a different name; see his 'Roger Bacon and the Origins of *perspectiva* in the West', in Edward Grant and John E. Murdoch, eds, *Mathematics and its Applications to Science and Natural Philosophy in the Middle Ages: Essays in Honor of Marshall Clagett*, Cambridge University Press, 1987, pp. 249–68. A. Mark Smith, 'Getting the Big Picture in Perspectivist Optics', *Isis*, 1981, **72**, pp. 568–89, quite correctly points out that the 'perspectivist' tradition was, in its technical aspects, concerned with sight not light, yet his account is based on the assumption that 'the ulterior concern of the perspectivists was epistemology'; hence his account omits God, ignores the religious dimension and motivation of the work and the Franciscan orientation of those who pursued it, and turns them all into Aristotelians.

80. A.I. Sabra, translator and editor, *The Optics of Ibn Al-Haytham, Books I-III On Direct Vision*, London, The Warburg Insitute, 2 vols, 1989, vol. 2, pp. lxxvi–vii. Sabra says that 'Without the first three chapters (especially the third)' of Ibn Al-Haytham's work, 'the Latin writers on optics were handed a truncated theory for which they had to provide a new foundation. The significance of this situation becomes even greater when we remember that Ptolemy's *Optics* also reached the Latin West (through

Eugenius' translation from the Arabic) without a theory of light radiation which had already been missing when the Arabic version was made, probably in the ninth century'. For the Latin text of Ptolemy (no Greek original or Arabic translation survives), see Albert Lejeune, *L'Optique de Claude Ptolémée dans la Version Latine d'après l'Arabe de l'Emir Eugène de Sicile: Edition Critique et Exégétique*, Louvain, Publications Universitaires de Louvain, 1956.

81. A. Mark Smith, for instance, in *Witelonis Perspectivae Liber Quintus*, p. 18, following Lindberg, writes that 'The medieval science of *perspectiva* was, in most respects, the bastard offspring of three basic Greek traditions in optics – the geometrical, the physical, and the anatomical'.

82. It is only fair to mention that the possibility of a specifically Franciscan interest in 'optics' (though not any possible Franciscan reason for it) has occasionally been discussed before by other scholars, but usually only to be dismissed. Lindberg, *Theories of Vision*, p. 107, for instance, says in this connection that 'one must beware of superficial correlations and of gratuitous causal inferences drawn from them ... We must avoid simplistic explanation of scientific achievement in terms of birthplace or membership in a religious order or education at a particular university'. It is not clear to us why Lindberg thinks that explanation by virtue of membership of a particular religious order is superficial and simplistic, given that such membership does, and is intended to, shape and involve the whole life and thinking of its members. Elsewhere Lindberg has acknowledged that 'among the English Franciscans a tradition of mathematical science had been initiated by Robert Grosseteste ... and advanced by Roger Bacon. There is no doubt that this tradition influenced Pecham ...', but he suggests no explanation for the existence of this tradition, nor of why it should be specific to Franciscans; see the entry 'Pecham, John', in the *Dictionary of Scientific Biography*, p. 474.

83. Birkenmajer writes, with respect to Witelo's *Perspectiva* (correctly to our minds), 'l'objectif principal et général de cet ouvrage n'est pas l'exposé de l'optique mais celui de l' "action des formes naturelles"'; he is quoting Witelo's term *forma naturalia* in his Dedication to Moerbeke. See 'Witelo est-il auteur de l'oposcule *De intelligentiis*?', the second of the 'Etudes sur Witelo' in his *Etudes d'Histoire des Sciences en Pologne*, Warsaw, Studia Copernica IV, Polish Academy of Sciences, 1972, pp. 259–339. (However, we disagree with much of the rest of the argument of this article.)

84. On the translation of the title of Al-Haytham's book, *Al-Manazir*, itself an Arabic rendering of the Greek 'optica', into Latin as *Perspectiva*, see Sabra, vol. 2, p. lxxv. Pecham refers to Al-Haytham's book simply as 'the *Perspectiva*'; see Lindberg, *John Pecham and the Science of Optics*, pp. 24–5.

85. On the sermons given within the convents of the friars, see Jacques Guy Bougerol, OFM, 'Les sermons dans les "studia" des mendiants', in *Le Scuole degli Ordini Mendicanti (Secoli XIII–XIV)*, Convegni del Centro di Studi sulla Spiritualità Medievale, XVII, Todi, 1978, pp. 249–80.

86. D.L. d'Avray, 'Sermons to the Upper Bourgeoisie by a Thirteenth Century Franciscan', *Studies in Church History* (the one published by the Ecclesiastical History Society) 1979, [no vol. number] pp. 187–199; the quotation is from p. 199; the Franciscan in question is Guibert of Tournai, a Parisian master and contemporary of St Bonaventure.

87. David L. Clarke, 'Optics for Preachers: The *De oculo morali* by Peter of Limoges', *Michigan Academician*, 1977, **9**, 329–43, esp. 333.
88. *Summa Theologica* 3a Q. 77 art. 1; in Henry Bettenson (ed.), *Documents of the Christian Church*, Oxford University Press, 1943, p. 210.
89. Heather Phillips, 'John Wyclif and the Optics of the Eucharist', in Anne Hudson and Michael Wilks (eds), *From Ockham to Wyclif*, Oxford, Blackwell for the Ecclesiastical History Society, 1987, pp. 245–58. For other aspects of the Franciscan objections to the Dominican account of transubstantiation, see David Burr, 'Eucharistic Presence and Conversion in Late Thirteenth-Century Franciscan Thought', *Transactions of the American Philosophical Society*, 1984, vol. 74, Part 3.
90. Phillips, 'John Wyclif and the Optics of the Eucharist', p. 251.
91. On Suger see Erwin Panofsky, ed., *Abbot Suger on the Abbey Church of St.-Denis and its Art Treasures*, Princeton University Press, 1946, second edition 1979; this includes the Latin texts and translations. See also Duby, *The Age of the Cathedrals*, pp. 98–108; and *Abbot Suger and Saint-Denis: A Symposium*, ed. Paula Lieber Gerson, New York: The Metropolitan Museum of Art, 1986. Brilliant on all these matters is Otto von Simson, *The Gothic Cathedral: Origins of Gothic Architecture and the Medieval Concept of Order*, Princeton University Press, 1962 (first published 1956); see also his 'The Gothic Cathedral: Design and Meaning', in Sylvia Thrupp, ed., *Change in Medieval Society: Europe North of the Alps 1050–1500*, London, Peter Owen, 1965, pp. 168–87. Peter Frankl, *The Gothic: Literary Sources and Interpretations through Eight Centuries*, Princeton University Press, 1960, is also very useful. On the subsequent history of Suger's church, see Caroline Astrid Bruzelius, *The 13th Century Church at St-Denis*, Yale University Press, 1985.
92. This is what Suger wrote on the importance of coloured light: 'Thus when, out of love for the beauty of the house of God, the beautiful many-colouredness of the jewels sometimes called me away from external cares, and devoted meditation persuaded me – by transferring [me] from the material to the immaterial – to dwell upon the diversity of the Divine Virtues, then I seem to see myself as if dwelling under some strange region of the orb of the earth which is neither wholly in the slime of the earth nor wholly in the purity of heaven, able by God's grace to be transferred in a spiritual manner (*anagogico more*) from this inferior to that higher world' (our translation from the Latin as given in Panofsky, *Abbot Suger on the Abbey Church of St.-Denis*, pp. 63–5). It would seem that for Suger coloured light coming through the windows had the same spiritually transporting effect; see Wim Swaan, *The Gothic Cathedral*, Omega Books 1984 (first published 1969), p. 48. On the surviving beautiful things Suger collected at St Denis, see *Le Trésor de Saint-Denis*, Paris, The Louvre, 1991.
93. A.R. Martin, *Franciscan Architecture in England*, Manchester University Press, 1937, for British Society of Franciscan Studies (vol. 18). See also Kurt Biebrach, *Die holzgedeckten Franziskaner- und Dominikaner-kirchen in Umbrien und Toskana*, (Dresden Techn. Hochschule, Doktor-Ingenieur dissertation) Berlin, Wasmuth a.g., 1908.
94. Emile Mâle, *The Gothic Image: Religious Art in France of the Thirteenth Century*, translated from the third edition by Dora Nussey, London, Collins, 1961 (first published in French in 1910); Sue A. Levine, *The*

Northern Foreportal Column Figures of Chartres Cathedral, Style and Dating; and Reflections of Vincent of Beauvais' 'Speculum Doctrinale', Frankfurt am Main, Peter Lang, 1984 (Kultstätten der Gallisch-Fränkischen Kirche, Band 3).

95. See James Macaulay, *The Gothic Revival 1747–1845*, Glasgow and London, Blackie, 1975. Pugin's *Contrasts* of 1836 is largely responsible for promoting the aesthetic argument for Gothic, at least in England, claiming that it was the spontaneous and perfect expression of true religious attitudes; his work on Gothic architecture is part of a plea for a return to Catholicism since, in his own words, 'the excellence of art was only to be found in Catholicism' and 'pointed architecture [Gothic] was produced by the Catholic faith' (pp. 15, iii). The expression 'Gothic revival' was established in England only in 1872, with the publication of C.L. Eastlake's *History of the Gothic Revival.*

CHAPTER ELEVEN

Epilogue

Natural philosophy in the schools

The Franciscans and Dominicans continued to practise their natural philosophy through the thirteenth century as long as they thought there was need for spiritual and learned guidance. Meanwhile, the regent masters of the universities, who had been familiar with the sources of the friars' philosophy before the friars came into existence, also constructed a natural philosophy. This proved to be remarkably long lived and survived inside the universities down to the middle of the seventeenth century. While the natural philosophies of the two Orders of friars never came close to each other, the secular masters and their students handled a constructed natural philosophy that contained elements of both. The story of the masters' natural philosophy is one for another book and we can note here only that, like the philosophy of the friars, it was called into existence for specific historical reasons.

The secular masters pursued their common interests by forming a fraternity, or guild, the *consortium*. Based on recently revived principles of Roman law, the *consortium* was a legal person and consequently a political force. It was dominated by the numerous masters of arts, and it represented the masters' interests against those of the chancellor, the pope, the townspeople and the monarch. The masters controlled entry into their group, that is, who became a master. The natural career progression of a new master was to teach in arts for two years and then depart to teach elsewhere, to serve a magnate or a bishop, or to study theology with a view to a master's degree and a higher teaching career. But the master faced difficulties with two of these choices. On the one hand, although he was a master of arts, the 'licence to teach anywhere' was the gift of the chancellor. One the other, many of the theology teaching posts were occupied by the friars, who had been conspicuously successful in inserting themselves into the universities. Many of the secular masters were obliged to disregard their own motto, 'don't grow old in arts', and remain as regent masters. In these circumstances the *consortium* of masters in Paris in the middle of the thirteenth century drew up statutes that specified that reading the Aristotelian *libri naturales* – the books that had been banned in 1210 and 1215 – was necessary for the bachelor in the arts faculty intending to become a master. In Oxford, where there had been no ban something similar may have already been in place.

These statutes helped to prepare the students for at least the Dominican form of theology, in which Aristotelian learning was so important. They were also designed to exclude the friars from the *consortium*, for the friars' arts education was in-house, not in the arts faculty. It was in the interests of the masters to insist on their statutes and to impose a rule on their members to cease teaching if the statutes were not obeyed. But they needed the co-operation of the chancellor so that new masters could obtain the licence to teach. The chancellor gave the licence after his own examination of the candidates: he was less interested in the masters' statutes than in ensuring that the licence was given to men sound in the doctrine of the Church. His examination consequently included a wider range of things, including the traditional liberal arts and material that was closer to the Franciscan natural philosophy.

In other words the secular masters used natural philosophy partly in a political way, to serve their own ends. Their appropriation of it raised misgivings. Individual Dominicans in later life sometimes regretted their earlier and vain 'curiosity' about natural things, and the Order as a whole increasingly turned its attentions to its proper theological purposes as the threat of heresy began to recede. The secular masters in promoting natural philosophy began to seem to the theologians as if they were sponsoring an Aristotelian view of the natural world, eternal and Godless. In a word, the autonomy of nature, the twelfth-century problem that had reached its climax with the dualism of the Cathars, seemed to be arising again. Franciscans and 'Augustinian' theologians, who had never been enthusiastic about the new Aristotle in the universities, were alarmed. The condemnation in 1277 of a large number of art-course propositions was intended to stop anyone thinking that nature was an autonomous principle.

The first statutes, those of the 1250s, had prompted the appearance of a textbook of natural philosophy, containing all the now-canonical Aristotelian physical works. Students hearing lectures in Oxford at least wrote down notes in the margins of their textbooks. In England this was a common gloss that all students wrote, a basic interpretation of the Latin versions of Aristotle. (The major commentaries of the great masters like Adam of Buckfield and Thomas Aquinas were addressed to a more sophisticated audience and written separately.) The textbook changed towards the end of the thirteenth century, perhaps following the condemnations of 1277, and certainly as teaching progressed from literal glosses to disputed questions. It still contained the statutory texts of Aristotle, but also now a wider range of Aristotelian texts, some of them spurious. The students' notes in both versions of the textbook indicate that in addition to the canonical texts of Aristotle, the students were being taught material from the Franciscans' natural philosophy such as Pecham's treatise on perspective. The secular masters had to prepare their students not only for the statutory and philosophical disputation that preceded inception (joining the *consortium*) but also for the chancellor's examination, where more traditional Augustinian material might be looked for.

Many new universities in the fourteenth century and later followed the model of Paris. The textbook of statutory texts was often copied out, sometimes with the legend that it was all that was required for the degree of master of arts in the university in question. It became known often as the *Octo Physicorum* because it invariably began with the eight books of Aristotle's *Physics*. It served its purpose through academic debates like that about nominalism and realism, and it was not greatly changed by the attentions of long-serving masters of arts like Buridan. Whatever the sophistications and new directions of the 'calculators' at Merton College, Oxford, in the fourteenth century, and of figures like Oresme, it still remained necessary to have a basic collection of texts on which to base discussions about and departures from natural philosophy, and with which to measure a student's progress through the course. Sometimes all that was needed was a summary of the text or a collection of textual fragments on which disputable questions could be based and for this purpose the textbook often appeared in the form known as the *Textus Abbreviatus*. From the late fifteenth century, printed versions of the textbook, like the manuscript forms, also sometimes announced that they contained all the texts needing to be read for the degree in this or that university, and they existed alongside major commentaries upon points contained in their texts. Sometimes these commentaries were systematic, working through the sequence of the *libri naturales*. The textbook and its commentaries played complementary roles, for the commentaries supplied interpretations of the text in line with the intellectual circumstances of the time and the text defined what had to be understood. *This* is what *studium* natural philosophy was: the understanding and teaching of a group of topics about nature, canonical in the sense of being expected for both the degree and the licence, shaped by the religious constraints and intellectual needs of successive periods and teachers and with a practical and sometimes political role in the university.

These remained features of natural philosophy throughout its career. At the Reformation the Catholic Church faced the greatest heresy since the time of the Cathars. It reacted, as it had done before, by insisting on features of its doctrine that differed from those of its opponents. When the Protestants said that it was not necessary to have a priestly hierarchy to explain God to man, the Catholics gave prominence to the learned tradition of the Church. That learning included natural philosophy, which was concerned with God's creation. The Protestants were more inclined than the Catholics to go and look at the physical world, mostly its living parts, and this was for them too a religious duty of seeking God directly through His works. But, apart from a brief period in the Protestant university of Wittenberg, neither side denied that Aristotle remained the authority on the physical world. Both sides were explicit that Aristotelian philosophy was a necessary foundation for true faith, and both feared that the stability of society would be threatened by abandoning it. Just as at the time of the Cathar heresy, so at the Reformation both sides saw the importance of firm doctrine at centres of education (and re-education). By the seventeenth century some Reformers had begun to think that the Catholic Aristotle was unReformed and hence scholastic, but this was by no means a general feeling. Certainly many Catholic commentators went back to Aristotle with more detailed attention to the text and more sophistication of argument than had been shown since the great commentaries of the thirteenth century; but this did not mean, for example, that the vigorous new scholarship of the Coimbran Jesuits was unacceptable even in so Protestant a place as Cambridge. Aristotle was equally valuable to both. Traditional and theocentric natural philosophy died only when the heat went out of the religious quarrels, and this did not happen until after the seventeenth century.

Natural philosophy or medieval science?

The differences between the natural philosophy created by the Franciscans, and that developed by their fellow friars, the Dominicans, are and were enormous. They differ from each other at the level of motive, in their preferences for particular ancient authorities and inspirations, in their concepts of cause, in their respective concerns with rationality or spirituality. They differ in what it is in nature that they choose to look at, and how they look at it, with the Dominicans obsessed with the *natures* of things, and the Franciscans with the *properties* of things.

Yet both of these natural philosophies were brought into existence to meet the same set of critical problems facing the Catholic Church at the end of the twelfth and the beginning of the thirteenth centuries. The orthodoxy of Catholic Europe had to be preserved; the spirituality of Catholic Europe in an age of materialism had to be promoted. It was in the pursuit of these twin goals that these professional Christian organizations, the friars, were brought into existence, turned their attentions to nature, and made their enquiries into nature central to the achievement of their religio-political goals. Both of their natural philosophies were about God and God's creation. They were Christian approaches to nature.

Should we, however, be distinguishing these clearly religio-political approaches to nature from some other, contemporaneous, 'objective' approach to nature? Did the thirteenth century witness not only the creation of natural philosophies – that is, *God-oriented* enterprises of looking at nature – but also an objective '*scientific*' tradition of looking at nature, 'scientific' in the modern sense of the word? Historians of science in the twentieth century, when dealing with the medieval centuries, have certainly written as if there was such an 'objective' and 'scientific' enterprise being undertaken at this time. And they use as some of their evidence the work of the same friars whose work we have been discussing here, work which we have been showing was actually religio-political in inspiration and nature. Our discussion of *perspectiva*, for instance, includes every Christian individual who appears in standard historical sourcebooks on the history of 'optics' in the thirteenth century. Were these individuals perhaps *simultaneously* engaged both in *perspectiva*, with all its religious characteristics as we have described them, and *also* in producing early versions of modern science, at one and the same time, with one and the same sentences? Similarly, the thirteenth-century so-called 'scientific encyclopaedists' who appear in conventional histories of science: these are the same people that we have shown were producing these very works for the service of Dominican preaching and Franciscan contemplation respectively. Were they simultaneously scientists and religious men, in one and the same works, and one and the same sentences?

No: there was no scientific tradition (in the modern sense of the term 'scientific') of looking at nature in the thirteenth century, only a religio-political way of doing so. Natural philosophy was not the same as modern science.

The creation, by historians, of a tradition of 'medieval science', is something which has taken place only over the last century or so. It derives from a number of nineteenth- and twentieth-century positions, and deserves a book to itself. Partly it comes from the liberals and positivists of the mid-nineteenth century, who attacked the Catholic Church as the enemy of freedom of thought. In the view of such liberals and positivists, science represented the greatest achievement of the human mind. They therefore presented the *history* of science as the story of the defeat, over time, of superstition by rationality: that is, as the defeat of Christianity, especially the Catholic Church, by science. This story was given its great heroes such as Galileo and Bruno, who were portrayed as defending the truth of science against the bigotry of religion. Propagandist works putting forward this interpretation included John William Draper's *History of the Conflict Between Religion and Science*, of 1874, and Andrew White's *A History of the Warfare of Science with Theology*, of 1896. In such stories the medieval period was a time when science was at its lowest level, as the Church (supposedly) suppressed free thought, and bound men's minds to the dictates of the Bible and Aristotle.

Subsequently Catholic scholars sought to demonstrate that the medieval period was not one where the Catholic Church suppressed freedom of thought, but rather was one where churchmen – bishops and friars amongst them – actively worked at science, and found that there were few if any conflicts between science and religion. In the central decades of the twentieth century, scholars with no allegiance to Catholicism have taken the bones of this revisionist story and developed it in highly sophisticated ways, hence creating a very scholarly 'history of medieval science', on which there are now many textbooks and detailed studies.

As scholars on both sides have worked out and developed these rival stories over the last century, the *modern* category of science, both as a form of knowledge and as an activity, has been retrospectively cast back on men of religion and on to the secular masters of the universities of the thirteenth and fourteenth centuries. The elision of the subject-area the medievals were pursuing in their work on nature (that is, natural philosophy) with the modern subject they were not pursuing, because it had not yet been created (that is, science), has not been noticed. Partly this is because modern scholars have been particularly concerned with those respects in which natural philosophy appears most to resemble modern science, and they have thus been least concerned with those respects in which they differ. Partly, as hinted above, it is because the achievements (or otherwise) of these medievals in their work on nature is, for modern writers, part of a larger modern dispute about the relative status of secular and religious values. What the medievals were actually concerned with in their discussions of nature has therefore not been a question that has been asked. Hence the God-oriented nature of natural philosophy and the religio-political motivation of those who invented natural philosophy and developed it – in short, its identity – have all been lost to sight. We hope that our account of the Dominicans and the Franciscans, and their respective grounds for being concerned with nature, will be a first step in helping to bring back into visibility the true nature of natural philosophy.

Bibliography of works cited

Abbreviation:
PL or Migne: Migne, J.P., ed., *Patrologiae Cursus Completus, seu Bibliotheca Universalis ... Omnium SS. Patrum, Doctorum Scriptorumque Ecclesiasticorum ... qui ab Aevo Apostolico ad Aetatem Innocenti III (ann. 1216) pro Latinis ... Floruerunt ...* , Latin series, 221 vols, Paris, Migne, 1844–.

Aegidius Zamorensis, Johannis, (Juan Gil de Zamora), *Historia Naturalis*, ed. Domínguez García, Avelino and García Ballester, Luis, 3 vols, Salamanca, 1994.

Alain of Lille, *Anticlaudianus*, in Migne, *PL*, vol. 210, col. 482.

———, *De Arte seu Articulis Catholice Fidei*, Migne, *PL*, vol. 210, col. 594.

———, *De Fide Catholica Contra Hereticos sui Temporis, Praesertim Albigenses*: Migne, *PL*, col. 210, col. 305.

———, *The Complaint of Nature*, translated by Moffat, D.M., New York, 1908.

Albertus Magnus, *De Vegetabilibus Libri VII. Historiae Naturalis Pars XVIII*, ed. Meyer, E., and Jessen, C., Berlin 1867.

———, *De Animalibus Libri XXVI*, ed. Stadler, H., 2 vols, Münster, 1916–21.

Aquinas, St Thomas, *Summae Contra Gentiles Libri Quatuor*, Rome, 1924.

———, *Summa Theologica*, 4 vols, Rome, 1925.

———, *Commentary on Aristotle's Physics*, translated by Blackwell, R.J., Spath, R.J., and Thirlkel, W.E., London, 1963.

Aristotle, *Metaphysics*.

———, *Parts of Animals*.

Armstrong, E.A., *Saint Francis, Nature Mystic. The Derivation and Significance of the Nature Stories in the Franciscan Legend*, Berkeley, California, 1973.

Ashley, B.M., 'St Albert and the Nature of Natural Science', in Weisheipl, *Albertus Magnus and the Sciences*.

Augustine, St., *On Christine Doctrine*, translated by Shaw, J.F., Edinburgh, 1873.

———, *S. Aurelii Augustini Confessiones*, ed. Dubois, M., Oxford,

1888. Translated by Pusey, E.B., as *The Confessions of S. Augustine*, Oxford, 1838.

Avi-Yonah, R.-S., *The Aristotelian Revolution: A Study of the Transformation of Medieval Cosmology, 1150–1250*, Harvard University, unpublished Ph.D. dissertation, 1986 (University Microfilms International).

Bacon, Roger, *Fr. Rogeri Bacon Opera Quaedam Hactenus Inedita, vol. 1 Containing I – Opus Tertium, II – Opus Minus, III – Compendium Philosophiae*, [only one volume published], ed. Brewer, J.S., London, Rolls Series, 1859.

———, *The 'Opus Majus' of Roger Bacon*, ed. Bridges, J.H., 2 vols, Oxford, 1897; Supplementary Volume, London, 1900.

———, *Opera Hactenus Inedita Rogeri Bacon.*, ed. Steele, R., 16 fascs, Oxford, ?1905–41.

———, *The Opus Majus of Roger Bacon*, translated by Burke, R.B., New York, 2 vols, 1962.

Baeumker, C., *Witelo. Ein Philosoph und Naturforscher des XIII. Jahrhunderts*, Münster, 1908 (*Beiträge zur Geschichte der Philosophie des Mittelalters* vol. 3, part 2).

Baldwin, J.W., *Masters, Princes and Merchants*, 2 vols, Princeton, New Jersey, 1970.

———, 'Masters at Paris from 1179 to 1215. A Social Perspective', in Benson and Constable, *Renaissance and Renewal*.

Barber, R., *The Knight and Chivalry*, New York, 1982 (originally published 1970).

Barbour, R., 'A Manuscript of Ps. -Dionysius Areopagita Copied for Robert Grosseteste', *Bodleian Library Record*, 1957–61, **6**, pp. 401–16.

Barnes, T.D., *Tertullian: A Historical and Literary Study*, Oxford, 1985.

Bartholomew Anglicus, *On the Properties of Things: John Trevisa's Translation of Bartholomaeus Anglicus De Proprietatibus Rerum*, Seymour, M.C., general editor, 3 vols, Oxford, 1975–88.

Bartholomew of Pisa, *Liber Aureus. Inscriptus Liber Conformitatum Vitae Beati ac Seraphici Patris Francisci ad Vitam Jesu Christi Domini Nostri*, Bologna, 1590.

Baur, L., *Die Philosophischen Werke des Robert Grosseteste, Bischofs von Lincoln*, Münster, 1912.

Bennett, R.F., *The Early Dominicans: Studies in Thirteenth-Century Dominican History*, Cambridge, 1937.

Benson, Robert L., and Constable, Giles, eds, *Renaissance and Renewal in the Twelfth Century*, Oxford, 1982.

Beresford, M., *New Towns of the Middle Ages: Town Plantation in England, Wales and Gasgony*, London, 1967.

Bettenson, H., ed., *Documents of the Christian Church*, Oxford, 1943.
Biebrach, K., *Die Holzgedeckten Franziskaner- und Dominikaner-Kirchen in Umbrien und Toskana*, (Dresden Techn. Hochschule, Doktor-Ingenieur dissertation) Berlin, 1908.
Biller, P., 'Heresy and Literacy: Earlier History of the Theme', in Biller and Hudson, *Heresy and Literacy*.
———, 'The Cathars of Languedoc and Written Materials', in Biller and Hudson, *Heresy and Literacy*.
Biller, Peter and Hudson, Anne, eds, *Heresy and Literacy, 1000–1530*, Cambridge, 1994.
Birkenmajer, A., 'La Rôle Jouée par les Médecins et les Naturalistes', in his *Etudes d'Histoire des Sciences et de la Philosophie du Moyen Age* (Studia Copernicana, 1), Warsaw, 1970.
———, 'Witelo Est-il Auteur de l'Oposcule *De Intelligentiis?*', the second of the 'Etudes sur Witelo' in his *Etudes d'Histoire des Sciences en Pologne*, (Studia Copernicana, **4**), Warsaw, 1972.
Blund, John, *Tractatus de Anima*, ed. Callus, D.A. and Hunt, R.W., London, 1970.
Boas, G., editor and translator, *The Mind's Road to God: Saint Bonaventura*, New York, 1953.
Boese, H., ed., *Thomas Cantimpratensis, Liber De Natura Rerum*, Berlin, 1973.
Bonacursus, *Vita Haereticorum*, Migne, *PL*, vol. 204, col. 772.
Bonaventure, St., *Opera Omnia*, 10 vols, Quaracchi, 1982–.
Bougerol, J.G., OFM, 'Les Sermons dans les "Studia" des Mendiants', in *Le Scuole degli Ordini Mendicanti (Secoli XIII–XIV)*, Convegni del Centro di Studi sulla Spiritualità Medievale, XVII, Todi, 1978.
———, *Saint Bonaventure: Etudes sur les Sources de sa Pensée*, London, 1989, I 'Saint Bonaventure et le Pseudo-Denys l'Aréopagite' (essay originally published in 1968).
Box, G.H., *Judaism in the Greek Period*, Oxford, 1932.
Brady, I.C. 'History of Philosophy (Ancient Philosophy)' in the *New Catholic Encyclopedia*, 17 vols, New York, 1967–79, vol. 11.
Breuning, W., *Die Hypostatische Union in der Theologie Wilhems von Auxerre, Hugos von St. Cher und Rolands von Cremona*, Trier, 1962.
Brooke, C., *Medieval Church and Society, Collected Essays*, London, 1971.
———, *The Monastic World, 1000–1300*, London, 1974.
Brooke, R.B., *The Coming of the Friars*, London, 1975.
Bruzelius, C.A., *The Thirteenth Century Church at St-Denis*, New Haven and London, 1985.
Burr, D., 'Eucharistic Presence and Conversion in Late Thirteenth-Century Franciscan Thought', *Transactions of the American*

Philosophical Society, 1984, **74**, Part 3.

Buttimer, C.H., ed., *Hugonis de Sancto Victore Didascalicon. De Studio Legendi*, Washington, 1939.

Cadden, Joan, 'Science and Rhetoric in the Middle Ages: The Natural Philosophy of William of Conches', *Journal of the History of Ideas*, 1995, **56**, pp. 1–24.

Callus, D.A., 'Introduction of Aristotelian Learning to Oxford', *Proceedings of the British Academy*, 1943, pp. 229–281.

———, ed., *Robert Grosseteste: Scholar and Bishop*, Oxford, 1955.

Carmody, F.J., 'Physiologus Latinus Versio Y', *University of California Publications in Classical Philology 12*, 1941, (7), pp. 95–134.

Carton, R., *L'Expérience Physique chez Roger Bacon: Contribution à l'Etude de la Méthode et de la Science Expérimentales au XIII*[e] *Siècle*, and *L'Expérience Mystique de l'Illumination Intérieure chez Roger Bacon*, Etudes de philosophie médiévale, nos. II and III, Paris, 1924.

Chadwick, H., *Early Christian Thought and the Classical Tradition*, Oxford, 1966.

Charles, E., *Roger Bacon, Sa Vie, Ses Ouvrages, et Ses Doctrines*, Paris, 1861.

Chartularium Universitatis Parisiensis, ed. Denifle, H., OP, Paris, vol. 1, 1889.

Chenu, M.-D., OP, *Toward Understanding St. Thomas* (published in French, 1950), translated by Landry, A.-M., OP, and Hughes, D., OP, Chicago, 1964.

Chevallier, P., *Dionysiaca, Recueil Donnant l'Ensemble des Traductions Latines des Ouvrages Attribués au Denys de l'Aréopage*, Paris, 2 vols, 1937, 1950.

Clarke, D.L., 'Optics for Preachers: The *De Oculo Morali* by Peter of Limoges', *Michigan Academician*, 1977, **9**, pp. 329–43.

Corbin, H., *History of Islamic Philosophy*, translated by Sherrard, L. and P., London and New York, 1993.

Cornford, F.M., *From Religion to Philosophy. A Study in the Origins of Western Speculation*, London, 1912, reprinted Sussex, 1980.

———, *Before and After Socrates*, Cambridge, 1932, reprinted 1979.

Creytens, R., 'Les Constitutions des Frères Prêcheurs dans les Rédactions de S. Raymond de Peñafort (1241)', *Archivum Fratrum Praedicatorum*, 1948, **18**, pp. 5–68.

———, 'L'Instruction des Novices Dominicains au XIIIe Siècle d'après le MS Toulouse 418', *Archivum Fratrum Praedicatorum*, 1950, **20**, pp. 114–93.

Crombie, A.C., *Robert Grosseteste and the Origins of Experimental Science 1000–1700*, Oxford, 1953.

———, 'Expectation, Modelling and Assent in the History of Optics:

Part I. Alhazen and the Medieval Tradition', *Studies in the History and Philosophy of Science*, 1990, **21**, pp. 605–32.

d'Alverny, M.-T., 'Translations and Translators', in Benson and Constable, *Renaissance and Renewal.*

d'Avray, D.L., 'Sermons to the Upper Bourgeoisie by a Thirteenth Century Franciscan', *Studies in Church History* (the series of that title published by the Ecclesiastical History Society) 1979, pp. 187–99.

Dales, R.C., and Gieben, Servus, OFM Cap., *Robert Grosseteste: Hexaemeron*, London, 1982.

Dales, R.C., *Roberti Grosseteste Episcopi Lincolniensis Commentarius in VIII Libros Physicorum Aristotelis*, Boulder, Colorado, 1963.

Denzinger, H., *The Sources of Catholic Dogma*, translated by Roy J. Deferrari, St Louis, 1957.

Dictionary of Scientific Biography, ed. Gillespie, C.C., New York, 1970–80, 18 vols.

Dionisotti, A.C., 'On the Greek Studies of Robert Grosseteste', in Dionisotti, A.C., Grafton, Anthony, and Kraye, Jill, *The Uses of Greek and Latin: Historical Essays*, London, 1988.

Dionysius the Areopagite, *The Divine Names*, translated by Rolt, C.E., London, 1920.

———, *Mystical Theology*, translated by Jones, John D., Milwaukee, 1980.

Dondaine, A., OP, *Un Traité Néo-Manichéen du XIIIe Siècle. Le Liber de Duobus Principiis, Suivi d'un Fragment de Rituel Cathare*, Rome, 1939.

———, 'Un Commentaire Scripturaire de Roland de Crémone "Le Livre de Job"', *Archivum Fratrum Praedicatorum*, 1941, **11**, pp. 109–137.

———, 'Le manuel de l'Inquisiteur (1230–1330)', *Archivum Fratrum Praedicatorum*, 1947, **17**, pp. 85–194.

———, 'La Hiérarchie Cathare en Italie', *Archivum Fratrum Praedicatorum*, 1950, **20**, pp. 234–324.

———, 'Durand de Huesca et la Polémique Anticathare', *Archivum Fratrum Praedicatorum*, 1959, **29**, pp. 228–76.

———, *Les Hérésies de l'Inquisition, XIIe–XIIIe Siècles. Documents et Etudes*, ed. Dossat, Y., Aldershot, 1990.

Dondaine, H.F., *Le Corpus Dionysien de l'Université de Paris au XIIIe Siècle*, Rome, 1953.

Draper, J.W., *History of the Conflict Between Religion and Science*, New York, 1874.

Dronke, P., ed., *Bernardus Sylvestris Cosmographia*, Leiden, 1978.

———, ed., *A History of Twelfth-Century Western Philosophy*, Cambridge, 1988.

Duby, G., *The Age of the Cathedrals: Art and Society, 980–1420*, translated by Levieux, Eleanor, and Thompson, Barbara, Chicago, 1981.

———, *The Knight, the Lady and the Priest: The Making of Modern Marriage in Medieval France*, London, 1984 (original French edition 1981).

Durantel, J., *Saint Thomas et le Pseudo-Denis* (Thèse pour le Doctorat à la Faculté des Lettres de l'Université de Paris), Paris, 1919.

Duvernoy, J., *Le Catharisme: L'Histoire des Cathares*, 2 vols, Toulouse, 1979.

Eastlake, C.L., *History of the Gothic Revival*, London, 1872.

Easton, S.C., *Roger Bacon and his Search for a Universal Science: A Reconsideration of the Life and Work of Roger Bacon in the Light of his own Stated Purposes*, Oxford, 1952.

Eastwood, B.S., 'Robert Grosseteste's Theory of the Rainbow: A Chapter in the History of Non-Experimental Science', *Archives Internationales d'Histoire des Sciences*, 1966, **19**, pp. 313–32.

Eco, Umberto, *The Name of the Rose* (originally published in Italian in 1980), London, 1983.

Evans, G.R., *The Mind of St Bernard of Clairvaux*, Oxford, 1983.

———, 'The Uncompleted Heptateuch of Thierry of Chartres', *History of Universities*, 1983, **3**, pp. 1–13.

———, *The Language and Logic of the Bible: The Earlier Middle Ages*, Cambridge, 1984.

Féret, H.-M., OP, 'Vie Intellectuelle et Vie Scolaire dans l'Ordre des Prêcheurs', *Archives d'Histoire Dominicaine*, 1946, **1**, pp. 1–37.

Ferruolo, S.C., *The Origins of the University*, Stanford, California, 1985.

Fleming, J.V., *An Introduction to the Franciscan Literature of the Middle Ages*, Chicago, 1977.

Fletcher, W.G.D., *The Black Friars of Oxford*, Oxford, 1882.

Flint, R., *Philosophy as Scientia Scientiarum: and a History of Classifications of the Sciences*, Edinburgh and London, 1904.

Frankl, P., *The Gothic: Literary Sources and Interpretations Through Eight Centuries*, Princeton, New Jersey, 1960.

French, R.K., 'A Note on the Anatomical Accessus of the Middle Ages', *Medical History*, 1979, **23**, pp. 461–8.

———, 'Gentile da Foligno and the Via Medicorum', in North, J.D. and Roche, J.J. eds, *The Light of Nature*, Dordrecht, 1985.

———, *Ancient Natural History: Histories of Nature*, London, 1994.

Gabriel, A.L., *The Educational Ideas of Vincent of Beauvais*, Notre Dame, Indiana, 1956 (*Texts and Studies in the History of Medieval Education*, IV, ed. Gabriel, A.L. and Garvin, J.N.).

Gadave, R., *Les Documents sur l'Histoire de l'Université de Toulouse*, Toulouse, 1910.

Garvin, J and Corbett, J., *The Summa Contra Haereticos Ascribed to Praepositinus of Cremona*, Notre Dame, Indiana, 1985.

Gerson, L.P., *God and Greek Philosophy*, London, 1990.

Gerson, P.L., ed., *Abbot Suger and Saint-Denis: A Symposium*, New York, 1986.

Gieben, S., 'Traces of God in Nature According to Robert Grosseteste', *Franciscan Studies*, 1964, **24**, pp. 144–58.

Gilson, E., *The Philosophy of St Bonaventure*, translated by Dom I. Trethowan and F.J. Sheed, London, 1938.

———, *History of Christian Philosophy in the Middle Ages*, London, 1980, (first published 1955).

Gimpel, J., *The Medieval Machine: The Industrial Revolution of the Middle Ages*, London, 1977.

Godfrey of St Victor, *The Fountain of Philosophy: A Translation of the Twelfth-Century Fons Philosophiae of Godfrey of St Victor*, translated by Synan, E.A., Toronto, 1972.

Goodich, M., 'The Politics of Canonization in the Thirteenth Century: Lay and Mendicant Saints', *Church History*, 1975, **44**, pp. 294–307.

Grant, E., ed., *A Source Book in Medieval Science*, Cambridge, Mass., 1974.

Grant, R.M., *Augustus to Constantine: the Thrust of the Christian Movement into the Roman World*, London, 1971.

Grosseteste, Robert, *Commentarius in Posteriorum Analyticorum Libros*, ed. Rossi, Pietro, Florence, 1981.

Guiraud, J., *Saint Dominic*, translated by de Mattos, K., London, 1901.

Gumbley, W., OP, *The Cambridge Dominicans*, Oxford, 1938.

Gundissalinus, *De Divisione Philosophiae*, in Baeumker, C, and Hertling, G.F. von, eds, *Beiträge zur Geschichte der Philosophie des Mittelalters*, Münster, 1906.

Guthrie, W.K.C., *A History of Greek Philosophy*, Cambridge, 6 vols, 1962–81.

Habig, M.A., ed., *St Francis of Assisi: Writings and Early Biographies. English Omnibus of the Sources for the Life of St Francis*, 3rd edition, Chicago, 1973.

Hamilton, B., 'The Cathar Council of Saint-Félix Reconsidered', *Archivum Fratrum Praedicatorum*, 1978, **48**, pp. 23–53.

Haskins, C.H., *The Renaissance of the Twelfth Century*, Cambridge, Mass., 1927.

Hastings, J., and Selbie, John A., eds, *Dictionary of the Bible*, Edinburgh, 1909.

Hedwig, K., *Sphaera Lucis: Studien zur Intelligibilität des Seienden im*

Kontext der mittelalterlichen Lichtspekulation, Münster (Beiträge zur Geschichte der Philosophie und Theologie des Mittelalters, Neue Folge, Band 18), 1980.

Heer, F., *The Medieval World. Europe from 1100 to 1350*, translated by Sondheimer, J., London, 1962.

Henderson, E.F., editor and translator, *Select Historical Documents of the Middle Ages*, London, 1925.

Hinnebusch,W.A., OP, *The Early English Friars Preachers*, Rome, 1951.

Hunt, R.W., 'English Learning in the Late Twelfth Century' in *Essays in Medieval History*, ed. Southern, R., London, 1968.

———, *The Schools and the Cloister. The Life and Writings of Alexander Nequam*, Oxford, 1984.

Ilarino da Milano, P., 'La "Manifestatio Heresis Catarorum quam fecit Bonacursus" secondo il cod. Otob. Lat. 136 della Biblioteca Vaticana', *Aevum*, 1938, **12**, pp. 281–333.

———, 'Fr. Gregorio OP, Vescovo di Fano et la "Disputatio inter Catholicum et Paterinum Hereticum"', *Aevum*, 1940, **14**, pp. 85–140.

———, 'Il "Liber supra Stella" del Piacentino Salvo Burci Contro i Catari e Altre Correnti Ereticali, *Aevum*, 1942, **16**, pp. 272–319.

———, 'Il "Liber supra Stella" del Piacentino Salvo Burci Contro i Catari et Altre Correnti Ereticali. 4 – Le Dottrine Catare', *Aevum*, 1945, **19**, pp. 281–341.

Jacquart, D., 'Aristotelian Thought in Salerno', in Dronke, *Twelfth-Century Western Philosophy*, 1988.

Jaeger, Werner, 'Greeks and Jews', in his *Scripta Minora*, 2 vols, Rome, 1960, vol. 2.

———, *Early Christianity and Greek Paideia*, Cambridge, Mass., 1961.

Jarrett, Bede, OP, *Life of St Dominic (1170–1221)*, London, 1924.

Jeanneau, E., *Note sur l'Ecole de Chartres*, Chartres, 1965 (also available in *Bulletin de la Société Archéologique d'Eure-et-Loire*, 4e Trimestre 1964: Mémoires, t. xxiii).

John of Salisbury, *Polycraticus*, in Migne, *PL*, vol. 199, col. 379.

———, *The Metalogicon of John of Salisbury: A Twelfth-Century Defense of the Verbal and Logical Arts of the Trivium*, translated with an Introduction and Notes by McGarry, Daniel D., Berkeley, California, 1955.

Jones, A.H.M., *Constantine and the Conversion of Europe*, London, 1948, repr. 1964.

Jordan, William, *Ancient Concepts of Philosophy*, London, 1990.

Kaeppelli, T., 'Une Somme Contre les Hérétiques de S Pierre Martyr(?)' *Archivum Fratrum Praedicatorum*, 1947, 17, pp. 295–335.

Kibre, P., *Scholarly Privileges in the Middle Ages*, New York, 1961.

Kilwardby, Robert, *De Ortu Scientiarum*, ed. Judy, A.G., Toronto, 1976.

Knowles, M.D., 'Some Aspects of the Career of Archbishop Pecham', *English Historical Review*, 1942, **57**, pp. 1–18, 178–201.

———, *Cistercians and Cluniacs: The Controversy between St Bernard and Peter the Venerable*, Oxford, 1955.

Koudelka, V.J., OP, 'Notes pour Servir à l'Histoire de Saint Dominique II', *Archivum Fratrum Praedicatorum*, 1973, **43**, pp. 5–27.

Kraye, Jill, Ryan, W.F., and Schmitt, C.B. eds, *Pseudo-Aristotle in the Middle Ages: The Theology and Other Texts*, London, 1986.

Kretzmann, N., 'Reason in Mystery', in *The Philosophy in Christianity*, ed. Vesey, G., Cambridge, 1989.

Kretzmann, N., Kenny, A., and Pinborg, J., eds, *The Cambridge History of Later Medieval Philosophy from the Rediscovery of Aristotle to the Disintegration of Scholasticism 1100–1600*, Cambridge, 1982.

Kristeller, P.O., 'The School of Salerno', *Bulletin of the History of Medicine*, 1945, **17**, pp. 138–194.

———, 'Bartholomaeus, Musandinus and Maurus of Salerno and other early Commentators of the "Articella" With a Tentative List of Texts and Manuscripts', *Italia Medioevale e Umanistica*, 1976, **19**, pp. 57–87.

———, 'Philosophy and Medicine in Medieval and Renaissance Italy' in Spicker, S.F., ed., *Organism, Medicine and Metaphysics*, Dordrecht, 1978.

Kuttner, S., 'The Revival of Jurisprudence', in Benson and Constable, *Renaissance and Renewal.*

Ladurie, E. Le Roy, *Montaillou: Cathars and Catholics in a French Village*, translated from French by Bray, B., London, 1978.

Lambert, M.D., *Franciscan Poverty. The Doctrine of the Absolute Poverty of Christ and the Apostles in the Franciscan Order 1210–1323*, London, 1961.

Lardner, G.B., 'Terms and Ideas of Renewal', in Benson and Constable, *Renaissance and Renewal.*

Latouche, R., *The Birth of Western Economy: Economic Aspects of the Dark Ages*, London, 1967 (original French edition 1956).

Lawn, B., *The Salernitan Questions*, Oxford, 1963.

Lawn, B., *The Prose Salernitan Questions*, London, 1979.

Lawrence, C.H., *The Friars. The Impact of the Early Mendicant Movement on Western Society*, London, 1994.

Le Scuole degli Ordini Mendicamenti (Secoli XIII–XIV), Convegni del Centro di Studi sulla Spiritualità Medievale XVII, Todi, 1978.

Le Trésor de Saint-Denis, Paris, 1991.

Lea, H.C., *An Historical Sketch of Sacerdotal Celibacy in the Christian Church*, Philadelphia, 1867.

Leclercq, J., 'The Renewal of Theology' in Benson and Constable, *Renaissance and Renewal.*

Lejeune, A., *L'Optique de Claude Ptolémée dans la Version Latine d'après l'Arabe de l'Emir Eugène de Sicile: Edition Critique et Exégétique*, Louvain, 1956.

Lemay, H.R., 'Guillaume de Conches' Division of Philosophy in the Accessus ad Macrobium', *Mediaevalia*, **1** (2), 1975, pp. 115–26.

Lemay, R., *Abu Ma'shar and Latin Aristotelianism in the Twelfth Century*, Beirut, 1962.

Levine, S.A., *The Northern Foreportal Column Figures of Chartres Cathedral, Style and Dating; and Reflections of Vincent of Beauvais' 'Speculum doctrinale'*, Frankfurt am Main, 1984 (Kultstätten der Gallisch-Fränkischen Kirche, Band 3).

Lewis, C.S., *The Allegory of Love. A Study in Medieval Tradition*, Oxford, 1977, (first published 1936).

Lewry P.O., OP, 'A Passiontide Sermon of Robert Kilwardby OP', *Archivum Fratrum Praedicatorum*, 1982, **52**, pp. 89–113.

Limborch, P. von, *The History of the Inquisition*, translated by Chandler, S., 2 vols, London, 1731.

Lindberg, D.C., 'Alhazen's theory of vision and its reception in the West', *Isis*, 1967, **58**, pp. 321–41.

———, *John Pecham and the Science of Optics: Perspectiva Communis*, Wisconsin, Michigan, 1970.

———, *John Pecham: Tractatus de Perspectiva*, New York, 1972.

———, *Theories of Vision from Al-Kindi to Kepler*, Chicago, 1976.

———, *Science in the Middle Ages*, Chicago, 1978.

———, 'The Transmission of Greek and Arabic Learning to the West', in Lindberg, *Science in the Middle Ages.*

———, *Roger Bacon's Philosophy of Nature: A Critical Edition, with English Translation, Introduction and Notes, of 'De Multiplicatione Specierum' and 'De Speculis Comburentibus'*, Oxford, 1983.

———, 'Laying the Foundations of Geometrical Optics: Maurolico, Kepler, and the Medieval Tradition', in Westman, R.S., ed., *The Discourse of Light from the Middle Ages to the Enlightenment*, Los Angeles, California, 1985.

———, 'The Genesis of Kepler's Theory of Light: Light Metaphysics from Plotinus to Kepler', *Osiris*, 1986 (second series), **2**, pp. 5–42.

———, 'Roger Bacon and the Origins of *Perspectiva* in the West', in Grant, Edward and Murdoch, John E., eds, *Mathematics and its Applications to Science and Natural Philosophy in the Middle Ages: Essays in Honor of Marshall Clagett*, Cambridge, 1987.

Lindberg, D.C., and Numbers, R.L., *God and Nature: Historical Essays on the Encounter Between Christianity and Science*, Berkeley,

California, 1986.

Little, A.G., *The Grey Friars in Oxford*, Oxford, 1892.

———, 'Educational Organisation of the Mendicant Friars in England (Dominicans and Franciscans)', *Transactions of the Royal Historical Society*, New Series, 1894, **8**, pp. 49–70.

———, 'The Franciscan School at Oxford in the Thirteenth Century', *Archivum Franciscanum Historicum*, 1926, **19**, pp. 803–74.

———, 'The Friars and the Foundation of the Faculty of Theology in the University of Cambridge', *Bibliothèque Thomiste*, 1930, **14**, pp. 389–401.

Lohr, C.H., 'The Pseudo Aristotelian Liber de Causis and Latin Theories of Science in the Twelfth and Thirteenth Centuries' in Kraye, Ryan and Schmitt, *Pseudo-Aristotle in the Middle Ages*.

Lohse, E., *The New Testament Environment*, London, 1976.

Long, R.J., ed., *Bartholomaeus Anglicus On the Properties of Soul and Body: De Proprietatibus Rerum Libri III et IV*, Toronto, 1979.

———, 'The Virgin as Olive-Tree: A Marian Sermon of Richard Fishacre and Science at Oxford', *Archivum Fratrum Praedicatorum*, 1982, **52**, pp. 77–87.

Lopez, R.S., *The Commercial Revolution of the Middle Ages, 950–1350*, Cambridge, 1976.

Lucks, H.A., 'Natura Naturans – Natura Naturata', *The New Scholasticism*, 1935, **9**, pp. 1–24.

Lynch, L.E., 'The Doctrine of Divine Ideas and Illumination in Robert Grosseteste, Bishop of Lincoln', *Mediaeval Studies*, 1941, **3**, pp. 161–73.

Macaulay, J., *The Gothic Revival 1747–1845*, Glasgow and London, 1975.

Maccagnolo, E., 'David of Dinant and the Beginnings of Aristotelianism in Paris', in Dronke, *Twelfth-Century Western Philosophy*, 1988.

Mackinney, L.C., *Bishop Fulbert and Education at the School of Chartres*, Notre Dame, Indiana, 1957.

Madaule, J., *The Albigensian Crusade. An Historical Essay*, London, 1967.

Mâle, E., *The Gothic Image: Religious Art in France of the Thirteenth Century*, translated from the third edition by Nussey, Dora, London, 1961 (first published in French in 1910).

Mandonnet, P., OP, *Saint Dominique. L'Idée, l'Homme et l'Oeuvre*, with additions by Vicaire, M.H., OP, 2 vols, Paris, 1938.

Manselli, R., 'Per la Storia dell'Eresia nel Secolo XII', *Bullettino dell'Istituto Storico Italiano per il Medio Evo e Archivio Muratoriano*, 1955, **67**, pp. 189–264.

Mansi, J.D., *Sacrorum Conciliorum Nova et Amplissima Collectio*, vol.

21, Venice, 1776.

Marenbon, J., *Later Medieval Philosophy (1150–1350): An Introduction*, London, 1987.

Marrone, S.P., *William of Auvergne and Robert Grosseteste: New Ideas of Truth in the Early Thirteenth Century*, Princeton, New Jersey, 1983.

Martin, A.R., *Franciscan Architecture in England*, Manchester, 1937.

Martin-Chabot, E., ed., *Les Classiques d'Histoire de France au Moyen Age*, vol. 21: *La Chanson de la Croisade Albigeoise*, vol. 1, Paris, 1931; vol. 24: *La Chanson*, vol. 2 (part 1), Paris, 1957; and vol. 25: *La Chanson*, vol. 3 (part 2), Paris, 1961.

Martines, L., *Power and Imagination: City-States in Renaissance Italy*, London, 1980.

McEvoy, James, 'The Metaphysics of Light in the Middle Ages', *Philosophical Studies*, 1979, **26**, pp. 126–45.

———, *The Philosophy of Robert Grosseteste*, Oxford, 1982.

McInerny, R., 'Beyond the Liberal Arts', in Wagner, David L., ed., *The Seven Liberal Arts in the Middle Ages*, Bloomington, Indiana, 1983.

McMenomy, C.A., *The Discipline of Astronomy in the Middle Ages*, University of California, Los Angeles, unpublished Ph.D. thesis (University Microfilms International, 1984).

Menzies, A., ed., *Ante-Nicene Christian Library: Additional Volume*, Edinburgh, Clark, 1897.

Migne, J.P., *Patrologiae Cursus Completus, seu Bibliotheca Universalis ... Omnium SS. Patrum, Doctorum Scriptorumque Ecclesiasticorum ... qui ab Aevo Apostolico ad Aetatem Innocenti III (ann. 1216) pro Latinis ... Floruerunt ...* , Latin series, 221 vols, Paris, Migne, 1866–. Referred to as Migne, *Patrologia Latina*, or *PL*.

Moneta of Cremona, *Adversus Catharos et Valdenses Libri Quinque*, Rome, 1743.

Moody, E.A., 'William of Auvergne and his Treatise "De Anima"', in his *Studies in Medieval Philosophy, Science and Logic*, Berkeley, California, 1975.

Moore, R.I., *The Birth of Popular Heresy*, London, 1975.

Moorman, J.R.H., *The Sources for the Life of S. Francis of Assisi*, Manchester, 1940.

———, *The Grey Friars in Cambridge 1225–1538*, Cambridge, 1952.

———, *A History of the Franciscan Order from its Origins to the Year 1517*, Oxford, 1968.

Mundy, J.H. 'Urban Society and Culture: Toulouse and its Region', in Benson and Constable, *Renaissance and Renewal*.

Murphy, J.C., OFM, 'The Early Franciscan Studium at the University of Paris', in Domonkos, Leslie S. and Schneider, Robert J., eds, *Studium*

Generale: Studies Offered to Astrik L. Gabriel, Notre Dame, 1967, pp. 159–203.

Neckam, Alexander, *De Naturis Rerum, De Laudibus Divinae Sapientie*, ed. Wright, T., London, 1863 (*Rerum Britannicarum Medii Aevi Scriptores*).

———, *Speculum Speculationum*, ed. Thomson, R.M., Oxford, 1980.

Packard, S.R., *Europe and the Church under Innocent III*, New York, 1927, reprinted 1968.

Pagels, E., *The Gnostic Gospels*, London, 1980.

Panofsky, E., ed., *Abbot Suger on the Abbey Church of St. -Denis and its Art Treasures*, Princeton, New Jersey, 1946, second edition 1979.

Parent, J.M., *La Doctrine de la Création dans l'Ecole de Chartres*, Paris and Ottowa, 1938.

Park, K., 'Albert's Influence on Late Medieval Psychology', in Weisheipl, *Albertus Magnus and the Sciences*.

Parker, J., *The Works of Dionysius the Areopagite*, 2 vols, London, 1897–99.

Paterson, Linda, M., *The World of the Troubadours: Medieval Occitan Society, c.1100–c.1300*, Cambridge, 1993.

Pegge, S., *The Life of Robert Grosseteste the Celebrated Bishop of Lincoln*, London, 1793.

Pera, C., OP, ed., *S. Thomae Aquinatis In Librum Beati Dionysii de Divinis Nominibus Expositio*, Rome, 1950.

Peters, E., *Heresy and Authority in Medieval Europe*, London, 1980.

Phillips, H., 'John Wyclif and the Optics of the Eucharist', in Hudson, A., and Wilks, M., eds, *From Ockham to Wyclif*, Oxford, 1987, pp. 245–258.

Physiologus, ed. Sbordone, F., Milan, 1936.

PL. See Migne.

Plato, *Phaedo*.

———, *Republic*.

Platt, C., *The English Medieval Town*, London, 1976.

———, *The Parish Churches of Medieval England*, London, 1981.

Powicke, F.M., 'Robert Grosseteste and the Nichomachean Ethics' *Proceedings of the British Academy*, 1930, **16**, pp. 85–104.

———, *Ways of Medieval Life and Thought: Essays and Addresses*, London, 1949.

Pugin, A., *Contrasts*, Salisbury, 1836.

Pullan, B., *Sources for the History of Medieval Europe from the Mid-Eighth Century to the Mid-Thirteenth Century*, Oxford, 1966.

Radcliff-Umstead, D., 'The Catharists and the Failure of Community', *Mediaevalia*, 1975, **1** (2), pp. 64–87.

Rashdall, H., *The Universities of Europe in the Middle Ages*, ed.

Powicke, F.M. and Emden, A.B., Oxford, 3 vols, 1936, reprinted 1958 (original edition 1895).

Raven, C., *English Naturalists from Neckam to Ray*, Cambridge, 1947.

Reeds, K., 'Albert on the Natural Philosophy of Plant Life', in Weisheipl, *Albertus Magnus and the Sciences.*

Riedl, C.C., *Robert Grosseteste On Light (De Luce), Translated from the Latin with an Introduction*, Milwaukee, 1942.

Risner, F., *Opticae Thesaurus*, Basle, 1572.

Roberts, Revd A., and Donaldson, James, eds, *Ante-Nicene Christian Library: Translations of the Writings of the Fathers down to 325 AD*, 24 vols, Edinburgh, 1867–72, vols 4 and 12.

Rohde, E., *Psyche. The Cult of Souls and Belief in Immortality among the Greeks*, London, 1925.

Roquebert, M., *L'Epopée Cathare 1198–1212: L'Invasion*, Toulouse, 1970.

Rouse, R.H. and M.A., *Preachers, Florilegia and Sermons: Studies on the Manipulus Florum of Thomas of Ireland*, Toronto, 1979.

———, 'Statim Invenire. Schools, Preachers and New Attitudes to the Page', in Benson and Constable, *Renaissance and Renewal.*

Rubin, M., *Corpus Christi. The Eucharist in Late Medieval Culture*, Cambridge, 1991.

Runciman, S., *The Byzantine Theocracy*, Cambridge, 1977.

———, *The Medieval Manichee. A Study of the Christian Dualist Heresy*, Cambridge, 1982.

Russell, J.C., *Twelfth-century Studies*, New York, 1982.

Sabra, A.I., translator and editor, *The Optics of Ibn Al-Haytham, Books I–III On Direct Vision*, 2 vols, London, 1989.

Sandys, Sir J.E., 'Roger Bacon in English Literature', in Little, A.G., ed., *Roger Bacon: Essays Contributed by Various Writers on the Occasion of the Commemoration of the Seventh Centenary of his Birth*, Oxford, 1914.

Sanjek, F., 'Raynerius Sacconi O.P. Summa de Catharis', *Archivum Fratrum Praedicatorum*, 1974, **44**, pp. 31–60.

Schaff, P., ed., *A Select Library of the Nicene and post Nicene Fathers of the Christian Church. Volume IV: St Augustine: the Writings against the Manicheans and against the Donatists*, Michigan, 1887.

Scheeben, H.C., 'Die Konstitutionen des Predigerordens unter Jordan von Sachsen, *Quellen und Forschungen zur Geschichte des Dominikanerordens in Deutschland*, vol. 38, Cologne and Leipzig, 1939.

Shank, M.H., *'Unless You Believe, You Shall Not Understand'. Logic, University and Society in late Medieval Vienna*, Princeton, New Jersey, 1988.

Shareshill, Alfred of, *De Motu Cordis*, in Barach, C.S., ed., *Excerpta a*

Libro Alfredi Anglici De Motu Cordis item Costa-ben-Lucae De Differentia Animae et Spiritus, Innsbruck, 1878.

Sharp, D.E., *Franciscan Philosophy at Oxford in the Thirteenth Century*, Oxford, 1930.

Simon, G., *Le Regard, l'Etre et l'Apparence dans l'Optique de l'Antiquité*, Paris, 1988.

Simson, O. von, *The Gothic Cathedral: Origins of Gothic Arthitecture and the Medieval Concept of Order*, Princeton, New Jersey, 1962 (first published 1956).

———, 'The Gothic Cathedral: Design and Meaning', in Thrupp, Sylvia, ed., *Change in Medieval Society: Europe North of the Alps 1050–1500*, London, 1965.

Siraisi, N., *Arts and Sciences at Padua: The Studium of Padua before 1350*, Toronto, 1973.

———, *Taddeo Alderotti and his Pupils. Two Generations of Italian Medical Learning*, Princeton, New Jersey, 1981.

———, *Avicenna in Renaissance Italy. The Canon and Medical Teaching in Italian Universities after 1500*, Princeton, New Jersey, 1987.

Smalley, B., 'Some Thirteenth-Century Commentaries on the Sapiental Books', *Dominican Studies*, 1949, **2**, pp. 318–55, and 1950, **3**, pp. 236–74.

———, *The Study of the Bible in the Middle Ages*, Oxford, third edition 1984 (first published 1941).

Smart, A., *The Assisi Problem and the Art of Giotto*, Oxford, 1971.

Smith, A.M., 'Getting the Big Picture in Perspectivist Optics', *Isis*, 1981, **72**, pp. 568–89.

———, *Witelonis Perspectivae Liber Quintus: Book V of Witelo's Perspectiva; An English Translation with Introduction and Commentary and Latin Edition of the First Catoptrical Book of Witelo's Perspectiva*, Warsaw, Studia Copernicana XXIII, 1983.

Sorrell, R.D., *St Francis of Assisi and Nature. Tradition and Innovation in Western Christian Attitudes Toward the Environment*, Oxford, 1988.

Southern, R.W., 'The Schools of Paris and the School of Chartres', in Benson and Constable, *Renaissance and Renewal.*

———, *Robert Grosseteste, The Growth of an English Mind in Medieval Europe*, Oxford, 1986; second edition 1992.

Stahl, W.H., *Roman Science: Origins, Development and Influence to the Later Middle Ages*, Madison, 1962.

Stahl, W.H., Johnson, R., and Burge, E.L., eds and translators, *Martianus Capella and the Seven Liberal Arts*, 2 vols, New York, 1971, 1977.

Stock, B., *Myth and Science in the Twelfth Century. A Study of Bernard Silvester*, Princeton, New Jersey, 1972.

———, 'Science, Technology and Economic Progress in the Early Middle Ages', in Lindberg, *Science in the Middle Ages.*

Strayer, J.R., *The Albigensian Crusade*, New York, 1971.

Stroumsa, Gedaliahu G., 'Anti-Cathar polemics and the *Liber De Duobus Principiis*', in Lewis, Bernard and Niewöhner, Friedrich, eds, *Religionsgespräche im Mittelalter*, Wolfenbütteler Mittelalter-Studien, vol. 4, Wiesbaden, 1992.

Sudhoff, K., 'Daniels von Morley Liber de Naturis Inferiorum et Superiorum', *Archiv für die Geschichte der Naturwissenschaften und der Technik*, 1917, **8**, pp. 1–40.

Sumption, J., *The Albigensian Crusade*, London, 1978.

Swann, W., *The Gothic Cathedral*, London, 1984 (first published 1969).

Taylor, J., *The Origin and Early Life of Hugh of St Victor: An Evaluation of the Tradition*, Indiana, 1957.

Taylor, R.C., 'The Kalam Fi Mahd al-Khair (*Liber de Causis*) in the Islamic Philosophical Milieu', in Kraye, Ryan and Schmitt, *Pseudo-Aristotle.*

Théry, G., OP, 'Autour du Décret de 1210: 1 – David de Dinant. Etude sur son Panthéisme Matérialiste', *Bibliothèque Thomiste*, 1925, **6**.

Thomas of Cantimpré, *Liber de Natura Rerum*: edn of Berlin and New York, 1973.

Thomson, S. Harrison, *The Writings of Robert Grosseteste, Bishop of Lincoln 1235–1253*, Cambridge, 1940.

Thorndike, Lynn, *A History of Magic and Experimental Science*, 8 volumes, New York, 1923–58.

Thouzellier, C., ed., *Une Somme Anti-Cathare. Le Liber Contra Manicheos de Durand de Huesca*, Louvain, 1964.

———, *Catharisme et Valdéisme en Languedoc à la Fin du XIIe et au Début de XIIIe Siècle*, Paris and Louvain, 1969.

Trigg, J.W., *Origen: the Bible and Philosophy in the Third-century Church*, London, 1985.

Tugwell, S., OP, *Early Dominicans: Selected Writings*, London, 1982.

Ullmann, W., *The Growth of Papal Government in the Middle Ages: A Study in the Ideological Relation of Clerical to Lay Power*, London, 1955.

Unguru, S, *Witelonis Perspectivae Liber Primus: Book One of Witelo's Perspectiva; An English Translation with Introduction and Commentary and Latin Edition of The Mathematical Book of Witelo's Perspectiva*, Warsaw, Studia Copernicana XV, 1977.

Vaissette, J., *Histoire Générale de Languedoc*, 15 vols, Toulouse, 1872–92.

Valois, N., *Guillaume d'Auvergne Evêque de Paris (1228–1249). Sa Vie et ses Ouvrages*, Paris, 1880.

van Steenbergen, J., *Aristotle in the West. The Origins of Latin Aristotelianism*, Louvain, 1970.

Vincentius Burgundus, *Bibliotheca Mundi, Speculum Quadruplex, Naturale, Doctrinale, Morale, Historiale*, 4 vols, Douai, 1624.

Wagner, D.L., *The Seven Liberal Arts in the Middle Ages*, Bloomington, Indiana, 1983.

Wailes, S.L., 'Why did Jesus Use Parables? The Medieval Discussion', *Medievalia et Humanistica*, ns 1985, **13**, pp. 43–64.

Wakefield, W.L., *Heresy, Crusade and Inquisition in Southern France*, London, 1974.

Warichez, J., ed., *Les Disputationes de Simon de Tournai*, Louvain, 1932.

Warner, M., *Alone of all her Sex: The Myth and the Cult of the Virgin Mary*, London, 1985 (first published 1976).

Webb, C.J., *Studies in the History of Natural Theology*, Oxford, 1915.

Weijers, O., *Pseudo-Boèce: De Disciplina Scolarium*, Leiden, 1976.

Weisheipl, J.A., 'Albertus Magnus and the Oxford Platonists' *Proceedings of the American Catholic Philosophical Association*, 1958, **32**, pp. 124–39.

———, ed., *Albertus Magnus and the Sciences. Commemorative Essays 1980*, Toronto, 1980.

———, 'The life and works of St Albert the Great', in Weisheipl, *Albertus Magnus and the Sciences.*

———, 'Aristotle's Concept of Nature: Avicenna and Aquinas', in Roberts, L.D., ed., *Approaches to Nature in the Middle Ages*, New York, 1982.

Wessley, S., 'The Composition of Georgius' Disputatio inter Catholicum et Paterinum Hereticum', *Archivum Fratrum Praedicatorum*, 1978, pp. 55–61.

White, A., *A History of the Warfare of Science With Theology*, London, 1896.

White, L., Jr., *Medieval Technology and Social Change*, Oxford, 1962.

———, *Medieval Religion and Technology*, University of California Press, 1978.

William of Auvergne (G. Alvernus), *Opera Omnia*, Rouen, 1674.

William of Conches, *Philosophia Mundi*, edited and translated into German by Maurach, G., Pretoria, 1980.

Wilson, S., ed., *Saints and Their Cults: Studies in Religious Sociology, Folklore and History*, Cambridge, 1983.

Wind, E., *Pagan Mysteries in the Renaissance*, Oxford, 1980 (first published 1958).

Index